READINGS IN GLOBAL HISTORY
Volume 2

Second Edition

Anthony Snyder
Sherri West
Brookdale Community College

KENDALL/HUNT PUBLISHING COMPANY
4050 Westmark Drive   Dubuque. Iowa 52002

Contents

Acknowledgments

We would like to thank Jane Scimeca and Jess Le Vine, our colleagues in World History at Brookdale Community College, for their suggestions and additions. Also, many thanks to the fine team of Brookdale adjunct instructors, who have regularly advised us on various aspects of the reader. Finally, thanks to the Brookdale students. It is for them that we have labored on this book, from them that we have learned its strengths and weaknesses, loud and clear, and for that reason, we owe them a debt of gratitude.

Anthony W. Snyder
Sherri L. West

1

Europe and the World: The Spice Trade

Anthony Esler, the author of a well-known text on World History, describes the pre-modern world of 1500 as a "world in balance . . . a world of separate zones of culture . . . a tidy little world (where) regional societies, great empires, and some of the most impressive civilizations the world has seen shared the earth." While some have argued that the major cultures were never as separate, the world never as tidy as Esler suggests, it was from this world that Columbus and da Gama set forth, shattering whatever balance existed, and setting in motion forces that would lead to the emergence of a "single human story." The result has been the globalization of history, "binding the peoples of the world in more and more elaborate nets of interdependence," a hallmark of the modern world. In this selection, the author provides a brief history of the spice trade in the Indian Ocean up to today, the role that Europeans would play in that trade, and the impact of that trade on European nations, on Asian states, as well as the cultivators of the spices "worth their weight in gold."

Discussion Questions

1. Why does the author state that the "modern age" begins with da Gama's travels to Asia?

2. What is the "Muslim Curtain" and what is its connection with European voyages of exploration?

3. Why do you suppose that Europeans were eventually successful in establishing commercial ties in Asia, and, ultimately, how successful were they?

4. What similarities between the spice trade of yesterday and the spice trade of today are referred to in the reading?

5. Why were spices "worth their weight in gold," and what were Europeans willing to do to claim some of them as their own? What impact would it have on the farmers cultivating spices, or the local leaders that controlled the trade? Are there commodities today that are as priceless as nutmeg and pepper of yesterday?

A Taste of Adventure
Kerala, India, and the Molucca Islands, Indonesia
The History of Spices Is the History of Trade

Soon after dawn on May 21st 1498, Vasco da Gama and his crew arrived at Calicut after the first direct sea voyage from Europe to Asia. If history's modern age has a beginning, this is it. Europe's ignorance of, and isolation from, the cosmopolitan intellectual and commercial life of Asia were ended forever. With ships, weaponry and a willingness to use them both, the countries of Europe were about to colonize the rest of the world. To support this expansion, its merchant classes would invent new forms of commercial credit and the first great corporations, vital parts of capitalism's operating system, and spread their trading networks across the seven seas. And what did the men shout as they came ashore? "For Christ and spices!"

The proselytizing part turned out to be disappointingly unnecessary: there were already plenty of Christians living on the Malabar coast, following the arrival of a Syrian contingent many centuries earlier. But as far as spice went, Da Gama and his crew were right on the money. Then, as now, Calicut was a gateway to the world's greatest pepper-growing region—indeed this was why the Syrians had moved there in the first place. As such it was at the heart of the spice trade, a network of sea routes and entrepôts in the making for Millennia: the world economy's oldest, deepest, most aromatic roots.

For thousands of years before Da Gama and hundreds of years afterwards, the secret of the spice trade was simple: great demand and highly controlled supply. Some of that control was enforced through political power or contrived through mercantile guile. Some was simply a gift from the gods of climate and botany. Legend has it that, before leaving, Da Gama dared to ask the zamorin of Calicut whether he could take a pepper stalk with him for replanting. His courtiers were outraged, but the potentate stayed calm. "You can take our pepper, but you will never be able to take our rains." He knew how important the region's unusual twin monsoon, both phases of which bring heavy rain, was to its fickle crop. To this day, though regions elsewhere grow pepper, Kerala reigns supreme in its quality, dominating the high end of the market.

If those vital downpours have not washed away what passes for the road, a few days travel into Kerala's rolling Western Ghats, where waterfalls roar and herds of wild elephants loom from soft mist, brings you to the ancestral home of *Piper nigrum*. High up in the middle of nowhere, Iddicki produces the finest pepper in the world, its peppercorns always dark and heavy, bursting with flavor. Its vines wind their way around almost every tree in sight, climbing ten meters or more into the sky.

After such a journey you might expect Iddicki to be a sleepy backwater. In its own idyllic way, though, it is a boomtown worthy of the Wild West. Fancy jeeps clog the narrow streets; shops overflow with the latest necessities of rural life, like washing machines and stereos. Giant satellite dishes shove their expensive snouts at the heavens from every other house. One of the world's largest stashes of gold is in rural India, and to judge by its glittering jewelry shops this town has considerably more than its fair share. "Black gold," explains one pepper farmer with a broad grin, is fetching top prices on the world market.

Until you talk to them about that world market, Iddicki's residents seem much like

farmers anywhere else in the developing world—scraping a living at the margins of the market economy. Thomas Thomas, one of the several hundred thousand small-holders who grow Kerala's pepper, is a good example. A humble man of the earth, he speaks softly and still wears his *dhothi*, a traditional loincloth, when he tills his soil. But with a little prompting he will give you an analysis of the pepper market sophisticated enough to make a Chicago commodities trader blush: current prices, the direction of the futures market, the costs versus benefits of holding stocks. A local spice dealer explains over a feast of fiery snapper and spiced tapioca at his spacious bungalow that "there is full price-discovery in this market." The farmers who sell their crops to him (for resale at the big market in Jewtown, which has replaced Calicut as the hub of Kerala's pepper trade) do so with the latest New York and Rotterdam prices in hand. One particularly sharp farmer, he moans, is cutting out the middlemen altogether and shipping his stocks directly to Europe.

The global aspect of the dealer's trade is nothing new. As far back as 2600BC, there are records of the Egyptians feeding spices obtained from Asia to laborers building the great pyramid of Cheops, to give them strength. Archeological evidence suggests that cloves were quite popular in Syria not long after, despite the fact that, like nutmeg and mace, they came only from the spice islands of what is now Indonesia. Long before the 6th century BC, when Confucius advocated the use of ginger, the Chinese were obtaining spices from the tropics. Europe imported them before Rome was founded.

Today spices are chiefly flavorings for food, but a hundred other uses have contributed to the demand through history. In ancient Egypt cassia and cinnamon fetched a high price because they were essential for embalming; so too were anise, marjoram and cumin, used to rinse out the innards of the worthy dead. Hammurabi's legal code, which called for severe punishment of sloppy or unsuccessful surgeons, did much to encourage the use of medicinal spices in Sumeria.

Particularly in Europe, though, food came to matter most. Spices preserve, and they also make the poorly preserved palatable, masking the appetite-killing stench of decay. After bad harvests and in cold winters the only thing that kept starvation at bay was heavily salted meat—with pepper. And there was never enough of it. Thus pepper began the association with gold it still has in the streets of Iddicki, often at a one-to-one exchange rate. In order to call off their siege of Rome in 408AD, the Visigoths demanded a bounty in gold, silver and pepper. In the Middle Ages plague added to the demand for medicinal spices; a German price table from the 14th century sets the value of a pound of nutmeg at seven fat oxen. At the same time "peppercorn rents" were a serious way of doing business. When the *Mary Rose*, an English ship that sank in 1545, was raised from the ocean floor in the 1980s, nearly every sailor was found with a bunch of peppercorns on his person—the most portable store of value available.

The great beneficiaries of Europe's need were the Arabs. Spices could change hands a dozen times between their source and Europe, soaring in value with each transaction, and the Arabs were the greatest of the middlemen. Keen to keep it that way, they did everything possible to confuse consumers about the spices' origins. As early as the 5th century BC an Arab cover story fooled Herodotus into believing that cinnamon was found only on a mountain range somewhere in Arabia. The spices were jealously guarded by vicious birds of prey, he wrote, which made their nests of the stuff on steep mountain slopes. Arabs would leave out large chunks of fresh donkey meat for the birds to take

back to their nests, which would crash to the ground under the weight The brave Arabs then grabbed the nests, from under the talons of their previous owners.

Not everyone was fooled. In the 1st century AD the Roman historian Pliny grew concerned at the way the empire's gold flowed ever to the east, and set out to expose the truth and undercut the Arab monopolists, who he reckoned to be selling pepper at prices a hundred times what they paid for it in India. It did not help that the gluttonous Romans were, in the words of Frederic Rosengarten, a spice historian, "the most extravagant users of aromatics in history." They used spices in every imaginable combination for their foods, wines and fragrances. Legionaries headed off to battle wearing perfume. The rich slept on pillows of saffron in the belief that it would cure hangovers.

Resentment against the Arab stranglehold had led Rome to launch an invasion of Arabia in 24BC, an ill-fated expedition that ended in humiliation. But where military means failed, market intelligence prevailed. In 40AD, Hippalus, a Greek merchant, discovered something the Arabs had long tried to obscure: that the monsoons which nourish India's pepper vines reverse direction midyear, and that trips from Egypt's Red Sea coast to India and back could thus be shorter and safer than the empire had imagined. Roman trade with India boomed: the Arab monopoly broke.

Early in the 7th century, an obscure spice merchant named Muhammad re-established Arab dominance of the spice trade by introducing an aggressive, expansionary Islam to the world. When the muslims took Alexandria in 641AD, they killed the trade which had long flourished between Rome and India. As they tightened their grip on the business over the next few centuries, prices in Europe rose dramatically. During the Middle Ages, spices became a luxury that only a few in

Europe could afford. This was bad news for the poor and good news for Venice. Its shrewd merchants struck a deal with the Arabs that made them the trade's preferred—indeed almost exclusive—European distributors. Even during the crusades, the relationship bought wealth to all concerned.

The rest of Europe did not care at all for the Muslim Curtain, as the Islamic empire separating west from east came to be called, or for the Venetians. The final blow came in 1453 when the Ottoman Turks took Constantinople, shutting down the small overland trade that had previously evaded the Arab-Venetian monopoly. The Egyptians, gatekeepers of the trade with Venice, felt confident enough to impose a tariff amounting to a third of the value of spices passing through their fingers.

Salvation for the palates and exchequers of Europe's kings lay in finding a sea route to the Indies. In particular, the hunt was on for Malacca, the most important entrepôt in the spice trade and the fabled gateway to the Spice Islands. Spain and Portugal financed dozens of exploration parties in its general direction; half would never make it back home. The rationale for this expense and danger was simple: "He who is lord of Malacca has his hand on the throat of Venice."

It was as part of Portugal's *Drang nach Osten* that Vasco da Gama rounded Africa's Cape of Good Hope to reach India in 1498. As waves of Portuguese explorers returned to Lisbon with their loads of spices, the Venetians and the Egyptians were stunned: the price of pepper in Lisbon fell to one-fifth that in Venice.

The Spaniards, too, were less than happy. They had sent Christopher Columbus to find a route to the Indies via the west, but he had failed, hitting upon the previously unknown Americas instead. In his zeal to convince his paymasters and himself that he had succeeded, he named the new world's natives as Indians and their sacred *chiles* "red" pepper—two unpardonable obfuscations that have confused people to this day.

Pope Alexander IV was drafted in to keep the two expansionist powers apart; the result was the treaty of Tordesillas, which granted all discoveries west of a mid-Atlantic meridian to Spain, and those east of it to Portugal. But the Spanish clung to the possibility of a western end-run to the Spice Islands, and financed Ferdinand Magellan on what would become the first circumnavigation of the earth. Magellan himself was killed in the Philippines, but his sidekick, Sebastian del Cano, completed the momentous journey—with a landfall at the Spice Islands en route. In 1522 his *Victoria* returned to Europe with a tonne of spices on board. The king awarded him a coat of arms embellished with two cinnamon sticks, three nutmegs and twelve cloves.

But the Portuguese had pipped Spain to the post. They had captured the vibrant free-trading port of Malacca, in what is now Malaysia, in 1511. Using the intelligence they gathered there, they made it to the promised land: the tiny Banda islands, the world's only source of nutmeg and mace, which they reached the following year. Nutmeg is the pit of the nutmeg tree's fruit, and mace, which commanded and still commands a higher price, is the delicate red aril which comes between the pit and the fruit's husky exterior. Chaucer extolled "nutemuge put in ale . . ." and it remains an essential part of Coca-Cola's secret formula.

After filling their holds, the Portuguese began their return. One ship ran aground, stranding its crew on a remote island. Hearing of a strange race of white men in his parts, the sultan of Ternate, the most powerful of the clove isles, sent for them—and so the Europeans found the last secret source of spice.

Look out from the expansive verandah of the sultan's palace in Ternate and one of history's great microcosms lies before you. Dominating one side is Gamalama, the island's temperamental volcano. Opposite it stands its equally fickle twin on the island of Tidore. The two spits of land, not a mile apart, are now almost unknown beyond their immediate vicinity. But five centuries ago their names were uttered with breathless excitement across Europe as their rulers, ancient rivals, played the new great powers off against each other with promises of limitless wealth.

Dark, husky aromas swirl through the palace as incense made specially of local spices finds its way into the thick tropical air. The place is overflowing with gifts from distant customers: priceless Chinese vases, exquisitely carved Indian daggers, fine Venetian glassware, all of them evidence of the influence these rulers once wielded. Ask politely, and you might be allowed to gaze—from a respectful distance, and only after much ceremony—at the sultan's magical crown, its hundred sparkling gemstones hanging heavy like ripe peaches. You are not the first impressionable tourist here. Francis Drake gushed about the palace, especially its 400-strong harem. And it seems that it's still good to be the king: one of the gifts on display is an enormous modern settee, helpfully labelled "Lazy chair: for the sultan to take naps."

For much of the 16th century, Spain and Portugal tried to win control of the trade in cloves that made such a lifestyle possible. This meant entangling themselves in the long-running rivalry between the rulers of the two islands, who were in-laws. The European powers would build alliances and forts in one place and then the other, only to find themselves kicked out or caught up in endless intrigues and feuds. After decades of this Machiavellian palaver the Portuguese emerged as the top European player in the clove market, but they never really made it a monopoly. Indeed, they allowed the Dutch, who were growing increasingly anxious for a piece of the action, to be their chief distributors in the north and west of Europe. After Spain gobbled up Portugal in 1580, though, the trade changed again. The Spanish tightened control of the market to which they now had exclusive access, cutting the Dutch out of the picture and raising prices across the continent.

Convinced that they had to find a way to control the source of the spices, the Dutch got their act together. In 1602 they formed the Dutch East India Company (the *Vereenigde Oost-Indische Compagnie,* VOC), an association of merchants meant to reduce competition, share risk and realize economies of scale. Other European countries also formed East India companies—everyone from Portugal to Sweden to Austria had a go—but none was ever as successful in the spice trade as the VOC. By 1670 it was the richest corporation in the world, paying its shareholders an annual dividend of 40% on their investment despite financing 50,000 employees, 30,000 fighting men and 200 ships, many of them armed. The secret of this success was simple. They had no scruples whatsoever.

The VOC's first conquest was the Banda archipelago. Unlike the sultans of the clove islands, who relished the attention lavished upon them by their European suitors and the opportunities for mischief that came with it, the fiercely independent Islamic merchants of the Bandas had never allowed Spain or Portugal to build forts on their islands: they insisted on their freedom to trade with all nations. This independence proved their undoing, since it encouraged the VOC to put the nutmeg trade first on its order of business.

For a taste of Banda's romance nothing beats a trip to Run, an explosion of nutmeg trees in the middle of a turquoise sea. Reaching it after a night aboard ship is a magical experience; scores of dolphins dart about

---

Hot Chile

"Oh Blessed Incomparable Chile, ruler of all things . . . I give thee thanks for my digestive health, I give thee thanks for my very life!" Thus the Transcendental Capsaicinophilic Society, one of the worrying number of cults devoted to *capsicum*: chiles or "red" pepper.

If it sounds as if they are on drugs then so, in a way, they are. Paul Bosland of the Chile Pepper Institute in New Mexico reckons they and all chileheads are high on endorphins, painkillers released by the body to block the sting of the capsaicin which gives chiles their bite.

The addicts are spread all over the world. Travelling on the back of the European spice trade, America's chiles have since colonized every corner of the earth so thoroughly that everyone thinks they have always been around. Even the top man at the Indian Spices Board refuses to accept that chiles are an import, pulling dubious sanskrit references from the Vedas to bolster his point. His clinching argument? "Indians can go months without touching black pepper. but not a day goes by that we don't eat chile peppers,"

This is fast becoming true everywhere else, too, Americans' consumption of chile has doubled over the past two decades; they now use the spice in almost everything. Salsa now outsells ketchup as America's top condiment. But black pepper still gets all the glory as the world's most important traded spice. Unlike its fickle namesake, red pepper grows like mad all over the place. So though there may be a great demand for it, no one makes much money out of trading it. Bad news for traders, good news for foodies.

---

your bow-wave as the first glints of sunrise streak across the sky. It feels much as it must have done when English adventurers first claimed the place, making it the country's first colony anywhere. Not much of a colony, it must be said: the island is so small that even a modest fishing vessel can come ashore only at high tide. Yet this seemingly insignificant toe-hold in nutmeg-land so exercised the Dutch that they traded away a promising young colony on the other side of the world to secure it. That island was New Amsterdam, now better known as Manhattan.

The purchase of Run demonstrates the VOC's persistence; it does not do justice to the company's cruelty (normally, but not exclusively, meted out to non-Europeans). Its most successful head, Jan Pieterszoon Coen, had earlier convinced the reluctant Bandanese of his firm's God-given right to monopolize the nut-

meg trade in a more typical style: he had had every single male over the age of fifteen that he could get his hands on butchered. Coen brought in Japanese mercenaries to torture, quarter and decapitate village leaders, displaying their heads on long poles. The population of the isles was 15,000 before the VOC arrived; 15 years later it was 600.

When they turned to the clove trade the Dutch had no time for the squabbling politics of Ternate and Tidore. The VOC uprooted all the Sultans' clove trees and concentrated production on Ambon, an island where its grip was tight. By 1681, it had destroyed three-quarters of all nutmeg trees in unwanted areas and reorganized farming into plantations. It imposed the death penalty on anyone caught growing, stealing or possessing nutmeg or clove plants without authorization. It drenched every nutmeg with lime before export, to ensure that not one fertile seed escaped its clutches. Yet high on its hillside Afo lives to tell its tale.

Climb through the dense, aromatic forests that cover the steep slopes of Ternate's volcano, and you will find this living testament to the ultimate futility of monopoly. Nearly 40 meters tall and over 4 meters round, Afo is the world's oldest clove tree, planted in defiance of the Dutch ban nearly four centuries ago. Despite the VOC's extreme precautions, Afo's sister seedlings, stolen in 1770 by an intrepid Frenchman (curiously, named Poivre), ended up flourishing on the Seychelles, Réunion and especially Zanzibar, which later became the world's largest producer of cloves. By the end of the 18th century the emergence of these rivals had broken the Dutch monopoly for good.

By that time the VOC was already a hollow mockery of its original ghastly self. As early as the end of the 17th century, careful analysis of the books shows that its volume of trade was reducing every year. Even a monopoly so ruthlessly enforced could not help but leak, and the VOC's overheads were huge—tens of thousands of employees, garrisons, warships. Decades of easy rents had created a corrupt and inefficient beast. By 1735, dwindling spice income had been overtaken by textiles in the company's profit column. In 1799, the most vicious robber baron of them all met its final end. The VOC went bankrupt.

The demise of the VOC was not just a pleasing comeuppance. It was evidence that, in just two centuries, Europeans had changed the spice trade forever. The spices that were once limited to tiny islands in hidden archipelagoes were being grown around the world and in large quantities. Trade routes that spanned oceans were becoming commonplace and, as such, competitive. The Dutch did their best to buck the trend, destroying their stocks so blatantly that, according to one observer, the streets of Amsterdam were

"flooded with nutmeg butter." But it was all in vain. Spices were no longer that hard to come by. Monopolies gave way to markets.

Those markets remained rich in romance; the allure of the trade, its role as a cultural crossroads, its many rival players, its uncertainties and its opportunities for smuggling (even relatively cheap spices carry a lot of value for a given weight) kept the spice bazaars of Kerala, Ambon and Rotterdam fascinating. And lucrative, too; though no one could control the overall flow of spice any more, information could still be rushed ahead fast enough—or sequestered behind long enough—for people in the know to make a killing. Now, though, the information itself has started to flow freely. "There just aren't so many secrets anymore," reflects a spice trader in Rotterdam. "The farmers in Vietnam are walking around with mobile phones. They know the market price as soon as I do."

Such traders are now caught in a trap. Their space for bargaining and trade, opened up with the end of monopoly production, is being hemmed in by ever more powerful purchasers—the food giants and spice multinationals. In an age of free-flowing information these buyers can bypass the markets and go directly to the source. From Jewtown, still the key pepper entrepôt, to Rotterdam, London and New York, the main international markets, spice traders are a dying breed. One industry veteran reckons that only a fifth of the trading concerns that flourished 30 years ago are still in business.

Their problems stem from men like Al Goetze. Meet him in his office near Baltimore, at the staid headquarters of McCormick, the world's largest spice firm, and his conservative suit and dry manner might lead you to mistake him for a stuffy corporate type. But to his admiring colleagues he is "a modern day Marco Polo."

Procurement managers at food-processing firms were once content to purchase spices through brokers, never leaving the comfort of their air-conditioned offices. Mr. Goetze hits the road. He and his men have travelled to nearly every country on earth that grows spices, again and again. McCormick has set up joint-ventures or wholly owned subsidiaries in over a dozen key spice-producing countries in recent years.

Once the reason for going to the source was price. Now, Mr. Goetze says, quality is what matters. Both American and European regulators, prompted by increasing consumer awareness of food safety, have been cracking down hard on impurities. Mr. Goetze points to an unlikely assortment of objects in a display case: stones, rusty nails, giant cockroaches, plastic beach sandals. All were crammed into bursting burlap bags and sold to McCormick with its spice. Big processing firms and marketers, frightened that such stuff—or worse, microscopic impurities that come with it—might make it to the dinner plates of litigious customers, are going straight to the source to clean things up.

Alfons van Gulick, the head of Rotterdam's Man Producten, the world's biggest and most influential spice-trading firm, is understandably unimpressed: "McCormick should stick to polishing its brand and selling, rather than telling countries how to produce spice." But the people for whose products McCormick and Man Producten compete have an interest in Mr. Goetze's strategy. The Indian Spices Board is already helping members improve standards and obtain seals of approval such as ISO certification. The hope is that, over time, producers can go downstream and capture more of the fat margins that come with the "value-added" processing now done in rich countries.

Industry analysts are skeptical about vertical integration. In other commodities it has not been much of a success. Cutting out the middleman may pose unexpected problems for conservative multinationals, unfamiliar with the culture and risks involved in going upstream. And then there is volatility, on which middlemen thrive and which farmers and multinationals dislike. Asked whether the trade has lost its mystery, one animated trader replies "Mystery? I experience it every day when I try to figure out what is going on with prices in this market!"

Producers hate this, and have made various attempts to iron out the market's ups and downs. The International Pepper Community—which includes India, Indonesia and Brazil among its members—has tried for decades to form a producers' cartel to boost prices, without any success. Price fixing by vanilla growers in Madagascar succeeded for a while, but then Uganda flooded the market with cheaper beans. Indonesia and Grenada, the top producers of nutmeg, managed to boost prices for a few years by limiting supply, but cheating quickly scuppered the arrangement. Quiet talks are underway between top cardamom producers in India and Guatemala, who produce nearly all the world's output, to restrict supply; it may work for a while, but not for long.

Every decade or so, an ambitious individual trader tries to do with money what the producers cannot do by agreement. To corner the pepper market would offer huge riches, and so people regularly have a go. Half a century ago, it was an Armenian; a decade ago, an American. Now it appears that a shadowy Indonesian tycoon may be making a play for at least the white pepper market. But history teaches that such grandiose efforts at monopoly face an uphill struggle. And though it may be possible to milk them for a while, the modern day economics of the trade ensure that they cannot last. The spice trade, once the stuff of legends, has become a market much like any other. And a taste of luxury beyond the dreams of almost every human in history is available to almost everyone, almost everywhere.

2

Transition to the Modern Era

From:	To:
Traditionalism and Stability	Change, Revolution, Progress
Religion and Faith	Science and Reason
Church	State
Agriculture	Industry
Rigid Social Structure	Mobility
Monarchy	Democracy and Dictatorship

Two Basic Currents in Western Civilization

1. Ancient, Pagan, Rational, Secular, Humanistic

2. Medieval, Christian, Faith-Based, Other-Worldly, Spiritualistic

3

The Scientific Revolution: Galileo

Written exactly midway between Copernicus' *On the Revolutions of the Heavenly Spheres* (1543) and Newton's *Mathematical Principles of Natural Philosophy* (1687), Galileo's letter to Christina, Grand Duchess of Tuscany, presents the conflicts involved in the Scientific Revolution. Most scientists remained committed to the Medieval-Ptolemaic geocentric worldview until after Newton's work was published and they did so for mostly scientific but also religious reasons. (In fact there was no proof that the earth moved until 1727.) Galileo, therefore, found himself in the midst of conflicts of faith (both scientific and religious) as well as of fact. The issues of the day involved not only what the truth was but also how it was to be ascertained. It was in the latter respect that Galileo raised the most important questions and made his most important contributions.

Discussion Questions

1. What motives does Galileo attribute to his critics? Does he think their chief objections to his opinions are religious?

2. Why doesn't he think the Bible should be the foundation of scientific knowledge? What does he think should be?

3. In the Middle Ages, theology was called "the Queen of the Sciences." Why does Galileo question that title? What are the differences he draws between religion and science?

Some years ago, as Your Serene Highness well knows, I discovered in the heavens many things that had not been seen before our own age. The novelty of these things, as well as some consequences which followed from them in contradiction to the physical notions commonly held among academic philosophers, stirred up against me no small numbers of professors—as if I had placed these things in the sky with my own hands in order to upset nature and overturn the sciences. They seemed to forget the increase of known truths stimulates the investigation, establishment, and growth of the arts; not their diminution or destruction.

Showing a greater fondness for their own opinions than for truth, they sought to deny and disprove the things which, if they had cared to look for themselves, their own senses would have demonstrated to them. To this end they hurled various charges and published numerous writings filled with vain arguments, and they made the grave mistake of sprinkling these with passages taken from places in the Bible which they had failed to understand properly, and which were ill suited to their purposes. . . .

Persisting in their original resolve to destroy me and everything mine by any means they can think of, these men are aware of my views in astronomy and philosophy. They know that as to the arrangement of the parts of the universe, I hold the sun to be situated motionless in the center of the revolution of the celestial orbs while the earth rotates on its axis and revolves about the sun. They know also that I support this position not only by refuting the arguments of Ptolemy and Aristotle, but by producing many counterarguments; in particular, some which relate to physical effects whose causes can perhaps be assigned in no other way. In addition there are astronomical arguments derived from many things in my new celestial discoveries that plainly confute the Ptomenaic system while admirably agreeing with and confirming the contrary hypothesis. Possibly because they are disturbed by the known truth of other propositions of mine which differ from those commonly held, and therefore mistrusting their defense so long as they confine themselves to the field of philosophy, these men have resolved to fabricate a shield for their fallacies out of the mantle of pretended religion and the authority of the Bible. These they apply, with little judgement, to the refutation of arguments that they do not understand and have not even listened to.

First they have endeavored to spread the opinion that such propositions in general are contrary to the Bible and are consequently damnable and heretical. . . . [And] they have had no trouble in finding men who would preach the damnability and heresy of the new doctrine from their very pulpits with unwonted confidence, thus doing impious and inconsiderate injury not only to that doctrine and its followers but to all mathematicians in general. . . .

Now as to the false aspersions which they so unjustly seek to cast upon me, I have thought it necessary to justify myself in the eyes of all men, whose judgement in matters of religion and of reputation I must hold in great esteem. I shall therefore discourse of the particulars which these men produce to make this opinion detested and to have it condemned not merely as false but as heretical. To this end they make a shield of their hypocritical zeal for religion. They go about invoking the Bible, which they would have minister to their deceitful purposes. Contrary to the sense of the Bible and the intention of the holy Fathers, if I am not mistaken, they would extend such authorities until even in purely physical matters—where faith is not involved—they would have us altogether abandon reason and the evidence of our senses in favor of some biblical passage, though under the surface meaning of its words this passage may contain a different sense. . . .

. . . I think that in discussions of physical problems we ought to begin not from the authority of scriptural passages, but from sense-experiences and necessary demonstrations; for the holy Bible and the phenomena of nature proceed alike from the divine Word, the former as the dictate of the Holy Ghost and the latter as the observant executrix of God's commands. It is necessary for the Bible, in order to be accommodated to the understanding of every man, to speak many things which appear to differ from the absolute truth so far as the bare meaning of the words is concerned. But Nature, on the other hand, is inexorable and immutable; she never transgresses the laws imposed upon her, or cares a whit whether her abstruse reasons and methods of operation are understandable to men. For that reason it appears that nothing physical which sense-experience sets before our eyes, or which necessary demonstrations prove to us, ought to be called in question

(much less condemned) upon the testimony of biblical passages which may have some different meaning beneath their words. For the Bible is not chained in every expression to conditions as strict as those which govern all physical effects; nor is God any less excellently revealed in Nature's actions than in the sacred statements of the Bible. . . .

I do not wish to place in the number of such lay writers some theologians whom I consider men of profound learning and devout behavior, and who are therefore held by me in great esteem and veneration. Yet I cannot deny that I feel some discomfort which I should like to have removed, when I hear them pretend to the power of constraining others by scriptural authority to follow in a physical dispute that opinion which they think best agrees with the Bible, and then believe themselves not bound to answer the opposing reasons and experiences. In explanation and support of this opinion they say that since theology is queen of all the sciences, she need not bend in any way to accommodate herself to the teachings of less worthy sciences which are subordinate to her; these others must rather be referred to her as to their supreme empress, changing and altering their conclusions according to her statues and decrees. . . .

First, I question whether there is not some equivocation in failing to specify the virtues which entitle sacred theology to the title of "queen." It might deserve that name by reason of including everything that is learned from all the other sciences and establishing everything by better methods and with profounder learning. It is thus, for example, that the rules for measuring fields and keeping accounts are much more excellently contained in arithmetic and in the geometry of Euclid than in the practices of surveyors and accountants. Or theology might be queen because of being occupied with a subject which excels in dignity all the subjects which compose the other sciences, and because her teachings are divulged in more sublime ways.

That the title and authority of queen belongs to theology in the first sense, I think will not be affirmed by theologians who have any skill in the other sciences. None of these, I think, will say that geometry, astronomy, music, and medicine are much more excellently contained in the Bible than they are in the books of Archimedes, Ptolemy, Boethius, and Galen. Hence it seems likely that regal pre-eminence is given to theology in the second sense; that is, by reason of its subject and the miraculous communication of divine revelation of conclusions which could not be conceived by men in any other way, concerning chiefly the attainment of eternal blessedness.

Let us grant then that theology is conversant with the loftiest divine contemplation, and occupies the regal throne among sciences by dignity. But acquiring the highest authority in this way, if she does not descend to the lower and humbler speculations of the subordinate sciences and has no regard for them because they are not concerned with blessedness, then her professors should not arrogate to themselves the authority to decide on controversies in professions which they have neither studied nor practiced. Why, this would be as if an absolute despot, being neither a physician nor an architect but knowing himself free to command, should undertake to administer medicines and erect buildings according to his whim—at grave peril of his poor patients' lives, and the speedy collapse of his edifices.

Again, to command that the very professors of astronomy themselves see to the refutation of their own observations and proofs as mere fallacies and sophisms is to enjoin something that lies beyond any possibility of accomplishment. For this would amount to commanding that they must not see what they see and must not understand what they know, and that in searching they must find the opposite of what they actually encounter. Before this could be done they would have to be taught how to make one mental faculty command another, and the inferior powers the superior, so that the imagination and the will might be forced to believe the opposite of what the intellect understands. I am referring at all times to merely physical propositions, and not to supernatural things which are matters of faith.

* * *

Besides, I question the truth of the statment that the church commands us to hold as matters of faith all physical conclusions bearing the stamp of harmonious interpretation by all the Fathers. . . . So far as I can find, all that is really prohibited is the "perverting into senses contrary to that of the holy Church or that of the concurrent agreement of the Fathers those passages, and those alone, which pertain to faith or ethics, or which concern the edification of Christian doctrine." . . . But the mobility or stability of the earth or sun is neither a matter of faith nor one contrary to ethics.

4

The Scientific Revolution: Newton

In 1998, Michael H. Hart issued the second edition of his book *The 100: A Ranking of the Most Influential Persons in History*. As in the first edition, he ranked Isaac Newton as the second most influential person in history behind Muhammad and ahead of Jesus. The following selection is his chapter on Newton in which he explains the choice he made. That Newton is the leading scientist of all time was seconded by a Nobel physicist at the University of Chicago who, on the 300th anniversary of the publication of Newton's *Principia Mathematica* in 1987, said that among scientists Einstein ranks "a very distant second" behind Newton.

Discussion Questions

1. What are the major fields in which Newton made his most important contributions?

2. What does Hart think is the most significant overall contribution Newton made to science?

3. In what ways does Hart think that Newton's contributions extend beyond science?

4. Do you think that Hart makes his case that Newton ought to rank number 2?

Isaac Newton (1642–1727)

Isaac Newton, the greatest and most influential scientist who ever lived, was born in Woolsthorpe, England, on Christmas Day, 1642, the same year that Galileo died. Like Muhammad, he was born after the death of his father. As a child, he showed considerable mechanical aptitude, and was very clever with his hands. Although a bright child, he was inattentive in school and did not attract much attention. When he was a teenager, his mother took him out of school, hoping that he would become a successful farmer. Fortunately, she was persuaded that his principal talents lay elsewhere, and at eighteen, he entered Cambridge University. There, he rapidly absorbed what was then known of science and mathematics, and soon moved on to his own independent research. Between his twenty-first and twenty-seventh years, he laid the foundations for the scientific theories that subsequently revolutionized the world.

The middle of the seventeenth century was a period of great scientific ferment. The invention of the telescope near the beginning of the century had revolutionized the entire study of astronomy. The English philosopher Francis Bacon and the French philosopher René Descartes had both urged scientists throughout Europe to cease relying on the authority of Aristotle and to experiment and observe for themselves. What Bacon and Descartes had preached, the great Galileo had practiced. His astronomical observations, using the newly invented telescope, had revolutionized the study of astronomy, and his mechanical experiments had established what is now known as Newton's first law of motion.

Other great scientists, such as William Harvey, who discovered the circulation of the blood, and Johannes Kepler, who discovered the laws describing the motions of the planets around the sun, were bringing new basic information to the scientific community. Still, pure science was largely a plaything of intellectuals, and as yet there was no proof that when applied to technology, science could revolutionize the whole mode of human life, as Francis Bacon had predicted.

Although Copernicus and Galileo had swept aside some of the misconceptions of ancient science and contributed to a greater understanding of the universe, no set of principles had been formulated that could turn this collection of seemingly unrelated facts into a unified theory with which to make scientific predictions. It was Isaac Newton who supplied that unified theory and set modern science on the course which it has followed ever since.

Newton was always reluctant to publish his results, and although he had formulated the basic ideas behind most of his work by 1669, many of his theories were not made public until much later. The first of his discoveries to be published was his groundbreaking work on the nature of light. In a series of careful experiments, Newton had discovered that ordinary white light is a mixture of all the colors of the rainbow. He had also made a careful analysis of the consequences of the laws of the reflection and refraction of light. Using these laws, he had in 1668 designed and actually built the first reflecting telescope, the type of telescope that is used in most major astronomical observatories today. These discoveries, together with the results of many other optical experiments which he had performed, were presented by Newton before the British Royal Society when he was twenty-nine years old.

Newton's achievements in optics alone would probably entitle him to a place on this list; however, they are considerably less important than his accomplishments in pure mathematics and mechanics. His major mathematical contribution was his invention of integral calculus, which he probably devised when he was twenty-three or twenty-four years old. That invention, the most important achievement of modern mathematics, is not merely the seed out of which much of modern mathematical theory has grown, it is also the essential tool without which most of the subsequent progress in modern science would have been impossible. Had Newton done nothing else, the invention of integral calculus by itself would have entitled him to a fairly high place on this list.

Newton's most important discoveries, however, were in the field of mechanics, the science of how material objects move. Galileo had discovered the first law of motion, which describes the motion of objects if they are not subjected to any exterior forces. In practice, of course, all objects are subjected to exterior forces, and the most important question in mechanics is how objects move under such circumstances. This problem was solved by Newton in his famous second law of motion, which may rightly be considered the most fundamental law of classical physics. The second law (described mathematically by the equation $F = ma$) states that the acceleration of an object (i.e., the rate at which its velocity changes) is equal to the net force on the object divided by the object's mass. To those first two laws, Newton added his famous third law of motion (which states that for each action—i.e., physical force—there is an equal and opposite reaction), and the most famous of his scientific laws, the law of universal gravitation. This set of four laws, taken conjointly, form a unified system by means of which virtually all macroscopic mechanical systems, from the swinging of a pendulum to the motion of the planets in their orbits around the sun, may be investigated, and their behavior predicted. Newton did not merely state these laws of mechanics; he himself, using the mathematical tools of the calculus, showed how these fundamental laws could be applied to the solution of actual problems.

Newton's laws can be and have been applied to an extremely broad range of scientific and engineering problems. During his lifetime, the most dramatic application of his laws was made in the field of astronomy. In this area, too, Newton led the way. In 1687, he published his great work, the *Mathematical Principles of Natural Philosophy* (usually referred to simply as the *Principia*), in which he presented his law of gravitation and laws of motion. Newton showed how these laws could be used to predict precisely the motions of the planets around the sun. The principal problem of dynamical astronomy—that is, the problem of predicting exactly the positions and motions of the stars and planets—was thereby completely solved by Newton in one magnificent sweep. For this reason, Newton is often considered the greatest of all astronomers.

What, then, is our assessment of Newton's scientific importance? If one looks at the index of an encyclopedia of science, one will find more references (perhaps two or three times as many) to Newton and to his laws and discoveries than to any other individual scientist. Furthermore, one should consider what other great scientists have said about Newton. Leibniz, no friend of Sir Isaac's, and a man with whom he engaged in a bitter dispute, wrote: "Taking mathematics from the beginning of the world to the time when Newton lived, what he has done is much the better part." The great French scientist Laplace wrote: "The *Principia* is preeminent above any other production of human genius." Lagrange frequently stated that Newton was the greatest genius who ever lived, while Ernst Mach, writing in 1901, said: "All that has been accomplished in mathematics since his day has been a deductive, formal, and mathematical development of mechanics on the basis of Newton's laws." This, perhaps, is the crux of Newton's great accomplishment: he found science a hodgepodge of isolated facts and laws, capable of describing some phenomena but of predicting only a few; he left us a unified system of laws, which were capable of application to an enormous range of physical phenomena, and which could be used to make exact predictions.

In a brief summary like this, it is not possible to detail all of Newton's discoveries; consequently, many of the lesser ones have been omitted, although they were important achievements in their own right. Newton made significant contributions to thermodynamics (the study of heat) and to acoustics (the study of sound); he enunciated the extremely important physical principles of conservation of momentum and conservation of angular momentum; he discovered the binomial theorem in mathematics; and he gave the

first cogent explanation of the origin of the stars.

Now, one might grant that Newton was by far the greatest and most influential scientist who ever lived but still ask why he should be ranked higher than such major political figures as Alexander the Great or George Washington, and ahead of such major religious figures as Jesus Christ and Gautama Buddha. My own view is that even though political changes are of significance, it is fair to say that most people in the world were living the same way 500 years after Alexander's death as their forebears had lived five centuries before his time. Similarly, in most of their daily activities, the majority of human beings were living the same way in 1500 A.D. as human beings had been living in 1500 B.C. In the last five centuries, however, with the rise of modern science, the everyday life of most human beings has been completely revolutionized. We dress differently, eat different foods, work at different jobs, and spend our leisure time a great deal differently than people did in 1500 A.D. Scientific discoveries have not only revolutionized technology and economics; they have also completely changed politics, religious thinking, art, and philosophy. Few aspects of human activity have remained unchanged by this scientific revolution, and it is for this reason that so many scientists and inventors are to be found on this list. Newton was not only the most brilliant of all scientists; he was also the most influential figure in the development of scientific theory, and therefore well merits a position at or near the top of any list of the world's most influential persons.

Newton died in 1727, and was buried in Westminster Abbey, the first scientist to be accorded that honor.

5

The Age of Enlightenment

The Norwegian author, Jostein Gaarder, has combined in her book, *Sophie's World: A Novel About the History of Philosophy,* what one book reviewer called, "a short history of Western philosophy . . . embedded in the wrapping of a suspense novel." In a series of exchanges between Sophie, a 14-year-old Norwegian girl, and her teacher, the mysterious Alberto, some two thousand years of philosophy is imparted in bits and pieces, and its meanings used to unravel a strange set of circumstances. Suspense aside, this excerpt highlights the key concepts of the 18th century intellectual movement known as the Enlightenment. Inspired by the scientific and rational theories of Newton, Galileo, Locke and Hobbes, a group of French writers known as the *philosophes,* not only popularized the new thinking of the day, but also sought to apply those principles to human society. The leaders of the movement, Voltaire, Rousseau and Montesquieu, attacked the so-called "unenlightened" institutions of monarchy, organized religion, mercantilism and class hierarchy presently existing in France, and advocated their reform. They reasoned that human society must, like the physical world, be governed by natural, universal laws that humans could employ to correct the abuses of the past and present. Modeling the institutions of government, the economy, social classes, the church and the schools, on the principles described in the following passage, would, so the *philosophes* believed, lead humankind into an era of unparalleled progress, indeed, would create a paradise on earth.

Discussion Questions

1. What similarities do the ideas in this passage share with those contained in Galileo's letter or in the sentiments of Tom Paine?

2. What meaning did the philosophes give to nature? Progress? Do they have the same meaning today?

3. Reason, or rationalism, is a key component of enlightenment thought. How was it used to support the arguments of the philosophes? Do you think it is as important in justifying present day institutions and policies as in the 18th century?

4. Would you consider yourself a philosophe, or do you think that too many of their ideas are wrong?

5. What was the long-term effect of the Enlightenment on Western values and society? Have the key ideas of the Enlightenment thinkers been discredited, or do they still apply to today's world?

Jostein Gaarder

“After Hume, the next great philosopher was the German, Immanuel Kant. But France also had many important thinkers in the eighteenth century. We could say that the philosophical center of gravity in Europe in the eighteenth century was in England in the first half, in France in the middle, and in Germany toward the end of it.”

“A shift from west to east, in other words.”

“Precisely. Let me outline some of the ideas that many of the French Enlightenment philosophers had in common. The important names are *Montesquieu, Voltaire, and Rousseau,* but there were many, many others. I shall concentrate on seven points.”

“Thanks, that I am painfully aware of.”

Sophie handed him the card from Hilde's father. Alberto sighed deeply, “He could have saved himself the trouble . . . the first key words, then, are *opposition to authority.* Many of the French Enlightenment philosophers visited England, which was in many ways more liberal than their home country, and were intrigued by the English natural sciences, especially Newton and his universal physics. But they were also inspired by British philosophy, in particular by Locke and his political philosophy. Once back in France, they become increasingly opposed to the old authority. They thought it was essential to remain skeptical of all inherited truths, the idea being that the individual must find his own answer to every question. The tradition of Descartes was very inspiring in this respect."

"Because he was the one who built everything up from the ground."

"Quite so. The opposition to authority was not least directed against the power of the clergy, the king, and the nobility. During the eighteenth century, these institutions had even more power in France than they had in England."

"Then came the French Revolution."

"Yes, in 1789. But the revolutionary ideas arose much earlier. The next key word is *rationalism.*"

"I thought rationalism went out with Hume."

"Hume himself did not die until 1776. That was about twenty years after Montesquieu and only two years before Voltaire and Rousseau, who both died in 1778. But all three had been to England and were familiar with the philosophy of Locke. You may recall that Locke was not consistent in his empiricism. He believed, for example, that faith in God and certain moral norms were inherent in human reason. This idea is also the core of the French Enlightenment."

"You also said that the French have always been more rational than the British."

"Yes, a difference that goes right back to the Middle Ages. When the British speak of 'common sense,' the French usually speak of 'evident.' The English expression means 'what everybody knows,' the French means 'what is obvious'—to one's reason, that is."

"I see."

"Like the humanists of antiquity—such as Socrates and the Stoics—most of the Enlightenment philosophers had an unshakable faith in human reason. This was so characteristic that the French Enlightenment is often called the Age of Reason. The new natural sciences had revealed that nature was subject to reason. Now the Enlightenment philosophers saw it as their duty to lay a foundation for morals, religion, and ethics in accordance with man's immutable reason. This led to the *enlightenment movement.*"

"The third point."

"Now was the time to start 'enlightening' the masses. This was to be the basis for a better society. People thought that poverty and oppression were the fault of ignorance and superstition. Great attention was therefore focused on the education of children and of the people. It is no accident that the science of pedagogy was founded during the Enlightenment."

"So schools date from the Middle Ages, and pedagogy from the Enlightenment."

"You could say that. The greatest monument to the enlightenment movement was characteristically enough a huge encyclopedia. I refer to the Encyclopedia in 28 volumes published during the years from 1751 to 1772. All the great philosophers and men of letters contributed to it. 'Everything is to be found here,' it was said, 'from the way needles are made to the way cannons are founded.'"

"The next point is *cultural optimism,*" Sophie said. . . .

"The Enlightenment philosophers thought that once reason and knowledge became widespread, humanity would make great progress. It could only be a question of time before irrationalism and ignorance would give way to an 'enlightened' humanity. This thought was dominant in Western Europe until the last couple of decades. Today we are no longer so convinced that all 'developments' are to the good.

"But this criticism of 'civilization' was already being voiced by French Enlightenment philosophers."

"Maybe we should have listened to them."

"For some, the new catchphrase was *back to nature*. But 'nature' to the Enlightenment philosophers meant almost the same as 'reason,' since human reason was a gift of nature rather than of religion or of 'civilization.' It was observed that the so-called primitive peoples were frequently both healthier and happier than Europeans, and this, it was said, was because they had not been 'civilized.' Rousseau proposed the catchphrase, 'We should return to nature.' For nature is good, and man is 'by nature' good; it is civilization which ruins him. Rousseau also believed that the child should be allowed to remain in its 'naturally' innocent state as long as possible. It would not be wrong to say that the idea of the intrinsic value of childhood dates from the Enlightenment. Previously, childhood had been considered merely a preparation for adult life. But we are all human beings—and we live our life on this earth, even when we are children."

"I should think so!"

"Religion, they thought, had to be made natural."

"What exactly did they mean by that?"

"They meant that religion also had to be brought into harmony with 'natural' reason. There were many who fought for what one could call *a natural religion,* and that is the sixth point on the list. At the time there were a lot of confirmed materialists who did not believe in a God, and who professed to atheism. But most of the Enlightenment philosophers thought it was irrational to imagine a world without God. The world was far too rational for that. Newton held the same view, for example. It was also considered rational to believe in the immortality of the soul. Just as for Descartes, whether or not man has an immortal soul was held to be more a question of reason than of faith."

"That I find very strange. To me, it's a typical case of what you believe, not of what you know."

"That's because you don't live in the eighteenth century. According to the Enlightenment philosophers, what religion needed was to be stripped of all the irrational dogmas or doctrines that had got attached to the simple teachings of Jesus during the course of ecclesiastical history."

"I see."

"Many people consequently professed to what is known as *Deism*."

"What is that?"

"By Deism we mean a belief that God created the world ages and ages ago, but has not revealed himself to the world since. Thus God is reduced to the 'Supreme Being' who only reveals himself to mankind through nature and natural laws, never in any 'supernatural' way. We find a similar 'philosophical God' in the writings of Aristotle. For him, God was the 'formal cause' or 'first mover.'"

"So now there's only one point left, *human rights*."

"And yet this is perhaps the most important. On the whole, you could say that the French Enlightenment was more practical than the English philosophy."

"You mean they lived according to their philosophy?"

"Yes, very much so. The French Enlightenment philosophers did not content themselves with theoretical views on man's place in society. They fought actively for what they called the 'natural rights' of the citizen. At first, this took the form of a campaign against censorship—for the freedom of the press. But also in matters of religion, morals, and politics, the individual's right to freedom of thought and utterance had to be secured. They also fought for the abolition of slavery and for a more humane treatment of criminals."

"I think I agree with most of that."

"The principle of the 'inviolability of the individual' culminated in the Declaration of the Rights of Man and Citizen adopted by the

French National Assembly in 1789. This Declaration of Human Rights was the basis for our own Norwegian Constitution of 1814."

"But a lot of people still have to fight for these rights."

"Yes, unhappily. But the Enlightenment philosophers wanted to establish certain rights that everybody was entitled to simply by being born. That was what they meant by natural rights.

"We still speak of a 'natural right' which can often be in conflict with the laws of the land. And we constantly find individuals, or even whole nations, that claim this 'natural right' when they rebel against anarchy, servitude, and oppression."

"What about women's rights?"

"The French Revolution in 1787 established a number of rights for all 'citizens.' But a citizen was nearly always considered to be a man. Yet it was the French Revolution that gave us the first inklings of feminism."

"It was about time!"

"As early as 1787 the Enlightenment philosopher *Condorcet* published a treatise on be rights of women. He held that women had the same 'natural rights' as men. During the Revolution of 1789, women were extremely active in the fight against the old feudal regime. For example, it was women who led the demonstrations that forced the king away from his palace at Versailles. Women's groups were formed in Paris. In addition to

the demand for the same political rights as men, they also demanded changes in the marriage laws and in women's social conditions."

"Did they get equal rights?"

"No. Just as on so many subsequent occasions, the question of women's rights was exploited in the heat of the struggle, but as soon as things fell into place in a new regime, the old male-dominated society was reintroduced."

"Typical!"

"One of those who fought hardest for the rights of women during the French Revolution was *Olympe de Gouges.* In 1791—two years after the revolution—she published a declaration on the rights of women. The declaration on the rights of the citizen had not included any article on women's natural rights. Olympe de Gouges now demanded all the some rights for women as for men.

"What happened?"

"She was beheaded in 1793. And all political activity for women was banned."

"How shameful!"

"It was not until the nineteenth century that feminism really got under way, not only in France but also in the rest of Europe. Little by little this struggle began to bear fruit. But in Norway, for example, women did not get the right to vote until 1913. And women in many parts of the world still have a lot to fight for."

"They can count on my support." . . .

6

The Enlightenment: Deism

Some historians describe the European Enlightenment of the 18th century as the first fully modern worldview in history. The agents of this movement, whom we usually call the *philosophes* (men like Voltaire, Diderot and Montesquieu), believed that earlier thinkers like Descartes, Locke and Newton had opened up an entirely new, and true, view of man, society and nature. They believed that using reason to understand the laws of nature would lead inevitably to progress and the universal improvement of the human condition. But they also recognized that progress could only be achieved through the destruction of what they called the *ancien regime* (essentially a combination of absolutism, the church and mercantilism). Believing that the liberation of the mind was the first step toward progress, they leveled their guns at institutionalized religion and created what they thought would be a benign "natural" religion, deism.

Among the first full-scale attacks against institutionalized Christianity was Thomas Paine's *Age of Reason*, written in 1794, which follows.

Discussion Questions

1. What does Paine say he believes in? What doesn't he believe in?

2. For what reasons does he reject most institutionalized religions like Christianity?

3. What is Paine's standard of evidence?

4. Why does he consider Christianity to be a "contrivance?"

5. What are the foundations on which he thinks we can build a "true" religion?

The Age of Reason

To My Fellow Citizens of the United States of America

I put the following work under your protection. It contains my opinion upon religion. You will do me the justice to remember that I have always strenuously supported the right of every man to his opinion however different that opinion might be to mine. He who denies to another this right makes a slave of himself to his present opinion, because he precludes himself the right of changing it.

The most formidable weapon against errors of every kind is reason. I have never used any other, and I trust I never shall.

Your affectionate friend and fellow citizen,

Thomas Paine
Luxembourg (Paris), 8th Pluvôise.
Second year of the French Republic, one and indivisible,
January 27th, O. S. 1791.

It has been my intention, for several years past, to publish my thoughts upon religion. I am well aware of the difficulties that attend the subject and, from that consideration, had reserved it to a more advanced period of life. I intended it to be the last offering I should make to my fellow Citizens of all nations, and that at a time when the purity of the motive that induced me to it could not admit of a question, even by those who might disapprove the work.

The circumstance that has now taken place in France of the total abolition of the whole national order of priesthood, and of everything appertaining to compulsive systems of religion, and compulsive articles of faith, has not only precipitated my intention, but rendered a work of this kind exceedingly necessary, lest in the general wreck of superstition, of false systems of government and false theology, we lose sight of morality, of humanity, and of the theology that is true.

As several of my colleagues, and others of my fellow citizens of France, have given me the example of making their voluntary and individual profession of faith, I also will make mine; and I do this with all that sincerity and frankness with which the mind of man communicates with itself.

I believe in one God, and no more; and I hope for happiness beyond this life.

I believe in the equality of man; and I believe that religious duties consist in doing justice, loving mercy, and endeavoring to make our fellow creatures happy.

But, lest it should be supposed that I believe in many other things in addition to these, I shall, in the progress of this work, declare the things I do not believe, and my reasons for not believing them.

I do not believe in the creed professed by the Jewish church, by the Roman church, by the Greek church, by the Turkish church, by the Protestant church, nor by any church that I know of. My own mind is my own church.

All national institutions of churches, whether Jewish, Christian, or Turkish, appear to me no other than human inventions, set up to terrify and enslave mankind, and monopolize power and profit.

I do not mean by this declaration to condemn those who believe otherwise; they have the same right to their belief as I have to mine. But it is necessary to the happiness of man that he be mentally faithful to himself. Infidelity does not consist in believing or in disbelieving; it consists in professing to believe what he does not believe.

It is impossible to calculate the moral mischief, if I may so express it, that mental lying has produced in society. When a man has so far corrupted and prostituted the chastity of his mind as to subscribe his professional belief to things he does not believe, he has prepared himself for the commission of every other crime. He takes up the trade of a priest for the sake of gain, and in order to qualify himself for that trade he begins with a perjury. Can we conceive anything more destructive to morality than this? . . .

Every national church or religion has established itself by pretending some special mission from God, communicated to certain individuals. The Jews have their Moses; the Christians their Jesus Christ, their apostles and saints; and the Turks their Mohammed, as if the way to God was not open to every man alike.

Each of those churches show certain books which they call "revelation," or the word of God. The Jews say that their word of God was given by God to Moses, face to face; the Christians say their word of God came by divine inspiration; and the Turks say that their word of God (the Koran) was brought by an angel from heaven. Each of those churches accuse the other of unbelief; and for my part I disbelieve them all. . . .

When Moses told the children of Israel that he received the two tables of the Commandments from the hands of God, they were not obliged to believe him, because they had no other authority for it than his telling them so; and I have no other authority for it than some historian telling me so. The Commandments carry no internal evidence of divinity with them; they contain some good moral precepts, such as any man qualified to be a lawgiver, or a legislator, could produce himself without having recourse to supernatural intervention.*

When I am told that the Koran was written in heaven and brought to Mohammed by an angel, the account comes too near the same kind of hearsay evidence and secondhand authority as the former. I did not see the angel myself, and therefore I have a right not to believe it.

When also I am told that a woman called the Virgin Mary said, or gave out, that she was with child without any cohabitation with a man, and that her betrothed husband, Joseph, said that an angel told him so, I have a right to believe them or not; such a circumstance required a much stronger evidence than their bare word for it; but we have not even this—for neither Joseph nor Mary wrote any such matter themselves; it is only reported by others that they said so—it is hearsay upon hearsay, and I do not choose to rest my belief upon such evidence. . . .

Nothing that is here said can apply, even with the most distant disrespect, to the real character of Jesus Christ. He was a virtuous and an amiable man. The morality that he preached and practiced was of the most benevolent kind; and though similar systems of morality had been preached by Confucius and by some of the Greek philosophers many years before, by the Quakers since, and by many good men in all ages, it has not been exceeded by any.

Jesus Christ wrote no account of himself, of his birth, parentage, or anything else; not a line of what is called the New Testament is

---

* It is, however, necessary to except the declaration which says that God visits *the sins of the fathers upon the children; it is contrary to every principle of moral justice.*

of his own writing. The history of him is altogether the work of other people; and as to the account of his resurrection and ascension, it was the necessary counterpart to the story of his birth. His historians, having brought him into the world in a supernatural manner, were obliged to take him out again in the same manner, or the first part of the story must have fallen to the ground.

The wretched contrivance with which the latter part is told exceeds everything that went before it. The first part, that of the miraculous conception, was not a thing that admitted of publicity; and therefore the tellers of this part of the story had this advantage that, though they might not be credited, they could not be detected. They could not be expected to prove it because it was not one of those things that admitted of proof, and it was impossible that the person of whom it was told could prove it himself.

But the resurrection of a dead person from the grave, and his ascension through the air, is a thing very different, as to the evidence it admits of, to the invisible conception of a child in the womb. The resurrection and ascension, supposing them to have taken place, admitted of public and ocular demonstration like that of the ascension of a balloon or the sun at noonday, to all Jerusalem at least. A thing which everybody is required to believe requires that the proof and evidence of it should be equal to all and universal; and as the public visibility of this last related act was the only evidence that could give sanction to the former part, the whole of it falls to the ground because that evidence never was given. Instead of this, a small number of persons, not more than eight or nine, are introduced as proxies for the whole world, to say they saw it, and all the rest of the world are called upon to believe it. But it appears that Thomas did not believe the resurrection and, as they say, would not believe without having ocular and manual demonstration himself. So *neither will I,* and the reason is equally

as good for me and for every other person as for Thomas. . . .

But some, perhaps, will say: Are we to have no word of God—no revelation? I answer, Yes; there is a word of God; there is a revelation.

The word of God is the creation we behold: and it is in this word, which no human invention can counterfeit or alter, that God speaketh universally to man. . . .

It is only in the *Creation* that all our ideas and conceptions of a *word of God* can unite. The Creation speaks a universal language, independently of human speech or human language, multiplied and various as they may be. It is an ever-existing original, which every man can read. It cannot be forged; it cannot be counterfeited; it cannot be lost; it cannot be altered; it cannot be suppressed. It does not depend upon the will of man whether it shall be published or not; it publishes itself from one end of the earth to the other. It preaches to all nations and to all worlds; and this *word of God* reveals to man all that is necessary for man to know of God. . . .

It has been by rejecting the evidence that the word or works of God in the creation afford to our senses, and the action of our reason upon that evidence, that so many wild and whimsical systems of faith and of religion have been fabricated and set up. There may be many systems of religion that, so far from being morally bad, are in many respects morally good; but there can be but one that is true; and that one necessarily must, as it ever will, be in all things consistent with the ever-existing word of God that we behold in his works. But such is the strange construction of the Christian system of faith that every evidence the Heavens afford to man either directly contradicts it or renders it absurd. . . .

It is certain that in one point all nations of the earth and all religions agree—all believe in a God; the things in which they disagree are the redundancies annexed to that belief; and, therefore, if ever a universal religion should prevail, it will not be by believing anything new, but in getting rid of redundancies and believing as man believed at first. Adam, if ever there were such a man, was created a Deist; but in the meantime, let every man follow, as he has a right to do, the religion and the worship he prefers.

7

The Declaration of Independence

One of the earliest and most profound statements reflecting the Enlightenment values of natural law, reason and progress is found in the Declaration of Independence, issued on the eve of the American Revolution in 1776. Most of the ideas contained in the *Declaration* did not originate with Jefferson, but can be traced back to various English political philosophers of the 17th century, chief among them, John Locke (1632–1704). In his *Two Treatises of Government*, Locke set forth the view that all humans were born with certain natural rights, which no government could abridge. Government itself was to be the instrument of the people's will, its powers restricted by a social contract, or constitution, that the people could alter, as they could elect their officials, thus preventing tyranny and abuse of power. If a tyranny did develop, the people had the right of rebellion. Thus, Locke's views, as well as those of Jefferson's, are thought to be classic statements associated with the liberal state—popular sovereignty, representative government and constitutionalism.

Discussion Questions

1. What are natural rights? Do you think they exist today? What natural rights does Jefferson identify in the *Declaration*? Do you think Americans accept the premises and values of the document today?

2. The *Declaration of Independence* is a rationale for the American revolution as much as it is a statement of colonial values. What was the rationale used by the Americans, and is similar justification used by revolutionaries today?

3. What do you think Jefferson meant by his statement that "all men are created equal?" Is there a contradiction between the liberty and equality of which Jefferson speaks?

4. Peoples around the world, from Mao to Meiji Japan to Bolivar to Mandela to Gandhi to Gorbachev have been inspired by the *Declaration of Independence*. How do you account for its universal appeal?

The American Declaration of Independence

In Congress, July 4, 1776 the Unanimous Declaration of the Thirteen United States of America

When in the course of human events it becomes necessary for one people to dissolve the political bands which have connected them with another, and to assume among the powers of the earth, the separate and equal station to which the Laws of Nature and of Nature's God entitle them, a decent respect to the opinions of mankind requires that they should declare the causes which impel them to the separation.

We hold these truths to be self-evident, that all men are created equal, that they are endowed by their Creator with certain unalienable Rights, that among these are Life, Liberty and the pursuit of Happiness.—That to secure these rights, Governments are instituted among Men, deriving their just powers from the consent of the governed.—That whenever any Form of Government becomes destructive of these ends, it is the Right of the People to alter or to abolish it, and to institute new Government, laying its foundation on such principles, and organizing its powers in such form, as to them shall seem most likely to effect their Safety and Happiness. Prudence, indeed, will dictate that Governments long established should not be changed for light and transient causes; and accordingly all experience hath shewn, that mankind are more disposed to suffer, while evils are sufferable, than to right themselves by abolishing the forms to which they are accustomed. But when a long train of abuses and usurpations, pursuing invariably the same Object, evinces a design to reduce them under absolute Despotism, it is their right, it is their duty to throw off such Government, and to provide

Thomas Jefferson, The Declaration of Independence, July 2, 1776.

new Guards for their future security.—Such has been the patient sufferance of these Colonies, and such is now the necessity which constrains them to alter their former Systems of Government. The history of the present King of Great Britain is a history of repeated injuries and usurpations, all having in direct object the establishment of an absolute Tyranny over these States. To prove this, let Facts be submitted to a candid world.

He has refused his Assent to Laws, the most wholesome and necessary for the public good.

He has forbidden his Governors to pass Laws of immediate and pressing importance, unless suspended in their operation till his Assent should be obtained; and when so suspended, he has utterly neglected to attend to them.

He has refused to pass other Laws for the accommodation of large districts of people, unless those people would relinquish the right of Representation in the Legislature, a right inestimable to them and formidable to tyrants only.

He has called together legislative bodies at places unusual, uncomfortable, and distant from the depository of their public Records, for the sole purpose of fatiguing them into compliance with his measures.

He has dissolved Representative Houses repeatedly, for opposing with manly firmness his invasions on the rights of the people.

He has refused for a long time, after such dissolutions, to cause others to be elected; whereby the Legislative powers, incapable of Annihilation, have returned to the People at large for their exercise; the State remaining in the mean time exposed to all the dangers of invasion from without, and convulsions within.

He has endeavored to prevent the population of these States; for that purpose obstructing the Laws for Naturalization of Foreigners; refusing to pass others to encourage their migrations hither, and raising the conditions of new Appropriations of Lands.

He has obstructed the Administration of Justice, by refusing his Assent to Laws for establishing judiciary powers.

He has made judges dependent on his will alone, for the tenure of their offices, and the amount of payment of their salaries.

He has erected a multitude of New Offices, and sent hither swarms of Officers to harrass our people, and eat out their substance.

He has kept among us, in times of peace, Standing Armies without the Consent of our legislatures.

He has affected to render the Military independent of and superior to the Civil power.

He has combined with others to subject us to a jurisdiction foreign to our constitution, and unacknowledged by our laws; giving his Assent to their Acts of pretended Legislation:

For quartering large bodies of armed troops among us:

For protecting them, by a mock Trial, from punishment for any Murders which they should commit on the Inhabitants of these States:

For cutting off our Trade with all parts of the world:

For imposing Taxes on us without our Consent:

For depriving us in many cases, of the benefits of Trial by Jury:

For transporting us beyond Seas to be tried for pretended offences:

For abolishing the free System of English Laws in a neighbouring Province, establishing therein an Arbitrary government, and enlarging its Boundaries so as to render it at once an example and fit instrument for introducing the same absolute rule into these Colonies:

For taking away our Charters, abolishing our most valuable Laws, and altering fundamentally the Forms of our Governments:

For suspending our own Legislatures, and declaring themselves invested with power to legislate for us in all cases whatsoever.

He has abdicated Government here, by declaring us out of his Protection and waging War against us.

He has plundered our seas, ravaged our Coasts, burnt our towns, and destroyed the lives of our people.

He is at this time transporting large Armies of foreign Mercenaries to compleat the works of death, desolation and tyranny, already begun with circumstances of Cruelty & perfidy scarcely paralleled in the most barbarous ages, and totally unworthy the Head of a civilized nation.

He has constrained our fellow Citizens taken Captive on the high Seas to bear Arms against their Country, to become the executioners of their friends and Brethren, or to fall themselves by their Hands.

He has excited domestic insurrections amongst us, and has endeavored to bring on the inhabitants of our frontiers; the merciless Indian Savages, whose known rule of warfare, is an undistinguished destruction of all ages, sexes and conditions.

In every stage of these Oppressions We have Petitioned for Redress in the most humble terms: Our repeated Petitions have been answered only by repeated injury. A Prince, whose character is thus marked by every act which may define a Tyrant, is unfit to be the ruler of a free people.

Nor have We been wanting in attentions to our British brethren. We have warned them from time to time of attempts by their legislature to extend an unwarrantable jurisdiction over us. We have reminded them of the circumstances of our emigration and settlement here. We have appealed to their native justice and magnanimity, and we have conjured them by the ties of our common kindred to disavow these usurpations, which would inevitably interrupt our connections and correspondence. They too have been deaf to the voice of justice and of consanguinity. We must, therefore, acquiesce in the necessity, which denounces our Separation, and hold them, as we hold the rest of mankind, Enemies in War, in Peace Friends.

We, therefore, the Representatives of the united States of America, in General Congress, Assembled, appealing to the Supreme Judge of the world for the rectitude of our intentions, do, in the Name, and by Authority of the good People of these Colonies solemnly publish and declare, That these United Colonies are, and of Right ought to be Free and Independent States; that they are Absolved from all Allegiance to the British Crown, and that all political connection between them and the State of Great Britain, is and ought to be totally dissolved; and that as Free and Independent States, they have full Power to levy War, conclude Peace, contract Alliances, establish Commerce, and to do all other Acts and Things which Independent States may of right do.

And for the support of this Declaration, with a firm reliance on protection of divine Providence, we mutually pledge to each other our Lives, our Fortunes and our sacred Honor.

8

The Dust Never Settled

As North Americans continued the process of nation-building with the establishment of the United States of America under the Constitution, their example also served to inspire revolutions in South and Central America in the late 18th and early 19th century. In addition to the example set by the North Americans, the French Revolution of 1789, and, particularly Napoleon's intervention in Spain and Portugal provided an opportunity for those influenced by Enlightenment ideas to act. A generation of revolutionary leaders in the late 18th and early 19th century, including Toussaint L'Ouverture who helped to free Haiti from the French in 1801; Simon Bolivar, "The Liberator," who won his title by creating the modern states of Colombia, Venezuela, Bolivia, Peru and Ecuador; Father Miguel Hildalgo, who pioneered in the independence of Mexico; and Jose de San Martin, whose work led to revolutions in Argentina and Chile by the early 1820's, would usher in a new era in American politics. Yet, as the title of this selection, published anonymously in an Ecuadorian newspaper in 1829 suggests, "the dust never settled."

Discussion Questions

1. To what is the author referring when he writes that "the dust never settled?" What went wrong in the Latin American wars for independence?

2. Compare the American, French and Latin American revolutions? What similarities in goals, ideologies, personalities and events can you identify? What differences existed?

3. Does the same pattern exist in Central and South America today? If not, what has changed?

The Dust Never Settled

Anonymous

On May 25, 1810, the city of Buenos Aires began its political existence. As its example was not followed by the other provinces, it was necessary to use force in order to compel them to espouse the revolutionary cause. While so engaged, the troops of Buenos Aires set a precedent for their subsequent harsh and ignorant behavior by killing the Viceroy Liniers, who had earlier freed that country from the British troops. At the same time they began to persecute the pastors of the Church, in the person of a bishop who was guilty of nothing more than obedience to his vows. . . .

The Rio de la Plata [Buenos Aires and vicinity] has had but one man who proved capable of serving his country nobly and well, Saavedra quickly proved himself capable of presiding over the destinies of that Republic, but his death soon deprived the country of its one remaining hope. Since that time there has been no order or pattern in Argentine affairs. The federal government took possession of the land, and the land became its victim. Every province recovered its individual sovereignty, which God has given to every man, but that every man tacitly relinquishes to society, which thereupon assumes responsibility for the individual's safety. Nothing is so perilous as inconsistency between a political system and natural law. Each province governed itself, and every

military expedition sent against them went down in humiliating defeat. The towns armed and fought each other like enemies. As a result of federation, the nation fell heir to blood, death, and crime of every description, due to the unleashing of the passions of a people who, although they had broken their chains, were devoid of the concepts of right and duty, and could only avoid enslavement by becoming tyrannical themselves.

Elections were characterized by riots and intrigue. Many times, armed soldiers marched to the polls in formation, something unknown even in ancient Rome or in the island of Haiti. Force, faction, and bribery determine everything. And to what purpose?—momentary control amidst times of trouble, battle, and sacrifice. Virtually every government official has been replaced by a blood-stained victor, and those who are removed are made to suffer the misfortune of banishment, proscription, or violent death. Rare are the elections that are free of terrible crimes, and fewer still are the government leaders who have held their posts for the term provided by law or have been succeeded by legally elected leaders. . . .

However, let us be fair to the Rio de la Plata. What we have just described is not peculiar to that country: its history is that of all Spanish America. We shall again see these same principles, these same processes, these

---

From an anonymous editorial in an Equadorian newspaper, 1829.

same consequences in every republic, one country differing from another only incidentally, and modified only by circumstances and regional variations.

Throughout America we shall see but a single trend in public affairs. The cycles are similar, varying at most according to time and conditions, but otherwise paralleling the stages and the events in the other newborn states.

Nowhere are there legal elections; nowhere do those elected come to office according to the law. . . . If a Dorrego has been assassinated, assassinations are also being committed in Mexico, Bolivia, and Colombia—September 25 is too recent a date to be forgotten. If Pueyrredon plunders the public treasury [of Buenos Aires], there are those in Colombia who do the same. If [the Argentine province of] Cordoba and Paraguay are ruled by bloody hypocrites, Peru has its General La Mar in a donkey-skin, with the claws of a tiger and an insatiable lust for American blood. If anarchic movements occur in every Argentine province, Chile and Guatemala set such horrible examples that we can scarcely hope for peace. In the Argentine provinces, Sarratea, Rodriguez, and Alvear have compelled their country to house, in the capital, bandits who call themselves liberators. . . . The lawful authorities have been removed; the provinces have rebelled against the capital; brother wars upon brother—a horror which the Spaniards had prevented—and this war is to the death. Town fights town; city stands against city, each with its own government, and every street is a self-constituted nation. In Central America all is bloodshed and terror!

Though it is true that a government in Buenos Aires lasts scarcely a week, it is equally certain that Bolivia has now followed this monstrous example. No sooner had the illustrious Sucre left that unfortunate country than the traitor Blanco seized, through in-

trigue, the government which legally belonged to General Santa Cruz. Yet Blanco did not hold it five days before he was captured and killed by a dissatisfied faction, to be followed by a legitimate head, Velazco, who was in turn succeeded by Santa Cruz. Thus, hapless Bolivia has had four different leaders in less than two weeks! Only the Kingdom of Hell could offer so appalling a picture discrediting humanity!

We are amazed at the almost infinite number of subdivisions in the territory of the Argentine, whose condition resembles that of the baronies of old, so that this federation under freedom is like the feudal estates under monarchy. The barons imposed levies, built castles, and ruled as they pleased; they thus defied their sovereign, and on occasion they even fought him. Buenos Aires, Chile, and Guatemala imitate and surpass the practices and doctrines of those barons; thus, extremes clash, and, for the same reasons, personal ambition. . . .

. . . From one end to the other, the New World is an abyss of abominations, and, were anything lacking to complete this terrible chaos, Peru could more than supply it. A partisan of the tyrannical Spaniards during the war for independence, Peru, with her liberty not yet fully won, in the very first days of her existence, was the scene of a fraticidal struggle. The country had been cleared of Spaniards from Trujillo to Ica by valorous General San Martin, at the head of the Chileans and Argentines. In the eyes of the people of Lima there was no more of Peru to liberate; thereupon, some promptly undertook to rid the country of San Martin, whose services were most urgently needed. This act of ingratitude interrupted all political progress in Peru. . . .

There is no good faith in America, nor among the nations of America. Treaties are scraps of paper; constitutions, printed matter; elections, battles; freedom, anarchy; and life,

a torment. Such, Fellow-Americans, is our deplorable situation. Unless we change it, death is to be preferred. Anything is better than endless conflict, the indignity of which appears to increase with the violence and the duration of the movement. Let us not delude ourselves—this evil, which increases revolts and mutinies in the armed forces, will eventually compel us to reject the very first constructive principles of political life. We lost all individual rights when, in an effort to obtain them in perfect form, we sacrificed our blood and all that we cherished most, prior to the war—for, if we look back at that time, who will deny that our rights were then more respected? Never were we as badly off as we are at present. At that time we enjoyed positive and tangible benefits, whereas today we have dreams bordering upon illusion, hope feeding upon the future, and disillusionment forever tortured with the bitterness of reality.
. . .

9

Freeing Spanish America: Mixed Blessing

The ideals that lay behind the wars for independence in Latin America were, like those in North America, largely derived from the European Enlightenment. Francesco de Miranda was one of the early leaders who had traveled to the United States and Europe and had imbibed the new ideas. He envisaged a future where "Colombia would be a great nation extending from the Mississippi to Cape Horn." But, unlike events as they unfolded in what became the United States, independence leaders in Latin America would encounter a series of forces and movements which prevented them from achieving their goals. As Simon Bolivar was to say, "Those who served the revolution plowed the sea."

Discussion Questions

1. Why didn't Miranda's vision of a single great nation become reality?

2. Were the revolutionary leaders and their supporters really inspired by democracy?

3. What problems in the social and economic realms thwarted the revolutionary leaders' dreams?

Freeing Spanish America: Mixed Blessing

During two days in July 1822, in a house in Guayaquil, a Pacific port of sticky tropical heat, Simon Bolivar and Jose de San Martin met for the first and last time. Each had come far in an uncoordinated pincer movement. their troops had wrested much of South America from Spanish control.

In 1817, San Martin had led his men from Argentina through the Andes to conquer Chile, thence organizing a seaborne expedition to Peru. Bolivar, after a long struggle in Venezuela, had outflanked the Spanish forces and, marching over flooded lowlands and Andean heights, had taken Bogota.

The Spaniards still controlled most of Peru. Who should take them on, and how, was one issue for the two liberators. Another was how the new free states should be governed. As republics, said Bolivar, an egocentric aristocrat. Invite European princes to take their thrones, said San Martin, Argentine-born but for 20 years an officer in Spain's European wars. Bolivar won his point. San Martin retired quietly to a long exile in Europe.

By 1825, Bolivar had ousted the remaining Spaniards from Peru and Bolivia. After 15 years of struggle, all of Spain's mainland possessions were free (Cuba and Puerto Rico remained colonies until 1898). In a world of mainly unfettered monarchy, some 17m people had been won, in theory at least, for the principles of representative government.

Imperial Spain had long been in decline. Royal attempts at reform in the late 18th century had done little but irritate colonial elites. Their chief grievance was the monopoly of trade and public office held by the Spanish-born, at the expense of locally born *criollos*. Another was added after Spain went to war with Britain in 1804, and tried to increase its colonial revenues, especially from Mexico.

Recent events and ideas inspired some *criollos*: independence and republicanism in the United States, the French Enlightenment, British liberalism. What set spark to tinder was the abdication of Spain's King Ferdinand VII, after a French invasion in 1808. Though Spanish liberals formed a government of resistance, royal authority had been undermined. Starting in Caracas and Buenos Aires, *criollos* set up governing juntas across the Americas. Often these proclaimed loyalty to Ferdinand. But with Spanish royalist officials refusing any autonomy, calls for independence soon followed.

Rarely did this involve popular rebellion. Mexico was the main exception: there, in 1810–11, Miguel Hidalgo, a parish priest, raised the Indian masses, and handed out land confiscated from whites. But he was defeated. His radicalism scared *criollo* landholders, and Mexico declared independence only in 1821, in conservative reaction to a liberal Spanish government. The *criollo* elite everywhere feared the poor masses of Indians and black slaves (especially after the bloody 1790s rebellion of the 1/2m slaves in France's St. Domingue led to the birth of black-run

Haiti there in 1804). Politically radical, the new leaders, with rare exceptions such as Uruguay's Jose Artigas, were socially conservative. The *criollos* wanted political power so that they could keep the old social order intact.

The new states paid lip service to republican ideas of equality before the law. The import of slaves was generally banned; blacks, notable in the armies of both San Martin and Bolivar, were freed; but slavery was not at once outlawed. In most places, the Indian tribute and forced labor were ended, but not the serfdom of Indians on the large estates. The colonial legacy of land inequality that these typified was preserved. In the Andes it was aggravated by well-intentioned liberalism: decrees granting Indians individual possession of communal land, and so the right to sell it, led to large areas being gobbled up by *criollo* landowners.

The new republics faced other problems. How should they be governed? Liberals favored elected congresses, with a franchise normally limited to property holders; and, often, a loose federal structure. Most conservatives wanted strong and centralized government. ("America can be ruled only by an able despotism," said Bolivar, who died in 1830, by then a pessimistic conservative heading for exile.) By the 1830s conservatives were in the ascendant. In Mexico in 1864, with French aid, they even briefly installed a monarch, Maximilian, a Habsburg

prince, deposed and executed in 1867. (And Brazil remained an "empire" under descendants of Portugal's royal family until 1889.) Liberals regained the upper hand later in the century. The argument still rages.

The new states faced another problem: their backward economies, further weakened by war. Most declared trade "free" (i.e., no longer a Spanish monopoly), but often with high tariffs. Industry was slow to develop, the region depended on exports from its mines, plantations and ranches. In 1822, Chile became the first of many countries to seek a loan in London, defaults would soon follow.

Large armies were a costly burden. With independence came two of Latin America's lasting political scourges: militarism, and the *caudillo*, the strongman. Bolivar's dreams of continental integration yielded to parochialism: the Central American Federation of 1825 was five countries by 1838.

"Independence is the only benefit we have gained, at the cost of every thing else," lamented a disillusioned Bolivar. A century later, liberation's unfinished business bred a new cycle of revolutions and a new kind of *caudillo*. Starting in Mexico, but including Brazil's Getulio Vargas, in 1930–45, and Argentina's Juan Peron ten years after him, these combined assertive nationalism with the political incorporation of sections of the excluded masses. They solved some old problems, but created new ones.

10

Latin American Constitutions

One of the major issues that plagued the emerging republics of Latin America after the wars of independence was the difficulty in establishing political legitimacy—how does one know which government is the valid, rightful, legal one in a particular country? In the United States, after fumbling with the Articles of Confederation, a constitution was promulgated in 1787 which established the "rules" of legitimacy—the rightful government is the one which comes to power according to the terms of the constitution. In Latin America this road was not followed and the constitution has often been the plaything of individual leaders who use it to reinforce their own legitimacy.

Discussion Questions

1. If the constitution itself does not set the standards for legitimacy, what does?

2. What forces prevented constitutions from establishing legitimacy in Latin America?

3. What explains why there have been so many "revolutions" in Latin America?

In Latin America, "The Constitution Is What I Say It Is"

Larry Rohter

There is an argument to be made that the favorite pastime of Latin American politicians is neither soccer nor baseball, but tinkering with their countries' constitutions.

Take Ernesto Pérez Balladares, the president of Panama. He doesn't like the prohibition against immediate re-election that has existed here since Theodore Roosevelt engineered this nation's breakaway from Colombia nearly a century ago, so Panamanians will trudge to the polls today to vote on a measure that would allow him to seek a second consecutive term next year.

Given the track record of some of their neighbors, Panamanians can consider themselves lucky. The Dominican Republic has had 32 different constitutions in just over 150 years, while Haiti, its neighbor on the Caribbean island of Hispaniola, has had 24 since 1804. Venezuela is South America's champion, with 25 separate charters in 187 years, and in Central America, El Salvador, Honduras and Nicaragua have each had 14 constitutions since splitting from Spain early in the 19th century.

"The constitutional history of Latin America is the most convulsive in the world," said José Luis Cordeiro, a Venezuelan economist and journalist who is the author of a recent book, "The Second Death of Bolívar," that examines the region's propensity to replace its charters. "Constitutions, seem to have become like shirts, not even suits, which rulers put on and take off at their whim."

To many Latin Americans, the roots of the phenomenon can be traced to colonial times. In those days, kings in Madrid or Lisbon and their viceroys were fond of issuing edicts that seemed lofty on paper but both rulers and their distant subjects knew could never be enforced. From that experience came a proverb still used across Latin America to describe the prevailing attitude toward laws and decrees: "I obey, but I do not comply."

In such an environment, constitutions have come to be seen as statements of aspirations rather than binding declarations of principles. Latin American constitutions tend to be lengthy documents with dozens of chapters and scores of articles, written in florid language that promises more safeguards and services than their American counterpart while specifying more obligations. Panama's current charter, for instance, has 322 articles.

"Constitutions in our countries tend to be a rigid compilation of regulations or a type of detailed administrative code, more formal than real," said Miguel Antonio Bernal, a prominent legal scholar and political commentator here. "They exist not to guarantee rights, but to legitimize abuses, to allow whoever is in power to leave the reflection of his own interests."

The end result for the average citizen, of course, is antipathy mixed with cynicism, as each ruler imposes a constitution tailored to his own needs and recruits jurists willing to bend to his will. Another proverb popular in Latin America warns that, "He who makes the law makes the loopholes." Or as a member of the Panamanian Supreme Court, put it recently in a lecture to law students here, "The constitution is what we, the judges, say it is."

Term Limits

Throughout modern Latin American history, the issue of re-election has been inextricably linked to that of constitutions. Since the typical caudillo, or strongman, always wants to modify or replace the existing charter with one of his own, one country after another has thought it logical to prevent the emergence of such strongmen by writing constitutions that simply forbid any president from serving two consecutive terms. Thus, the Mexican Revolution took as its slogan, "Effective suffrage and no re-election."

Today's heads of state, though democratically elected, persist in seeking to mold their societies and institutions to their own desires. Mr. Pérez Balladares is by no means an aberration: over the past five years, other "modernizers," including Alberto Fujimori of Peru, Carlos Saúl Menem of Argentina and Fernando Henrique Cardoso of Brazil, have all sought, and gained, constitutional changes that allowed them to seek re-election. Indeed, Peru's Congress on Thursday told Mr Fujimori, the originator of the trend, that he could go after a third term without getting public approval in a referendum.

"What we are seeing is the revival of the old Latin American tradition of caudillismo in technocratic clothing," said Ricardo Arias

New Beginnings

The number of constitutions each nation has had since achieving independence. The year of independence is at left and the year the most recent constitution went into effect is at right.

Year of independence	Nation	Number	Year of most recent constitution
1844	Dominican Republic	32	1966
1811	Venezuela	25	1961
1804	Haiti	24	1987
1822	Ecuador	19	1979
1825	Bolivia	15	1967
1821	El Salvador	14	1983
1821	Nicaragua	14	1987
1821	Honduras	14	1982
1821	Peru	13	1993
1810	Columbia	12	1991

Sources: "The Second Death of Bolivar," by José Luis Cordeiro: "The Constitutions of the World."

Calderón, a former vice president of Panama. These new leaders "say they have found the magic formula and are the only ones who know how to apply it," he said. That is dangerous, Mr. Calderón added, because "in Latin America, unlike North America, a president is almost a king during his reign" and thus has the means to impose "a civilian dictatorship."

Words of Advice

Yet there are few signs that Latin America's procession of constitutions is about to stop. Colombia, Paraguay and Peru have all approved new charters since 1990, and with the United States and Latin America formally committed to a hemispheric free trade agreement by 2005, other countries will soon be obliged to follow suit. No one has asked him, but Mr. Cordeiro has a few words of advice to those who will draft those texts: Less is better.

"The experience of Latin America has clearly demonstrated that the answer to po-litical crises is not to pass more and more laws each time, above all if these are defec-tive or are not applied, but in having a few good laws that are respected," he said. "If laws are neither institutionalized nor imple-mented, they are useless."

11

A Thumbnail Sketch of Modernity

Though pre-industrial societies are the focus of her book, Patricia Crone also identifies the chief elements of modern societies. Closely associated with the process of industrialization, which was at first an exclusively European phenomenon, the author paints a picture of modern life in its political, economic, cultural, social and ideological contexts, while at the same time contrasting modernity with its predecessor, the pre-industrial society. As you read, take note of the characteristics of modern societies that Crone points to, and compare her characterization with that of Kennedy and others.

Discussion Questions

1. What are some specific examples of the "high degree of political, cultural and economic integration" Crone refers to as being an essential element of modern societies?

2. How do modern societies foster both equality and inequality? Individualism and mass politics? What does Crone mean when she writes, "Society must be like a pack of cards that can be reshuffled any time?" Has Crone described life, attitudes, ideologies and institutions of modern societies today, or have we entered into a new era?

3. How did nationalism arise, according to Crone? What is the connection between nationality (or ethnicity) and the nation-state? Does the nationalism that Crone describes bear any resemblance to the nationalism of the present day?

From Poverty to Affluence

Scarcity was a hallmark of pre-industrial society. By contrast, industrialization means wealth to the point that income is used as its defining characteristic: an industrial revolution is deemed to have taken place where real income per head has increased progressively over several decades to levels substantially above those characteristic of pre-industrial economics. A progressive and substantial increase of real income is what all industrializing countries are trying to achieve.

From Pre-Industrial Polity to Nation

Pre-industrial society was characterized by low degrees of economic, political and cultural integration. By contrast, a high degree of integration in all three respects is the hallmark of modernity.

Economic Integration

Economically, modernity breeds integration by its systematic division of labour. All members of modern society specialize in a single economic activity, offering their labour, skill or capital on the market and receiving monetary payment in return. All are thus dependent on the market (be it free, or more or less so, as in capitalist countries, or wholly regulated by the state, as in socialist ones).

Systematic division of labour goes hand in hand with mass production and mass markets: technology has made it possible to produce very large quantities of goods for distribution among very large numbers of people spread over very large distances; and economically it has become profitable to do so because the masses are not just producers, but also consumers, having completely ceased to be self-sufficient.

All members of modern society are thus abjectly dependent upon one another for their nourishment, clothing, fuel, education, medical attention and a wide array of other services; differently put, all are members of a single economy, the national one, which plays the same role in the life of the modern workforce as did the household in that of the pre-industrial peasantry. Indeed, without a national economy they would not constitute a single workforce at all.

Cultural Integration

Culturally, modernity breeds integration by prising loose the masses from their local communities, getting them together in the same factories and the same cities, subjecting them to the same schooling in the same language from early childhood to late adolescence, bombarding them via the same mass media, and putting an end to the isolation of the communities from which they came.

Modern industry needs a literate and numerate workforce able to communicate in the same language at all levels and trained in the assimilation of information of all kinds. Once all members of society have come together in a single workforce, moreover, they need a shared value system of a more unitary kind than the traditional high culture superimposed over a multiplicity of local traditions. In short, industry means that the masses have to be integrated culturally.

Unlike pre-industrial children, who began their specialist training early and automatically picked up such general knowledge as they needed in the course of growing up, modern children spend years on the same general education before being allowed to specialize: modern society is much too complex for general knowledge to be transmitted by osmosis alone. All children are educated in the virtues of the elite, not just in the sociological sense that those who control the educational apparatus decide what values and skills it ought to impart, but also in the historical sense that mass education disseminates the high culture with associated literary language that used to be restricted to a privileged few.

In many countries the functions performed by schools were (and are) assisted by the army, which would take in recruits from a wide variety of ethnic and social groups, teach them the same national language, commit them to the same national policy, and send them out again as acculturated citizens. Both schools and the army had (and have) the additional advantage of keeping the young off the streets without putting them into the workforce, or in other words keeping them occupied without swamping the labour market.

The formation of a single national culture is everywhere assisted by the national press, radio, television and other forms of telecommunication which spread the same language and outlook to all who listen and watch. At the same time improved means of transporta-

tion open up traffic between hitherto isolated communities, which are gradually integrated in the national economy too. Local dialects thus disappear along with local costume, cooking and other customs, except in so far as they get picked up by cookery books and tourist brochures destined for national or international circulation. In short, the high culture no longer coexists with, but rather suppresses local diversity, regional accents and other survivals notwithstanding.

Socio-Political Integration

In social and political terms modernity breeds integration by attaching all individuals directly to a bureaucratic state which processes them mechanically without regard for their social, ethnic or religious background. Privileged and excluded groups give way to persons endowed with identical legal and political rights, though not with the same wealth, or in other words to sharply defined citizens fuzzily divided into classes. Differently put, modernity breeds nation states, that is to say polities composed of free individuals who each bear the same relationship to the government. (Nation states are also identified as polities composed of people who share the same ethnicity, language, history and culture; I shall come back to this definition, and amplify the first, in the next section.) The nation state made its appearance before the arrival of industry, being first proclaimed in the French Revolution; but industry gave it reality to the point that industrialization and nation-building are two sides of the same modernizing process today.

Progress required all members of society to be identical legal units for easy administration and placement wherever their skills were needed (a point to which I shall come back in a moment), and all were duly given identical civil status: aristocrats, serfs, Jews and other minorities were transformed into citizens in most parts of Europe in the course of the nineteenth century, and even royalty can be fined for speeding in the twentieth.

It was this erosion of the socio-political hierarchy on the one hand and the emergence of a national economy on the other which led to the perception of society as divided into classes. The class system identifies people with reference to their position in the workforce. Differently put, the concept of class developed in tandem with the creation of a nation, being increasingly adopted by the members of a given nation to envisage a society that could no longer be adequately described in terms of functional orders, estates or aristocrats versus commoners.

The same process encouraged equal distribution of political rights, or in other words the emergence of democracy. Industrialization endows the masses with a political presence because workers congregating in cities, where they learn to read and write and acquire means of mass communication, are considerably harder to ignore than a dispersed and illiterate peasantry sunk in "the idiocy of rural life" (as Marx called it). Once the peasants are transformed into workers, they invariably organize themselves for collective action. In the cities they become interdependent (wage-rates accepted by workers in one city will affect those of workers in another); and constant interaction endows them with awareness of their shared situation.

With or without mass participation in government, however, industrial states are characterized by mass political membership: all citizens are directly affiliated to the state, not to intermediate groups; all have rights in it of one kind or another (if not political or civil, then at least social—social rights being those to education, medical care, pension and so on); and their loyalty to it normally overrides the claims of rival political or religious organizations, or so at any rate where nation-building has succeeded. In short, the pre-in-

dustrial pattern whereby a far-flung elite and a cosmopolitan culture lord it over a plurality of peasant societies has been replaced by one in which blocks of people ruled by states of their own share the language, culture and political status. Differences between elites and masses in these repects are greatly attenuated, being typically far weaker than those between the nation and its neighbours. Within each block, all members are tied to nationwide institutions by which they are educated and administered, in which an enormous number of jobs are available, and in which they have economic, social and political entitlements of various kinds. Modern people are wedded to their states to a degree unknown in pre-industrial times, being linguistically incompetent outside them (except in so far as the same language happens to be spoken in several states) and endowed with a host of rights difficult to transfer or unobtainable abroad. To some extent this is changing now that the world is shrinking, but the supremacy of the nation still has not been seriously dented.

Nationalism

Nation-building in Europe bred nationalism, a political ideology which is now of great importance in the non-European world, rival creeds in the form of Marxism, Maoism and fundamentalist Islam notwithstanding.

Nationalism is a doctrine to the effect that political and national borders must coincide: each nation must have its own political house (nations being peoples with a shared ethnicity, language, history and culture). The doctrine assumes nations to exist prior to and independently of state structures. In fact, however, it was the political houses of western Europe (or some of them) that created nations, not the other way round. Europe had always accommodated a plurality of political houses, and its once uniform high culture had long been broken up into vernacular forms. As each state integrated its local communities in the same economy, exposed them to its own variety of high culture and eventually granted them identical political rights, whole peoples came to be differentiated from their neighbours by language, culture, history and political membership alike: each state, in other words, came to accommodate a nation. Elsewhere, by contrast, states only integrated the elite, as we have seen; the masses below them might be divided into "nations" on the basis of ethnicity, language, religious allegiance or a combination thereof, but these divisions were antithetical to political membership and mastery of the high culture, not, as in Europe, the outcome of participation in both.

Nationalism condemned this antithesis as intolerable. It did not however argue that all states must amalgamate their masses, but on the contrary that the divisions which prevailed among the masses ought to form the basis of states. It thus validated a European development, but reversed cause and effect, and this made it immensely explosive: there were plenty of empires to blow up and local communities to fuse in the name of supposed national identities, partly in Europe itself and more particularly outside it; in due course it blew up the colonial empires established by the Europeans themselves.

But whether it validated an existing or a future situation, it played, and still plays, a crucial role in nation-building by instilling a sense of togetherness among its adherents, telling them where their collective future lies with reference to their real or supposed common past, and thus in inducing them to transfer their loyalties from their local communities or supra-national church to the nation state. Its aim is the creation of polities in which all individuals are directly affiliated to the state as identical legal units in which all can communicate in the same language (oc-

casionally two or more) on the basis of a shared body of ideas, and, not least, in which all are prepared to defend this state of affairs. Where this has been achieved, a nation-state exists, however great the ethnic, cultural and religious diversity it may contain. The nationalist definition of the nation is prescriptive rather than descriptive: a considerable amount of diversity can and frequently does persist without being politically divisive. But the constant harping on the theme of shared identity on the one hand and the persistent influence of old communal divisions on the other can also do immense damage to minorities (as it did to the Jews of Germany, the Armenians of the Ottoman empire and many others besides).

Nationalism is invariably coupled with populism in the sense of admiration for the ways and the will of the masses. Thus national culture is invariably presented as popular culture, though in fact nation-building involves mass dissemination of the high culture of the elite, as has been seen; and national politics are equated with the popular will, though the people may be completely deprived of political rights, as has been seen too. Nationalism thus has both an ethnic and a social aspect to it, being directed against empires in respect of borders and against elites in respect of government: in principle all nations are democracies. Rival creeds such as Marxism, Maoism and fundamentalist Islam lack the ethnic aspect, but venerate the people too. In fact all ideologues do today.

All venerate the people because nation-building is about the reception of the masses. Nations are the outcome of economic, cultural and political integration. Differently put, nation-building amounts to the formation of one huge horizontal linkage: all the masses that formerly had to be kept apart now have to come together in a single world. Ideology "mobilizes" them (as sociologists put it), taking them out of their autarkic villages and political self-help groups into cities, education and the reach of the modern state. Old community ties are broken, national ones are still embryonic, the rewards are hard to see: industrialization and nation-building are two sides of the same extremely painful process. Ideology plays a key role in keeping people committed to the process, and the more difficult the process, the shriller the ideology is likely to be, total commitment being required. Conversely, where the process is completed the fervour dies down: western European countries still validate their policies with reference to the nation and democracy, but they are only shrill when they are under military threat.

Nationalism being a peculiarly European product, it is not surprising that it is thinly attested in the non-European past. A species of it is documented for Tokugawa Japan, where the political house built by barbarians was also distinct from universal truth (neo-Confucianism imported from China), and there may well be other examples. Generally speaking, however, ethnicity was not used to identify or defend polities in preindustrial times unless ethnicity was sanctified by religion, in which case the ideology was almost invariably imperialist; and even where the state came to be identified in purely ethnic as distinct from religious or cultural terms, as in Europe and Japan, premodern nationalism (or proto-nationalism, as one might call it) lacked the populist element: it was an elite sentiment destined for elite consumption. It took industrialization for the nativism of the masses and the proto-nationalism of the elite to merge.

Tradition Versus Progress

The pre-industrial scenario may be summarized as follows. Society is tied to a superior being or beings (ancestors, spirits, gods or God), or principles (such as cosmic order or filial piety) or laws (such as *karma*): an enduring truth above mere human beings generates a socio-political ideal with corresponding institutions. Since the truth cannot change, the institutions it spawns ought likewise to retain their original form, only minor changes to meet the needs of the times being acceptable; and since the truth is whole rather than partial, it ought to govern all aspects of life. Society was thus dominated by a tradition, a time-honoured way of doing and looking at things; and conscious attempts at change were usually envisaged as restoration: the ideal was a concrete order exemplified in the past, not an unknown future.

By contrast, industrial society has abandoned tradition. Its crucial concept is that of growth or progress, in other words change assumed to be for the better. Progress was once understood as a law (as in the Marxist vision in which it inexorably leads to the elimination of the state from complex society); nowadays, it is only an ideal, but it is still something bigger and more enduring than ourselves in that it is meant to be for the common good.

However, an enduring truth to the effect that human society must always change cannot generate a time-honoured way of doing and perceiving things; the ideal is not a specific order exemplified in the past, but on the contrary something new which has never been tried out before. The supreme truth to which modern society subscribes can only sanctify a *process*, more precisely one of constant demolition and re-organisation. Society having committed itself to change, all obstacles to it must be kept out of the way: above all, religion must be pushed aside.

This is not to say that industrial society is hostile to religion; you may have as much of it as you like (communist countries being partial exceptions). But it will not allow you to embroil your religion in matters of public importance, be they political, social or cognitive.

Religion is not allowed to impinge on such matters because it may not underpin: wherever an ultimate truth underpins a phenomenon, it creates a sacred cow, a holy institution, a dogma, something that cannot be changed. Dogmas would mean the end of modern science and scholarship. Both have expanding frontiers, and neither could go on expanding if religious truths were allowed to interfere with them or alternatively if scientific or scholarly theories were allowed to become religious truths. If God's view of things as presented in the Bible had been allowed to shape scientific and scholarly research, a host of scientists and scholars would have had to be executed as heretics; and if the law of gravity been allowed to acquire sacred status, Einstein too would have had to be burnt at the stake. Modern science and scholarship are cumulative, meaning that one insight is assumed to lead to another which will lead to a third, outmoding the first in the process. Nothing is sacred; everything is preliminary. Neither science nor scholarship today ever leads to the discovery of that final truth which will enable us all to rest, satisfying ourselves with the transmission of the truth to future generations.

Religion thus becomes "purely religious", as some would put it, or in other words that it becomes a highly specialized activity as opposed to the multi-purpose phenomenon that it was in pre-industrial times; and as such it is threatened with irrelevance.

Egalitarianism

Just as dogmas would mean the end of modern science and technology, so sacred institutions would mean the end of the society which supports them in the expectation of benefitting from their advance. Modern society must keep itself open to a constant demand for labour, talent and new skills in whatever shape or size they may come (male/female, black/white, Christian/Jewish, privileged/ working-class, able-bodied/ handicapped, etc.), at the same time preparing itself for constant demolition of social arrangements in tandem with the decline of well-established occupations (printers go out as computers come in, and so on).

If the social order were to congeal into stable hierarchies and ghettos, the labour market would come to be dominated by ascription rather than talent (women, blacks, Jews, workers, aristocrats and so on being preordained for certain roles by birth), while at the same time society would be too rigid to benefit from technological advance (with the result that it would stop paying for such advances, paying scientists and scholars to underpin the social hierarchy instead). In short, an economy geared to science and technology requires a fluid society with unimpeded social and geographical mobility. Society must be like a pack of cards that can be reshuffled any time, and to some extent it is.

What our egalitarian ideologies do succeed in doing is thus to prevent socio-political differentiation from freezing. At the same time, mobility in conjunction with a high standard of living helps to keep the egalitarian ideology alive.

Individualism

Modern society is not just egalitarian, but also individualistic. The individual is generally seen as having a right, or indeed duty, to fulfil himself above all other considerations; we are no longer identical with our social roles, nor do we automatically accept the rights and duties vested in them.

This is partly because industrial society reduces the number of inherited roles. Since occupational roles are not inherited or enacted at home, children cannot train for theirs from an early age by imitation of their parents. At the same time, however, institutional differentiation means that an individual may occupy very different positions at home, at work, in his church, his club and so on, adopting different moral codes and types of behaviour in each connection. Having very different and indeed incompatible roles to play, he cannot identify fully with any of them: the search for the real self begins.

In addition, modernity drastically reduces the control exercised by kinsmen and neighbours over individual behaviour. Modern states insist on dealing directly with individuals rather than collectivities, and they also take over most of the functions previously performed by self-help groups, thus depriving the latter of their leverage. The individual remains a member of a family, of course, and modern governments generally profess belief in the tenet that the family is "the foundation of society". But in actual fact parental control is undermined by the immense power over the national offspring vested by modern governments in educational, medical and welfare institutions on the grounds that "the interests of the children come first", or in other words that the nation knows better than mere progenitors (a view to which social workers are particularly addicted). Possibly, the indiscriminate dissemination of information and (more importantly) values practised by television undermines parental authority too: the parental view of right and wrong is reduced to one among many. At all events, since the family is no longer a unit of production, as opposed to one of consumption and exchange of services, the economic control enjoyed by parents is also limited, and both geographical and social mobility further reduce their influence. Independent income for wives similarly reduces the control exercised by husbands. Urbanization, mobility and the disappearance of self-help groups mean that neighbours are superficial acquaintances or wholly anonymous persons incapable of exercising pressures of a signifi-

cant kind. The search for the real self is thus conducted in considerable freedom from external control. The cost of this freedom, of course, is loneliness and a widespread sense of dissolution of identity.

It should be noted, however, that individualism has gone much further in the West (above all America) than in Japan, where group pressure is still strong and role identification more pronounced as a result. Industrialization may have an inherent tendency to promote certain developments, but the actual result clearly depends on the cultural context with which it interacts, and it is only because industrialization has so far been enacted almost entirely within a single civilization that we implicitly assume it to have much the same outcome wherever it takes place.

Fragmentation

All in all, progress generates a world which is fragmented rather than coherent, unstable rather than enduring, and rich in contemporary rather than historical experience. It is fragmented because countless bits of the world conflict with other bits. One and the same God or morality has ceased to preside over all. You may adhere to one set of values as politician, doctor, director or worker, another as a supporter of wildlife and nature, a third as church-goer, and a fourth as spouse and parent. The contrast between pre-modern and modern societies in this respect can easily be exaggerated: conflicting beliefs and norms were commonplace in the pre-industrial world (what else is tragedy about?); and the industrial world is less incoherent than it may seem at first sight once religion is discounted. But even so, it would be hard to deny that the lack of an overarching world view, or more precisely, the unsatisfactory nature of "growth" in this role, increases the number of dilemmas.

Being fragmented, the industrial world is unstable. More precisely, it is kept fragmented because it *wishes* to be unstable, the expansion of cognitive, technological and economic boundaries being its aim. Rapid change means that past experience rapidly loses intelligibility and relevance: children grow up in a world appreciably different from that in which their parents had their formative years, radically different from that of their grandparents, and totally unlike that of remoter generations. Communication across time is thus impeded. (This is known as the generation gap in so far as communication between parents and children are concerned, but in fact it is an entire culture gap.) But the mass media greatly intensify communication over space. The present is extremely rich in human experience, but it does not lock in with either past or future, the former being irrelevant and the latter unknown. Far from being anchored in a tradition, the modern individual is liable to drift: he has to decide for himself who he is and where he is going. All this is what defenders of traditional societies have in mind when they dwell on the "moral bankruptcy" of the West.

Bankrupt or creditworthy, the industrial West is the world in which most readers of this book will have grown up. How they should evaluate it is a moral, not a scholarly question: just as science cannot tell you whether or not to forsake tobacco, only the effects of its use, so scholarship cannot tell you whether or not to accept modernity, only the manner in which it works. What matters here is simply the trivial point that it works quite differently from its pre-industrial predecessors.

12

The Age of Romanticism

This selection from Jostein Gaarder's *Sophie's World* discusses the Romantic movement of the late eighteenth and early nineteenth centuries. The emphasis is on some of the key thinkers of the era, their main ideas and how they differed from the Enlightenment of the eighteenth century.

Discussion Questions

1. In what ways did the Romantics challenge the ideas of the Enlightenment?

2. What were the most important Romantic ideas concerning nature, art and human beings?

3. What are the differences between universal and national Romanticism?

4. In what specific ways did Romanticism contribute to the new ideology of nationalism?

Sophie's World

Jostein Gaarder

Alberto Knox was sitting on the step again when Sophie arrived.

"Have a seat," he said, getting straight down to work.

"Previously we spoke of the Renaissance, the Baroque period, and the Enlightenment. Today we are going to talk about *Romanticism,* which could be described as Europe's last great cultural epoch. We are approaching the end of a long story, my child."

"Did Romanticism last that long?"

"It began toward the end of the eighteenth century and lasted till the middle of the nineteenth. But after 1850 one can no longer speak of whole 'epochs' which comprise poetry, philosophy, art, science, and music."

"Was Romanticism one of those epochs?"

"It has been said that Romanticism was Europe's last common approach to life. It started in Germany, arising as a reaction to the Enlightenment's unequivocal emphasis on reason. After Kant and his cool intellectualism, it was as if German youth heaved a sigh of relief."

"What did they replace it with?"

"The new catchwords were 'feeling,' 'imagination,' 'experience,' and 'yearning.' Some of the Enlightenment thinkers had drawn attention to the importance of feeling—not least Rousseau—but at that time it was a criticism of the bias toward reason.

What had been an undercurrent now became the mainstream of German culture."

"So Kant's popularity didn't lost very long?"

"Well, it did and it didn't. Many of the Romantics saw themselves as Kant's successors, since Kant had established that there was a limit to what we can know of 'das Ding an sich.' On the other hand, he had underlined the importance of the ego's contribution to knowledge, or cognition. The individual was now completely free to interpret life in his own way. The Romantics exploited this in an almost unrestrained 'ego-worship,' which led to the exaltation of artistic genius."

"Were there a lot of these geniuses?"

"*Beethoven* was one. His music expresses his own feelings and yearnings. Beethoven was in a sense a 'free' artist—unlike the Baroque masters such as Bach and Handel, who composed their works to the glory of God, mostly in strict musical forms."

"I only know the Moonlight Sonata and the Fifth Symphony."

"But you know how romantic the Moonlight Sonata is, and you can hear how dramatically Beethoven expresses himself in the Fifth Symphony."

"You said the Renaissance humanists were individualists too."

"Yes. There were many similarities between the Renaissance and Romanticism. A typical one was the importance of art to human cognition. Kant made a considerable contribution here as well. In his aesthetics he investigated what happens when we are overwhelmed by beauty—in a work of art, for instance. When we abandon ourselves to a work of art with no other intention than the aesthetic experience itself, we are brought closer to an experience of 'das Ding an sich.'"

"So the artist can provide something philosophers can't express?"

"That was the view of the Romantics. According to Kant, the artist plays freely on his faculty of cognition. The German poet *Schiller* developed Kant's thought further. He wrote that the activity of the artist is like playing, and man is only free when he plays, because then he makes up his own rules. The Romantics believed that only art could bring us closer to 'the inexpressible.' Some went as far as to compare the artist to God."

"Because the artist creates his own reality the way God created the world."

"It was said that the artist had a 'universe-creating imagination.' In his transports of artistic rapture he could sense the dissolving of the boundary between dream and reality.

"*Novalis,* one of the young geniuses, said that 'the world becomes a dream, and the dream becomes reality.' He wrote a novel called *Heinrich von Ofterdingen* set in Medieval times. It was unfinished when he died in 1801, but it was nevertheless a very significant novel. It tells of the young Heinrich who is searching for the 'blue flower' that he once saw in a dream and has yearned for ever since. The English Romantic poet *Coleridge* expressed the same idea; saying something like this:

> What if you slept? And what if, in your sleep, you dreamed? And what if, in your dream, you went to heaven and there plucked a strange and beautiful flower? And what if, when you awoke, you had the flower in your hand? Ah, what then?"

"How pretty!"

"This yearning for something distant and unattainable was characteristic of the Romantics. They longed for bygone eras, such as the Middle Ages, which now become enthusiastically reappraised after the Enlightenment's negative evaluation. And they longed for distant cultures like the Orient with its mysticism. Or else they would feel drawn to Night, to Twilight, to old ruins and the supernatural. They were preoccupied with what we usually refer to as the dark side of life, or the murky, uncanny, and mystical."

"It sounds to me like an exciting period. Who were these Romantics?"

"Romanticism was in the main an urban phenomenon. In the first half of the last century there was, in fact, a flourishing metropolitan culture in many parts of Europe, not least in Germany. The typical Romantics were young men, often university students, although they did not always take their studies very seriously. They had a decidedly anti-middle class approach to life and could refer to the police or their landladies as philistines, for example, or simply as the enemy."

"I would never have dared rent a room to a Romantic!"

"The first generation of Romantics were young in about 1800, and we could actually call the Romantic Movement Europe's first student uprising. The Romantics were not unlike the hippies a hundred and fifty years later."

"You mean flower power and long hair, strumming their guitars and lying around?"

"Yes. It was once said that 'idleness is the ideal of genius, and indolence the virtue of the Romantic.' It was the duty of the Romantic to experience life—or to dream himself away from it. Day-to-day business could be taken care of by the philistines."

"Byron was a Romantic poet, wasn't he?"

"Yes, both Byron and Shelley were Romantic poets of the so-called Satanic school.

Byron, moreover, provided the Romantic Age with its idol, the Byronic hero—the alien, moody, rebellious spirit—in life as well as in art. Byron himself could be both willful and passionate, and being also handsome, he was besieged by women of fashion. Public gossip attributed the romantic adventures of his verses to his own life, but although he had numerous liaisons, true love remained as illusive and as unattainable for him as Novalis's blue flower. Novalis became engaged to a fourteen-year-old girl. She died four days after her fifteenth birthday, but Novalis remained devoted to her for the rest of his short life."

"Did you say she died four days after her fifteenth birthday?"

"Yes . . ."

"I am fifteen years and four days old *today*."

"So you are."

"What was her name?"

"Her name was Sophie."

"What?"

"Yes, it was

"You scare me. Could it be a coincidence?"

"I couldn't say, Sophie. But her name was Sophie."

"Go on!"

"Novalis himself died when he was only twenty-nine. He was one of the 'young dead.' Many of the Romantics died young, usually of tuberculosis. Some committed suicide . . ."

"Ugh!"

"Those who lived to be old usually stopped being Romantics at about the age of thirty. Some of them went on to become thoroughly middle-class and conservative."

"They went over to the enemy, then."

"Maybe. But we were talking about romantic love. The theme of unrequited love was introduced as early as 1774 *by Goethe* in his novel *The Sorrows of Young Werther*. The book ends with young Werther shooting himself when he can't have the woman he loves."

"Was it necessary to go that far?"

"The suicide rate rose after the publication of the novel, and for a time the book was banned in Denmark and Norway. So being a Romantic was not without danger. Strong emotions were involved."

"When you say 'Romantic,' I think of those great big landscape paintings, with dark forests and wild, rugged nature . . . preferably in swirling mists."

"Yes, one of the features of Romanticism was this yearning for nature and nature's mysteries. And as I said, it was not the kind of thing that arises in rural areas. You may recall Rousseau, who initiated the slogan 'back to nature.' The Romantics gave this slogan popular currency. Romanticism represents not least a reaction to the Enlightenment's mechanistic universe. It was said that Romanticism implied a renaissance of the old *cosmic consciousness."*

"Explain that, please."

"It means viewing nature as a whole; the Romantics were tracing their roots not only back to Spinoza, but also to Plotinus and Renaissance philosophers like Jakob Böhme and Giordano Bruno. What all these thinkers had in common was that they experienced a divine 'ego' in nature."

"They were Pantheists then . . ."

"Both Descartes and Hume had drawn a sharp line between the ego and 'extended' reality. Kant had also left behind him a sharp distinction between the cognitive 'I' and nature 'in itself.' Now it was said that nature is nothing but one big 'I.' The Romantics also used the expressions 'world soul' or 'world spirit.'"

"I see."

"The leading Romantic philosopher was *Schelling,* who lived from 1775 to 1854. He wanted to unite mind and matter. All of nature—both the human soul and physical reality—is the expression of one Absolute, or world spirit, he believed."

"Yes, just like Spinoza."

"Nature is visible spirit, spirit is invisible nature, said Schelling, since one senses a 'structuring spirit' everywhere in nature. He also said that matter is slumbering intelligence."

"You'll have to explain that a bit more clearly."

"Schelling saw a 'world spirit' in nature, but he saw the same 'world spirit' in the human mind. The natural and the spiritual are actually expressions of the some thing."

"Yes, why not?"

"World spirit can thus be sought both in nature and in one's own mind. Novalis could therefore say 'the path of mystery leads inwards.' He was saying that man bears the whole universe within himself and comes closest to the mystery of the world by stepping inside himself."

"That's a very lovely thought."

"For many Romantics, philosophy, nature study, and poetry formed a synthesis. Sitting in your attic dashing off inspired verses and investigating the life of plants or the composition of rocks were only two sides of the some coin because nature is not a dead mechanism, it is one living world spirit."

"Another word and I think I'll become a Romantic."

"The Norwegian-born naturalist *Henrik Steffens*—whom Wergeland called 'Norway's departed laurel leaf' because he had settled in Germany—went to Copenhagen in 1801 to lecture on German Romanticism. He characterized the Romantic Movement by saying, 'Tired of the eternal efforts to fight our way through raw matter, we chose another way and sought to embrace the infinite. We went inside ourselves and created a new world . . .'"

"How can you remember all that?"

"A bagatelle, child."

"Go on, then."

"Schelling also saw a development in nature from earth and rock—to the human mind. He drew attention to very gradual transitions from inanimate nature to more complicated life forms. It was characteristic of the Romantic view in general that nature was thought of as an organism, or in other words, a unity which is constantly developing its innate potentialities. Nature is like a flower unfolding its leaves and petals. Or like a poet unfolding his verses."

"Doesn't that remind you of Aristotle?"

"It does indeed. The Romantic natural philosophy had Aristotelian as well as Neoplatonic overtones. Aristotle had a more organic view of natural processes than the mechanical materialists . . ."

"Yes, that's what I thought . . ."

"We find similar ideas at work in the field of history. A man who came to have great significance for the Romantics was the historical philosopher Johann Gottfried von *Herder,* who lived from 1744 to 1803. He believed that history is characterized by continuity, evolution, and design. We say he had a 'dynamic' view of history because he saw it as a process. The Enlightenment philosophers had often had a 'static' view of history. To them, there was only one universal reason which there could be more or less of at various periods. Herder showed that each historical epoch had its own intrinsic value and each nation its own character or 'soul.' The question is whether we can identify with other cultures."

"So, just as we have to identify with another person's situation to understand them better, we have to identify with other cultures to understand them too."

"That is taken for granted nowadays. But in the Romantic period it was a new idea. Romanticism helped strengthen the feeling of national identity. It is no coincidence that the Norwegian struggle for national independence flourished at that particular time—in 1814."

"I see."

"Because Romanticism involved new orientations in so many areas, it has been usual to distinguish between two forms of Romanticism. There is what we call *Universal Romanticism,* referring to the Romantics who were preoccupied with nature, world soul, and artistic genius. This form of Romanticism flourished first, especially around 1800, in Germany, in the town of Jena."

"And the other?"

"The other is the so-called *National Romanticism,* which become popular a little later, especially in the town of Heidelberg. The National Romantics were mainly interested in the history of 'the people,' the language of 'the people,' and the culture of 'the people' in general. And 'the people' were seen as an organism unfolding its innate potentiality—exactly like nature and history."

"Tell me where you live, and I'll tell you who you are."

"What united these two aspects of Romanticism was first and foremost the key word 'organism.' The Romantics considered both a plant and a nation to be a living organism. A poetic work was also a living organism. Language was an organism. The entire physical world, even, was considered one organism. There is therefore no sharp dividing line between National Romanticism and Universal Romanticism. The world spirit was just as much present in the people and in popular culture as in nature and art."

"I see."

"Herder had been the forerunner, collecting folk songs from many lands under the eloquent title *Voices of the People.* He even referred to folktales as 'the mother tongue of the people.' The *Brothers Grimm* and others began to collect folk songs and fairy tales in Heidelberg. You must know of *Grimm's Fairy Tales.*"

"Oh sure, Snow White and the Seven Dwarfs, Rumpelstiltskin, The Frog Prince, Hansel and Gretel . . ."

"And many more. In Norway we had *Asbøjørnsen and Moe,* who traveled around the country collecting 'folks' own tales.' It was like harvesting a juicy fruit that was suddenly discovered to be both good and nourishing. And it was urgent—the fruit had already begun to fall. Folk songs were collected; the Norwegian language began to be studied scientifically. The old myths and sagas from heathen times were rediscovered, and composers all over Europe began to incorporate folk melodies into their compositions in an attempt to bridge the gap between folk music and art music."

"What's art music?"

"Art music is music composed by a particular person, like Beethoven. Folk music was not written by any particular person, it came from the people. That's why we don't know exactly when the various folk melodies date from. We distinguish in the same way between folktales and art tales."

"So art tales are . . .?"

"They are tales written by an author, like *Hans Christian Andersen.* The fairy tale genre was passionately cultivated by the Romantics. One of the German masters of the genre was *E.T.A. Hoffmann.*"

"I've heard of *The Tales of Hoffmann.*"

"The fairy tale was the absolute literary ideal of the Romantics—in the same way that the absolute art form of the Baroque period was the theater. It gave the poet full scope to explore his own creativity."

"He could play God to a fictional universe."

"Precisely. And this is a good moment to sum up."

"Go ahead."

"The philosophers of Romanticism viewed the 'world soul' as an 'ego' which in a more or less dreamlike state created everything in the world. The philosopher *Fichte* said that nature stems from a higher, unconscious imagination. Schelling said explicitly that the world is 'in God.' God is aware of some of it, he believed, but there are other aspects of nature which represent the unknown in God. For God also has a dark side."

"The thought is fascinating and frightening. It reminds me of Berkeley."

"The relationship between the artist and his work was seen in exactly the same light. The fairy tale gave the writer free rein to exploit his 'universe-creating imagination.' And even the creative act was not always completely conscious. The writer could experience that his story was being written by some innate force. He could practically be in a hypnotic trance while he wrote."

"He could?"

"Yes, but then he would suddenly destroy the illusion. He would intervene in the story and address ironic comments to the reader, so that the reader, at least momentarily, would be reminded that it was, after all, only a story."

"I see."

"At the some time the writer could remind his reader that it was he who was manipulating the fictional universe. This form of disillusion is called 'romantic irony.' *Henrik Ibsen,* for example, lets one of the characters in *Peer Gynt* say: 'One cannot die in the middle of Act Five.'"

"That's a very funny line, actually. What he's really saying is that he's only a fictional character."

"The statement is so paradoxical that we can certainly emphasize it with a new section."

13

Romanticism: Wordsworth

The Romantic movement of the early nineteenth century emerged as a reaction to the Enlightenment. In almost every respect, the Romantics contradicted the basic assumptions of the *philosophes* of the eighteenth century. One of the most obvious points of disagreement was in their respective approaches toward nature. The *philosophes* had emphasized the rational, scientific analysis of the physical universe as a path to progress in human society—to them nature was a thing, an entity, to be observed and studied with the goal of discovering the laws that govern it and are embedded within it.

In the following poem from 1798, William Wordsworth (1770–1850) presents the Romantic approach to nature.

Discussion Questions

1. What passages show that Wordsworth rejects the Enlightenment assessment of nature?

2. What, according to Wordsworth, is the value of nature to human beings?

3. What human qualities does Wordsworth emphasize? How do they differ from those emphasized by the *philosophes*?

The Tables Turned
An Evening Scene on the Same Subject

William Wordsworth (1770–1850)

UP! up! my Friend, and quit your books;
Or surely you'll grow double:
Up! up! my Friend, and clear your looks;
Why all this toil and trouble?

The sun, above the mountain's head,
A freshening lustre mellow
Through all the long green fields has spread,
His first sweet evening yellow.

Books! 'tis a dull and endless strife:
Come, hear the woodland linnet,   10
How sweet his music! on my life,
There's more of wisdom in it.

And hark! how blithe the throstle sings!
He, too, is no mean preacher:
Come forth into the light of things,
Let Nature be your teacher.

She has a world of ready wealth,
Our minds and hearts to bless—
Spontaneous wisdom breathed by health,
Truth breathed by cheerfulness.   20

One impulse from a vernal wood
May teach you more of man,
Of moral evil and of good,
Than all the sages can.

Sweet is the lore which Nature brings;
Our meddling intellect
Mis-shapes the beauteous forms of things:—
We murder to dissect.

Enough of Science and of Art;
Close up those barren leaves;   30
Come forth, and bring with you a heart
That watches and receives.

1798.

14

A Definition of Nationalism

Modern nationalism emerged out of the dual revolutions of the 18th century, the French and the Industrial Revolutions. Along with the liberty and equality that were rallying cries of French citizens, were also those of "La Patrie!," the nation, conveying a sense of patriotic community. As Napoleon's armies poured throughout Europe, they carried these inflammatory ideas with them, awakening many to the cause of revolution. The Industrial Revolution created national markets, with railroads and other forms of transportation and communication knitting together heretofore autonomous regions to form a national economic community. Another influence in the emergence of nationalism came from the Romantic Movement, whose championing of individual freedom, emphasis on the emotions rather than reason, and love of nature, encouraged people to "find their roots." Thus, cultural or romantic nationalism was born, particularly among the Germans, whose search for their past led them to conclude that each culture had a heritage and a destiny that was unique to it. In this selection, the contemporary political scientist, Hans Kohn, offers a definition of nationalism that incorporates the earliest expressions of nationalism, with those that developed later in the 19th century, linking nationality with creation of the nation-state.

Discussion Questions

1. Is nationalism a liberal idea, like that of liberty and equality? Did the Liberals of the 19th century advocate nationalism? To whom would nationalism appeal?
2. Has the definition of nationalism changed over time? Is nationalism like religion?
3. What does national or ethnic identity have to do with the creation of a nation-state? Does every nationality or ethnic group that can identify itself as such have the right to a separate, sovereign state?

4. Has nationalism been a largely positive or negative force in world history? What is its present role?

The Roots of Nationalism

What is Nationalism? Nationalism is a state of mind, in which the supreme loyalty of the individual is felt to be due the national-state. A deep attachment to one's native soil, to local traditions and to established territorial authority has existed in varying strength throughout history. But it was not until the end of the eighteenth century that nationalism in the modern sense of the word became a generally recognized sentiment increasingly molding all public and private life. Only very recently has it been demanded that each nationality should form a state, its own state, and that the state should include the whole nationality. Formerly, man's loyalty was due not to the nation-state, but to differing other forms of social authority, political organization and ideological cohesion such as the tribe or clan, the city-state or the feudal lord, the dynastic state, the church or religious group. Throughout many centuries the political ideal was not the nation-state but the, at least, theoretically world-wide empire comprising various nationalities and ethnic groups on the basis of a common civilization and for the assurance of a common peace.

Nationalities are the products of the living forces of history, and therefore fluctuating and never rigid. They are groups of the utmost complexity and defy exact definition. Most of them possess certain objective factors distinguishing them from other nationalities like common descent, language, territory, political entity, customs and traditions, or religion. But it is clear that none of these factors is essential to the existence or definition of nationality. Thus the people of the United States do not claim common descent to form a nationality, and the people of Switzerland speak three or four languages and yet form one well-defined nationality. Although objective factors are of great importance for the formation of nationalities, the most essential element is a living and active corporate will. It is this will which we call nationalism, a state of mind inspiring the large majority of a people and claiming to inspire all of its members. It asserts that the nation-state is the ideal and the only legitimate form of political organization and that the nationality is the source of all cultural creative energy and of economic well-being.

From Hans Kohn, *Nationalism: Its Meaning and History*, Revised edition, copyright © 1965 by D. Van Nostrand Co., New York, pp. 9–10.

15

Aspects of Nationalism

1. **Feeling of uniqueness identified with a "nationality" group as seen in:**
   a. Common language, culture, territory, history and ethnic background (*"Ethnic Nationalism"*)
   b. Common institutions and interests (economic, political, social)
   c. Pride in achievements and sorrow in tragedies (victimization)

2. **Leads to:**
   a. Preference for fellow nationals and indifference or hostility to others
   b. Desire for political self-determination (independent, sovereign state)
   c. Devotion to the nation and nationality

3. **Four types of nationalism**
   a. *Traditional Nationalism ("Civic Nationalism")*
      - People identify with their country (loyalty)
      - Symbols: flag, holidays, national anthems, heroes
      - Education in the nation's history and greatness
      - "We-they" sentiments
   b. *Striving Nationalism*
      - Nationality group ruled by others
      - Desire for self-determination
   c. *Protective Nationalism*
      - Nation under severe threat from within or without
      - Plea for national unity expressed by leadership
   d. *Imperialistic Nationalism*
      - National mission requires control over others
      - Conquest of others shows national greatness/superiority
      - Make other people accept one's nation's values and way of life

16

Working Conditions in the Industrial Revolution

British public policy during the nineteenth century was under the sway of the principle of laissez faire. Unquestionably it contributed to tremendous advances in the economy as a whole, but also led to terrible working conditions. Several parliamentary committees gathered information from both the working and manufacturing classes in order to make recommendations for reform. The selections below come from the Sadler Committee and Lord Ashley's Mines Commission.

Discussion Questions

1. What view of children did English industrial society apparently have?

2. Do you think the conditions they had to endure were much different from the children of farmers?

3. What forms of discipline were employed in factories?

4. What position did Thomas Wilson take on the question of governmental regulation of working conditions?

5. Would any governmental reform be consistent with laissez faire doctrine?

The Sadler Report

VENERIS, 18° DIE MAII, 1832

Michael Thomas Sadler, Esquire, in the chair

* * *

MR. MATTHEW CRABTREE, *called in;
and Examined.*

What age are you?————Twenty-two.

What is your occupation?————A blanket
manufacturer.

Have you ever been employed in a factory?————Yes.

At what age did you first go to work in
one?————Eight.

How long did you continue in that occupation?————Four years.

Will you state the hours of labour at the
period when you first went to the factory, in
ordinary times?————From 6 in the morning
to 8 at night.

Fourteen hours?————Yes.

With what intervals for refreshment and
rest?————An hour at noon.

Then you had no resting time allowed in
which to take your breakfast, or what is in
Yorkshire called your "drinking"?————No.

When trade was brisk what were your
hours?————From 5 in the morning to 9 in
the evening.

Sixteen hours?————Yes.

With what intervals at dinner?————An
hour.

How far did you live from the mill?————
—About two miles.

Was there any time allowed for you to get
your breakfast in the mill?————No.

Did you take it before you left your
home?————generally.

During those long hours of labour could
you be punctual; how did you awake?————I
seldom did awake spontaneously; I was most
generally awoke or lifted out of bed, sometimes asleep, by my parents.

Were you always in time?————No.

What was the consequence if you had been
too late?————I was most commonly beaten.

Severely?————Very severely, I thought.

In whose factory was this?————Messrs.
Hague & Cook's, of Dewsbury.

Will you state the effect that those long
hours had upon the state of your health and
feelings?————I was, when working those
long hours, commonly very much fatigued
at night, when I left my work; so much so
that I sometimes should have slept as I
walked if I had not stumbled and started
awake again; and so sick often that I could
not eat, and what I did eat I vomited.

Did this labour destroy your appetite?————
—It did.

In what situation were you in that mill?——
——I was a piecener.

Will you state to this Committee whether
piecening is a very laborious employment for
children, or not?————

It is a very laborious employment. Piecen-
ers are continually running to and fro, and on
their feet the whole day.

Reports from the Sadler Committee, *Parliamentary Papers* (1831–1832) and Lord Ashley's Mines Commission,
Parliamentary Papers (1842).

The duty of the piecener is to take the cardings from one part of the machinery, and to place them on another?———Yes.

So that the labour is not only continual, but it is unabated to the last?———It is unabated to the last.

Do you not think, from your own experience, that the speed of the machinery is so calculated as to demand the utmost exertions of a child supposing the hours were moderate?———It is as much as they could do at the best; they are always upon the stretch, and it is commonly very difficult to keep up with their work.

State the condition of the children toward the latter part of the day, who have thus to keep up with the machinery.———It is as much as they can do when they are not very much fatigued to keep up with their work, and toward the close of the day, when they come to be more fatigued, they cannot keep up with it very well, and the consequence is that they are beaten to spur them on.

Were you beaten under those circumstances?———Yes.

Frequently?———Very frequently.

And principally at the latter end of the day?———Yes.

And is it your belief that if you had not been so beaten, you should not have got through the work?———I should not if I had not been kept up to it by some means.

Does beating then principally occur at the latter end of the day, when the children are exceedingly fatigued?———It does at the latter end of the day, and in the morning sometimes, when they are very drowsy, and have not got rid or the fatigue of the day before.

What were you beaten with principally?———A strap.

Anything else?———Yes, a stick sometimes; and there is a kind of roller which runs on the top of the machine called a billy, perhaps two or three yards in length, and perhaps an inch and a half, or more in diameter; the circumference would be four or five inches; I cannot speak exactly.

Were you beaten with that instrument?———Yes.

Have you yourself been beaten, and have you seen other children struck severely with that roller?———I have been struck very severely with it myself, so much so as to knock me down, and I have seen other children have their heads broken with it.

You think that it is a general practice to beat the children with the roller?———It is.

You do not think then that you were worse treated than other children in the mill?———No, I was not, perhaps not so bad as some were.

In those mills is chastisement towards the latter part of the day going on perpetually?———Perpetually.

So that you can hardly be in a mill without hearing constant crying?———Never an hour, I believe.

Do you think that if the overlooker were naturally a humane person it would be still found necessary for him to beat the children, in order to keep up their attention and vigilance at the termination of those extraordinary days of labour?———Yes, the machine turns off a regular quantity of cardings, and of course they must keep as regularly to their work the whole of the day; they must keep with the machine, and therefore however humane the slubber may be, as he must keep up with the machine or be found fault with, he spurs the children to keep up also by various means but that which he commonly resorts to is to strap them when they become drowsy.

At the time when you were beaten for not keeping up with your work, were you anxious to have done it if you possibly could?———Yes; the dread of being beaten if we could not keep up with our work was a sufficient impulse to keep us to it if we could.

When you got home at night after this labour, did you feel much fatigued?———Very much so.

Had you any time to be with your parents, and to receive instruction from them?———No.

What did you do?———All that we did when we got home was to get the little bit of supper that was provided for us and go to bed immediately. If the supper had not been ready directly, we should have gone to sleep while it was preparing.

Did you not, as a child, feel it a very grievous hardship to be roused so soon in the morning?———I did.

Were the rest of the children similarly circumstanced?———Yes, all of them; but they were not all of them so far from their work as I was.

And if you had been too late you were under the apprehension of being cruelly beaten?———I generally was beaten when I happened to be too late; and when I got up in the morning the apprehension of that was so great, that I used to run, and cry all the way as I went to the mill.

That was the way by which your punctual attendance was secured?———Yes.

And you do not think it could have been secured by any other means?———No.

Then it is your impression from what you have seen, and from your own experience, that those long hours of labour have the effect of rendering young persons who are subject to them exceedingly unhappy?———Yes.

You have already said it had a considerable effect upon your health?———Yes.

Do you conceive that it diminished your growth?———I did not pay much attention to that; but I have been examined by some persons who said they thought I was rather stunted, and that I should have been taller if I had not worked at the mill.

What were your wages at that time?———Three shillings [per week].

And how much a day had you for over-work when you were worked so exceedingly long?———A halfpenny a day.

Did you frequently forfeit that if you were not always there to a moment?———Yes; I most frequently forfeited what was allowed for those long hours.

You took your food to the mill; was it in your mill, as is the case in cotton mills, much spoiled by being laid aside?———It was very frequently covered by flues from the wool; and in that case they had to be blown off with the mouth, and picked off with the fingers before it could be eaten.

So that not giving you a little leisure for eating your food, but obliging you to take it at the mill, spoiled your food when you did get it?———Yes, very commonly.

And that at the same time that this overlabour injured your appetite?———Yes.

Could you eat when you got home?———Not always.

What is the effect of this piecening upon the hands?———It makes them bleed; the skin is completely rubbed off, and in that case they bleed in perhaps a dozen parts.

The prominent parts of the hand?———Yes, all the prominent parts of the hand are rubbed down till they bleed; every day they are rubbed in that way.

All the time you continue at work?———All the time we are working. The hands never can be hardened in that work, for the grease keeps them soft in the first instance, and long and continual rubbing is always wearing them down, so that if they were hard they would be sure to bleed.

Is it attended with much pain?———Very much.

Do they allow you to make use of the back of the hand?———No; the work cannot be so well done with the back of the hand, or I should have made use of that.

Is the work done as well when you are so many hours engaged in it, as it would be if you were at it a less time?————I believe it is not done so well in those long hours; toward the latter end of the day the children become completely bewildered, and know not what they are doing, so that they spoil their work without knowing.

Then you do not think that the masters gain much by the continuance of the work to so great a length of time?————I believe not.

Were there girls as well as boys employed in this manner?————Yes.

Were they more tenderly treated by the overlookers, or were they worked and beaten in the same manner?————There was no difference in their treatment.

Were they beaten by the overlookers, or by the slubber?————By the slubber.

But the overlooker must have been perfectly aware of the treatment that the children endured at the mill?————Yes; and sometimes the overlooker beat them himself; but the man that they wrought under had generally the management of them.

Did he pay them their wages?————No; their wages were paid by the master.

But the overlooker of the mill was perfectly well aware that they could not have performed the duty exacted from them in the mill without being thus beaten?————I believe he was.

You seem to say that this beating is absolutely necessary, in order to keep the children up to their work; is it universal throughout all factories?————I have been in several other factories, and I have witnessed the same cruelty in them all.

Evidence Before Lord Ashley's Mines Commission

THOMAS WILSON, Esq., OF THE BANKS, SILKSTONE, OWNER OF THREE COLLIERIES

I object on general principles to government interference in the conduct of any trade, and I am satisfied that in the mines it would be productive of the greatest injury and injustice. The art of mining is not so perfectly understood as to admit of the way in which a colliery shall be conducted being dictated by any person, however experienced, with such certainty as would warrant an interference with the management of private business. I should also most decidedly object to placing collieries under the present provisions of the Factory Act with respect to the education of children employed therein. First, because, if it is contended that coal-owners, as employers of children, are bound to attend to their education, this obligation extends equally to all other employers, and therefore it is unjust to single out one class only; secondly, because, if the legislature asserts a right to interfere to secure education, it is bound to make that interference general; and thirdly, because the mining population is in this neighborhood so intermixed with other classes, and is in such small bodies in any one place, that it would be impossible to provide separate schools for them.

17

An Industrial Town

Charles Dickens' *Hard Times,* Written in 1854, is one of the most evocative novels about England's industrial age. Few writers could describe the sights, sounds and even smells of factory work and life as well as he did for his avid readers. England had just celebrated its progress at the Crystal Palace Exposition, but Dickens finds in Coketown greedy capitalists like Bounderby and "efficiency experts" like Gradgrind who see none of life's beauty. In the following selection, Dickens describes Coketown, the model of an industrial town.

Discussion Questions

1. What does Dickens mean by saying Coketown was "a triumph of fact?"

2. Why didn't the laboring people go to church?

3. Why does Dickens say that the millers of Coketown were as fragile as China-ware?

4. How would a modern environmentalist describe Coketown?

5. What connections could you make between the testimony before the Sadler committee and Dickens' description of Coketown?

Coketown, to which Messrs. Bounderby and Gradgrind now walked, was a triumph of fact; it had no greater taint of fancy in it than Mrs. Gradgrind herself. Let us strike the keynote, Coketown, before pursuing our tune.

It was a town of red brick, or of brick that would have been red if the smoke and ashes had allowed it; but as matters stood it was a town of unnatural red and black like the painted face of a savage. It was a town of machinery and tall chimneys, out of which interminable serpents of smoke trailed themselves forever and ever, and never got uncoiled. It had a black canal in it, and a river that ran purple with ill-smelling dye, and vast piles of building full of windows where there was a rattling and a trembling all day long, and where the piston of the steam-engine worked monotonously up and down like the head of an elephant in a state of melancholy madness. It contained several large streets all very like one another, and many small streets still more like one another, inhabited by people equally like one another, who all went in and out at the same hours, with the same sound upon the same pavements, to do the same work, and to whom every day was the same as yesterday and tomorrow; and every year the counterpart of the last and the next.

These attributes of Coketown were in the main inseparable from the work by which it was sustained; against them were to be set off comforts of life which found their all over the world, and elegancies of life which made, we will not ask how much of the fine-lady, who could scarcely bear to hear the place mentioned. The rest of its features were voluntary, and they were these.

You saw nothing in Coketown but what was severely workful. If the members of a religious persuasion built a chapel there—as the members of eighteen religious persuasions had done—they made it a pious warehouse of red brick, with sometimes (but this is only in highly ornamental examples) a bell in a bird-cage on the top of it. The solitary exception was the New Church; a stuccoed edifice with a square steeple over the door, terminating in four short pinnacles like florid wooden legs. All the public inscriptions in the town were painted alike, in severe characters of black and white. The jail might have been the infirmary, the infirmary might have been the jail, the townhall might have been either, or both, or anything else, for anything that appeared to the contrary in the graces of their construction. Fact, fact, fact, everywhere in the material aspect of the town; fact, fact, fact, everywhere in the immaterial. The McChoakum child school was all fact, and the school of design was all fact, and the relations between master and man were all fact, and everything was fact between the lying in hospital and the cemetery, and what you couldn't state in figures, or show to be purchasable in the cheapest market and saleable in the dearest, was not, and never should be, world without end, Amen.

A town so sacred to fact, and so triumphant in its assertion, of course got on well? Why no, not quite well. No? Dear me!

No. Coketown did not come out of its own furnaces in all respects like gold that had stood the fire. First, the perplexing mystery of the place was, Who belonged to the eighteen denominations? Because, whoever did, the labouring people did not. It was very strange to walk through the streets on a Sunday morning and note how few of *them*; the barbarous jangling of bells that was driving the sick and nervous mad called away from their own quarter, from their own close rooms, from the comers of their own streets, where they lounged listlessly, gazing at all the church- and chapel-going, as at a thing with which they had no manner of concern. Nor was it merely the stranger who noticed this, because there was a native organization in Coketown itself whose members were to be heard of in the House of Commons every session, indignantly petitioning for acts of Parliament that should make these people religious by main force. Then—came the Teetotal Society, who complained that these same people *would* get drunk, and showed in tabular statements that they did get drunk, and proved at tea parties that no inducement, human or divine (except a medal), would induce them to forgo their custom of getting drunk. Then came the chemist and druggist, with other tabular statements, showing that when they didn't get drunk they took opium. Then came the experienced chaplain of the jail, with more tabular statements, outdoing all the previous tabular statements, and showing that the same people *would* resort to low haunts, hidden from the public eye, where they heard low singing and saw low dancing, and mayhap joined in it; and where A.B., aged twenty-four next birthday, and committed for eighteen months' solitary, had himself said—not that he had ever shown himself particularly worthy of belief—his ruin began, as he was perfectly sure and confident that otherwise he would have been a tip-top moral specimen.

* * *

I entertain a weak idea that the English people are as hard-worked as any people upon whom the sun shines. I acknowledge to

this ridiculous idiosyncrasy as a reason why I would give them a little more play.

In the hardest working part of Coketown; in the innermost fortifications of that ugly citadel, where Nature was as strongly bricked out as killing airs and gases were bricked in; at the heart of the labyrinth of narrow courts upon courts, and close streets upon streets, which had come into existence piecemeal, every piece in a violent hurry for some one man's purpose, and the whole an unnatural family, shouldering, and trampling, and pressing one another to death; in the last close nook of this great exhausted receiver, where the chimneys, for want of air to make a draught, were built in an immense variety of stunted and crooked shapes, as though every house put out a sign of the kind of people who might be expected to be born in it; among the multitude of Coketown, generically called "the Hands"—a race who would have found more favour with some people if Providence had seen fit to make them only hands, or, like the lower creatures of the seashore, only hands and stomachs—lived a certain Stephen Blackpool, forty years of age.

Stephen looked older, but he had had a hard life. It is said that every life has its roses and thorns; there seemed, however, to have been a misadventure or mistake in Stephen's case, whereby somebody else had become possessed of his roses, and he had become possessed of the same somebody else's thorns in addition to his own. He had known, to use his words, a peck of trouble. He was usually called Old Stephen, in a kind of rough homage to the fact.

A rather stooping man, with a knitted brow, a pondering expression of face, and a hard-looking head sufficiently capacious on which his iron-grey hair lay long and thin, Old Stephen might have passed for a particularly intelligent man in his condition. Yet he was not. He took no place among those remarkable "Hands," who, piecing together their broken intervals of leisure through many years, had mastered difficult sciences and acquired a knowledge of most unlikely things. He held no station among the Hands who could make speeches and carry on debates. Thousands of his compeers could talk much better than he, at any time. He was a good power-loom weaver, and a man of perfect integrity. What more he was, or what else he had in him, if anything, let him show for himself.

The lights in the great factories, which looked, when they were illuminated, like Fairy Palaces—or the travellers by express-train said so—were all extinguished; and the bells had rung for knocking off for the night, and had ceased again; and the Hands, men and women, boy and girl, were clattering home. Old Stephen was standing in the street with the old sensation upon him which the stoppage of the machinery always produced—the sensation of its having worked and stopped in his own head.

* * *

A sunny midsummer day. There was such a thing sometimes, even in Coketown.

Seen from a distance in such weather, Coketown lay shrouded in a haze of its own, which appeared impervious to the sun's rays. You only knew the town was there, because you knew there could have been no such sulky blotch upon the prospect without a town. A blur of soot and smoke, now confusedly tending this way, now that way, now aspiring to the vault of Heaven, now murkily creeping along the earth, as the wind rose and fell, or changed its quarter: a dense formless jumble, with sheets of cross light in it, that showed nothing but masses of darkness—Coketown in the distance was suggestive of itself, though not a brick of it could be seen.

The wonder was, it was there at all. It had been ruined so often that it was amazing how it had borne so many shocks. Surely there never was such fragile china-ware as that of which the millers of Coketown were made. Handle them never so lightly and they fell to pieces with such ease that you might suspect them of having been flawed before. They were ruined when they were required to send labouring children to school; they were ruined when inspectors were appointed to look into their works; they were ruined when such inspectors considered it doubtful whether they were quite justified in chopping people up with their machinery; they were utterly undone when it was hinted that perhaps they need not always make quite so much smoke. Besides Mr. Bounderby's gold spoon which was generally received in Coketown, another prevalent fiction was very popular there. It took the form of a threat. Whenever a Coketowner felt he was ill-used—that is to say, whenever he was not left entirely alone, and it was proposed to hold him accountable for the consequences of any of his acts—he was sure to come out with the awful menace that he would "sooner pitch his property into the Atlantic." This had terrified the Home Secretary within an inch of his life on several occasions.

However, the Coketowners were so patriotic, after all, that they never had pitched their property into the Atlantic yet, but, on the contrary, had been kind enough to take mighty good care of it. So there it was, in the haze yonder, and it increased and multiplied.

The streets were hot and dusty on the summer day, and the sun was so bright that it even shone through the heavy vapour drooping over Coketown, and could not be looked at steadily. Stokers emerged from low underground doorways into factory yards, and sat on steps, and posts, and palings, wiping their swarthy visages, and contemplating coals. The whole town seemed to be frying in oil. There was a stifling smell of hot oil everywhere. The steam-engines shone with it, the dresses of the Hands were soiled with it, the mills throughout their many stories oozed and trickled it. The atmosphere of those Fairy Palaces was like the breath of the simoom, and their inhabitants, wasting with heat, toiled languidly in the desert. But no temperature made the melancholy mad elephants more mad or more sane. Their wearisome heads went up and down at the same rate, in hot weather and cold, wet weather and dry, fair weather and foul. The measured motion of their shadows on the walls was the substitute Coketown had to show for the shadows of rustling woods; while, for the summer hum of insects, it could offer, all the year round, from the dawn of Monday to the night of Saturday, the whirr of shafts and wheels.

Drowsily they whirred all through this sunny day, making the passenger more sleepy and more hot as he passed the humming walls of the mills. Sun-blinds, and sprinklings of water, a little cooled the main streets and the shops, but the mills, and the courts and alleys, baked at a fierce heat. Down upon the river that was black and thick with dye, some Coketown boys who were at large—a rare sight there—rowed a crazy boat, which made a spumous track upon the water as it jogged along, while every dip of an oar stirred up vile smells. But the sun itself, however beneficent generally, was less kind to Coketown than hard frost, and rarely looked intently into any of its closer regions without engendering more death than life. So does the eye of Heaven itself become an evil eye, when incapable or sordid hands are interposed between it and the things it looks upon to bless. . . .

18

The Impact of the Industrial Revolution on Women

Women have always worked, constantly, continuously, always and everywhere, in every type of society in every part of the world since the beginning of human time.

Heather Gordon Cremonesi

"I know that," you may be saying to yourself, yet "women's work," has come to be seen as somehow different, and usually of less value than men's work. Was that an idea that always existed, or did it develop at a particular time? In this selection from Rosalind Miles' *A Women's History of the World*, the impact of the Industrial Revolution on the lives of women and children is discussed. The conventional view of the Industrial Revolution is that it improved the lives and opportunities of all people, especially women, whose role became that of housewife and supporter to her husband, the "breadwinner." As the dictates of "Bourgeois Respectability," the social creed which developed in the 19th century suggested, "a woman's place is in the home," the so-called private sphere, while the man occupied the public sphere, that of office or factory. As the Industrial Revolution transformed the place of work, it also redefined the value and meaning of work, and changed the daily lives of all. As you read the following selection, evaluate the impact of industrialization on women's lives and women's work.

Discussion Questions

1. Did the machine age improve the work, status, economic and/or political position of women? If not, why not?

2. What impact did industrialization have on the lives of women and children? How does Miles' account compare with earlier readings? Could most of the women in this selection identify with the ideals which some have labelled "the Cult of True Womanhood?"

3. Would you agree with Miles that of the revolutions of the 18th century— "each was a revolution for some and not for all . . . with the most enduring (ideas) prove(ing) to be the natural superiority of man?"

Iron, coal, steam—the new sources of power developed in the Britain of the eighteenth century revolutionized more than manufacturing technology. In an astonishingly short time their effect was to shatter the traditional structure of women's lives by splitting apart what had previously been the one indivisible whole of husband, home and family. The work of the pre-industrial housewife combined all these elements without strain, and centered her strongly both in her own world and in the wider scheme of things as a person of some significance:

> In their role as agriculturalists, women produced the bulk of the country's food supply. The entire management of the dairy, including the milking of cows and the making of butter and cheese, was in women's hands, and the women were also responsible for the growing of flax and hemp, for the milling of corn, for the care of the poultry, pigs, orchards and gardens.

With the shift from an agricultural to an industrial economy, from country to town, from home to factory, women lost the previous flexibility, status and control of their work. In its place they were granted the privilege of low-grade, exploited occupations, the double burden of waged and domestic labor, and the sole responsibility for child care that has weighed them down ever since. Each of the changes of the Industrial Revolution proved to have an adverse impact upon women's lives; coming together, the result was devastating, in ways that could never have been foreseen.

At the simplest level, the shift from home to factory production had a number of damaging consequences for women workers. Among the first was the loss of any previous partnership status, when a wife was denied the opportunity to share her husband's work. Before industrialization, women frequently worked alongside their menfolk or in close harmony with them, reaping, gleaning, binding, threshing, digging; a central image of the Middle Ages, and a metaphor for the mutual interdependence of the well-balanced couple, was the husbandman ploughing the furrow while his wife follows behind sowing the seed. This primitive pastoral which had endured through so many thousands of years was one of the first casualties of the revolution in labor.

Another was the control women had enjoyed as the head of their own home units of production, along with the often considerable sums of money they could generate. The pre-industrial housewife made little or no distinction between domestic or commercial activities; she brewed, baked, wove, collected eggs or raised pigs, and whatever she had left over from her own household requirements she would sell. The harder she worked, and the more successful her sidelines, the more money she made. As with the shared outdoor work of the agricultural calendar, the division of labor was reciprocal, and there was no concept of the only or principal male breadwinner supporting his wife and children—all were productive, the wife doubly so. As a waged laborer, by contrast, a woman was on a fixed weekly sum, fixed moreover at a rate often lower than that of children, let alone that of men, for reasons which were crystal clear to the boss-persons:

> The low price of female labour makes it the most profitable as well as the most agreeable occupation for a female to superintend her own domestic establishment, and her low wages do not tempt her to abandon the care of her own children [i.e., because she cannot be tempted to what she cannot afford, a nurse or mother-substitute] . . . Mr. E., a manufacturer, employs females exclusively . . . [with] a decided preference to married females, especially those who have families at home dependent on them for support; they are attentive, docile, more so than unmarried females, and are compelled to use their utmost exertions to produce the necessities of life.

As this shows, the factory system both reduced and dehumanized its operatives, regarding them "in no other light than as tools let out to hire." It also from the first created a hierarchy even of the exploited, for women were universally worked harder than their male fellow sufferers and paid less, employers everywhere agreeing that women were "more easily induced to undergo severe bodily fatigue than men," hence a better investment for "the master," as "a more obedient servant to himself, and an equally efficient slave to his machinery"—"cruelty!" wrote one reformer passionately, "though it may be voluntary, for God help them, the hands dare not refuse."

So women, previously autonomous, now economically crippled, were forced into dependence on men, which in turn reinforced and indeed recreated for the modern world fresh notions of women's natural inferiority. Female subordination to males also took a new turn with the relocation of women's work from home to factories; subjection to the power of males was one thing when the patriarch was your own husband or father, and quite another under industrial organization, when the authority of the absent owner was vested in and expressed through the daily tyranny of a brutal and bullying overseer, as in this report on the first factories in America, deploring the use of "the cowhide, or well-seasoned strap of American manufacture":

> We could show *many* females who have had corporeal punishment inflicted on them; one girl, 11 years of age, who had her leg broken with a billet of wood; another who had a board split over her head by a heartless monster in the shape of an overseer of a cotton-mill . . . *foreign overseers* are frequently placed over American women and children, and we are sorry to add that sometimes *foreigners in this country* have employed American overseers to carry into effect their tyrannical rule in these mills.

For the women catapulted out of their home-based working lives into a factory routine, the harsh discipline was only one of a number of shocks. First came the hours of unremitting labor: a working day of 5 AM to 8 PM was common, and at peak times work would begin at 3 AM continuing till 10 PM, without any extra pay. The hours themselves would not have been so different from the workload of a home-based woman. But the forced pace of the labor, with the inability to break off, to rest or to vary the work in any way, made it a mental as well as physical torment.

And even the humblest homes compared favorably with factories where the heat of the machines kept the temperature at a constant 80 to 84 degrees; where the workers were not allowed to break off to have a drink, even the rainwater being locked up to prevent any such temptation; and where all doors and windows were kept locked, on pain of a fine of one shilling for anyone trying to open them. (This, interestingly enough, was exactly the same as that imposed for any homosexual activity in the factory lavatory: "Any two spinners *found together* in the *necessary*, each man . . . 1s.[shilling].") A contemporary eye (or rather nose) witness reported the effect of these working conditions on the victims of them:

> . . . not a breath of sweet air . . . the abominable and pernicious stink of the gas to assist in the murderous effects of the heat . . . noxious effluvia, mixed with the steam . . . the dust, and what is called cotton-flyings, or fuz, which the unfortunate creatures have to inhale . . .

Any consideration of the lives of the female laborers of the Industrial Revolution bears out to its fullest the savage attack of Margaret, Duchess of Newcastle in the seventeenth century: "Women live like *bats* or *owls*, labor like *beasts* and die like *worms*." Yet even the appalling work, snuffed-out hopes and truncated lives, these women had more to suffer still.

Themselves often enough exploited child slaves—little girls began down the mines, opening doors for the coal wagons to pass, as young as five, "invariably set to work at an earlier age than boys . . . from a notion very generally entertained among the parents, that girls are more acute and capable of making themselves useful at an earlier age than boys"—they had no alternative but to see their own children ruined in their turn. What this meant for both mother and child can be seen in this examination of a 17-year-old textile worker who had been laboring for ten years in a factory in the North of England:

> When I had worked about half a year, a weakness fell into my knees and ankles; it continued, and it got worse and worse. In the morning I could scarcely walk, and my brother and sister used out of kindness to take me under each arm, and run with me, a good mile, to the mill, and my legs dragged on the ground in consequence of the pain; I could not walk. If we were five minutes late, the overlooker would take a strap and beat us till we were black and blue. . . . I was as straight and healthful as any when I was seven years and a quarter old . . .
>
> Your mother being a widow . . . could not afford to take you away?—No.
>
> Was she made very unhappy by seeing that you were getting crooked and deformed?— I have seen her weep sometimes, and I have asked her why she was weeping, but she would not tell me then, but she has told me since . . .

Condemned to work the same hours as their parents, and to shoulder as nearly as possible an adult workload (several cases were reported in which a full-grown male miner ruptured himself by lifting his child's load of coals on to its back) the "offspring of the laboring poor" were children only in name. If they faltered under these unreasonable demands, the punishments could be brutal and sadistic: a "bad" boy nail-maker would have his ear nailed to his workbench, a "disobedient" girl risked being dragged the length of the factory by her hair. Between fear of a repetition of the punishment, and fear of losing the "place" and with it the child's income, most families were powerless to challenge the abusers of their children. For one woman, however, when her young son was beaten with a "billy-roller" (a wooden loom-shaft between two and three yards long, and about five inches in diameter) till he vomited blood, it was too much. In the boy's own words:

> I entreated my mother not to make a complaint, lest I be further beaten. The next morning after I went to work, she followed me, and came to the slubber that had used me in that way, and gave him a sharp lecture . . . as soon as she was gone, he beat me again severely for telling, when one of the young men . . . went out and found my mother, and told her, and she came in again and enquired of me what instrument it was I was beaten with, but I durst not do it; some of the bystanders pointed out the instrument, the billy-roller, and she seized it immediately, and beat it about the fellow's head, and gave him one or two black eyes . . .

Stories like this provide welcome evidence that the experience of the Industrial Revolution was not one of unrelieved female submission to the purgatory of cruelty, suffering and deprivation. Nor was pre-industrial life the rosy pastoral that it has often seemed; there was no sudden pantomimic scene-change from agrarian utopia to dark satanic mills, and the country women described by La Bruyère as living, working and dying in holes in the ground "like wild animals" would have been most surprised to learn that theirs was about to become a paradise lost. Nor can all the evils of this crowded century be blamed on factory organization. The soaring population, for instance, as more babies survived their birth and infancy and more women survived childbirth to complete their reproductive years, certainly contrib-

uted to the contemporary evils of urban overcrowding and desperate poverty; but it was itself a force of nature, attributable to the oldest source of power, not to any of the newfangled discoveries.

It has been argued, too, that the Industrial Revolution, despite the sufferings of those who went down in the struggle against the machine, was a convulsion unavoidably necessary for society to survive. "He that will not apply new remedies, must expect new evils," warned Francis Bacon, one of the earliest social philosophers of the modern age; and the alternative scenario, of the disaster averted rather than the cataclysm that occurred, is forcefully outlined by a leading historian on the period, T. S. Ashton:

> The central problem of the age was how to feed and clothe and employ generations of children outnumbering by far those of any earlier time. Ireland was faced with the same problem. Failing to solve it, she lost in the forties about a fifth of her people by emigration or starvation and disease. If England had remained a nation of cultivators and craftsmen, she could hardly have escaped the same fate. . . . There are today on the plains of India and China men and women, plague-ridden and hungry, living lives little better, to outward appearance, than those of the cattle that toil with them by day and share their places of sleep by night. Such Asiatic standards, and such unmechanized horrors, are the lot of those who increase their number without passing through an Industrial Revolution.

As a counterbalance to the doomsday version of these historical events, this argument has much to commend it. The march of progress, however, is rarely welcomed by those it tramples underfoot. To the women faced with feeding the machines brought into being by man's resistless innovation, women condemned to serve the new gods of power for an insult of a pittance, invention was truly the mother of necessity. With this work, on these wages, women could not live. Married or marriageable women were therefore manacled to matrimony by the steel-strong fetter of the survival imperative, while single women paid for their anomalous state with all they had—or, brutally, did not have.

Every revolution is a revolution of ideas— yet to innovate is not to reform. The revolutions of the eighteenth century, so different from each other in some of their most profound particulars, yet had one simple truth in common—each was a revolution for some, and not for all. And only some ideas were overturned in the general *bouleversement*. Of those that survived, the most enduring proved to be that of the natural superiority of man. And when borne on the great wave of expansion, as adventurers and empire-builders struck out for foreign fields, this antique nostrum travelled with them like a plague virus. Unexamined and unchecked, it was the first of the items of the white man's burden to be distributed throughout his new dominions.

19

Industrialization and Women

In the following selection the authors Louise Tilly and Joan Scott review the complex changes that industrialization has had on the roles of women in the family and in society at large since about 1700.

Discussion Questions

1. What was the nature of what the authors call the "family economy" in the pre-industrial era and how did women fit into it?

2. How did the new "family wage economy" differ? How were productive and reproductive activities related to each other?

3. As industrialism proceeded, what role did consumption come to play? What was the new position of women and children?

4. What do the authors mean by a "U-shaped pattern of female productive activity?"

5. What factors influenced the supply of and the demand for women as workers?

6. What role did the family play in the various periods of transition from around 1700 to around 1900?

What was the impact of industrialization on women's work? There is no simple or single answer. Changes in the mode of production did not immediately or automatically transform women's work. Nor did they directly alter reproductive strategies and family organization, both of which influenced women's productive activities. Yet important changes have occurred. We can best answer the question about the impact of industrialization by conceiving of a process of change which affected the economy, demography and family organization in different ways and which also changed the relationships among them.

Let us review briefly the changing relationships among the economic, demographic and family influences on the work of women of the popular classes in Britain and France since 1700. In the household mode of production typical of the preindustrial economy, the unit of production was small and productivity was low. All household members worked at productive tasks, differentiated by age and sex. We have called this form of organization the *family economy*. Within marriage, fertility was high. High mortality was, however, an involuntary check on net reproduction. Children were potential workers, but they were also potential heirs to limited resources. So households controlled the size of future generations by late marriage and enforced celibacy for some members. Parental control of limited resources limited the autonomy of

children. High fertility, high mortality, a small-scale household organization of production, and limited resources meant that women's time was spent primarily in productive activity. Unmarried women worked in their parents' households or in other households if there was no need for their labor at home. Married women were both producers and mothers. The household setting of work facilitated the combination of productive and domestic activities. Married women adjusted their time to meet the demands of production in the interest of the family economy.

During industrialization, the size of productive units grew and productive activity moved out of the household to workshops and factories. Increasingly, people worked for wages. Early industrialization, particularly in the textile industry, relied heavily on the labor of women and children. Families adapted older expectations about work and strategies of reproduction to the new circumstances. The result was the *family wage economy*. Under this organization the family continued to allocate the labor of its members. Now the household's need for wages rather than for labor determined the productive activity, of women when they were daughters as well as wives and mothers. Families continued to bear many children, and infant mortality remained very high. This high mortality and the fact that surviving children were potential family wage earners made the continuation of earlier high fertility strategies feasible. Yet high fertility in the new circumstances created problems for married women. As in the past, they had to balance their time between productive and reproductive activities, but work now took them away from home. Under the family wage economy, married women worked when the household needed their wages. A woman's time was not invested exclusively in child care or domestic activity when subsistence had to be earned. But the domestic and reproductive needs of the household also claimed much of her time. So, her work tended to be episodic and irregular. If possible, she improvised cash-producing activities connected to her domestic work. When other family members, particularly children, were available to replace her as wage earners, the married woman withdrew from wage-earning activity. Over the course of her lifetime, a woman alternated productive and reproductive activity. Family needs determined when she worked. As a daughter, a woman was usually a family wage earner. As a mother and wife, the time she spent earning money depended on the need of the family for wages and therefore on the wages and work of other family members.

Technological change, the growth of heavy industry, and the increased scale of industrial organization led to increased productivity and greater prosperity by the end of the nineteenth century. The new organization of manufacturing required an adult male labor force primarily. In the tertiary sector, however, an increasing number of white-collar jobs were available for women. Men's wages in this period increased, and the standard of living of many working-class families rose above the subsistence level. The family economy became a *family consumer economy*, as households specialized in reproduction and consumption. Nonetheless, the family continued to allocate the labor of its members. Children of both sexes were family wage earners, usually after they had completed school. The state now required some schooling for all children and, increasingly, one's ability to find a regular, well-paying job depended on a minimum level of education. Married women, too, worked when their wages were needed, but increasingly this meant finding a temporary job during a family crisis. These crises of unemployment, illness, or death of the primary wage earner tended more and more to cluster in old age. During most of her married life a woman served as a specialist in child rearing and consumer activities for her family. These tasks filled important and economically useful needs for the working-class family. Managing family finances and buying goods and services required time and skill. Moreover, new fertility strategies demanded that women spend more time nurturing children. By the end of the nineteenth century, families had begun to restrict fertility. New health measures and a decline in infant mortality developed only later—in the first decades of the twentieth century. As families bore fewer children it became important to invest more time in their care so they would survive to maturity. Family needs thus allocated the mother's time away from wage earning and toward domestic responsibilities and child care.

After World War II, economic conditions and family needs exerted a different influence on women's work. The tertiary sector expanded and the demand for women in white-collar jobs grew. More part-time work was also available, particularly in Britain. Fertility continued to decline, but new levels of health reduced the fragility of infant and child life. Children remained in school for longer periods of their lives and spent less time as family wage earners. The result was an increase in the time married women spent in wage-earning activity.

The historical record shows a U-shaped pattern of female productive activity—from relatively high in the preindustrial household economy to a lower level in industrial economies. Married women's productive work contributed to this pattern. The fact that married as well as single women worked in the household economy and work today in the consumer economy raises the level of female productive activity in these two time periods.

There is no neat complementary curve for reproductive activity. Reproductive patterns have changed in the following manner: from relatively low nuptiality, high marital fertility, and high infant and child mortality; to high nuptiality, lower fertility, and lower infant and child mortality (dependent on women's increased investment of time in child nurture); to low fertility and low infant mortality (no longer dependent exclusively on a mother's time). Yet at any point in time, patterns of female productive activity have influenced and been influenced by the prevailing family fertility strategies.

Determinants of Women's Productive Activity

In this book we have compared aggregate features of two nation-states over a 250-year period. We have compared several cities with special economic and ecological characteristics. We also have studied women in families in their roles as daughters, wives, and mothers. The comparative examination of women and work at several different levels permits us to offer some general explanations of changes in patterns of women's work.

At the most general level we conclude that the interplay between a society's productive and reproductive systems within the household influences the *supply* of women available for work. The characteristics of the economy and its mode of production, scale of organization, and technology influence the *demand* for women as workers.

Historically, the likelihood of women participating in production is strongly correlated with the household mode of production. The closer in time that a given household is to the experience of household production, the more likely it is that women will do productive work and that they will subordinate time spent in reproductive activity to that work. During the entire nineteenth century the French economy was marked by the continuing importance of a small-scale, household organization of production. Britain, on the other hand, early developed a large-scale, factory-based system. As a result, French rates of female work-force participation were consistently higher than British rates.

Once the industrial mode of production predominates, once people work for wages outside of households, aggregate and local economic organization influence the demand for women in paid employment. An important constraint operates here: the almost universal segregation of occupations by sex. The degree of occupational segregation has varied somewhat over time, but there has been a continuing tendency for societies, employers, and workers to accept sex-typing of occupations. Women, then, are most likely to work when the demand for workers in female occupations is high. When there is a shortage of the supply of male workers (during or after a war, for example) more women will be drawn into nonfemale occupations. The analysis of the economic structure of the different cities demonstrated that levels of female employment were highest where female jobs were most numerous.

The supply of female workers, of course, is shaped in part by demographic, social, and economic factors. Single women are best able to work, since they have few other claims on their time. Married women, on the other hand, must adjust reproductive and domestic activity with paid employment. The difficulties of such an adjustment were evident during the early period of industrialization, particularly in textile towns. Then the economic need for women workers and the family's need for wages led to high levels of married women's employment at high costs to themselves and, even more, to their infants. Even in the textile towns, however, the demographic situation—the proportions in the population of married and single women—shaped the supply of women workers. In later periods, when demand for women was great and the supply of single women small, employers might change work conditions to accommodate the special needs of married women.

Household needs also influence the supply of women workers. The division of labor within the household is based on the family's economic needs. Under the household mode of production, the labor needs of the unit defined the work of all members. For wage-earning families, subsistence requirements replaced labor needs. Poor households sent as many members as possible into wage-earning employment. When possible, however, the family division of labor allocated time for domestic and child care activity to married women. Increased productivity and higher male wages permitted a sharper division of labor and a differentiation of activity within the household. Single women became preferred wage earners, while married women were preferred as child-care and consumer specialists.

Of course, household needs were not simply economic. The emphasis placed on children and childcare also influenced the supply of women, particularly of married women, to the labor market. In the earliest period of high fertility and high mortality there was no notion that infants and children required special care. Beyond time spent in childbirth and suckling an infant, little time was spent on children. With the decline in fertility and improved prospects for children to survive to

adulthood, there developed a new emphasis on the needs of children. Mothers were assumed to be responsible for children's physical, mental, and moral health. The time they spent caring for children was considered valuable by the family. Indeed the value of time spent at home began to outweigh time spent in wage-earning activity. After the Second World War, yet another change in conceptions of child care occurred. Continuing low fertility and dramatically improved prospects for infant and child survival mean that there are less demands on a mother's time for the nurture and care of young children. Not the physical survival, but the social and economic future of the child, his or her education and training, have become increasingly important. This kind of investment in children requires additional funds from the family and, increasingly, married women have sought paid employment to help earn those funds.

By looking not only at work, but at workers as members of households, we have been able to assess the role of the family. We have found that the family provided a certain continuity in the midst of economic change. Values, behavior, and strategies shaped under one mode of production continued to influence behavior as the economy changed. The older practices only slowly were adapted to the new circumstances. In the period we have examined, the family economy was modified from a productive unit to a wage unit. Yet membership in a family continued to define the work roles and relationships of parents and children. Our study challenges an older view which held that industrialization separated the family and work, isolating one sphere from another. We have found that industrialization did deprive the family unit of its productive activity. Nonetheless, the family continued to influence the productive activities of its members. That point was well understood by the three commentators we cited at the beginning of this book. Despite the vastly different conclusions they drew, Jules Simon, Jules Turgan, and Friedrich Engels all agreed that women's work had to be assessed in terms of the family.

Throughout this book we have described and analyzed changes in patterns of women's productive activity. Our analysis has been enriched by the insights of other disciplines, particularly economics, anthropology, and demography. Although we have focused on the history of women in Britain and France since 1700, our conclusions have wider appli-

cability. In the past, as in the present, patterns of women's work are shaped by the intersection of economy, demography, and family. Specific historical contexts differ and so do the experiences, attitudes and choices women make in different situations. The excitement and interest of social history lies in exploring and specifying the differences. The use of an interdisciplinary perspective yields important insights both for those seeking to understand women's position in the past and for those seeking to change and improve it in the present and future.

20

Women in the Victorian Age

The following selections offer a number of perspectives on the position and attitudes of women in the nineteenth century.

Discussion Questions

1. Why did Maria Deraismes decline to be considered an "angel?"

2. How did the French Civil Code of 1895 define the position of women?

3. Would the Countess of Flavigny and Ernest Legouve' agree with Maria Deraismes about the role of women?

4. Is there any way to harmonize the views of Barbara Bodichon and the minister Jonathan Stearns? What does Stearns believe to be the "peculiar advantages" of being a woman?

5. What are the differences in the lifestyles of the middle class woman and the working woman as described by Jeanne Deroin?

Maria Deraismes (Late 1860s)

Of all woman's enemies, I tell you that the worst are those who insist that woman is an angel. To say that woman is an angel is to impose on her, in a sentimental and admiring fashion, all duties, and to reserve for oneself all rights; it is to imply that her specialty is self-effacement, resignation, and sacrifice; it is to suggest to her that woman's greatest glory, her greatest happiness, is to immolate herself for those she loves; it is to let her understand that she will be generously furnished with every opportunity for exercising her aptitudes. It is to say that she will respond to absolutism by submission, to brutality by meekness, to indifference by tenderness, to inconstancy by fidelity, to egotism by devotion.

In the face of this long enumeration, I decline the honor of being an angel. No one has the right to force me to be both dupe and victim. Self-sacrifice is not a habit, a custom; it is an extra! It is not on the program of one's duties. No power has the right to impose it on me. Of all acts, sacrifice is the freest, and it is precisely because it is free that it is so admirable.

The French Civil Code (1895)

Of the Respective Rights and Duties of Husband and Wife

Husband and wife owe each other fidelity, support, and assistance.

A husband owes protection to his wife; a wife obedience to her husband.

A wife is bound to live with her husband and to follow him wherever he deems proper to reside. The husband is bound to receive her, and to supply her with whatever is necessary for the wants of life, according to his means and condition.

A wife cannot sue in court without the consent of her husband, even if she is a public tradeswoman or if there is no community or she is separated as to property.

From *Victorian Women: A Documentary Account of Women's Lives in 19th Century England, France and the United States*, edited by Erna Olafson Hellerstein, Leslie Parker Hume and Karen M. Offen, copyright © 1981 by the Board of Trustees of the Leland Stanford Junior University, pp. 140, 162–165, 304–305. Permission for Documents 33 (i–iv) and Document 64 (ii) given by Stanford University Press, Stanford.

The husband's consent is not necessary when the wife is prosecuted criminally or in a police matter.

A wife, even when there is no community, or when she is separated as to property, cannot give, convey, mortgage, or acquire property, with or without consideration, without the husband joining in the instrument or giving his written consent.

A wife may, if she is a public tradeswoman, bind herself without the husband's consent with respect to what relates to her trade, and in that case she also binds her husband if there is community of property between them. She is not considered a public tradeswoman if she merely retails the goods of her husband's business, but only when she has a separate business.

Louise-Mathilde de Montesquiou-Fezensac, Comtesse de Flavigny (1861)

Lord, it is You who have given me
In the husband with whom you have united me,
A guide for my inexperience,
A protector for my weakness—
Grant that, after the pleasure of pleasing you,

The attachment to my husband,
The care of making him happy
Will occupy me completely
Grant that by the abnegation of my will,
And deference to his least desires,
I will make his life agreeable and sweet.

Ernest Legouvé (1848)

Marriage alone can give to this feminine influence a character of continuity and of purity. . . . To live for another, to disappear in a glory or a virtue of which she is the principle, to dispense benefits while concealing the benefactress, to learn so that another may know, to think so that another may speak, to seek the light so that another may shine, there is no more beautiful destiny for woman, for all of this signifies devotion. And what more noble profession than that of devotion? What employment for life is more appropriate to all the qualities of woman? Every wife who is truly a wife has for a career the career of her husband.

Barbara Leigh Smith Bodichon (1854)

A man and wife are one person in law; the wife loses all her rights as a single woman, and her existence is entirely absorbed in that of her husband. He is civilly responsible for her acts; she lives under his protection or cover, and her condition is called coverture.

A woman's body belongs to her husband; she is in his custody, and he can enforce his right by a writ of habeas corpus.

What was her personal property before marriage, such as money in hand, money at the bank, jewels, household goods, clothes, etc., becomes absolutely her husband's, and he may assign or dispose of them at his pleasure whether he and his wife live together or not. . . .

The legal custody of children belongs to the father. During the life-time of a sane father, the mother has no rights over her children, except a limited power over infants, and the father may take them from her and dispose of them as he thinks fit.

Jonathan Stearns (1837)

Beware, then, how you forfeit your peculiar advantages. Beware how you do any thing to diminish that delicate and chivalrous respect, which the feminine character now commands from all who are not lost to every principle of honor. The refined and high minded woman, while she never presumes upon her privilege as an apology for selfishness and wrong, will rejoice to avail herself of every just advantage it affords her, in the cause of truth, benevolence and piety.

On you, ladies, depends, in a most important degree, the destiny of our country. In this day of disorder and turmoil, when the foundations of the great deep seem fast breaking up, and the flood of desolation threatening to roll over the whole face of society, it peculiarly develops upon you to say what shall be the result. Yours it is to determine, whether the beautiful order of society, a system of many members in one body, and all the members not having the same office, shall continue as it has been, to be the source of blessings to the world; or whether, despising all forms and distinctions, all boundaries and rules, society shall break up and become a chaos of disjointed and unsightly elements. Yours it is to decide, under God, whether we shall be a nation of refined and high minded christians, or whether, rejecting the civilities of life, and throwing off the restraints of morality and piety, we shall become a fierce race of semi-barbarians, before whom neither order, nor honor, nor chastity can stand.

And be assured, ladies, if the hedges and borders of the social garden should be broken up, the lovely vine, which now twines itself so gracefully upon the trellis, and bears such rich clusters, will be the first to fall and be trodden under foot.

Jeanne Deroin (1848)

It is in the household that woman's work is the most tiresome and the least appreciated.

We are not speaking of a household where there is a live-in nurse and a maid for each child, and domestic servants to do all the work; we are speaking of the minority, of the proletarian household, where the mother alone cares for several children, where there is not always means to pay the laundress, where the wife must get up before dawn, often exhausted by having had to nurse her newest child through part of the night. She lights her stove and prepares her wash water, in order to wash her children's clothing and the diapers. Moreover, she hasn't enough of anything to be able to wait a week; the lodging is small, the basins inconvenient; the sink is either one floor up or two floors down, and the stairway is dark. Her husband gets up to go to work; his pants are torn and must be mended but a child cries or the clay casserole tips over; the woman runs; the husband gets impatient; the repair gets done. He leaves and the washing begins. The two biggest children get up and ask for their breakfast; the littlest ones cry to be gotten up; the sudsing finished, she hangs out the wash as best she can, wipes up the spilt water, makes the soup, dresses the littlest children and gives everybody breakfast; she puts some bread in the baskets of the bigger children and sends them off to school; she has not yet had time to sit down for an instant in order to nurse the little one who is crying loudly.

The landlord's wife enters: she is an early riser, a woman of order, a good housewife who does her own canning and makes her own jam, repairs her laces, cleans her own ribbons and embroiders her collars. Everything is neat and tidy in her quarters before nine o'clock. She rouses her man and her domestic at five A.M. and supervises them, pushes them, prods them, so that the tasks get done promptly and well. Thus, upon entering, she is indignant at the laziness and disorderliness of her renter. The beds are not yet made, the room is not swept; the chipped bowls used for breakfast are still sitting unwashed on the floor; the poorly bleached diapers hang on the line, the torn caps and socks full of holes dry on the back of a chair. She concludes from all this that her renter doesn't get up early enough and doesn't work hard enough. She asks for the rent more severely than she might have otherwise and leaves, threatening to throw them all out if it isn't paid by the fourteenth.

Upset and already exhausted with fatigue, the poor wife nurses her infant, changes it and puts it back in the cradle, and leaves it in the charge of an obliging neighbor's children so that she can run to the central market to buy potatoes a bit cheaper. She returns in haste, loaded down, breathless and perspiring. She nurses the infant to stop its crying, puts her irons on to heat, peels her vegetables, irons the caps, mends the vests and pants, fixes the shirts, darns the socks, repairs the slippers, and prepares dinner.

The children come home from school: one has torn his blouse, the other has a bump on his head. She scolds the first one and bandages the second. During this time the potatoes have burned; her husband returns, and the soup is not yet poured over the bread. He is tired and in a bad mood, and displays his astonishment that a woman who has nothing to do but take care of her house is incapable of getting up dinner. He sulks or flies into a rage and, when dinner is over, he goes to bed. The wife undresses and puts the children to bed, washed the dishes, and is able to mend the most urgent items. But she has to interrupt her work every few minutes to calm the baby, whose cries are waking up the father, who gets upset at not being able to sleep and recover from the fatigue of the day. Often the poor baby has been changed with a diaper that is still wet; he gets colic, and the mother spends part of the night calming him. She scarcely gets a few hours of sleep and wakes up only to recommence the same life. And they say, in speaking of her, that only her husband works; she doesn't do anything. She has only her household and her children to take care of.

21

Marxism: The Communist Manifesto

The *Communist Manifesto* is the most famous work, and its author Karl Marx the most famous figure, in the history of socialism. The *Manifesto* contains most of the key ideas we identify collectively today as "Marxism," an ideology that represents an entire worldview, though its focal point is the industrial revolution. In it we see Marx the historian, Marx the sociologist, Marx the economist and even Marx the scientist. Indeed, Marx called his version of socialism, "Scientific Socialism," and he is therefore in the mainstream of European thought in the 19th century, especially those currents which reflect the 18th century Enlightenment values of reason, natural law and progress. In summarizing his contributions, the eleventh edition of the Encyclopedia Britannica (1911) said:

> The great scientific achievement of Marx lies . . . in the details and yet more in the method and principles of his investigations in his philosophy of history. Here he has, as is now generally admitted, broken new ground and opened new ways and new outlooks. Nobody before him had so clearly shown the role of the productive agencies in historical evolution; nobody so masterfully exhibited their great determining influence on the forms and ideologies of social organisms. The passages and chapters dealing with this subject form, notwithstanding occasional exaggerations, the crowning parts of his works. If he has been justly compared with Darwin, it is in these respects that he ranks with that great genius. . . . In the same year as Darwin's epoch-making work on the origin of species there also appeared Marx's work Critique of Political Economy, where he explains in concise sentences in the preface that philosophy of history which has for the theory of the transformation or evolution of social organisms the same significance that the argument of Darwin had for the transformation of biological organisms.

Discussion Questions

1. What is the significance of "class struggle" in Marx's view of history?

2. To what does Marx attribute the emergence of the bourgeoisie as the "ruling" class of Europe?

3. What is to be the historical role of the proletariat?

4. What aspect of the Manifesto might be called "scientific?"

5. Why does Marx want to get rid of private property?

6. Marx concludes the Manifesto with the exhortation "Working men of all countries, unite!" What did he mean by that? What about nationalism?

The Communist Manifesto

1

Bourgeois and Proletarians

The history of all hitherto existing society is the history of class struggles.

Freeman and slave, patrician and plebeian, lord and serf, guild-mastery and journeyman, in a word, oppressor and oppressed, stood in constant opposition to one another, carried on an uninterrupted, now hidden, now open fight, a fight that each time ended, either in a revolutionary reconstitution of society at large, or in the common ruin of the contending classes.

In the earlier epochs of history, we find almost everywhere a complicated arrangement of society into various orders, a manifold gradation of social rank. In ancient Rome we have patricians, knights, plebeians, slaves; in the Middle Ages, feudal lords, vassals, guild-masters, journeymen, apprentices, serfs; in almost all of these classes, again, subordinate gradations.

The modern bourgeois society that has sprouted from the ruins of feudal society has not done away with class antagonisms. It has but established new classes, new conditions of oppression, new forms of struggle in place of the old ones.

Our epoch, the epoch of the bourgeoisie, possesses, however, this distinctive feature: it has simplified the class antagonisms. Society as a whole is more and more splitting up into two great hostile camps, into two great classes directly facing each other: Bourgeoisie and Proletariat.

From the serfs of the Middle Ages sprang the chartered burghers of the earliest towns. From these burgesses the first elements of the bourgeoisie were developed.

The discovery of America, the rounding of the Cape, opened up fresh ground for the rising bourgeoisie. The East-Indian and Chinese markets, the colonization of America, trade with the colonies, the increase in the means of exchange and in commodities generally, gave to commerce, to navigation, to industry, an impulse never before known, and thereby, to the revolutionary element in the tottering feudal society, a rapid development.

The feudal system of industry, under which industrial production was monopolized by closed guilds, now no longer sufficed for the growing wants of the new market. The manufacturing system took its place. The guild-masters were pushed on one side by the manufacturing middle class; division of labour between the different corporate guilds vanished in the face of division of labour in each single workshop.

Meantime the markets kept ever growing, the demand ever rising. Even manufacture no longer sufficed. Thereupon, steam and machinery revolutionized industrial production. The place of manufacture was taken by the giant, Modern Industry, the place of the industrial middle class, by industrial millionaires, the leaders of whole industrial armies, the modern bourgeois.

Modern industry has established the world market, for which the discovery of America paved the way. This market has given an immense development to commerce, to navigation, to communication by land. This development has, in its turn, reacted on the extension of industry; and in proportion as industry, commerce, navigation, railways extended, in the same proportion the bourgeoisie developed, increased its capital, and pushed into the background every class handed down from the Middle Ages.

We see, therefore, how the modern bourgeoisie is itself the product of a long course of development, of a series of revolutions in the modes of production and of exchange. . . .

The bourgeoisie, historically, has played a most revolutionary part.

The bourgeoisie, wherever it has got the upper hand, has put an end to all feudal, patriarchal, idyllic relations. It has pitilessly torn asunder the motley feudal ties that bound man to his 'natural superiors.' and has left remaining no other nexus between man and man than naked self-interest, than callous 'cash payment.' It has drowned the most heavenly ecstasies of religious fervour, of chivalrous enthusiasm, of philistine sentimentalism, in the icy water of egotistical calculation. It has resolved personal worth into exchange value, and in place of the numberless indefeasible chartered freedoms, has set up that single, unconscionable freedom— Free Trade. In one word, for exploitation, veiled by religious and political illusions, it has substituted naked, shameless, direct, brutal exploitation.

The bourgeoisie has stripped of its halo every occupation hitherto honoured and looked up to with reverent awe. It has converted the physician, the lawyer, the priest, the poet, the man of science, into its paid wage-labourers.

The bourgeoisie has torn away from the family its sentimental veil, and has reduced the family relation to a mere money relation. . . .

We see then: the means of production and of exchange, on whose foundation the bourgeoisie built itself up, were generated in feudal society. At a certain stage in the development of these means of production and of exchange, the conditions under which feudal society produced and exchanged, the feudal organization of agriculture and manufacturing industry, in one word, the feudal relations of property became no longer compatible with the already developed productive forces; they became so many fetters. They had to be burst asunder; they were burst asunder.

Into their place stepped free competition, accompanied by a social and political constitution adapted to it, and by the economical and political sway of the bourgeois class.

A similar movement is going on before our own eyes. Modern bourgeois society with its relations of production, of exchange and of property, a society that has conjured up such gigantic means of production and of exchange, is like the sorcerer, who is no longer able to control the powers of the nether world whom he has called up by his spells. For many a decade past the history of industry and commerce is but the history of the revolt of modern productive forces against modern conditions of production, against the property relations that are the conditions for the existence of the bourgeoisie and of its rule. It is enough to mention the commercial crises that by their periodical return put on its trial, each time more threateningly, the existence of the entire bourgeois society. In these crises a great part not only of the existing products, but also of the previously created productive forces, are periodically destroyed. In these crises there breaks out an epidemic that, in all earlier epochs, would have seemed an absurdity—the epidemic of overproduction. . . .

And how does the bourgeoisie get over these crises? On the one hand by enforced destruction of a mass of productive forces; on the other, by the conquest of new markets, and by the more thorough exploitation of the old ones, That is to say, by paving the way for more extensive and more destructive crises, and by diminishing the means whereby crises are prevented.

The weapons with which the bourgeoisie felled feudalism to the ground are now turned against the bourgeoisie itself.

But not only has the bourgeoisie forged the weapons that bring death to itself; it has also called into existence the men who are to wield those weapons—the modern working class—the proletarians. . . .

Modern industry has converted the little workshop of the patriarchal master into the great factory of the industrial capitalist. Masses of labourers, crowded into the factory, are organized like soldiers. As privates of the industrial army they are placed under the command of a perfect hierarchy of officers and sergeants. Not only are they slaves of the bourgeois class, and of the bourgeois State; they are daily and hourly enslaved by the machine, by the overlooker, and, above all, by the individual bourgeois manufacturer himself. The more openly this despotism proclaims gain to be its end and aim, the more

petty, the more hateful and the more embittering it is. . . .

The lower strata of the middle class—the small tradespeople shopkeepers, and retired tradesmen generally, the handicraftsmen and peasants—all these sink gradually into the proletariat, partly because their diminutive capital does not suffice for the scale on which Modern Industry is carried on, and is swamped in the competition with the large capitalists, partly because their specialized skill is rendered worthless by new methods of production. Thus the proletariat is recruited from all classes of the population. . . .

But with the development of industry the proletariat not only increases in number; it becomes concentrated in greater masses, its strength grows, and it feels that strength more. The various interests and conditions of life within the ranks of the proletariat are more and more equalized, in proportion as machinery obliterates all distinctions of labour, and nearly everywhere reduces wages to the same low level. The growing competition among the bourgeois, and the resulting commercial crises, make the wages of the workers ever more fluctuating. The unceasing improvement of machinery, ever more rapidly developing, makes their livelihood more and more precarious; the collisions between individual workmen and individual bourgeois take more and more the character of collisions between two classes. Thereupon the workers begin to form combinations (Trades Unions) against the bourgeois; they club together in order to keep up the rate of wages; they found permanent associations in order to make provision beforehand for these occasional revolts. Here and there the contest breaks out into riots.

Now and then the workers are victorious, but only for a time. The real fruit of their battles lies, not in the immediate result, but in the ever-expanding union of the workers. This union is helped on by the improved means of communication that are created by modern industry and that place the workers of different localities in contact with one another. It was just this contact that was needed to centralize the numerous local struggles, all of the same character, into one national struggle between classes. But every class struggle is a political struggle. And that union, to attain which the burghers of the Middle Ages, with their miserable highways, required centuries, the modern proletarians, thanks to rail-ways, achieve in a few years.

This organization of the proletarians into a class, and consequently into a political party, is continually being upset again by the competition between the workers themselves. But it ever rises up again, stronger, firmer, mightier. . . .

Further, as we have already seen, entire sections of the ruling classes are, by the advance of industry, precipitated into the proletariat, or are at least threatened in their conditions of existence. These also supply the proletariat with fresh elements of enlightenment and progress.

Finally, in times when the class struggle nears the decisive hour, the process of dissolution going on within the ruling class, in fact within the whole range of old society, assumes such a violent, glaring character, that a small section of the ruling class cuts itself adrift, and joins the revolutionary class, the class that holds the future in its hands. Just as, therefore, at an earlier period, a section of the nobility went over to the bourgeoisie, so now a portion of the bourgeoisie goes over to the proletariat, and in particular, a portion of the bourgeois ideologists, who have raised themselves to the level of comprehending theoretically the historical movement as a whole. . . .

2

Proletarians and Communists

In what relation do the Communists stand to the proletarians as a whole?

The Communists do not form a separate party opposed to other working-class parties.

They have no interests separate and apart from those of the proletariat as a whole.

They do not set up any sectarian principles of their own, by which to shape and mould the proletarian movement.

The Communists are distinguished from the other working-class parties by this only: 1. In the national struggles of the proletarians of the different countries, they point out and bring to the front the common interests of the entire proletariat, independently of all nationality. 2. In the various stages of development which the struggle of the working class against the bourgeoisie has to pass through, they always and everywhere represent the interests of the movement as a whole

The Communists, therefore, are on the one hand, practically, the most advanced and resolute section of the working-class parties of every country, that section which pushes forward all others; on the other hand, theoretically, they have over the great mass of the proletariat the advantage of clearly understanding the line of march, the conditions, and the ultimate general results of the proletarian movement.

The immediate aim of the Communists is the same as that of all the other proletarian parties: formation of the proletariat into a class, overthrow of the bourgeois supremacy, conquest of political power by the proletariat. . . .

The distinguishing feature of Communism is not the abolition of property generally, but the abolition of bourgeois property. But modern bourgeois private property is the final and most complete expression of the system of producing and appropriating products, that is based on class antagonisms, on the exploitation of the many by the few.

In this sense, the theory of the Communists may be summed up in the single sentence: Abolition of private property. . . .

You are horrified at our intending to do away with private property. But in your existing society, private property is already done away with for nine-tenths of the population; its existence for the few is solely due to its non-existence in the hands of those nine-tenths. You reproach us, therefore, with intending to do away with a form of property the necessary condition for whose existence is the non-existence of any property for the immense majority of society.

In one word, you reproach us with intending to do away with your property. Precisely so; that is just what we intend. . . .

The Communists are further reproached with desiring to abolish countries and nationality.

The working men have no country. We cannot take from them what they have not got. . . .

National differences and antagonisms between peoples are daily more and more vanishing, owing to the development of the bourgeoisie, to freedom of commerce, to the world market, to uniformity in the mode of production and in the conditions of life corresponding thereto.

The supremacy of the proletariat will cause them to vanish still faster. United action, of the leading civilized countries at least, is one of the first conditions for the emancipation of the proletariat.

In proportion as the exploitation of one individual by another is put an end to, the exploitation of one nation by another will also be put an end to. In proportion as the antagonism between classes within the nation vanishes, the hostility of one nation to another will come to an end.

The charges against Communism made from a religious, a philosophical, and, generally, from an ideological standpoint, are not deserving of serious examination.

Does it require deep intuition to comprehend that man's ideas, views and conceptions, in one word, man's consciousness, changes with every change in the conditions of his material existence, in his social relations and in his social life?

What else does the history of ideas prove, than that intellectual production changes in character in proportion as material production is changed? The ruling ideas of each age have ever been the ideas of its ruling class. . . .

. . . the first step in the revolution by the working class, is to raise proletariat to the position of ruling class, to win the battle of democracy.

The proletariat will use its political supremacy to wrest, by degrees, all capital from the bourgeoisie, to centralize all instruments of production in the hands of the State, i.e., of the proletariat organized as the ruling class; and to increase the total of productive forces as rapidly as possible.

Of course, in the beginning, this cannot be effected except by means of despotic inroads on the rights of property, and on the conditions of bourgeois production; by means of measures, therefore, which appear economically insufficient and untenable, but which, in the course of the movement, outstrip themselves, necessitate further inroads upon the old social order, and are unavoidable as a means of entirely revolutionizing the mode of production.

These measures will of course be different in different countries.

Nevertheless, in the most advanced countries, the following will be pretty generally applicable:

1. Abolition of property in land and application of all rents of land to public purposes.
2. A heavy progressive or graduated income tax.
3. Abolition of all right of inheritance.
4. Confiscation of the property of all emigrants and rebels.
5. Centralization of credit in the hands of the State, by means of a national bank with State capital and an exclusive monopoly.
6. Centralization of the means of communication and transport in the hands of the State.
7. Extension of factories and instruments of production owned by the State; the bringing into cultivation of wastelands, and the improvement of the soil generally in accordance with a common plan.
8. Equal liability of all to labour. Establishment of industrial armies, especially for agriculture.
9. Combination of agriculture with manufacturing industries; gradual abolition of the distinction between town and country, by a more equable distribution of the population over the country.
10. Free education for all children in public schools. Abolition of children's factory la-bour in its present form. Combination of education with industrial production, &c., &c.

When, in the course of development, class distinctions have disappeared, and all production has been concentrated in the whole nation, the public power will lose its political character. Political power, properly so called, is merely the organized power of one class for oppressing another. If the proletariat during its contest with the bourgeoisie is compelled, by the force of circumstances, to organize itself as a class, if, by means of a revolution, it makes itself the ruling class, and, as such, sweeps away by force the old conditions of production, then it will, along with these conditions, have swept away the conditions for the existence of class antagonisms and of classes generally, and will thereby have abolished its own supremacy as a class.

In place of the old bourgeois society, with its classes and class antagonisms, we shall have an association, in which the free development of each is the condition for the free development of all. . . .

22

Race and Nation

During the last third of the nineteenth century, in the wake of the emergence of Darwin's theory of natural selection, there appeared a series of efforts to put the study of human society, nations and race on a scientific biological basis. The first result of this was the concept of Social Darwinism proposed by Herbert Spencer, who had invented the phrase "survival of the fittest." Social Darwinism suggested that human society operated according to Darwinian evolutionary principles and that therefore competition showed that certain individuals were biologically superior to others—an idea very popular among the business classes and free market advocates. Before long some people were suggesting that certain nations were superior to other nations. From this a new "scientific" basis for racism emerged, with white Europeans at the top of the evolutionary scale—this idea became very popular among nationalists and imperialists. A "logical" deduction of these assumptions (because that is what they were) was the so-called science of eugenics which argued that superior races could be designed or preserved, especially by eliminating or isolating allegedly "inferior" persons from the human gene pool. This idea became particularly popular in the United States during the first half of the twentieth century (and was the one thing Hitler said he liked about the United States.)

Houston Stewart Chamberlain (1855–1926) was in this tradition. He was the son of a British admiral, son-in-law of the composer Richard Wagner and a professed Germanophile. His major work was *The Foundations of the Nineteenth Century* which he wrote in German in 1899. It sold well and was especially popular later with the Nazis. The following selections from his work illustrate his view of the importance of race in the history of nations and the world.

Discussion Questions

1. What is the link between nationality and race?

2. How is the consciousness of race a product of science?

3. Is racialism a valid science? Or is it a pseudo-science?

4. Is Chamberlain's comparison of breeds of dogs and human beings a valid one?

5. Does history demonstrate that Teutons are the superior race? Just who are the Teutons he refers to?

Ranke had prophesied that our century would be a century of nationality; that was a correct political prognostic, for never before have the nations stood opposed to each other so clearly and definitely as antagonistic unities. It has, however, also become a century of races, and that indeed is in the first instance a necessary and direct consequence of science and scientific thinking. I have already said at the beginning of this introduction that science does not unite but dissects. That statement has not contradicted itself here. Scientific anatomy has furnished such conclusive proofs of the existence of physical characteristics distinguishing the races from each other that they can no longer be denied; scientific philology has discovered between the various languages fundamental differences which cannot be bridged over; the scientific study of history in its various branches has brought about similar results, especially by the exact determination of the religious history of each race, in which only the most general of general ideas can raise the illusion of similarity, while the further development has always followed and still follows definite, sharply divergent lines. The so-called unity of the human race is indeed still honoured as a hypothesis, but only as a personal, subjective conviction lacking every material foundation. The ideas of the eighteenth century with regard to the brotherhood of nations were certainly very noble but purely sentimental in their origin; and in contrast to these ideas to which the Socialists still cling, limping on like reserves in the battle, stern reality has gradually asserted itself as the necessary result of the events and investigations of our time.

---

* * *

To this day these two powers—Jews and Teutonic races—stand, wherever the recent spread of the Chaos has not blurred their features, now as friendly, now as hostile, but always as alien forces face to face. If we look around, we see that the importance of each nation as a living power to-day is dependent upon the proportion of genuinely Teutonic blood in its population. Only Teutons sit on the thrones of Europe.

* * *

And as if the scientific rearing of animals and plants did not afford us an extremely rich and reliable material, whereby we may become acquainted not only with the conditions but with the importance of "race"! Are the so-called (and rightly so-called) "noble" animal races, the draught-horses of Limousin, the American trotter, the Irish hunter, the absolutely reliable sporting dogs, produced by chance and promiscuity? Do we get them by giving the animals equality of rights, by throwing the same food to them and whipping them with the same whip? No, they are produced by artificial selection and strict maintenance of the purity of the race. Horses and especially dogs give us every chance of observing that the intellectual gifts go hand in hand with the physical; this is especially true of the moral qualities: a mongrel is frequently very clever, but never reliable; morally he is always a weed. Continual promiscuity between two pre-eminent animal races leads without exception to the destruction of the pre-eminent characteristics of both. Why should the human race form an exception? . . . In spite of the broad common foundation, the human races are, in reality, as different from one another in character, qualities, and above all, in the degree of their individual capacities, as greyhound, bull-dog, poodle and Newfoundland dog. Inequality is a state towards which nature inclines in all spheres; nothing extraordinary is produced without "specialisation"; in the case of men, as of animals, it is this specialisation that produces noble races; history and ethnology reveal this secret to the dullest eye. Has not every genuine race its own glorious, incomparable physiognomy? . . .

* * *

Nothing is so convincing as the consciousness of the possession of Race. The man who belongs to a distinct, pure race, never loses the sense of it. The guardian angel of his lineage is ever at his side, supporting him where he loses his foothold, warning him like the Socratic Daemon where he is in danger of going astray, compelling obedience, and forcing him to undertakings which, deeming them impossible, he would never have dared to attempt. Weak and erring like all that is human, a man of this stamp recognises himself, as others recognise him, by the sureness of his character, and by the fact that his actions are marked by a certain simple and peculiar greatness, which finds its explanation in his distinctly typical and super-personal qualities. Race lifts a man above himself: it endows him with extraordinary—I might almost say supernatural—powers, so entirely does it distinguish him from the individual who springs from the chaotic jumble of peoples drawn from all parts of the world: and should this man of pure origin be perchance gifted above his fellows, then the fact of Race strengthens and elevates him on every hand, and he becomes a genius towering over the rest of mankind, not because he has been thrown upon the earth like a flaming meteor by a freak of nature, but because he soars heavenward like some strong and stately tree, nourished by thousands and thousands of roots—no solitary individual, but the living sum of untold souls striving for the same goal.

* * *

There is one point which I have not expressly formulated, but it is self-evident from all that I have said; the conception of Race has nothing in it unless we take it in the narrowest and not in the widest sense: if we follow the usual custom and use the word to denote far remote hypothetical races, it ends by becoming little more than a colourless synonym for "mankind"—possibly including the long-tailed and short-tailed apes: Race only has a meaning when it relates to the experiences of the past and the events of the present.

Here we begin to understand what nation signifies for race. It is almost always the nation, as a political structure, that creates the conditions for the formation of race or at least leads to the highest and most individual activities of race.

* * *

. . . since race is not a mere word, but an organic living thing, it follows as a matter of course that it never remains stationary; it is ennobled or it degenerates, it develops in this or that direction and lets this or that quality decay. This is a law of all individual life. But the firm national union is the surest protection against going astray: it signifies common memory, common hope, common intellectual nourishment; it fixes firmly the existing bond of blood and impels us to make it ever closer.

23

The World Revolution
of Westernization

In this selection a contemporary author, Theodore H. Von Laue, offers a provocative view of what he feels has been the "central force" that has shaped the 20th century world—the world revolution of westernization. The West's expansion, beginning with Columbus' voyages in the late 15th century, led to a global revolution and transformation that eventually led to the "unification of the world," a phenomenon that has produced some surprising consequences. As you read, consider the evidence Von Laue uses to support his arguments, and the biases reflected in his views.

Discussion Questions

1. What does Von Laue mean by the "world revolution of Westernization." Has it been largely a success or a failure?

2. What changes have resulted from the unification of the world and its domination by the West? Do you accept his arguments, and, if not, why not?

3. When he speaks of a "cultural limbo," to what and whom is he referring?

4. Why does Von Laue state that all counterrevolutions have been futile, and do you agree?

This book offers a novel look at the conditions of the anarchic world community in which we live, a look reasonably free of the illusions buttressing liberal complacency. It aims at the detachment that allows true impartiality as well as a better sense of control over our destiny. It explains the 20th century, the most momentous and still largely uncomprehended age in all history, in terms of the central force that shaped it: the world revolution of Westernization. That gigantic, all-inclusive, and still incomplete historic process may be briefly outlined as follows.

The Expansion of the West

For the first time in all human experience the world revolution of Westernization brought together, in inescapably intimate and virtually instant interaction, all the peoples of the world, regardless of their prior cultural evolution or their capacity—or incapacity—for peaceful coexistence. Within a brief time, essentially within half a century, they were thrust into a common harness, against their will, by a small minority commonly called "The West"—the peoples of Western Europe and their descendants in North America. As a result, the human condition in the present and the future can only be understood within the framework of the Westernized world.

This massive confluence of the world's peoples, infinitely exceeding in intensity all previous interdependence and transforming the world's ecosystem on which human life depends, was started by irresistible force, by guns, supported by a vast and complex array of cultural skills, adding up to an overwhelming political presence that excelled also in the arts of peace. In creating an interdependent world through conquest, colonization, and expanded opportunities for all, that Western minority imposed its own accomplishments as a universal standard to which all others, however reluctantly, had to submit. Robbed of their past freedom to go their own ways politically and culturally, non-Western peoples were subjected to a world order that perpetuated or even deepened their helplessness. Henceforth equality could be attained only on the terms imposed by the West.

Western ascendancy was so complete that it left only one rational response: abject imitation as a condition of survival and self-affirmation. Decolonization and the formation of Western-inspired nation-states among the former colonial and semi-colonial peoples merely escalated the imitation and hardened the grip of Western institutions and values over the entire world. Even the most heated protests against Western power—and they were never lacking—were expressed in Western concepts and propagated by Western technology in Western languages. Yet inequality continued.

Submission and cultural imitation, however, were not without elemental advantage, individually and collectively. Overall material conditions improved, increasing individual welfare and tripling the volume of human life on earth within less than a century. Yet the survival of the ever growing and more demanding human multitudes led to yet greater dependence, calling for a further copying of essential aspects of Western culture. For the sake of feeding, housing, transporting, educating, and employing the world's population, "Westernization" is now pressed forward by non-Westerners themselves. Culturally neutralized, it has become "modernization" or simply "development," the common goal of all peoples and governments no matter how handicapped in achieving it.

Seen in a superficial light, the unification of the world was the work of all humanity. In expanding their power around the world the Europeans freely drew on the ingenuity, riches, and labor of non-Europeans; all humanity gained as the achievements of its separate peoples became accessible to all. Yet, examined more closely, the Europeans merely copied on their own terms whatever strengthened their might; they exploited the world's resources, hitherto mostly dormant, for their own gain; they enlisted the prowess and resilience of people around the world to make themselves masters. The will to power and the capacity for taking advantage of all opportunities for their own aggrandizement—the initiative for the world revolution of Westernization—sprang from Europe, from the hothouse competition among the Europeans themselves. In expanding around the world and enlarging their base from Europe into the "the West," they foisted their singular qualities on the unwilling and unprepared majority of humanity, dynamically transforming the entire world in their own image and establishing a hierarchy of prestige defined by the success of imitation. In the world revolution of Westernization, Western political ambition and competitiveness became universal—and fiercer because of the fury born of persistent inequality.

The Consequences of Western Expansion

The major effect of the world revolution of Westernization—generally down-played in the West—has been to undermine and discredit all non-Western cultures. The victorious Westerners, their own ways and self-confidence boosted by their worldwide sway, left the rest of the world humiliated and in cultural limbo. Under the Western impact traditional authorities and local customs had no future; they crumbled away. Meanwhile the imported ways of the West remained superficial or even incomprehensible; they did not fit societies whose cultural sovereignty had been crushed.

The subversion of traditional cultures admittedly took different forms in different parts of the world. It was perhaps least painful in Japan, a unique case where native tradition proved miraculously compatible with Western imports. Elsewhere, among the majority of peoples around the world, the results were cultural chaos characterized by a loss of purpose, moral insensibility, and a penchant for violence; by social and political fragmentation, and by the psychological misery of knowingly belonging to a "backward" society. Never before had the extremes of inequality been so great. Now the Great Confluence carried the wealth and glory of the richest instantly into the presence and conscience of the poorest. Expectations were raised and crushed, opportunities advanced and denied in the same instant. No wonder that violence spread and turned more vicious.

Traditional culture and society in non-Western parts of the world were subverted just as the pace of political competition was accelerated to worldwide intensity. After World War I, and even more after World War II, Western democracy, with the United States in the lead, stood out as the universal model of power in the world, of good government, and of economic prosperity; however imperfect, unfinished, and vilified by its critics, it proved elementally persuasive by comparison. Who among the onlookers did not feel envious? Who among the envious did not feel morally entitled—and tempted—to make the world even safer by their own ideals? Equality in political power, though deftly omitted from the Western-inspired inventory of human rights, certainly was claimed as an entitlement by proud non-Westerners. Few states possessed the wherewithal to take up the challenge, yet the aspiration became embedded in the new competition for global power, a source of heightened instability and conflict. But how could ambitious leaders of polities caught in cultural disorientation and social fragmentation mobilize their peoples to match this mighty model on their own terms?

Futile Counterrevolutions

The search for answers among culturally subverted countries with political potential, so this book argues, led to the totalitarian experiments of communism and fascism in the wake of World War I; from them, after World War II, communist Russia emerged as the most powerful challenger to the Western model. Simultaneously, the totalitarian experiments inspired state-builders among the new states emerging from decolonization. What was wanted, it turned out, was not self-affirmation but further Westernization through "reculturation" (to coin an ugly term for an ugly process), through an unnatural revamping of unsuitable indigenous institutions and human values under external pressure to meet alien goals. Leaving people to their own devices under these conditions, as tried by short-lived democratic regimes, merely enhanced the common disorientation and political weakness. Command and indoctrination had to be substituted for the lacking appropriate voluntary motivation, while a furious anti-Westernism covered up the blatant imitation.

In the West the experiments of totalitarianism have been castigated as outrages of inhumanity and terror; yet as counterrevolutions they merely carried the world revolution of Westernization one step further. Western-oriented indigenous leaders impressed by the fullness of Western power applied to their own peoples the violence that had characterized the elemental expansion of the West. They tried to convert their subjects by force into organization-minded citizens as disciplined, loyal, and cooperative as their counterparts in the Western democracies. They had to accomplish, in a hurry and by conscious design, what in the West had been achieved over centuries of largely invisible cultural conditioning (accompanied too, we should remember, by ferocious violence in war, civil war, and revolution). Seen in this light, communism and fascism were no more than idealized versions of Western (or "capitalist") society dressed up to inspire the humiliated and disadvantaged. Their statecraft was merely a disguised form of cultural colonialism creating, out of helpless and resentful people, a "new man" and a "new society" capable of competing with the West on more equal terms. Yet the results of all totalitarian experiments have refuted the high hopes for matching, let alone outpacing, the Western model. Inasmuch as they relied on compulsion, they remained tragically non-Western and inferior because compulsion can never match the cultural creativity of spontaneous civic cooperation.

Not all past experiments of Westernization (or modernization), fortunately, were as extreme in ambition or execution as Hitler's or Stalin's. Some were favored by newfound wealth, others by long association with Westerners or, as in the case of Japan (always the exception), by an element of cultural compatibility. Yet all of them suffered from intense partisanship, violence, and mismanagement; indigenous ways did not harmonize with the imported modern ways. Alienation and anger brooded under the surface (even in Japan, certainly in the twenty years before 1945), directed against Westernized natives or the ultimate source of all misery, the West itself. Tragic indeed is the record of state-building and development through the non-Western world in the past and in the present; ominous are the prospects for the future. The political competition and cultural disorientation of the Great Confluence continue to accelerate unabated, promoted in large part by Western ignorance of the consequences of Westernization.

Cultural Incomprehension and Confusion

The world's population is now organized in states patterned after the European nation-state. The relations between states are both cooperative and competitive within a common framework of an anarchic community governed by the rules of power; preparation for war and war itself characterize the new world system as much as it did the old European system of states. For better or worse, the whole world has now become a furnace of human creativity in intense competitive political and cultural interaction. The world-wide rivalry for wealth and power has stimulated an unprecedented rise in material prosperity; it has quickened the pace of scientific and technological discovery; it has advanced human mobility and built, on the surface, a global metropolis remarkably uniform in appearance and standards, glittering with the splendor of human ingenuity, forever eager to advance its vision of human rights in all lands.

Yet that global city is also crammed full with deadly fears and explosive anger. The larger the volume of life on earth, the greater also the common willingness to sacrifice human beings for the sake of power, as one can see from the rising casualty rates of two world wars and the projected carnage of nuclear conflict. The tensions, playing havoc with human rights, are constantly escalating—for obvious reasons.

To this day all-too-few people in the immensely privileged West realize the depths of despair, frustration, and fury to which the world revolution of Westernization has reduced its victims; public opinion, denying all responsibility, still prefers to look only at its positive aspects. All-too-few observers admit the legitimacy of the counterrevolutions which, in bloody experiments, have tried to recreate the fullness of Western power from recalcitrant non-Western peoples—peoples gladly taking the latest fruits of modernity (including the pride of leadership in the world) yet unwilling or unable to submit to the demanding work routines and civic obligations which constitute the invisible aspects of effective power. In the old Europe cultural diversity was a source of tension and war. In a shrunken world the tensions are even greater. Incompatible cultures and historical traditions are compressed into even closer association among people utterly incapable of dealing constructively with cultural incompatibility. Their ignorance has raised hostility to hitherto unmatched ferocity.

The world revolution of Westernization, in short, has not created a peaceful world order guided by the ascetic and all-inclusive humane rationalism, the best quality in Western civilization. Universalizing the tensions inherent in its own dynamic evolution, it has rather produced a worldwide association of peoples compressed against their will into an inescapable but highly unstable interdependence laced with explosive tensions. Underneath the global universals of power and its most visible supporting skills—literacy, science and technology, large-scale organization—the former diversities persist. The traditional cultures, though in mortal peril, linger under the ground floors of life. Rival political ideologies and ambitions clash head-on. The world's major religions vie with each other as keenly as ever. Attitudes, values, lifestyles from all continents mingle freely in the global marketplace, reducing in the intensified invidious comparison all former absolute truths to questionable hypotheses.

Viewed in this manner, the global confluence thus far has produced not a shiny global city but a global Tower of Babel in which the superficial and ignorant comparison of everything with everything else is undermining all subtle distinctions between right and wrong, good and evil, worth and worthlessness. Even the centers of Western culture, whose traditions were until recently affirmed by their political power, are now inundated by alien ideas and practices, with subversive effects on the very convictions responsible for Western ascendance. An aimless cultural relativism threatens all moral energies; it encourages withdrawal into an illusory shelter of tradition while glorifying brute force perfected by sophisticated technology as the ultimate authority and source of security. Where in this global Babylon do we find the transcendent moral absolutes that can restrain the rising penchant for violence? . . .

24

European Expansion and Imperialism

	The Old Imperialism ca. 1400–1600	Free Trade Imperialism ca.1600–1830 [*]	The New Imperialism ca. 1870–1945
Chief Players:	Spain, Portugal	England, France, Holland	England, France, Germany, Italy, USA, Japan
Major Agents:	Explorers, Missionaries, Conquistadors	Chartered Monopolies, Merchants	Nations, Missions, Corporations
Main Areas of Activity:	Americas, Indian Ocean (periphery)	Americas, Indian Ocean and China (periphery)	Asia & Africa (Land empires)
Chief Commodities:	Gold, Spices, Slaves	Luxury goods (spices, silk, porcelain, gems, tea) Slaves	Raw materials
Motivations, Rationalizations:	Proselytizing, wealth, individual advancement ("God, Gold, Glory")	Dynastic competition, wealth; "Man-on-the-spot"	National Prestige; Social Darwinism (racism), Cultural & religious superiority, "Dual-Mandate," Humanitarianism; Markets
Relationships to Indigenous People:	Conquest, Trade, Accommodation	Accommodation, Trade, Conquest	Colonialism (pol. subjugation)
Approx % of World Land Area Ruled:	(ca. 1600) 16%	(ca. 1830) 25%	(ca. 1914) 85%

*ca. 1830–1880: The Industrial Revolution and nationalism begin to have major effects in transforming the relationships between Europe and the rest of the world:

1. Trade in luxury goods declines relative to bulk raw materials and the search for markets for European manufactured goods; the slave trade is abolished (1807 and after).
2. European accommodation gives way to educating indigenous peoples in European languages, religion, etc.; this was accompanied by growing disdain and contempt for non-Western cultures.
3. There is some additional territorial acquisition (esp. Britain in India, Australia and New Zealand and the United States to the Pacific Ocean).

25

"The White Man's Burden"

The famous English writer, Rudyard Kipling, composed this poem as a way of celebrating America's annexation of the Philippines after the Spanish-American War of 1898. Though the Americans would not only have to defeat the Spanish in order to lay claim to the Philippines, but also to suppress an independence movement by Filipinos under the leadership of Emiliano Aquinaldo, the acquisition of this strategic outpost in the Pacific, along with Hawaii, placed America in the ranks of a leading world power. As you read this selection, compare Kipling's view of the situation with those of Albert Beveridge, as well as Lugard and other European imperialists, and try to imagine how the Filipinos reacted, both to the event and to the poem.

Discussion Questions

1. What does Kipling mean by "the White Man's Burden?" How did the anti-imperialists respond? Was there a "Brown Man's Burden," and, if so, what was it?

2. How were the Filipinos characterized in this poem? What assumptions about the people of the Philippines, and the Westerners, does Kipling make?

3. How do you suppose the people of the Philippines reacted to the tone and message of this poem?

4. How are race, gender and class used by Kipling in his poem? Were his views typical of attitudes at that time? Do attitudes such as these still exist?

"The White Man's Burden"

Rudyard Kipling

Take up the White Man's burden—
Send forth the best ye breed—
Go, bind your sons to exile
To serve your captives' need;
To wait, in heavy harness,
On fluttered folk and wild—
Your new-caught sullen peoples,
Half devil and half child.

Take up the White Man's burden—
In patience to abide,
To veil the threat of terror
And check the show of pride;
By open speech and simple,
An hundred times made plain,
To seek another's profit
And work another's gain.

Take up the White Man's burden—
The savage wars of peace—
Fill full the mouth of Famine,
And bid the sickness cease;
And when your goal is nearest
(The end for others sought)
Watch sloth and heathen folly
Bring all your hope to nought.

Take up the White Man's burden—
No iron rule of kings,
But toil of serf and sweeper—
The tale of common things.

The ports ye shall not enter,
The roads ye shall not tread,
Go, make them with your living
And mark them with your dead.

Take up the White Man's burden,
And reap his own reward—
The blame of those ye better
The hate of those ye guard—
The cry of hosts ye humour
(Ah, slowly!) toward the light:—
"Why brought ye us from bondage,
Our loved Egyptian night?"

Take up the White Man's burden—
Ye dare not stoop to less—
Nor call too loud on Freedom
To cloke your weariness.
By all ye will or whisper,
By all ye leave or do,
The silent sullen peoples
Shall weigh your God and you.

Take up the White Man's burden!
Have done with childish days—
The lightly-proffered laurel,
The easy ungrudged praise;
Comes now, to search your manhood
Through all the thankless years,
Cold, edged with dear-bought wisdom
The judgment of your peers.

Rudyard Kipling, "The White Man's Burden," *McClure's Magazine*, Volume XII, Number 4 (February 1899), pp. 290–291.

26

Social History of the Machine Gun—Imperialism

In this reading, Robert Ellis, a contemporary social historian, explains some of the connections between technology and racism as causal factors in the New Imperialism of the late 19th century.

Discussion Questions

1. What role did the machine gun play in the colonialization of Africa? How do Ellis' views compare with those of Headrick's in the "Legacy of Imperialism?" Did the machine gun facilitate Lugard's rule of thumb regarding imperialism, "to keep the peace and to make the colonies pay?"

2. What did the racism of the late 19th century have to do with the decision to use the machine gun against indigenous peoples in Africa, and throughout the world? Do you see similar attitudes today between the use of technology and the assumptions that are made about different cultures or subcultures?

3. What do you think was the African response to the introduction of the machine gun?

4. If the use of the machine gun was as effective as Ellis suggests, why did the "brass back home," consider it more a "tiresome gimmick," unsuitable for use on a European battlefield?

Making the Map Red

"And the white man had come again with his guns that spat bullets as the heavens sometimes spit
hail, and who were the naked Matabele to stand up against these guns?"

A great gulf existed between the effectiveness of military firepower and the soldiers' total lack of respect for its potential. Their contemptuous attitude persisted, even in the teeth of mounting evidence of the unparalleled efficacy of modern firearms. Nor had that evidence been manifested only in parts of the world not very familiar to European military establishments. The machine gun had also been put to use in an area of the world with which most European armies had close connections, and there its effectiveness had become shatteringly obvious.

In Africa automatic weapons were used to support the seizure of millions of square miles of land and to discipline those unfortunates who wished to eschew the benefits of European civilisation. With machine guns in their armoury, mere handfuls of white men, plunderers and visionaries, civilians and soldiers, were able to scoff at the objections of the Africans themselves and impose their rule upon a whole continent.

Without examining all the reasons for imperialist expansion it is certain that the search for markets, strategical considerations and the question of national prestige were all contributory factors, though historians have argued about the exact importance of each. But of one thing there is no doubt. Whatever the general causes, or the personal motives of the individual colonisers, the whole ethos of the of the imperialist drive was predicated upon racism. Attitudes to the Africans varied from patronising paternalism to contempt and outright hatred, but all assumed that the white man was inherently superior to the black.

A central strand of this racialism was the crude interpretation of Darwinian theories about "the survival of the fittest." Projected back into the past, such theories enabled people to put forward the relative superiority of Western civilisation as a reason for arguing that the white man was the dominant race. One could also extrapolate from them to predict that eventually this race would physically dominate the whole world. An extreme version of this prediction was given in 1881, by W. D. Hay, in a book called *Three Hundred Years Hence*. He described the future paradise:

> The old idea of universal fraternity had worn itself out; or rather it had become modified when elevated into the practical law of life. Throughout the Century of Peace . . . men's minds had become opened to the truth, had become sensible of the diversity of species, had become conscious of Nature's law of development . . . The stern logic of facts proclaimed the Negro and Chinaman below the level of the Caucasian, and incapacitated from advance towards his intellectual standard. To the development of the White Man, the Black Man and the Yellow must ever remain infe-

rior, and as the former raised itself higher and yet higher, so did these latter seem to sink out of humanity and appear nearer and nearer to the brutes. . . . It was now incontrovertible that the faculty of Reason was not possessed by them in the same degree as the White Man, nor could it be developed by them beyond a very low point. This was the essential difference that proved the worthlessness of the Inferior Races as contrasted with ourselves, and that therefore placed them outside the pale of Humanity and its brotherhood.

Clearly, working from such a theory of human development, it was easy, even natural, to go on to regard superior military technology as a God-given gift for the suppression of these inferior races. A popular history of science of 1876 offers a perfect example of such an attitude. In the chapter on firearms the author tells us:

We often hear people regretting that so much attention and ingenuity as are shown by the weapons of the present day should have been expended upon instruments of destruction. . . . The wise and the good have in all ages looked forward to a time when sword and spear shall be everywhere finally superseded by the ploughshare and the reaping–hook. . . . Until that happy time arrives . . . we may consider that the more costly and ingenious and complicated the instruments of war become, the more certain will be the extension and the permanence of civilisation. The great cost of such appliances as those we are about to describe, the ingenuity needed for their contrivance, the elaborate machinery required for their construction, and the skill implied in their use, are such that these weapons can never be the arms of other than wealthy and intelligent nations. We know that in ancient times opulent and civilised communities could hardly defend themselves against poor and barbarous races. . . . In our day it is the poor and barbarous tribes who are everywhere at the mercy of the wealthy and cultivated nations.

Europeans had superior weapons because they were the superior race. With regard to the machine gun, for example, one writer assured his readers that "the tide of invention which has . . . developed the 'infernal machine' of Fieschi into the mitrailleur (sic) and Gatling Battery of our own day—this stream took its rise in the God–like quality of reason." Thus when the Europeans opened their bloody dialogue with the tribes of Africa it was only natural that they should make them see reason through the ineluctable logic of automatic fire.

The British Army had decided to purchase twelve Gatlings in October 1869 but they were not sent on active service until 1874, on the occasion of the first campaign against the Ashantis. It was decided that Wolseley's small expeditionary force should take along some Gatlings to even up the odds. The Times heard of this decision in late 1873 and it prompted them to express some rather bloodthirsty hopes:

The Gatling guns . . . we presume are mainly intended for the defence of stockaded positions. For fighting in the bush a Gatling would be as much use as a fire engine, but if by any lucky chance Sir Garnet Wolseley manages to catch a good mob of savages in the open, and at a moderate distance, he cannot do any better than treat them to a little Gatling music. . . . Altogether we cannot wish the Ashantees worse luck than to get in the way of a Gatling well served . . .

For men like Cecil Rhodes and Frederick Lugard, and organizations like the British South Africa Company and the Imperial East African Trading Company, the Maxim gun was an indispensable tool for the imposition of European control. Maxim himself was only too pleased that his invention should be used in such a role. In 1887 an expedition led by Stanley set off for Wadelai, near Lake Albert, to rescue Emin Pasha (Eduard Schnitzer), who had established a bizarre dominion among the natives of that region. This expedition of mercy attracted the imagination of Europe and Maxim donated one of his guns to help them on their way.

In 1890 the somewhat battered gun was taken up by Lugard when he left Mombasa to travel to Uganda. By the Anglo–German Treaty of that year Uganda had been recognised as falling within the British sphere of influence, and Lugard lost no time in revealing the reality of that influence. Missionaries had already exacerbated tribal tensions there and relations between Protestant and Catholic Africans became increasingly bitter. In 1892 open warfare broke out, with the Catholics demanding the expulsion of the British. Lugard immediately threw his support, which included his Maxims, behind the Protestant Ingleza tribe. This support was decisive, despite Catholic over–optimism. During the preparation for the uprising, Mwanga, its leader, had drawn some faulty conclusions from the tatty appearance of Lugard's much–travelled Maxim. One of his envoys "had circulated the most extraordinary reports, saying that we were cowards who dare not fight . . . that our Maxim was merely for show, and fired single bullets like a gun." Clearly the usual efficacy of such weapons had already been noised abroad in Africa. But even a battered Maxim was better than no Maxim at all. At the Battle of Mango Hill Lugard and his Sudanese mercenaries threw their weight behind the Protestants, the former taking charge of the machine gun: "Firing the Maxim hastily, Lugard scored a pair of freak hits on the legs of two Fransa chiefs. . . . He then traversed to cover an open potato patch that the attackers would have to cross. The Maxim was now jamming at almost every other shot . . . but the few rounds Lugard got off sufficed to hold the Fransa back."

Perhaps Mwanga's original concern with the potential of the Maxim gun had been aroused by events in Tanganyika. In 1890 certain German opportunists had established the German East African Company. They almost immediately encountered African opposition and in 1891 the Company was involved in a savage war with the Hehe tribe under their chief Mkwawa. At one stage Hehe warriors had ambushed a German column and massacred almost everyone. But it turned out to be a Pyrrhic victory at best. Towards the end of the battle, "the German officer–surgeon, helped by *askaris*, dragged two machine guns, with plenty of ammunition into a mud hut, and from there turned the tables on the Hehe. He is said to have killed about one thousand of them."

For the rest of the century, and into the twentieth, the use of machine guns was limited to consolidating the Europeans' hold on the African continent, and to the suppression of any native dissent. In 1897 Sir Arthur Hardinge gave a succinct definition of the true nature of European rule. His remarks referred to British policy in Kenya but they are applicable to all nations who had established a foothold on the "dark continent." As he said: "These people must learn submission by bullets—it is the only school. . . . In Africa to have peace you must first teach obedience and the only person who teaches the lesson properly is the sword." The choice of weapon is a little confused but the message is clear. The only adequate response to native discontent was violence. And despite Harding's rhetorical reference to the *arme blanche*, it was the machine gun that offered the most economical solution to the problem of keeping down the whole population of a continent with small bodies of police and soldiers.

Another group who were prepared to come out into the open about the harsh realities of imperialism were certain British poets of the turn of the century. Perhaps because it was 'only poetry' people felt that their words had less real significance. Nevertheless, the message sometimes came through loud and clear. Even Rudyard Kipling, usually so piously smug about the duties of Empire and the thankless self-sacrifice involved in them, gave at least one scathing definition of Christian civilisation. In 1897 he wrote a poem called "Pharaoh and the Sergeant," dedicated to the Sergeant–Instructors sent to Egypt to help train that country's ramshackle army. It begins thus:

> Said England unto Pharaoh, 'I must make a man of you,
> That will stand upon his feet and play the game;
> That will Maxim his oppressor as a Christian ought to do.'
> And she sent old Pharaoh Sergeant Whatsisname.

Hilaire Belloc was equally blunt in a poem called "The Modern Traveller." In it a typical, somewhat languid colonial figure utters the perfect motto for the triumph of British imperialism:

> I shall never forget the way
> That Blood stood upon this awful day
> Preserved us all from death.
> He stood upon a little mound
> Cast his lethargic eyes around,
> And said beneath his breath:
> "Whatever happens, we have got
> The Maxim Gun, and they have not."

So the slaughter continued. In 1900 the Ashanti had once again to bear the brunt of British displeasure. At first the British fared rather badly. One force was besieged by the Ashanti in the fort at Kumasi, and the relief column, under Captain Aplin, which was sent from Lagos, was continually harassed by the natives. The main reason for Aplin's plight was that the inevitable Maxims accompanying the column were of an old and unreliable model, and whenever they were brought into action they never failed to overheat and jam. But Aplin's force eventually reached the fort and found that the plight of its occupants was not as desperate as had at first been feared. Yet again Maxim guns had saved the day, for "at first the Ashantis had tried to attack the fort itself, but the machine guns on the bas-

tions had proved too effective for them and they had settled down to a long and patient siege. More troops were thrown into the campaign as swiftly as possible, mainly from the Gold Coast Constabulary and the West African Frontier Force, all these units possessing large numbers of Maxims. They were used to effect in the final battle of Aboasu in which Ashanti resistance was crushed for good.

As was common practice at this time, almost all the troops used in this campaign were African, only the officer being British. One of the most important duties of these officers was to operate the Maxim guns. It would clearly be too dangerous to teach natives, even though they might be wearing a British uniform, the secrets of the white man's ultimate weapon.

In 1898 the U.S. Government also took on colonial responsibilities of a sort when they annexed the Philippines, which had been under Spanish dominion for the preceding four centuries. In the following year they received the honour of having one of Kipling's poems addressed to them. In it he warned them of their heavy responsibilites:

> Take up the White Man's burden—
> Send forth the best ye breed—
> Go bind your sons to exile
> To serve your captives' need;
> To wait in heavy harness
> On fluttered folk and wild—
> Your new-caught, sullen peoples,
> Half devil and half child.

At the time few people in either Britain or the United States objected to such smug assumptions about the superiority of Western civilization. Theodore Roosevelt described it as "rather poor poetry, but good sense from the expansionist view point." But there was in England a small group of radical anti-imperialists, known as the Little Englanders, who did find such patronizing guff rather offensive. Their most prominent spokesperson was Henry Labouchere, who as well as being an emphatic opponent of imperialism in general, was also keenly aware of the intimate links between "paternal" British control and the power of automatic weapons. In a reply to Kipling's poem, published in *Truth*, a journal of which he was the editor, Labouchere banged his point home.

> Pile on the Brown Man's burden!
> And if ye rouse his hate
> Meet his old-fashioned reasons
> With Maxims—up to date,
> With shells and Dum–Dum bullets
> A hundred times make plain
> The Brown Man's loss must never
> Imply the White Man's gain.

In the same journal he also lampooned writing that was generally regarded as being even more sacred than Kipling's verse. His *Pioneers' Hymn* began thus:

> Onward Christian Soldiers, on to heathen lands,
> Prayer-books in your pockets, rifles in your hands,
> Take the glorious tidings where trade can be done:
> Spread the peaceful gospel—with a Maxim gun.

By now then, the picture should be clear. The machine gun was a vitally useful tool in the colonisation of Africa. Time and time again automatic fire enabled small groups of settlers and soldiers to stamp out any indigenous resistance ot their activities and to extend their writ over vast areas the African continent. Yet, as has already been indicated, this gruesome test of the machine gun's efficiency had almost no effect upon the military High Command in Britain. For "brass" back home automatic fire was still a tiresome gimmick, not likely to play any significant role upon a European battlefield. The reasons for this complacency are not hard to find.

They are to be found in the ideology of British imperialism, whose very essence was an unquestioning belief in the innate superiority of the white race, and the British in particular. Without such beliefs it would have been impossible for the original colonisers to set such a low price on African lives. For only by holding them so cheap could the slaughter of the natives seem to be morally acceptable. The belief in white supremacy was the very bedrock of imperialist attitudes, and is evident in all their manifestations. At best the Europeans regarded those they slaughtered with little more than amused contempt. Thus Winston Churchill in a letter home from the Sudan:

> It is like a pantomime scene at Drury Lane. These extraordinary foreign figures . . . march one by one from the dark wings of Barbarism up to the bright footlights of civilisation . . . And the world audience clap their hands, amused yet impatient . . . and their conquerors, taking their possessions, forget even their names. Nor will history record such trash . . . Perhaps the time will come when the supply will be exhausted and there will be no more royal freaks to conquer . . . The good old times will have passed away, and the most cynical philosopher will be forced to admit that though the world may not be much more prosperous it can scarcely be so merry.

This feeling of contempt is obviously functional within a colonial situation. It dehumanises one's opponent and makes it easier to seize his lands and his labour, and to stamp ruthlessly on any sparks of resistance. Thus when it becomes necessary to kill those who stand in one's way, the problem is seen in technical rather than human terms. It is simply a matter of "bagging" as many natives as possible with the minimum effort. The machine gun filled these requirements admirably.

27

The Legacy of Technological Imperialism

In Daniel Headrick's introduction to his book, *The Tools of Empire*, he distinguishes the "new" imperialism from its predecessors in two respects—its extent and its legacy. "In the year 1800 Europeans occupied or controlled thirty-five percent of the land surface of the world; by 1878 this figure had risen to sixty-seven percent, and by 1914 over eighty-four percent of the world's land area was European-dominated." How had this occurred? While conventional examinations have focused on political, economic and even socio-cultural factors, such as was exemplified in Kipling's "White Man's Burden," little attention has been given to the role of technology as a causal factor. If technology was mentioned at all, it was often disregarded as an important motive for imperialism, or rejected as portraying human actions in too deterministic a way. Yet, as Headrick argues, if history "results from the interactions of human decisions," then the choices about technology that Europeans made at the time, both as motive for actions, and means, providing the wherewithal to carry out those actions, need to be included in any study of a complex process like imperialism. In this selection the author summarizes the key ways in which technology and the motives and means of the "new" imperialism interacted.

Discussion Questions

1. Headrick refers to the European empires that formed in the 19th century as "economy empires." What does he mean by this, and do you find his arguments convincing?

2. Why is it necessary to understand the "flow of information" among Western and non-Western peoples in the 19th century in order to understand the ways that the diffusion of technology occurred?

3. Do you think he places too much importance on technology as a causal factor in the imperialism of the 19th century? If so, what factors would you rank as more important?

4. Do you accept his statement that the "true" legacy of imperialism was a "fascination with machinery and innovation?" How do Headrick's views compare with those of Von Laue?

The Legacy of Technological Imperialism

The history of European imperialism in the nineteenth century still contains a number of paradoxes, which an understanding of technology can help elucidate. One of them is the expansion of Britain in the mid-century, a world power claiming to want no more imperial responsibilities yet reluctantly acquiring territories "in a fit of absent–mindedness." Was this really a case, as Fieldhouse put it, of "a metropolitan dog being wagged by its colonial tail?" A more appropriate metaphor might be the pseudonym Macgregor Laird used in writing to *The Spectator*: Cerberus, the many-headed dog.

For the imperialist drive did not originate from only one source. In the outposts of empire, and most of all in Calcutta and Bombay, were eager imperialists, adventurous and greedy for territory. They lacked, however, the industry to manufacture the tools of conquest. Had they been able to create the instruments appropriate to their ambitions, they might well have struck out on their own, like the settlers in the Thirteen Colonies of North America. But against Burma, China, the Middle East, and Africa they needed British technology.

In Britain, meanwhile, the politicians were at times reluctant; the lengthy delay in occupying Egypt is an example of this. But the creators of the tools of empire—people like Peacock, the Lairds, the arms manufacturers—were provisioning the empire with the equipment that the peripheral imperialists required. The result was a secondary imperialism, the expansion of British India, sanctioned after the fact by London.

Imperialism in the mid–century was predominantly a matter of British tentacles reaching out from India toward Burma, China, Malaya, Afghanistan, Mesopotamia, and the Red Sea. Territorially, at least, a much more important impressive demonstration of the new imperialism was the scramble for Africa in the last decades of the century. Historians generally agree that from a profit–making point of view, the scramble was a dubious undertaking. Here also, technology helps explain events.

Inventions are most easily described one by one, each in its own technological and socioeconomic setting. Yet the inner logic of innovations must not blind us to the patterns of chronological coincidence. Though advances occurred in every period, many of the innovations that proved useful to the imperialists of the scramble first had an impact in the two decades from 1860 to 1880. These were the years in which quinine prophylaxis made Africa safer for Europeans; quick-firing breech-loaders replaced muzzle-loaders among the forces stationed on the imperial frontiers; and the compound engine, the Suez Canal, and the submarine cable made steamships competitive with sailing ships, not only on government-subsidized mail routes, but for ordinary freight on distant seas as well. Europeans who set out to conquer new lands in 1880 had far more power over nature and over the people they encountered than their predecessors twenty years earlier had; they could accomplish their tasks with far greater safety and comfort.

Few of the inventions that affected the course of empire in the nineteenth century were indispensable; quinine prophylaxis comes closest, for it is unlikely that many Europeans would willingly have run the risks of Africa without it. The muzzle-loaders the French used in fighting Abd-el Kader could also have defeated other non-Western peoples; but it is unlikely that any European nation would have sacrificed for Burma, the Sudan, or the Congo as much as France did for Algeria.

Today we are accustomed to important innovations being so complex—computers, jet aircraft, satellites, and weapons systems are but a few examples—that only the governments of major powers can defray their research and development costs; and generally they are eager to do so. In the nineteenth century European governments were preoccupied with many things other than imperialism. Industrialization, social conflicts, international tensions, military preparedness, and the striving for a balanced budget all competed for their attention. Within the ruling circles of Britain, France, Belgium, and Germany, debates raged on the need for colonies and the costs of imperialism.

What the breech–loader, the machine gun, the steamboat and steamship, and quinine and other innovations did was to lower the cost, in both financial and human terms of penetrating conquering, and exploiting new territories. So cost–effective did they make imperialism that not only national governments but lesser groups as well could now play a part in it. The Bombay Presidency opened the Red Sea Route; the Royal Niger Company conquered the Caliphate of Sokoto; even individuals like Macgregor Laird, William Mackinnon, Henry Stanley, and Cecil Rhodes could precipitate events and stake out claims to vast territories which later became parts of empires. It is because the flow of new technologies in the nineteenth century made imperialism so cheap that it reached the threshold of acceptance among the peoples and governments of Europe, and led nations to become empires. Is this not as important a factor in the scramble for Africa as the political, diplomatic, and business motives that historians have stressed?

All this only begs a further question. Why were these innovations developed, and why were they applied where they would prove useful to imperialists? Technological innovations in the nineteenth century are usually described in the context of the Industrial Revolution. Iron shipbuilding was part of the growing use of iron in all areas of engineering; submarine cables resulted from the needs of business and the development of the electrical industry. Yet while we can (indeed, we must) explain the invention and manufacture of specific new technologies in the context of general industrialization, it does not suffice to explain the transfer and application of these technologies to Asia and Africa. To understand the diffusion of new technologies, we must consider also the flow of information in the nineteenth century among both Western and non–Western peoples.

In certain parts of Africa, people are able to communicate by "talking drums" which imitate the tones of the human voice. Europeans inflated this phenomenon into a great myth, that Africans could speak to one another across their continent by the throbbing of tom-toms in the night. This myth of course reflected the Westerners' obsession with long–range communication. In fact, nineteenth–century Africans and Asians were quite isolated from one another and ignorant of what was happening in other parts of the world. Before the Opium War, the court of the Chinese emperor was misinformed about events in Canton and ignorant of the ominous developments in Britain, Burma, and Nigeria. People living along the Niger did not know where the river came from, nor where it went. Stanley encountered people in the Congo who had never before heard of firearms or white men. Throughout Africa, warriors learned from their own experiences but rarely from those of their neighbors.

To be sure, there were cases in which Africans or Asians adopted new technologies. Indian princes hired Europeans to train their troops. The Ethiopian Bezbiz Kasa had an English sergeant make cannons for him, while Samori Touré sent a blacksmith to learn gunsmithing from the French. Mehemet Ali surrounded himself with European engineers and officers in a crash program to modernize his country. What is remarkable about these efforts is their rarity and, in most cases, their insufficiency. In the nineteenth century, only Japan succeeded in keeping abreast of Western technological developments.

In contrast, Western peoples—whether Europeans or descendants of Europeans settled on other continents—were intensely interested in events elsewhere, technological as well as otherwise. Physicians in Africa published their findings in France and Britain. American gun manufacturers exhibited their wares in London, British experts traveled to America to study gunmaking, and General Wolseley paid a visit to the American inventor Hiram Maxim to offer suggestions. Macgregor Laird was inspired by news of events on the Niger to try out a new kind of ship. Dutch and British botanists journeyed to South America to obtain plants to be grown in Asia. Scientists in Indonesia published a journal in French and German for an international readership. The latest rifles were copied in every country and sent to the colonies for testing. The mails and cables transmitted to and from the financial centers of Europe up–to–date information on products, prices, and quantities of goods around the world. And the major newspapers, especially the London Times, sent out foreign correspondents and published detailed articles about events in faraway lands. Then, as now, people in the Western world were hungry for the latest news and interested in useful technological innovations. Thus what seemed to work in one place, whether iron river steamers, quinine prophylaxis, machine guns, or compound engines, was quickly known and applied in other places. In every part of the world, Europeans were more knowledgeable about events on other continents than indigenous peoples were about their neighbors. It is the Europeans who had the "talking drums."

European empires of the nineteenth century were economy empires, cheaply obtained by taking advantage of the new technologies, and, when the cost of keeping them rose a century later, quickly discarded. In the process, they unbalanced world relations, overturned ancient ways of life, and opened the way for a new global civilization.

The impact of this technologically based imperialism on the European nations who engaged in it is still hotly debated. The late nineteenth and early twentieth centuries were a time of overweening national pride, of frantic, often joyful, preparations for war. The cheap victories on the imperial frontiers, the awesome power so suddenly acquired over the forces of nature and over whole kingdoms and races, were hard to reconcile with the prudence and compromises which the delicate European balance required.

The era of the new imperialism was also the age in which racism reached its zenith. Europeans, once respectful of some non-Western peoples—especially the Chinese—be-gan to confuse levels of technology with levels of culture in general, and finally with biological capacity. Easy conquests had warped the judgment of even the scientific elites.

Among Africans and Asians the legacy of imperialism reflects their assessment of the true value of the civilization that conquered them. Christianity has had little impact in Asia, and its spread in Africa has been overshadowed by that of Islam. Capitalism that supposed bedrock of Western civilization, has failed to take root in most Third World countries. European concepts of freedom and the rule of law have fared far worse. The mechanical power of the West has not brought, as Macgregor Laird had hoped, "the glad tidings of 'peace and good will toward men' into the dark places of the earth which are now filled with cruelty."

The technological means the imperialists used to create their empires, however, have left a far deeper imprint than the ideas that motivated them. In their brief domination, the Europeans passed on to the peoples of Asia and Africa their own fascination with machinery and innovation. This has been the true legacy of imperialism.

28

Belgian Congo: The Rubber Terror

At the Berlin Conference of 1884–85, the huge central African region of the Congo was accepted as King Leopold II of Belgium's personal possession (which it remained until 1908 when Leopold was pressured into granting it to the Belgian government.) Leopold, who never visited the Congo, exploited the region ruthlessly—making a fortune for his efforts—even though his well-honed publicity presented his goals as strictly benevolent and "civilizing."

The following selection from Adam Hochschild's *King Leopold's Ghost* shows the role of rubber harvesting in making the Congo pay dividends to Leopold and other private investors. (This sort of system was common in many imperialist possessions around the world.)

Glossary:

Kuba—a kingdom deep in the Congo interior; the people are among the greatest artists in Africa; valued their isolation; had a sophisticated political system.

William Sheppard—a black American Presbyterian missionary and explorer.

Chicotte—a whip of raw, sun-dried hippopotamus hide, cut into a long, sharp-edged corkscrew strip; chicotte beatings were very common and sometimes fatal.

Force Publique—formed in 1888 as an army for the Congo; composed of African mercenaries and European officers; the most powerful army in central Africa; often acted as a corporate labor police force.

Discussion Questions

1. Why was rubber such an important global commodity by the end of the nineteenth century?

2. What role did private corporations play in the Congo rubber trade and how were they related to Leopold and the Congo state?

3. What methods were used to encourage the inhabitants of the Congo to provide rubber to the companies?

4. Was the expansion of the rubber trade beneficial to the indigenous people of the Congo?

5. Can the global trade in commodities ever be beneficial to indigenous people?

The Rubber Terror

Adam Hochschild

Not surprisingly, the Kuba were happy with their existing way of life, and, despite their friendliness toward Sheppard, showed little interest in Christianity. The mission station Sheppard ran among them made few converts. But Sheppard had become so well known back home for his discoveries that the Presbyterians were afraid of an adverse public reaction if they closed his mission to the Kuba and stationed him elsewhere.

The entire Kasai region, like the rest of the Congo, in time succumbed to the tightening grip on the Congo state. Some eight years after Sheppard's historic visit, Leopold's forces finally reached and looted the Kuba capital.

The raid on the capital, like many other events in the Congo, was triggered by a discovery far away. One day a few years before William Sheppard first embarked for Africa, a veterinary surgeon with a majestic white beard was tinkering with his son's tricycle at his home in Belfast, Ireland. John Dunlop was trying to solve a problem that had bedeviled bicyclists for many years: how do you get a gentle ride without springs? Dunlop finally devised a practical way of making a long-sought solution, an inflatable rubber tire. In 1890 the Dunlop Company began making tires—setting off a bicycle craze and starting a new industry just in time, it turned out, for the coming of the automobile.

Europeans had known about rubber ever since Christopher Columbus noticed it in the West Indies. In the late 1700s, a British scientist gave the substance its English name when he noticed it could rub out pencil marks. The Scot Charles Macintosh contributed his name to the language in 1823 when he figured out a mass-production method for doing something long practiced by the Indians of the Americas: applying rubber to cloth to make it waterproof. Sixteen years later the American inventor Charles Goodyear accidentally spilled sulfur into some hot rubber on his stove. He discovered that the resulting mixture did not turn stiff when cold or smelly and gooey when hot—major problems for those trying to make rubber boots or raincoats before then. But it was not until the early 1890s, half a decade after Dunlop fitted the pneumatic tire onto his son's tricycle wheel, that the worldwide rubber boom began. The industrial world rapidly developed an appetite not just for rubber tires, but for hoses, tubing, gaskets, and the like, and for rubber insulation for the telegraph, telephone, and electrical wiring now rapidly encompassing the globe. Suddenly factories could not get enough of the magical commodity, and its price rose throughout the 1890s. Nowhere did the boom have a more drastic impact on people's lives than in the equatorial rain forest, where wild rubber vines snaked high into the trees, that covered nearly half of King Leopold's Congo.

For Leopold, the rubber boom was a godsend. He had gone dangerously into debt with his Congo investments, but he now saw that the return would be more lucrative than he had ever imagined. The world did not lose its desire for ivory, but by the late 1890s wild rubber had far surpassed it as the main source of revenue from the Congo. His fortune assured, the king eagerly grilled functionaries returning from the Congo about rubber harvests; he devoured a constant stream of tele-grams and reports from the territory, marking them up in the margins and passing them on to aides for action. His letters from this period are filled with numbers: commodity prices from world markets, interest rates on loans, quantities of rifles to be shipped to the Congo, tons of rubber to be shipped to Europe, and the exact dimensions of the triumphal arch in Brussels he was planning to build with his newfound profits. Reading the king's correspondence is like reading the letters of the CEO of a corporation that has just developed a profitable new product and is racing to take advantage of it before competitors can get their assembly lines going.

The competition Leopold worried about was from cultivated rubber, which comes not from a vine but a tree. Rubber trees, however, require much care and some years before they grow large enough to be tapped. The king voraciously demanded ever greater quantities of wild rubber from the Congo, because he knew that the price would drop once plantations of rubber trees in Latin America and Asia reached maturity. This did indeed happen, but by then the Congo had had a wild-rubber boom nearly two decades long. During that time the search knew no bounds.

As with the men bringing in ivory, those supplying rubber to the Congo state and private companies were rewarded according to the amount they turned in. In 1903, one particularly "productive" agent received a commission eight times his annual salary. But the big money flowed directly back to Antwerp and Brussels, in the capital mostly to either side of the rue Bréderode, the small street that separated the back of the Royal Palace from several buildings holding offices of the Congo state and Congo business operations.

Even though Leopold's privately controlled state got half of concession-company profits, the king made vastly more money from the land the state exploited directly. But because the concession companies were not managed so secretively, we have better statistics from them. In 1897, for example, one of the companies, the Anglo-Belgian India Rubber and Exploration Company, or A.B.I.R., spent 1.35 francs per kilo to harvest rubber in the Congo and ship it to the company's headquarters at Antwerp—where it was sold for prices that sometimes reached 10 francs per kilo, a profit of more than 700 percent. By 1898, the price of A.B.I.R.'s stock was nearly thirty times what it had been six years earlier. Between 1890 and 1904, total Congo rubber earnings increased ninety-six times over. By the turn of the century, the État Indépendant du Congo had become, far and away, the most profitable colony in Africa. The profits came swiftly because, transportation costs aside, harvesting wild rubber required no cultivation, no fertilizers, no capital investment in expensive equipment. It required only labor.

How was this labor to be found? For the Congo's rulers, this posed a problem. They could not simply round up men, chain them together, and put them to work under the eye of an overseer with a *chicotte,* as they did with porters. To gather wild rubber, people must disperse widely through the rain forest and often climb trees.

Rubber is coagulated sap; the French word for it, *caoutchouc,* comes from a South American Indian word meaning "the wood that weeps" The wood that wept in the Congo was a long spongy vine of the *Landolphia* genus. Up to a foot thick at the base, a vine would twine upward around a tree to a hundred feet or more off the ground, where it could reach sunlight. There, branching, it might wind its way hundreds of feet through the upper limbs of another half-dozen trees. To gather the rubber, you had to slash the vine with a knife and hang a bucket or earthenware pot to collect the slow drip of thick, milky sap. You could make a small incision to tap the vine, or—officially forbidden but widely practiced—cut through it entirely,

which produced more rubber but killed the vine. Once the vines near a village were drained dry, workers had to go ever deeper into the forest until, before long, most harvesters were traveling at least one or two days to find fresh vines. As the lengths of vine within reach of the ground were tapped dry, workers climbed high into the trees to reach sap. "We . . . passed a man on the road who had broken his back by falling from a tree while . . . tapping some vines," wrote one missionary. Furthermore, heavy tropical downpours during much of the year turned large areas of the rain forest, where the rubber vines grew, into swampland.

No payments of trinkets or brass wire were enough to make people stay in the flooded forest for days at a time to do work that was so arduous—and physically painful. A gatherer had to dry the syrup-like rubber so that it would coagulate, and often the only way to do so was to spread the substance on his arms, thighs, and chest. "The first few times it is not without pain that the man pulls it off the hairy parts of his body," Louis Chaltin, a Force Publique officer, confided to his journal in 1892. "The native doesn't like making rubber. He must be compelled to do it."

How was he to be compelled? A trickle of news and rumor gradually made its way to Europe. "An example of what is done was told me up the Ubangi [River]," the British vice consul reported in 1899. "This officer[s] . . . method . . . was to arrive in canoes at a village, the inhabitants of which invariably bolted on their arrival; the soldiers were then landed, and commenced looting, taking all the chickens, grain, etc., out of the houses; after this they attacked the natives until able to seize their women; these women were kept as hostages until the Chief of the district brought in the required number of kilogrammes of rubber. The rubber having been brought, the women were sold back to their owners for a couple of goats apiece, and so he continued from village to village until the requisite amount of rubber had been collected."

Sometimes the hostages were women, sometimes children, sometimes elders or chiefs. Every state or company post in the rubber areas had a stockade for hostages. If you were a male villager, resisting the order to gather rubber could mean death for your wife. She might die anyway, for in the stockades food was scarce and conditions were harsh. "The women taken during the last raid at Engwettra are causing me no end of trouble," wrote Force Publique officer Georges Bricusse in his diary on November 22, 1895. "All the soldiers want one. The sentries who are supposed to watch them unchain the prettiest ones and rape them."

Leopold, of course, never proclaimed hostage-taking as official policy; if anyone made such charges, authorities in Brussels indignantly denied them. But out in the field, far from prying eyes, the pretense was dropped. Instructions on taking hostages were even given in the semiofficial instruction book, the revealing *Manuel du Voyageur et du Résident au Congo,* a copy of which the administration gave to each agent and each state post. The manual's five volumes cover everything from keeping servants obedient to the proper firing of artillery salutes. Taking hostages was one more routine piece of work:

> In Africa taking prisoners is . . . an easy thing to do, for if the natives hide, they will not go far from their village and must come to look for food in the gardens which surround it. In watching these carefully, you will be certain of capturing people after a brief delay . . . When you feel you have enough captives, you should choose among them an old person, preferably an old woman. Make her a present and send her to her chief to begin negotiations. The chief, wanting to see his people set free, will usually decide to send representatives.

Seldom does history offer us a chance to see such detailed instructions for those carrying out a regime of terror. The tips on hostage-taking are in the volume of the manual called *Practical Questions,* which was compiled by an editorial committee of about thirty people. One member—he worked on the book during a two-year period following his stint as the head-collecting station chief at Stanley Falls—was Léon Rom.

Hostage-taking set the Congo apart from most other forced-labor regimes. But in other ways it resembled them. As would be true decades later of the Soviet gulag, another slave labor system for harvesting raw materials, the Congo operated by quotas. In Siberia the quotas concerned cubic meters of timber cut or tons of gold ore mined by prisoners each day; in the Congo the quota was for kilos of rubber. In the A.B.I.R. concession company's rich territory just below the Congo River's great half-circle bend, for example, the normal quota assigned to each village was three to four kilos of dried rubber per adult male per fortnight which essentially meant full-time labor for those men. Elsewhere, quotas were higher and might be raised as time went on. An official in the Mongala River basin in the far north, controlled by another concession company, the Société Anversoise du Commerce au Congo, estimated that to fill their quota, rubber gatherers had to spend twenty-four days a month in the forest, where they built crude cages to sleep in for protection—not always successful—against leopards.

To get at parts of the vine high off the ground, men frantic to get every possible drop of rubber would sometimes tear down the whole vine, slice it into sections, and squeeze the rubber out. Although the Congo state issued strict orders against killing the vines this way, it also applied the *chicotte* to men who didn't bring in enough rubber. The *chicotte* prevailed. One witness saw Africans who had to dig up roots in order to find enough rubber to meet their quotas.

The entire system was militarized. Force Publique garrisons were scattered everywhere, often supplying their firepower to the companies under contract. In addition, each company had its own militia force, euphemistically called "sentries" In military matters as in almost everything else, the companies operated as an extension of the Congo state, and when hostages had to be taken or a rebellious village subdued, company sentries and Force Publique soldiers often took to the field together.

Wherever rubber vines grew, the population was tightly controlled. Usually you had to get a permit from the state or company agent in order to visit a friend or relative in another village. In some areas, you were required to wear a numbered metal disk, attached to a cord around your neck, so that company agents could keep track of whether you had met your quota. Huge numbers of Africans were conscripted into this labor army: in 1906, the books of A.B.I.R. alone, responsible for only a small fraction of the Congo state's rubber production, listed forty-seven thousand rubber gatherers.

All along the rivers, columns of exhausted men, carrying baskets of lumpy gray rubber on their heads, sometimes walked twenty miles or more to assemble near the houses of European agents, who sat on their verandas and weighed the loads of rubber. At one collection point, a missionary counted four hundred men with baskets. After the sap was turned in, it was formed into rough slabs, each the size of a small suitcase, and left to dry in the sun. Then it was shipped downriver, on a barge or scow towed by a steamboat, the first stage of the long journey to Europe.

The state and the companies generally paid villagers for their rubber with a piece of cloth, beads, a few spoonfuls of salt, or a knife. These cost next to nothing, and the knives were essential tools for gathering

more rubber. On at least one occasion, a chief who forced his people to gather rubber was paid in human beings. A legal dispute between two white officials near Stanley Falls put the following exchange on record in 1901. The witness being questioned was Liamba, chief of a village named Malinda:

> *Question:* Did M. Hottiaux [a company official] ever give you living women or children?
>
> *Answer.* Yes, he gave me six women and two men.
>
> *Question:* What for?
>
> *Answer.* In payment for rubber which I brought into the station, telling me I could eat them, or kill them, or use them as slaves—as I liked.

The rain forest bordering the Kasai River was rich in rubber, and William Sheppard and the other American Presbyterians there found themselves in the midst of a cataclysm. The Kasai was also the scene of some of the strongest resistance to Leopold's rule. Armed men of a chief allied with the regime rampaged through the region where Sheppard worked, plundering and burning more than a dozen villages. Floods of desperate refugees sought help at Sheppard's mission station.

In 1899 the reluctant Sheppard was ordered by his superiors to travel into the bush, at some risk to himself, to investigate the source of the fighting. There he found blood-stained ground, destroyed villages, and many bodies; the air was thick with the stench of rotting flesh. On the day he reached the marauders' camp, his eye was caught by a large number of objects being smoked. The chief "conducted us to a framework of sticks, under which was burning a slow fire, and there they were, the right hands, I counted them, 81 in all." The chief told Sheppard, "See! Here is our evidence. I always have to cut off the right hands of those we kill in order to show the State how many we have killed." He proudly showed Sheppard some of the bodies the hands had come from. The smoking preserved the hands in the hot, moist climate, for it might be days or weeks before the chief could display them to the proper official and receive credit for his kills.

Sheppard had stumbled on one of the most grisly aspects of Leopold's rubber system. Like the hostage-taking, the severing of hands was deliberate policy, as even high officials would later admit. "During my time in the Congo I was the first commissioner of the Equator district," recalled Charles Lemaire after his retirement. "As soon as it was a question of rubber, I wrote to the government, 'To gather rubber in the district . . . one must cut off hands, noses and ears.'"

If a village refused to submit to the rubber regime, state or company troops or their allies sometimes shot everyone in sight, so that nearby villages would get the message. But on such occasions some European officers were mistrustful. For each cartridge issued to their soldiers they demanded proof that the bullet had been used to kill someone, not "wasted" in hunting or, worse yet, saved for possible use in a mutiny. The standard proof was the right hand from a corpse. Or occasionally not from a corpse. "Sometimes," said one officer to a missionary, soldiers "shot a cartridge at an animal in hunting; they then cut off a hand from a living man" In some military units there was even a "keeper of the hands"; his job was the smoking.

Sheppard was not the first foreign witness to see severed hands in the Congo, nor would he be the last. But the articles he wrote for missionary magazines about his grisly find were reprinted and quoted widely, both in Europe and the United States, and it is partly due to him that people overseas began to associate the Congo with severed hands. A half-dozen years after Sheppard's stark discovery, while attacking the expensive public works Leopold was building with his Congo profits, the socialist leader Émile Van-

dervelde would speak in the Belgian Parliament of "monumental arches which one will someday call the Arches of the Severed Hands." William Sheppard's outspokenness would eventually bring down the wrath of the authorities and one day Vandervelde, an attorney, would find himself defending Sheppard in a Congo courtroom. But that is getting ahead of our story.

As the rubber terror spread throughout the rain forest, it branded people with memories that remained raw for the rest of their lives. A Catholic priest who recorded oral histories half a century later quotes a man, Tswambe, speaking of a particularly hated state official named Léon Fiévez, who terrorized a district along the river three hundred miles north of Stanley Pool:

> All the blacks saw this man as the Devil of the Equator. . . . From all the bodies killed in the field, you had to cut off the hands. He wanted to see the number of hands cut off by each soldier, who had to bring them in baskets. . . . A village which refused to provide rubber would be completely swept clean. As a young man, I saw [Fiévezs] soldier Molili, then guarding the village of Boyeka, take a big net, put ten arrested natives in it, attach big stones to the net, and make it tumble into the river. . . . Rubber caused these torments; that's why we no longer want to hear its name spoken. Soldiers made young men kill or rape their own mothers and sisters.

A Force Publique officer who passed through Fiévez's post in 1894 quotes Fiévez himself describing what he did when the surrounding villages failed to supply his troops with the fish and manioc he had demanded: "I made war against them. One example was enough: a hundred heads cut off, and there have been plenty of supplies at the station ever since. My goal is ultimately humanitarian. I killed a hundred people . . . but that allowed five hundred others to live."

With "humanitarian" ground rules that included cutting off hands and heads, sadists like Fiévez had a field day. The station chief at M'Bima used his revolver to shoot holes in Africans' ear lobes. Raoul de Premorel, an agent working along the Kasai River, enjoyed giving large doses of castor oil to people he considered malingerers. When villagers, in a desperate attempt to meet the weight quota, turned in rubber mixed with dirt or pebbles to the agent Albéric Detiège, he made them eat it. When two porters failed to use a designated latrine, a district commissioner, Jean Verdussen, ordered them paraded in front of troops, their faces rubbed with excrement.

As news of the white man's soldiers and their baskets of severed hands spread through the Congo, a myth gained credence with Africans that was a curious reversal of the white obsession with black cannibalism. The cans of corned beef seen in white men's houses, it was said, did not contain meat from the animals shown on the label; they contained chopped-up hands.

29

The Rod of Empire

The role that women played in the history of imperialism is the focus of this selection. In the introduction of her book, *The Women's History of the World*, contemporary English historian Rosalind Miles seeks not only to "fill in the gaps left by conventional history's preoccupation with male doings," but also to make the point that "women have not ultimately been victims either of men or of history, but have emerged as strong, as survivors, as invincible . . . Women have been active, competent and *important* through all the ages of man, and it is devastating for us if we do not understand this." As you read consider whether Miles' has accomplished her goal, as well as how her views compare with other readings regarding the role of the imperialists.

Discussion Questions

1. What were the various roles played by women in the history of imperialism? How and who determined these roles, according to Miles, and do you agree?

2. How was gender, that is, the sex of an individual, used as a "weapon of empire?" Is gender still used to define and to characterize relationships of power? What other factors are also used?

3. Who is the culprit in Miles' account of imperialism, and do you agree? What is patriarchy? Does it still exist?

4. What is the "paradox of empire" that Miles' mentions? Do you agree that the message of imperialism was simple—"dominion and domination?"

The Rod of Empire

Whoever sees Virginia,
This he shall surely find
A land for men . . .

MICHAEL DAYTON, "Ode
to the Virginian Voyage," 1605

Women therefore must go into the Colonies as well as men, that the plantations may spread into
generations, and not be forever pieced from without.

FRANCIS BACON, addressing the
English Royal Council for Virginia, 1609

No, no—surely not! My God—not more of those damned whores!

LIEUTENANT CLARK OF THE FIRST FLEET ON
SIGHTING A FEMALE CONVICT TRANSPORT SHIP
COMING INTO SYDNEY HARBOUR, JUNE 1790

Women are women the world over, whatever their color.

RIDER HAGGARD, *King Solomon's Mines* (1886)

If the Industrial Revolution brought the rape of nature, the imperial thrust which stimulated its growth and provided its market meant the rape of the world. Between 1796 and 1818, Britain seized Ceylon, South Africa, India, Burma, and Assam. By the Opium War of 1842, the body count had risen to include Hong Kong, the Punjab, Kashmir, Afghanistan and Singapore. Nor was empire a purely British theme — Dutch, Spanish, French and Portuguese all scrambled to the global carve-up like boys to a brawl, while the American expansion westward echoed the imperial theme of the country's first founders and gave it an internal empire within its own shores greater than many beyond. The sum of these moments has

proved a decisive legacy in the shaping of the modern world; in everything from apartheid in South Africa to the firearms *folie* of the USA, the spoor of the great imperial male stalking gun in hand across the sands of time may be detected to this day.

In song, story, myth and memory, and above all in official history, empire has always been seen in this way as an heroic male endeavor. Since Alexander the Great broke through to the limits of the last known frontier, then wept because there were no more worlds to conquer, women have been absent from the annals. Of those who sailed in the historic *Mayflower* voyage of 1620, the names of the Pilgrim Fathers are memorialized in stone on the Plymouth quayside—of the eighteen women who sailed too, there is no mention. And as the bounds of empire spread wider still and wider, pushed onward by Kipling's coldeyed adventurers "that smell of tobacco and blood," the classic fiction of men–against–the–odds is summed up by the boast of the hero of the Rider Haggard epic, *King Solomon's Mines*: "I can safely say that there is not a *petticoat* in the whole history."

Yet as the place names from Port Elizabeth to Maryland indicate, the female influence cannot be denied. For women were always there, active as colonizers from the days of the Greeks, essential to the survival of empire, as Bacon had insisted from the outset. In the North American venture, the first–ever imperial baby was a girl, the aptly named Virginia Dare, safely delivered on Roanoke Island on Ascension Day 1587. Similarly the first white Australian was the baby Rebekah Small, who arrived shortly after the First Fleet landed in 1788; although born to one of the "damned whores" who had so disgusted Lieutenant Ralph Clark, Rebekah lived this down to marry a missionary and to present her new country with no less than fourteen little Australians.

In the history of empire, women were always there because, quite simply, the men could not manage without them. Worldwide, secure, and long–term settlement was virtually impossible without female workers; the first governor of the Cape Colony, the Dutch Colonel Van Riebeck, was horrified at his men's inability to tend cattle, make butter and cheese, or to do anything for themselves. An immediate draft of girls from orphanages in Amsterdam and Rotterdam had to be ordered to supply the deficiency. England, alerted by Bacon, recognized the problem from the outset—the London Company responsible for the successful foundation of the Jamestown settlement in Virginia systematically despatched to the New World "young

women to make wives," to be "planted" alongside the men. These had to be "handsome and honestly educated maids," and "specially recommended into the colony for their good bringing–up." But neither their looks, education nor upbringing were to save them from being treated like the merchandise they were, and on arrival in Virginia they were "sold" for 120 pounds of best tobacco, the equivalent of $500 dollars apiece and thereafter committed to the colonists who took them, as servants or wives, for life.

Essentially, though, women were required for much, much more than their working capacity. There is no doubt that the primary production of imperial women was reproduction, the more so as hostile climates, disease and danger maximized infant mortality everywhere. The wife of the Reverend Samuel Sewall of Massachusetts bore him 14 children in 40 years of marriage, yet within four months of her death the patriarch was looking out for a new bride, "one young enough to bear." Women were equally expected to keep up their less tangible sexual duties, of setting a tone, maintaining standards and civilizing the men. Dismayed by the number of colonial administrators who fell victim to the temptation of "going native," the British government exported "English roses" by the shipload. These soon sent native concubines packing with a double–barrelled blast of Christianity and carbolic, to the open admiration of traveller Baron von Hubner: "It is the Englishwoman, courageous, devoted, well–educated, well–trained—the Christian guardian of the domestic hearth—who by her magic wand has brought this wholesome transformation." As this shows, English women were consciously used as a weapon of empire, to keep the master–race pure and to avoid the contemporary bogey of "miscegenation." Even the presence of his sister, old imperialists felt, "saved many a young fellow from drink and *ruin* [intercourse with native women]. Exquisitely pink and white, fresh and fragile, innocent and inviolable, the Englishwoman incarnated all the values of England, home and beauty" for which so many men suffered and died. But the task of keeping the moral conscience of the race was not merely a preoccupation of multi–racial imperial outposts, nor merely of patriarchal males. In 1847 the philanthropist Caroline Chisholm, whose devotion to the welfare of women was beyond question, issued this directive to the British government as a recipe for "the formation of a good and great people" in Australia: "For all the clergy you can dispatch, all the schoolmasters you can appoint, all the churches you can build, and all the books you can export, you will never do much good without what a gentleman in that Colony very appropriately called 'God's police'—good and virtuous women." Even women whose own mothers could not have called them good or virtuous had a key role to play in keeping the menfolk in line, according to a historian of the "old Wild West": "When one considers the crudity of what was predominantly a male society, it must be admitted that the scarlet representatives of the gentler sex played an important part in taming the West." As one old Montanan put it, "many's the miner who'd never wash his face or comb his hair if it wasn't for thinkin' of the sportin' girls he might meet in the saloons."

From the first, then, women only entered the empire adventure on male terms, as instruments of the overriding imperative of the patriarch: dominion and domination. Once they were there, strong systems continually reminded them of their purpose, and reinforced their status as the perennial underclass.

Gold-diggers, "business girls," female travellers, traders, and simple opportunists, these women colonizers had had at least some element of choice in their own lives. Most hapless and unprepared of all the women of the empire were those who were colonized; who simply by being born into a particular country fell victim to the domination of white males in addition to their own. For as the "gaming girls" remind us, one of the invisible exports of colonization was the age–old patriarchal division of women into madonna and whore, imposing on the women of the new worlds all the values and oppression of the old. Nor were these "virgin lands," in the preferred imperial imagery, supinely awaiting the thrust of the great white male to rouse them from their primeval slumber. All had their own existing social and political systems, in most of which women were subordinate to men. With colonization, then, in a grim and unavoidable concatenation of interests, white male supremacy meshed with preexisting male domination to ensure that native women, when all the permutations of sexism and racism were completed, found themselves at the very bottom of the pile, the lowest of the low. On the credit side of the balance, relations between conquerors and conquered were not always so unrelievedly black. Empire women in particular were often strongly motivated by religious or humanitarian principles, to help those who would certainly receive no other help on the earthly side of the grave. One public health instructor in turn–of–the–century Lahore was called to a difficult delivery in circumstances that were by no means out of the way:

> Three o'clock one cold winter's morning
> . . . the house of an outcaste, a little mud hut
> with an interior perhaps eight by twelve feet
> square. In the room were ten people, three
> generations of the family, all save the patient fast asleep. Also a sheep, two goats,
> some chickens and a cow, because the
> owner did not trust his neighbors. No light
> but a glim in an earthen pot. No heat but that
> from the bodies of man and beast. No aperture but the door, which was closed. In a
> small alcove at the back of the room four
> cot beds planted one upon another, all oc-

cupied by members of the family. In the cot third from the ground, a woman in advanced labor.

The midwife–instructor was, however, too short to reach the patient, although there was not a moment to be lost. But, by good fortune, the cow lay wedged against the bottom of the cot–pile—so standing on the back of the uncomplaining animal, the midwife, after a prolonged struggle, successfully delivered "a pair of tiny Hindus—boy and girl!"

Nor was the exchange between the women of empire always confined to a one-way flow of benefits from the colonizers to the colonized. The Scots missionary Mary Moffat wrote endearingly of learning from her African neighbors how to keep house in the Kuruman Valley of the Kalahari desert, "You will perhaps think it curious that we smear on our room floors with cow dung once a week at least." On her own admission, Mary had tried very hard to manage without "that dirty trick." But as she confessed:

> I had not been here long but I was glad to have it done and I had hardly patience to wait till Saturday. It lays the dust better than anything, kills fleas which would otherwise breed abundantly, and is a fine, clear green . . . it is mixed with water and laid on as thinly as possible. I now look on my floor smeared with cow dung with as much complacency as I used to do upon our best rooms when well scoured.

On the whole, though, the advancement of empire meant not cooperation with the indigenous peoples, but the establishment of mastery, an aim which hardened rather than diminished as time went on. In South Africa, for instance, the white settlers bitterly resented any progress towards equality made by the black people who had hitherto, in true patriarchal style, been their "dependents," and who could, if freed, compete for land with their own sons. This was one of the principal spurs to the Great Trek of 1835–48, when the Cape was abandoned by those who

could not stomach black emancipation. In the new republics of Natal, the Transvaal and the Orange Free State, there was an avowed rededication to the color bar just as it was beginning to fade away in the parent colony. This policy was pursued with such success that after the union of the new territories with the Cape in 1910, their descendants were strong enough to destroy any vestige of liberalism in its own homeland, and to impose the tyranny which subsequently proved so destructive and so durable.

As races, so individuals went under the heel, all suffering in different ways the imposition of the alien values of the white male. It is one of the graver ironies of imperial rule that colonial administrators, while powerless or disinclined to terminate traditions often brutally oppressive of women, had no compunction in striking at established customs that gave women some authority or economic control. In West Africa, for instance, women have always dominated the market economy, often rising to become major entrepreneurs. White colonialists, disapproving of this structure and determined to bring it in line with Western patterns, systematically set about suppressing the market women, and despite the women's agitation and demonstration finally succeeded in vesting this power in the hands of the males. Omu Okwei therefore became the last "Market Queen" when she was elected chair woman of the ancient Council of Mothers, a survival of the matriarchy which was finally destroyed when the British transferred supervision of all retailing from the women's council to the local city authorities after Okwei's death in 1943. This then was the paradox of empire: that while some women discovered new and unknown worlds, "Britannia's daughters" in particular seizing the hope of escaping the stifling narrowness of home to become doctors, teachers, leaders, fighters or farmers in the field, others were condemned to the spiral of the old degradation from which women are still struggling to be free. Stories of the early pioneers show women adapting with great skill, courage and resourcefulness to the mixed message of their inherently inferior status, and yet at the same time of the vital necessity of their input to their infant communities. But as time went on, the toils of empire, itself only the parent country and society writ large, grew tighter, working to strangle women's newborn independence and initiative before it had a chance to thrive and take root.

In harsh contradiction to the jingoistic self–glorification in which the tales of empire have been couched, it is hard to look back on the entire historical episode as anything other than a massive bungled opportunity. For what the world has finally inherited in every instance is simply another version of the white male patriarchy that the imperialists had nominally left behind, and a restatement in the usurped name of the "mother" country of everything father wanted, needed, and stood to gain from since time began. The pattern was established at the very dawn of democracy in America, when the Founding Fathers chose to reproduce the two–tier system, in the teeth of the forceful plea of Abigail Adams to her husband John: "I desire you would remember the ladies, and be more favourable to them than your ancestors . . . put not such power in the hands of husbands. Remember all men would be tyrants if they could."

They could, and they did. The machine of the patriarchs ground on, crushing women, children and native races as it went, consigning the flower of its youth to dusty death miles from home, making those same women, children, youths and natives the excuse for all its own self-serving, self-deluding obses-

sions. And when sexism combined with racism in the vicious circle of supremacy, women were victimized from both sides as in the worst atrocity of the Indian Mutiny when the rebel sepoy troops imprisoned the British women after the fall of Cawnpore in the very *bibighar* (women's house) where the white officers had previously kept their Indian concubines. When the soldiers refused to pollute themselves with the women's blood, butchers were sent in.

The British army recaptured Cawnpore only to find the *bibighar* running with blood. The house was littered with female underwear, hair, scattered limbs and naked, mutilated bodies. The soldiers shared out the tresses of one of the young girls and swore that, for every hair, a sepoy should die. The British commander, General Neil, decreed that the rebels' punishment should be "the heaviest, the most revolting to their feelings, and what they must ever remember." Accordingly the captives were forced to lick the *bibighar* clean of blood, dooming them in their religion to eternal torment in perdition, before being whipped and hanged in "a frenzy of retributive savagery which is one of the most shameful episodes of British history."

In this horrifying massacre and its aftermath, the imperial theme swells up loudly and unmistakably beneath all the contemporary cant. The message was simple—dominion and domination. Empire movements, in defiance of all the new freedoms they purported to offer, merely served to confirm women as the world's underclass, the perpetual subject race. But beneath the gentle swell of that eternal golden calm, something was stirring. After thousands of years of the human struggle, it was the turning of the tide.

30

American Imperialism

In his book, *The World Revolution of Westernization*, Theodore Von Laue, a contemporary historian, analyzes the relative success of the 19th century imperialists, as well as characterizing the motives, means and consequences of their colonization. Looking at America, which acquired an empire fairly late in the history of the "new" imperialism, with its victory in the Spanish-American War of 1898–1900, Von Laue explains the reasons for his conclusion that the Americans were the "most successful" of the expansionists. As you read, also compare his explanation of American imperialism with the others that we will examine—the Europeans and the Japanese.

Discussion Questions

1. What did American imperialism have in common with its European and Japanese counterparts? What were the differences?
2. Why does Von Laue conclude that the Americans were the most successful of the expansionists, and would you agree? If not, why not?
3. What ideals and institutions motivated the American imperialists? Would you agree with Emily Rosenberg, a contemporary diplomatic historian, who has characterized the American expansionists as "Capitalists, Christians and Cowboys" whose goal was to "spread the American Dream?"
4. What did Manifest Destiny mean to Americans, both before and after 1898? Did America's "bloody 'taste of empire,'" begin in 1898, or, as Von Laue suggests, from the beginning of the encounter between Europeans and the native Americans?
5. How would you answer the last questions Von Laue poses in this selection? How were they answered by Americans, and other expansionists, at the end of the 19th century?

American Imperialism

Americans—to put now their most characteristic qualities into this thumbnail sketch—certainly were the most successful expansionists in the world. From the start, expansion was an elemental necessity of self-preservation and self-affirmation, self-righteously viewed in moral terms. As the Rev. Increase Mather wrote in 1676: the "Lord God of our Fathers has given us for a rightful Possession" the land of "the heathen People amongst whom we live," to which he added his thanks for ". . . the wonderful Providence of God, who did . . . lay the fear of the English and the dread of them upon all the Indians. The terror of God was upon them round about." In this spirit the white man claimed dominion over all lands from the eastern seaboard to the Rocky Mountains and beyond. Resenting the encroachment of arrogant strangers, the Indians fought back, sometimes in utter desperation, to no avail; in the ceaseless Indian wars the best Indian, as the saying went, was a dead Indian. Between the Indians and the frontiersmen backed up by the U.S. army, the contests of power were so unequal that by the end of the 19th century the Indians had ceased to be a political factor deserving recognition or serious attention; the Indian wars, while nurturing romantic fantasies, left no scars on the civic creed. In the process of fighting the Indians the seaboard settlers grew into proud Americans adding new states to the United States from the Atlantic to the Pacific.

In the westward thrust through the continent lateral security posed no problem. To the north the British in Canada offered few incentives for territorial expansion, although in one instance, over a border dispute in the Northwest, Americans threatened to fight if they did not get their way; through the 19th century Canada was eyed as a potential enemy. The temptations were greater to the south, towards the countries of Latin America. Here Americans, some decades after declaring independence, took a sweeping view, claiming to be the protectors of the entire hemisphere against European intervention. In the famous statement by President Monroe (1823), the American government declared that it would regard any attempt by European nations "to extend their system to any portion of this hemisphere as dangerous to [its] peace and safety." Much depended, of course, on the interpretation of "peace and safety," but the Monroe Doctrine projected a bold pretension to an American hegemony over the Western Hemisphere. How bold was shown not long afterwards, when trouble brewed over American settlers in Mexican Texas. For their sake Americans went to war with their southern neighbor, conquering Mexico City in 1847 and annexing California as well as Texas; all told, the Americans took two-fifths of Mexico's territory.

The Mexican war marked the culmination of a feverish expansionism in the name of an American "manifest destiny to overspread the continent allotted by Providence for the free development of our yearly multiplying

---

From *The World Revolution of Westernization: The Twentieth Century in Global Perspective* by Theodore H. Von Laue.

millions." Its exultation was perhaps best expressed by a senator from New York in January 1848:

> Whoever will look back upon the past and forward to the present, must see that, allured by the justice of our institutions, before the close of the present century, this continent will teem with a free population of a hundred million souls. Nor have we yet fulfilled the destiny allotted to us. New territory is spread out for us to subdue and fertilize; new races are presented for us to civilize, educate, and absorb; new triumphs for us to achieve in the cause of freedom.

Subsequently, however, Americans respected Mexico's territorial integrity (with minor infringements under President Wilson). Why fight a country when it posed no threat militarily, economically, or politically? By 1900 American capital dominated Mexican finance; Americans owned 78% of the mines, 72% of the smelters, 58% of the oil, 68% of the rubber plantations, and about two-thirds of the railroads. Almost as attractive as Canada, it offered opportunities for the peaceful expansion of American business.

Tempting opportunities also beckoned further afield. After the Mexican war Americans began looking across the Pacific. "Westward will the course of empire take its way," observed Commodore Perry after forcibly opening Japan to Western commerce in 1853, adding that "to me it seems that the people of America will, in some form or other, extend their dominion and their power until they shall have brought within their mighty embrace multitudes of the Islands of the great Pacific, and placed the Saxon race upon the eastern shores of Asia."

After the issue of slavery had been resolved and the West been settled, "Manifest Destiny" reemerged, encouraged by the final thrust of European colonial expansion at the end of the 19th century. "Whether they will or no, Americans must now begin to look

outward," wrote Captain Mahan, the prophet of American seapower. And outwardly they looked, especially on their own continent and in the Pacific. As for the Americas, Secretary of State Olney in 1896 announced that "the United States is practically sovereign on this continent, and its fiat is law upon the subjects to which it confines its interpretations." It soon showed its strength by annexing Puerto Rico, exercising protectorates over Cuba, Panama, and Nicaragua, as well as by making the British government toe the American line in a South American border dispute. In the Pacific Admiral Perry's vision came closer to reality with the annexation of the islands of Hawaii, Midway, Guam, and Wake; after the war with Spain the Philippine islands were added. In West Africa Liberia, settled by American blacks, constituted a more inconspicuous (and often overlooked) outpost of American influence.

By 1900 the United States—now come of age, as it was said—had acquired colonial dependencies and become a world power. Reflecting a common sentiment and setting an American model for the great anti-Western challengers of the 20th century, the influential Senator Henry Cabot Lodge wrote, "Small states are of the past, and have no future. The great nations are rapidly absorbing for their future expansion and their present defence all the waste places of the earth. It is a movement which makes for civilization and the advancement of the race. As one of the great nations of the world the United States must not fall out of the line of march." The "advancement of the race" sometimes took rather uncivilized forms, as in an incident during the conquest of the Philippines when the people of a rebellious village, men, women, and children, were herded into an extinct crater and cold-bloodedly gunned to death from the rim. As the *Washington Post* in 1898 summed up the new American mood: "A new consciousness seems to have come upon us—the consciousness of strength, and with it a new appetite, a yearning to show our strength. . . . Ambition, interest, land-hunger, pride, the mere joy of fighting, whatever it may be, we are animated by a new sensation. . . . The taste of empire is in the mouth of the people, even as the taste of blood is in the jungle."

That bloody "taste of empire" in all encounters with alien peoples and creeds had been an ingredient in the American character from the start nourished by the Indian wars, it was not channeled, especially under Theodore Roosevelt's New Nationalism, into global politics. It remained, however, subordinate to the idealism of the American civic creed, held in check by isolationist sentiments or even morally deplored. As compared with the urgency of foreign policy in European states, American foreign relations remained a peripheral issue in public awareness. In any case, territorially secure, the country could expand its sway more effectively in nonterritorial ways and more in line with its ideals.

In reaction against the blatant imperialism of the previous decade President Taft argued that dollars were better than bullets. In an increasingly interdependent world, one of his spokesmen asserted that "international commerce conduces powerfully to international sympathy." Aware of the rapidly growing strength of the American economy, American businessmen had long looked for opportunities abroad, in Europe, Latin America, the Far East, and the Middle East too. Now they worked hand in glove with the government as agents of American policy, eager to spread American influence and promote prosperity. Thus in the Progressive Era American expansionism took an economic turn, demanding an Open Door wherever it saw new opportunities. Thus began the age of the ubiquitous American multinational corporations, led by Standard Oil. Superior technology of mass production aided the process, introducing mechanican novelties like the telephone, phonograph, typewriter, sewing machine, electric streetcars, and, of course, the automobile.

Promoting American business in an interdependent world could easily be fitted into the door-opening American civic creed. American business would draw together the whole world in mutually advantageous relationships, as happened within the American polity. This vision contained even a pacifist strain. Traditional power politics impeded the peaceful flow of goods and people. For that reason President Taft advocated the settlement of international disputes by arbitration.

It was President Wilson, however, who completed the idealist reinterpretation of American expansionism, drawing together the best in the American experience as a model for global cooperation. Under the banner of making the world safe for democracy and guaranteeing lasting peace under the League of Nations (as told in an earlier chapter), he presided over the peace conference which ended World War I. Prompted by the current globalization of power politics, Wilson, the most high-minded among American presidents, projected the American ideal over the world at large. He annexed it to the American dream, holding out the vision of an Americanized humanity.

His initiative, as we have seen, impressed another idealist, Lenin, whose vision by contrast was based on theory rather than on an exceptional historic fate. But he raised a basic question: did the American vision, abstracted from its moorings, really possess universal validity or was its export merely another form of imperialist expansionism? Admittedly, Americans carried with them the benefits of their historical exceptionality and the fruits ot their prosperity, in sharp contrast with Lenin's backward Russians. Yet, however attractive their gifts, did Americans in-fuse into international relations the equality so stressed at home? In their pride of global mission they let their ego grow large in 1917, ready to face the sacrifices of war. Yet, giving victory to the countries upholding the Western liberal-democratic tradition, were they aware at their moment of glory that they inspired others, who were outsiders to their traditions, to attempt the same preeminence? What they felt to be idealism might appear to the others merely as raw power disguised as moral righteousness. Who, for that matter, was morally entitled to reshape the world in their own image? Did there exist a universally accepted political morality?

31

The March of the Flag

Senator Albert Beveridge of Indiana (1862–1927) delivered the following speech during his campaign for office in 1898 at the time of the Spanish-American War. He was an enthusiastic advocate of American imperialism in which he was joined by many influential people such as Presidents McKinley and Theodore Roosevelt.

Discussion Questions

1. How does Beveridge demonstrate that Americans are God's chosen people?

2. Why does he argue that the consent of the governed should not be considered in the case of American imperialist expansion?

3. On what bases does he justify imperialism?

4. What duties does he imagine America has in the world? In this respect are his views the same as those of Rudyard Kipling in "The White Man's Burden?"

The March of the Flag

It is a noble land that God has given us; a land that can feed and clothe the world; a land whose coastlines would inclose half the countries of Europe; a land set like a sentinel between the two imperial oceans of the globe, a greater England with a nobler destiny.

It is a mighty people that He has planted on this soil; a people sprung from the most masterful blood of history; a people perpetually revitalized by the virile, man–producing working–folk of all the earth; a people imperial by virtue of their power, by right of their institutions, by authority of their Heaven–directed purposes the propagandists and not the misers of liberty.

It is a glorious history our God has bestowed upon His chosen people; a history heroic with faith in our mission and our future; a history of statesmen who flung the boundaries of the Republic out into unexplored lands and savage wilderness; a history of soldiers who carried the flag across blazing deserts and through the ranks of hostile mountains, even to the gates of sunset; a history of a multiplying people who overran a continent in half a century; a history of prophets who saw the consequences of evils inherited from the past and of martyrs who died to save us from them; a history divinely logical, in the process of whose tremendous reasoning we find ourselves today.

Therefore, in this campaign, the question is larger than a party question. It is an American question. It is a world question. Shall the American people continue their march toward the commercial supremacy of the world? Shall free institutions broaden their blessed reign as the children of liberty wax in strength, until the empire of our principles is established over the hearts of all mankind?

Have we no mission to perform, no duty to discharge to our fellow-man? Has God endowed us with gifts beyond our deserts and marked us as the people of His peculiar favor, merely to rot in our own selfishness, as men and nations must, who take cowardice for their companion and self for their deity—as China always has, as India has, as Egypt has?

Shall we be as the man who had one talent and hid it, or as he who had ten talents and used them until they grew to riches? And shall we reap the reward that waits on our discharge of our high duty; shall we occupy new markets for what our farmers raise, our factories make, our merchants sell-aye, and please God, new markets for what our ships shall carry?

Hawaii is ours; Puerto Rico is to be ours; at the prayer of her people Cuba finally will be ours; in the islands of the East, even to the gates of Asia, coaling stations are to be ours at the very least; the flag of a liberal government is to float over the Philippines, and may it be the banner that Taylor unfurled in Texas and Fremont carried to the coast.

The Opposition tells us that we ought not to govern a people without their consent. I answer, The rule of liberty that all just government derives its authority from the consent of the governed, applies only to those who are capable of self-government. We govern the Indians without their consent, we govern our territories without their consent, we

---

By Senator Albert Beveridge. Delivered as a campaign speech on September 16, 1898.

govern our children without their consent. How do they know what our government would be without their consent? Would not the people of the Philippines prefer the just, humane, civilizing government of this Republic to the savage, bloody rule of pillage and extortion from which we have rescued them?

And, regardless of this formula of words made only for enlightened, self–governing people, do we owe no duty to the world? Shall we turn these peoples back to the reeking hands from which we have taken them? Shall we abandon them, with Germany, England, Japan, hungering for them? Shall we save them from those nations, to give them a self–rule of tragedy?

They ask us how we shall govern these new possessions. I answer: Out of local conditions and the necessities of the case methods of government will grow. If England can govern foreign lands, so can America. If Germany can govern foreign lands, so can America. If they can supervise protectorates, so can America. Why is it more difficult to administer Hawaii than New Mexico or California? Both had a savage and an alien population; both were more remote from the seat of government when they came under our dominion than the Philippines are today.

Will you say by your vote that American ability to govern has decayed; that a century's experience in self–rule has failed of a result? Will you affirm by your vote that you are an infidel to American power and practical sense? Or will you say that ours is the blood of government; ours the heart of dominion; ours the brain and genius of administration? Will you remember that we do but what our fathers did—we but pitch the tents of liberty farther westward, farther southward—we only continue the march of the flag?

The march of the flag! In 1789 the flag of the Republic waved over 4,000,000 souls in thirteen states, and their savage territory which stretched to the Mississippi, to Canada, to the Floridas. The timid minds of that day said that no new territory was needed, and, for the hour, they were right. But Jefferson, through whose intellect the centuries marched; Jefferson, who dreamed of Cuba as an American state; Jefferson, the first Imperialist of the Republic—Jefferson acquired that imperial territory which swept from the Mississippi to the mountains, from Texas to the British possessions, and the march of the flag began!

The infidels to the gospel of liberty raved, but the flag swept on! The title to that noble land out of which Oregon, Washington, Idaho and Montana have been carved was uncertain; Jefferson, strict constructionist of constitutional power though he was, obeyed the Anglo-Saxon impulse within him, whose watchword then and whose watchword throughout the world to–day is, "Forward!": another empire was added to the Republic, and the march of the flag went on!

Those who deny the power of free institutions to expand urged every argument, and more, that we hear, to–day; but the people's judgment approved the command of their blood, and the march of the flag went on!

A screen of land from New Orleans to Florida shut us from the Gulf, and over this and the Everglade Peninsula waved the saffron flag of Spain; Andrew Jackson seized both, the American people stood at his back, and, under Monroe, the Floridas came under the dominion of the Republic, and the march of the flag went on! The Cassandras prophesied every prophecy of despair we hear, to–day, but the march of the flag went on!

Then Texas responded to the bugle calls of liberty, and the march of the flag went on! And, at last, we waged war with Mexico, and the flag swept over the southwest, over peerless California, past the Gate of Gold to Oregon on the north, and from ocean to ocean its folds of glory blazed.

And, now, obeying the same voice that Jefferson heard and obeyed, that Jackson heard and obeyed, that Monroe heard and obeyed, that Seward heard and obeyed, that Grant heard and obeyed, that Harrison heard and obeyed, our President today plants the flag over the islands of the seas, outposts of commerce, citadels of national security, and the march of the flag goes on!

Distance and oceans are no arguments. The fact that all the territory our fathers bought and seized is contiguous, is no argument. In 1819 Florida was farther from New York than Puerto Rico is from Chicago to-day; Texas, farther from Washington in 1845 than Hawaii is from Boston in 1898; California, more inaccessible in 1847 than the Philippines are now. Gibraltar is farther from London than Havana is from Washington; Melbourne is farther from Liverpool than Manila is from San Francisco.

The ocean does not separate us from lands of our duty and desire—the oceans join us, rivers never to be dredged, canals never to be repaired. Steam joins us; electricity joins us—the very elements are in league with our destiny. Cuba not contiguous? Puerto Rico not contiguous! Hawaii and the Philippines not contiguous! The oceans make them contiguous. And our navy will make them contiguous.

But the Opposition is right—there is a difference. We did not need the western Mississippi Valley when we acquired it, nor Florida, nor Texas, nor California, nor the royal provinces of the far northwest. We had no emigrants to people this imperial wilderness, no money to develop it, even no highways to cover it. No trade awaited us in its savage fastnesses. Our productions were not greater than our trade. There was not one reason for the land-lust of our states-men from Jefferson to Grant, other than the prophet and the

Saxon within them. But, to-day, we are raising more than we can consume, making more than we can use. Therefore we must find new markets for our produce.

And so, while we did not need the territory taken during the past century at the time it was acquired, we do need what we have taken in 1898, and we need it now. The resources and the commerce of these immensely rich dominions will be increased as much as American energy is greater than Spanish sloth. In Cuba, alone, there are 15,000,000 acres of forest unacquainted with the ax, exhaustless mines of iron, priceless deposits of manganese, millions of dollars' worth of which we must buy, to-day, from the Black Sea districts. There are millions of acres yet unexplored.

The resources of Puerto Rico have only been trifled with. The riches of the Philippines have hardly been touched by the finger-tips of modern methods. And they produce what we consume, and consume what we produce—the very predestination of reciprocity—a reciprocity "not made with hands, eternal in the heavens." They sell hemp, sugar, cocoanuts, fruits of the tropics, timber of price like mahogany; they buy flour, clothing, tools, implements, machinery and all that we can raise and make. Their trade will be ours in time. Do you endorse that policy with your vote?

Cuba is as large as Pennsylvania, and is the richest spot on the globe. Hawaii is as large as New Jersey; Puerto Rico half as large as Hawaii; the Philippines larger than all New England, New York, New Jersey and Delaware combined. Together they are larger than the British Isles, larger than France, larger than Germany, larger than Japan.

If any man tells you that trade depends on cheapness and not on government influence, ask him why England does not abandon South Africa, Egypt, India. Why does France seize South China, Germany the vast region whose port is Kaou–chou?

Our trade with Puerto Rico, Hawaii and the Philippines must be as free as between the states of the Union, because they are American territory, while every other nation on earth must pay our tariff before they can compete with us. Until Cuba shall ask for annexation, our trade with her will, at the very least, be like the preferential trade of Canada with England. That, and the excellence of our goods and products; that, and the convenience of traffic; that, and the kinship of interests and destiny, will give the monopoly of these markets to the American people.

The commercial supremacy of the Republic means that this Nation is to be the sovereign factor in the peace of the world. For the conflicts of the future are to be conflicts of trade struggles for markets—commercial wars for existence. And the golden rule of peace is impregnability of Position and invincibility of preparedness. So, we see England, the greatest strategist of history, plant her flag and her cannon on Gibraltar, at Quebec, in the Bermudas, at Vancouver, everywhere.

So Hawaii furnishes us a naval base in the heart of the Pacific; the Ladrones another, a voyage further on; Manila another, at the gates of Asia—Asia, to the trade of whose hundreds of millions American merchants, manufacturers, farmers, have as good right as those of Germany or France or Russia or England; Asia, whose commerce with the United Kingdom alone amounts to hundreds of millions of dollars every year; Asia, to whom Germany looks to take her surplus products; Asia, whose doors must not be shut against American trade. Within five decades the bulk of Oriental commerce will be ours.

No wonder that, in the shadows of coming events so great, free–silver is already a memory. The current of history has swept past that episode. Men understand, to–day, that the greatest commerce of the world must be conducted with the steadiest standard of value and most convenient medium of exchange human ingenuity can devise. Time, that unerring reasoner, has settled the silver question. The American people are tired of talking about money—they want to make it.

* * *

There are so many real things to be done—canals to be dug, railways to be laid, forests to be felled, cities to be builded, fields to be tilled, markets to be won, ships to be launched, peoples to be saved, civilization to be proclaimed and the flag of liberty flung to the eager air of every sea. Is this an hour to waste upon triflers with nature's laws? Is this a season to give our destiny over to word–mongers and prosperity–wreckers? No! It is an hour to remember our duty to our homes. It is a moment to realize the opportunities fate has opened to us. And so it is an hour for us to stand by the Government.

Wonderfully has God guided us. Yonder at Bunker Hill and Yorktown His providence was above us. At New Orleans and on ensanguined seas His hand sustained us. Abraham Lincoln was His minister and His was the altar of freedom the Nation's soldiers set up on a hundred battle–fields. His power directed Dewey in the East and delivered the Spanish fleet into our hands, as He delivered the elder Armada into the hands of our English sires two centuries ago [in 1588—ed.]. The American people can not use a dishonest medium of exchange; it is ours to set the world its example of right and honor. We can not fly from our world duties; it is ours to execute the purpose of a fate that has driven us to be greater than our small intentions. We can not retreat from any soil where Providence has unfurled our banner; it is ours to save that soil for liberty and civilization.

32

Roots of Chinese Stability

The comments of Thomas Meadows, a 19th century British observer of Chinese culture, serve as a brief summary of those values and institutions which had served China since the beginning of its imperial history in the 2nd century b.c.

Discussion Questions

1. What are the values that author attributes to the Chinese that have created the stability of which he speaks?

2. How does Meadows describe Chinese government? What checks and balances existed?

3. If rebellion was a legitimate and accepted part of Chinese society, how did China achieve its great stability?

4. How did the values and institutions of Chinese society in the 19th century compare with those of the West?

Roots of Chinese Stability

The real causes of the unequalled duration and constant increase of the Chinese people, as one and the same nation . . . consists of three doctrines, together with an institution. . . . The doctrines are

I. That the nation must be governed by moral agency in preference to physical force.
II. That the services of the wisest and ablest men in the nation are indispensable to its good government.
III. That the people have the right to depose a sovereign who, either from active wickedness or vicious indulgence, gives cause to oppressive and tyrannical rule.

The institution is . . .

The system of public service competitive examinations. . . .

The institution of Public Service Examinations (which have long been strictly competitive) is the cause of the continued duration of the Chinese nation: it is that which preserves the other causes and gives efficacy to their operation. By it all parents throughout the country, who can compass the means, are induced to impart to their sons an intimate knowledge of the literature which contains the three doctrines above cited, together with many others conducive to a high mental cultivation. By it all the ability of the country is enlisted on the side of that Government which takes care to preserve it in purity. By it, with its impartiality, the, poorest man in the country is constrained to that if his lot in life is a low one it is so in virtue of the "will of Heaven," and that no unjust barriers created by his fellow men prevent him from elevating himself. . . .

The normal Chinese government is essentially based on moral force: it is not a despotism. A military and police is maintained sufficient to crush merely factious risings, but totally inadequate both in numbers and in nature, to put down a disgusted and indignant people. But though no despotism, this same government is in form and machinery a pure autocracy. In his district the magistrate is absolute; in his province, the governor; in the empire, the Emperor. The Chinese people have no right of legislation, they have no right of self-taxation, they have not the power of voting out their rulers or of limiting or stopping supplies. They have therefore the right of rebellion. Rebellion is in China the old, often exercised, legitimate, and constitutional means of stopping arbitrary and vicious legislation and administration.

From T. T. Meadows, *The Chinese and Their Rebellions* (Smith, Elder, London, 1856), pp. 23, 24, 401–403.

33

China and the West Evaluate Each Other before the Opium War

This selection highlights some conclusions reached by the Chinese and the Europeans after their initial encounters in the eighteenth century.

The Chinese Concluded That:

1 These barbarians from Europe wouldn't accept the fact that they *were* barbarians! Even though they had no proper system of ceremonial etiquette and little understanding of "the distinction between Superior and Inferior."

2 Some barbarians behaved violently and aggressively like pirates. (Old Chinese proverb: "He who knows not the 'rites' has nothing to shape his character.")

3 The barbarians had cultural values and intellectual standards of their own. In some fields, barbarian knowledge was even ahead of theirs. (Few admitted this.)

4 The barbarians were also clever at inventing things such as telescopes and instruments for measuring time and space. *But* what real use were these little gadgets?

5 The barbarians also possessed effective weapons which they used with courage and skill. *But* there were enough people in China to defeat any puny barbarian horde.

6 Though barbarians all looked alike, they came from different countries. They quarrelled among themselves. It was easy to exploit their national jealousies.

7 The European barbarians were all Christians, but they believed in different varieties of Christianity. It was easy to make use of these religious differences.

8 The barbarians were a money-grubbing lot, interested only in buying and selling. (But what kind of "barbarians" did the Chinese most frequently encounter?)

9 The barbarians, all in all, were a nuisance. Why didn't they stay at home? (What didn't the Chinese find out?)

The Europeans Concluded That:

1 On the other side of the globe lay rich, well-ordered, highly civilized countries whose people thought *they* were barbarians. It was a geographical, economic and cultural shock. They were impressed by the size of

From Pat Barr, *Foreign Devils: Westerners in the Far East*, copyright © 1970 by Penguin Books Ltd., Harmondsworth, England, pp. 44–45. Reprinted with permission.

China, its wealth of natural resources, the splendour of the Oriental courts.

2 According to the highly coloured Jesuit accounts, China was a land that venerated learning, moral principles, social harmony. It was a model of "benevolent despotism." The philosophers of the Enlightenment were quite bowled over. Wrote Voltaire: "The constitution of their Empire is the most excellent the world has ever seen." Confucius was venerated as a great man. Leibnitz wrote, "Certainly the condition of our affairs, slipping into ever greater corruption, seems to me such that we need missionaries from the Chinese to teach us the use and practice of natural religion." (But the Jesuit accounts rather ignored the tyranny of the Emperor and Chinese officialdom, the economic disorder, the existence of many brutal customs.)

3 Much Oriental art was subtle and beautiful. Oriental silks, porcelain, ivories, lacquer became fashionable. Oriental motifs were adopted in architecture and landscape gardening.

4 The Far East had great trading potential. Merchants longed to introduce European manufactures to the people, who seemed strangely reluctant to buy their goods.

5 Throughout the Orient law was strictly, often cruelly enforced. (And in England during the seventeenth century, 180 crimes were punishable by death.)

6 The Orientals also practised benevolence, industriousness, obedience and other virtues that, in the past, Christians had assumed to be their monopoly.

7 The Japanese, in particular, were admirably clean. They bathed *every* day and the floors of their homes were so clean that "I would not dare to spit on them," said one Englishman.

8 There were distinct differences between Chinese and Japanese, though they looked alike. In general, the Chinese were more haughty, suspicious and culturally sophisticated than the Japanese. The Chinese were amazingly incurious about the West. (Imagine a shipload of mandarins sailing up the River Thames—what a furore of interest and excitement there would have been!) The Japanese seemed more eager to learn, more open-minded and hospitable, *but* also more warlike. The Chinese seemed to be almost defenceless; the Japanese practised the martial arts and their leaders were also warriors.

34

Chinese and Western Civilization Compared

The following selection provides some insight as to the way a Westerner would assess Chinese culture as compared to his own. Taking the position of a Chinese, Goldsworthy L. Dickinson, highlights the chief features of Chinese civilization, while also pointing to the differences between East and West.

Discussion Questions

1. What does the writer identify as the key values and institutions of the Chinese? Do you think that his assessment is an accurate one?

2. How does Dickinson characterize European values and institutions? Would you agree with his characterization? What additional qualities would you add?

3. How does Dickinson define the European idea of "progress," and what does he say is the Chinese view? How might the Chinese define progress?

4. Does the writer identify any similarities between the two cultures, and, if not, were there? Could these similarities have been used to forge a more workable relationship, or, as the saying goes, "East is east, West is west, and never the twain shall meet?"

Our civilization is the oldest in the world. It does not follow that it is the best; but neither, I submit, does it follow that it is the worst. On the contrary, such antiquity is, at any rate, a proof that our institutions have guaranteed to us a stability for which we search in vain among the nations of Europe. But not only is our civilization stable, it also embodies, as we think, a moral order; while in yours we detect only an economic chaos. Whether your religion be better than ours, I do not at present dispute; but it is certain that it has less influence on your society. You profess Christianity, but your civilization has never been Christian; whereas ours is Confucian through and through. But to say that it is Confucian, is to say that it is moral; . . . Whereas, with you (so it seems, to us) economic relations come first, and upon these you endeavor, afterward, to graft as much morality as they will admit.

This point I may illustrate by a comparison between your view of the family and ours. To you, so far as a foreigner, can perceive, the family is merely a means for nourishing and protecting the child until he is of age to look after himself. . . . As soon as they are of age, you send them out, as you say, to "make their fortune"; and from that moment, often enough, as they cease to be dependent on their parents, so they cease to recognize obligations toward them. They may go where they will, do what they will, earn and spend as they choose; and it is at their own option whether or not they maintain their family ties. With you the individual is the unit, and all the units are free. No one is tied, but also no one is rooted. Your society, to use your own word, is "progressive" you are always "moving on." Everyone feels it a duty (and in most cases it is a necessity) to strike out a new line for himself. To remain in the position in which you were born you consider a disgrace; a man, to be a man, must venture, struggle, compete, and win. To this characteristic of your society is to be attributed, no doubt, its immense activity, and its success in all material arts. But to this, also, is due the feature that most strikes a Chinaman—its unrest, its confusion, its lack (as we think) of morality. Among you no one is contented, no one has leisure to live, so intent are all on increasing the means of living.

Now, to us of the East all this is the mark of a barbarous society. We measure the degree of civilization not by accumulation of the means of living, but by the character and value of the life lived. Where there are no humane and stable relations, no reverence for the past, no respect even for the present, but only a cupidinous ravishment of the future, there, we think, there is no true society.

From Goldsworthy L. Dickinson, *Letters From a Chinese Official: Being an Eastern View of Western Civilization*, (New York: McClure, Phillips, 1907). Published in 1901 (London: R.B. Johnson), as *Letters From John Chinaman.*

35

Qianlong's Letter to George III

When the Chinese emperor Qianlong wrote this letter to George III, he was writing as a well-established monarch of a powerful, prosperous dynasty, the Manchu, or Qing, established in 1644. Two long-reigning emperors, Qianlong (1726–1795) and his predecessor and considered to be China's ideal leader, K'ang Hsi (1661–1722), would bring China to its peak of greatness, with increases in economic prosperity, population, agricultural innovations and foreign conquests. Yet this dynasty, founded by non-Chinese Manchurians, won respect from the Chinese by sinifying, that is, adopting Chinese values and institutions, in essence, trying to be more Chinese than the Chinese. This sinification included an especially conservative Confucianism that placed importance on self-sufficiency and, in terms of the outside world, a culture-centrism that viewed China as superior to all other cultures. The Chinese had had little contact with other nations, and those in East Asia with whom China had contact, were seen as inferior and expected to pay tribute in the form of regular missions which included the performance of the kowtow to the Chinese emperor. The Tribute System, as these missions were called, was applied to the Europeans when they came to call. In light of their worldview, perhaps it is not surprising that the Manchu (Qing) Dynasty was to be China's last, its decline beginning in 1800, soon after Qianlong's abdication.

Discussion Questions

1. What were the English demands, and what arguments does Qianlong make in refusing those demands? Which position, the English or the Chinese, seems the most rational to you? The most fair?

2. How do you think Qianlong viewed the English? How do you think the English reacted to Qianlong's letter?

3. From Qianlong's letter, how do you think the Tribute System worked? What Chinese attitudes did it reflect? How did it differ from Western views of the relations between nations?

You, O King, live beyond the confines of many seas, nevertheless, impelled by your humble desire to partake of the benefits of our civilisation, you have dispatched a mission respectfully bearing your memorial. Your Envoy has crossed the seas and paid his respects at my Court on the anniversary of my birthday. To show your devotion, you have also sent offerings of your country's produce.

"I have perused your memorial: the earnest terms in which it is couched reveal a respectful humility on your part, which is highly praiseworthy. In consideration of the fact that your Ambassador and his deputy have come a long way with your memorial and tribute, I have shown them high favour and have allowed them to be introduced into my presence. To manifest my indulgence, I have entertained them at a banquet and made them numerous gifts. I have also caused presents to be forwarded to the Naval Commander and six hundred of his officers and men, although they did not come to Peking, so that they too may share in my all-embracing kindness.

"As to your entreaty to send one of your nationals to be accredited to my Celestial Court and to be in control of your country's trade with China, this request is contrary to all usage of my dynasty and cannot possibly be entertained. It is true that Europeans, in the service of the dynasty, have been permitted to live at Peking, but they are compelled to adopt Chinese dress, they are strictly confined to their own precincts and are never permitted to return home. You are presumably familiar with our dynastic regulations. Your proposed Envoy to my Court could not be placed in a position similar to that of European officials in Peking who are forbidden to leave China, nor could be, on the other hand, be allowed liberty of movement and the privilege of corresponding with his own country; so that, you would gain nothing by his residence in our midst.

"Moreover, Our Celestial dynasty possesses vast territories, and tribute missions from the dependencies are provided for by

From The Emperor Qianlong's "Mandates" in *Annals and Memoirs of the Court of Peking*, by E. Backhouse and J. P. P. Bland, London, 1914, pp. 322–334.

the Department for Tributary States, which ministers to their wants and exercises strict control over their movements. It would be quite impossible to leave them to their own devices. Supposing that your Envoy should come to our Court, his language and national dress differ from that of our people, and there would be no place in which to bestow him. It may be suggested that he might imitate the Europeans permanently resident in Peking and adopt the dress and customs of China, but, it has never been our dynasty's wish to force people to do things unseemly and inconvenient. Besides, supposing I sent an Ambassador to reside in your country, how could you possibly make for him the requisite arrangements? Europe consists of many other nations besides your own: if each and all demanded to be represented at our Court, how could we possibly consent? The thing is utterly impracticable. How can our dynasty alter its whole procedure and system of etiquette, established for more than a century, in order to meet your individual views? If it be said that your object is to exercise control over your country's trade, your nationals have had full liberty to trade at Canton for many a year, and have received the greatest consideration at our hands. Missions have been sent by Portugal and Italy, proffering similar requests. The Throne appreciated their sincerity and loaded them with favours, besides authorising measures to facilitate their trade with China. You are no doubt aware that, when my Canton merchant, Wu Chao-ping, was in debt to the foreign ships, I made the Viceroy advance the monies due, out of the provincial treasury, and ordered him to punish the culprit severely. Why then should foreign nations advance this utterly unreasonable request to be represented at my Court? Peking is nearly two thousand miles from Canton, and at such a distance what possible control could any British representative exercise?

"If you assert that your reverence for Our Celestial dynasty fills you with a desire to acquire our civilisation, our ceremonies and code of laws differ so completely from your own that, even if your Envoy were able to acquire the rudiments of our civilisation, you could not possibly transplant our manners and customs to your alien soil. Therefore, however adept the Envoy might become, nothing would be gained thereby.

"Swaying the wide world, I have but one aim in view, namely, to maintain a perfect governance and to fulfil the duties of the state: strange and costly objects do not interest me. If I have commanded that the tribute offerings sent by you, O King, are to be accepted, this was solely consideration for the spirit which prompted you to dispatch them from afar. Our dynasty's majestic virtue has penetrated unto every country under Heaven, and Kings of all nations have offered their costly tribute by land and sea. As your Ambassador can see for himself, we possess all things. I set no value on objects strange or ingenious, and have no use for your country's manufactures. This then is my answer to your request to appoint a representative at my Court, a request contrary to our dynastic usage, which would only result in inconvenience to yourself. I have expounded my wishes in detail and have commanded your tribute Envoys to leave in peace on their homeward journey. It behooves you, O King, to respect my sentiments and to display even greater devotion and loyalty in future, so that, by perpetual submission to our Throne, you may secure peace and prosperity for your country hereafter. Besides making gifts (of which I enclose an inventory) to each member of your Mission, I confer upon you, O King, valuable presents in the number usually bestowed on such occasions, including silks and curios—a list of which is likewise enclosed. Do you reverently receive them and take note of goodwill towards you! A special mandate."

A further mandate to King George III dealt in detail with the British Ambassador's proposals and the Emperor's reasons for declining them: "You, O King, from afar have yearned after the blessings of our civilisation, and in your eagerness to come into touch with our converting influence have sent an Embassy across the sea bearing a memorial. I already taken note of your respectful spirit of submission, have treated your mission with extreme favour and loaded it with gifts, besides issuing a mandate to you, O King, and honouring with the bestowal of valuable presents. Thus has my indulgence been manifested.

"Yesterday your Ambassador petitioned my Ministers to memorialise me regarding your trade with China, but his proposal is not consistent with our dynastic usage and cannot be entertained. Hitherto, all European nations, including your own country's barbarian merchants, have carried on their trade with Our Celestial Empire at Canton. Such has been the procedure for many years, although Our Celestial Empire possesses all things in prolific abundance and lacks no product within its own borders. There was therefore no need to import the manufactures of outside barbarians in exchange for our own produce. But as the tea, silk and porcelain which the Celestial Empire produces, are absolute necessities to European nations and to yourselves, we permitted, as a signal mark of favour, that foreign *hongs* should be established at Canton, so that your wants might be supplied and your country thus participate in our beneficence. But your Ambassador has now put forward new requests which completely fail to recognise the Throne's principle to 'treat strangers from afar with indulgence,' and to exercise a pacifying control over barbarian tribes, the world over. Moreover, our dynasty, swaying the myriad races

of the globe, extends the same benevolence towards all. Your England is not the only nation trading at Canton. If other nations, following your bad example, wrongfully importune my ear with further impossible requests, how will it be possible for me to treat them with easy indulgence? Nevertheless, I do not forget the lonely remoteness of your island, cut off from the world by intervening wastes of sea, nor do I overlook your excusable ignorance of the usages of Our Celestial Empire. I have consequently commanded my Ministers to enlighten your Ambassador on the subject, and have ordered the departure of the mission. But I have doubts that, after your Envoy's return he may fail to acquaint you with my view in detail or that he may be lacking in lucidity, so that I shall now proceed to take your requests *seriatim* and to issue my mandate on each question separately. In this way you will, I trust, comprehend my meaning. . . .

[The emperor then lists the seven requests of the British; only the seventh is included here—Ed.]

"(7) Regarding your nation's worship of the Lord of Heaven, it is the same religion as that of other European nations. Ever since the beginning of history, sage Emperors and wise rulers have bestowed on China a moral system and inculcated a code, which from time immemorial has been observed by the myriads of my subjects. There has been no hankering after heterodox doctrines. Even the European (missionary) officials in my capital are forbidden to hold intercourse with Chinese subjects; they are restricted within the limits of their appointed residences, and may not go about propagating their religion. The distinction between Chinese and barbarian is most strict, and your Ambassador's request that barbarians shall be given full liberty to disseminate religion is utterly unreasonable.

"It may be, O King, that the above proposals have been wantonly made by your Ambassador on his shown responsibility, peradventure you yourself are ignorant of our dynastic regulations and had no intention of transgressing them when you expressed these wild ideas and hopes. I have ever shown the greatest condescension to the tribute missions of all States which sincerely yearn after the blessings of civilization, so as to manifest my kindly indulgence. I have even gone out of my way to grant any requests which were in any way consistent with Chinese usage. Above, all, upon you, who live in a remote and inaccessible region, far across the spaces of ocean, but who have shown your submissive loyalty by sending this tribute mission, I have heaped benefits far in excess of those accorded to other nations. But the demands presented by your Embassy are not only a contravention of dynastic tradition, but would be utterly unproductive of good result to yourself, besides being quite impracticable. I have accordingly stated the facts to you in detail, and it is your bounden duty reverently to appreciate my feelings and to obey these instructions henceforward for all time, so that you may enjoy the blessings of perpetual peace. If, after the receipt of this explicit decree, you lightly give ear to the representations of your subordinates and allow your barbarian merchants to proceed to Chêkiang and Tientsin, with the object of landing and trading there, the ordinances of my Celestial Empire are strict in the extreme, and the local officials, both civil and military, are bound reverently to obey the law of the land. Should your vessels touch the shore, your merchants will assuredly never be permitted to land or to reside there, but will be subject to instant expulsion. In that event your barbarian merchants will have had a long journey for nothing. Do not say that you were not warned in due time! Tremblingly obey and show no negligence! A special mandate!

36

The Morality of the Opium Trade

Two differing perspectives regarding the morality of trading opium are presented in these selections. The first reading is the personal experience of a American merchant with forty years of experience in China, and the second selection is from another merchant in Canton, writing to a British magazine in 1837.

Discussion Questions

1. What is your opinion of the first writer's suggestion that smoking opium and drinking wine are the same? How does the second writer respond to this comparison?

2. What is the first merchant's conclusion as to the ethics of opium smoking? What underlying motives might influence his attitude?What arguments does the second merchant use to refute the views of the first merchant, and others whom you've read?

3. "That which, sold in chests, is commerce, and to be applauded, becomes vulgar and mean when doled out in small lots. Admirable logic!" What is the second merchant's point in this statement, and do you find merit in his argument?

4. Are the views regarding the morality of using and trading opium in the 19th century similar to present attitudes and arguments? Is is appropriate to use the standards of the present to evaluate past actions, such as the morality of the opium traders?

The Opium Question from the Moral Point of View

An American Merchant in Canton

While the opium trade was going on, discussions often occurred as to the morality of it, as well as to the effect of smoking on the Chinese. None of the Hong merchants ever had anything to do with it, and several of the foreign houses refrained from dealing in it on conscientious grounds. As to its influence on the inhabitants of the city and suburbs at large, they were a healthy, active, hard-working, and industrious people, withal cheerful and frugal. They were intelligent in business, skillful in manufactures and handicrafts. These traits are inconsistent with habitual smoking, while the costliness of the prepared drug was such as to render a dilution of it (to bring it within the means of the masses) utterly harmless. Amongst the wealthier classes, no doubt it was more or less common, this we knew; but I myself, and I think I may safely say the entire foreign community, rarely, if ever, saw any one physically or mentally injured by it. No evidences of a general abuse, rarely of the use of the pipe, were apparent. I remember one man having been brought to a missionary hospital to be treated for excessive smoking of opium, but he was looked upon as a Lion and much was made of him. In fact, smoking was a habit, as the use of wine was with us, in moderation. As compared with the use of spirituous liquors in the United States and in England, and the evil consequences of it, that of opium was infinitesimal. This is my personal experience during a residence at Canton, Macao, and Hong Kong of forty years.

From W. C. Hunter, *The "Fan Kwae" at Canton Before Treaty Days: 1825–1844*, Shanghai, 1911, pp. 79–80; and "A British Merchant's Answer," from *The Chinese Repository*, Vol. V, pp. 407–412.

A British Merchant's Answer

Were the traffickers in this poison,—for such no one in possession of his senses can deny it to be, to state that they deal in it merely as a matter of gain; and that, with them, this determination supersedes every consideration of right or wrong, then their premises could be at once seen, and opposition or reasoning would be vain, since all conviction would be fruitless; but when, as now, the practice, evil in itself, and necessarily felt to be so, is upheld by anxious sophistication, it is but right that it be exposed. . . . Were not great capital, skill, and enterprise embarked in this trade, it would never have arrived at its present magnitude. . . . Constantly, avowedly, notoriously, in the practice of a trade, directly opposed to the laws of the empire; not less opposed to morality and propriety; the purveyors of a most powerful incentive to vice; a fierce moral destroying agent—on what has the opium merchant to plume himself, beyond his brother smuggler and law breaker, the contraband gin-importer into Great Britain? The one risks his life—the other, shielding himself behind the corruption of the local officers, or the weakness of the marine, carries on deeds of unlawfulness, without even the risk or excitement of personal danger; and coolly comments on the injustice of the Chinese government in refusing the practice of international law and reciprocity to countries, whose subjects it knows only as engaged in constant and gross infraction of laws, the breaking of which affects the basis of all good government, the morals of the country. . . .

Reverse the picture. Suppose, by any chance, that Chinese junks were to import into England, as a foreign and fashionable luxury, so harmless a thing as arsenic, or corrosive sublimate—that, after a few years, it became a rage—that thousands—that hundreds of thousands used it—and that its use was, in consequence of its bad effects, prohibited. Suppose that, in opposition to the prohibition, junks were stationed in the St. George's channel, with a constant supply, taking occasional trips to the isle of Wight, and the mouth of the Thames, when the governmental officers were sufficiently attentive to their duty, at the former station, to prevent its introduction there. Suppose the consumption to increase annually, and to arouse the attention of government, and of those sound thinking men who foresaw misery and destruction from the rapid spread of an insidious, unprofitable, and dangerous habit. . . .

The comparison of opium to wine is, I beg to say, mere "fudge," and the attempt at argument, thence deduced, no better than nonsense: but, even did the parallel hold, what would it prove? That because people in the western world poison themselves with wine, it is light and expedient that the Chinese should be poisoned with opium. . . . Such is the opinion entertained of it, *in all countries where it is used*, that he, who has once become a prey to the infatuation, is regarded as lost to society, his family, and himself—he is looked on as a reprobate, a debauchee, an incurable; and experience proves, by the innumerable wrecks which the fatal habit marks on its page, the truth of the observation. I will refer you for proof of this, to all the writers* on Turkey, Persia, and other countries, where the habit prevails. You will find all agree in the remark, above made. Does not our own experience confirm it? Who would have in his house a servant who smokes opium? Is not such a man a marked one, by his own countrymen and foreigners; and is he not looked down on with pity or scorn in consequence? The Chinese, who may be allowed to know somewhat of their own people, denounce the habit, as prejudicial and destructive. When once it is indulged in, renunciation is all but impossible; and the appetite, "growing by what it feeds on," increases till premature decay and death close the scene of dissipation and vice. This picture is by no means so agreeable a one to contemplate, as the *fancy* one of using it—being merely "a rational and sociable article of luxury and hospitality; but, what it wants in pleasing imagery, it makes up in truth. Ask any Chinese (who does not use this rational and sociable thing), what it is, and hear what he will tell you. . . .

. . . The saving clause in the opium-smuggling profession is that it is, not *a vulgar* one. It is a wholesale trade. Sales are made in thousands of dollars' worth. The amount is gentlemanly. Single balls would be low. Sales by retail would be indefensible. The seller of a pipe or two, the poor pander to a depraved appetite, should be pursued by justice—for none of these can be gentlemen. That which, sold in chests, is commerce, and to be applauded, becomes vulgar and mean when doled out in small lots. Admirable logic! with which one may hug one's self, satisfied that it is nothing more than "supplying an important branch of the Indian revenue safely and peaceably." . . . The trade may be a profitable one—it may be of importance to the Indian government, and to individuals—but to attempt a defense on the ground of its not having a dangerous and pernicious influence on health and morals, is to say what cannot be borne out, by fact or argument; and what all, who reason on the subject, cannot but feel to be an impotent attempt to defend what is, in itself, manifestly indefensible.

---

* Hope, Chardin, Fraser, Madden, Raffles, and a host of others.

37

Lord Palmerston

This brief selection contains a suggested way to ease the growing tensions over the opium trade. Lord Palmerston, the British Foreign Secretary is writing to the British Envoy in China.

Discussion Questions

1. Do you think Palmerston's suggestion would have removed the tensions between the English and the Chinese? Would the Chinese have accepted it?

2. Do you agree with Palmerston's statement that it was impossible for the English to help the Chinese prevent the importation of opium? What do you think is his underlying message?

3. How did Palmerston view the role and the power of the Chinese government?

May, 1841

Experience has shown that it is entirely beyond the power of the Chinese Government to prevent the introduction of opium into China; and many reasons render it impossible that the British Government can give the Chinese Government any effectual aid toward the accomplishment of that purpose. But while the opium trade is forbidden by law it must inevitably be carried on by fraud and violence; and hence must arise frequent conflicts and collisions between the Chinese preventive service and the parties who are engaged in carrying on the opium trade. These parties are generally British subjects, and it is impossible to suppose that this private war can be carried on between British opium smugglers and the Chinese authorities, without events happening which must tend to put in jeopardy the good understanding between the Chinese and British Governments.

H. M. Government makes no demand in this matter; for they have no right to do so. The Chinese Government is fully entitled to prohibit the importation of opium, if it pleases; and British subjects who engage in a contraband trade must take the consequences of doing so. But it is desirable that you should avail yourself of every favorable opportunity to strongly impress upon the Chinese Plenipotentiary, and through him upon the Chinese Government how much it would be for the interest of the Chinese Government itself to alter the law of China on this matter, and to legalize, by a regular duty, a trade which they cannot prevent.

From Lord Palmerston's Instructions to Sir Henry Pottinger respecting Opium, May, 1841, from S. Couling, *Encyclopedia Sinica*, London, 1917, p. 406.

38

Commissioner Lin's Letter

Lin Zexu, appointed to be the customs inspector at Canton shortly before the outbreak of the Opium War, addressed this letter to Queen Victoria as part of his campaign to eradicate opium from Chinese society. As the governor-general of the two central provinces of Hupei and Hunan, he had earlier distinguished himself by dealing with the opium menace through a policy of confiscating smoking equipment and the drug itself, as well as helping addicts overcome their addiction. He had never dealt with foreigners, however, and this is perhaps apparent in his entreaties to Queen Victoria, as well as in his actions in Canton. His confiscation of Westerners' opium and his blockading of Western enclaves would increase Chinese-British tensions that eventually led to war.

Discussion Questions

1. What is Commissioner Lin's view of the Westerners? Of Chinese?

2. What arguments does he make regarding the reasons that the English should stop the opium trade immediately? Do you find his arguments convincing?

3. How do Lin's views compare with those of the Emperor Qianlong in his letter to George III? Can you detect any differences in attitude or values in the two letters?

4. Besides stopping the trade of opium, what other changes in the Chinese-Western relationship do you think Lin would have welcomed?

A communication: magnificently our great emperor smoothes and pacifies China and the foreign countries, regarding all with the same kindness. If there is profit, then he shares it with the peoples of the world; if there is harm, then he removes it on behalf of the world. This is because he takes the mind of Heaven and earth as his mind.

The kings of your honorable country by a tradition handed down from generation to generation have always been noted for their politeness and submissiveness. We have read your successive tributary memorials saying: "In general our countrymen who go to trade in China have always received His Majesty the Emperor's gracious treatment and equal justice," and so on. Privately we are delighted with the way in which the honorable rulers of your country deeply understand the grand principles and are grateful for the Celestial grace. For this reason the Celestial Court in soothing those from afar has redoubled its polite and kind treatment. The profit from trade has been enjoyed by them continuously for two hundred years. This is the source from which your country has become known for its wealth.

But after a long period of commercial intercourse, there appear among the crowd of barbarians both good persons and bad, unevenly. Consequently there are those who smuggle opium to seduce the Chinese people and so cause the spread of the poison to all provinces. Such persons who only care to profit themselves, and disregard their harm to others, are not tolerated by the laws of Heaven and are unanimously hated by human beings. His Majesty the Emperor, upon hearing of this, is in a towering rage. He has especially sent me, his commissioner, to come to Kwangtung, and together with the governor-general and governor jointly to investigate and settle this matter. . . .

We find that your country is sixty or seventy thousand *li* from China. Yet there are barbarian ships that strive to come here for trade for the purpose of making a great profit. The wealth of China is used to profit the barbarians. That is to say, the great profit made by barbarians is all taken from the rightful share of China. By what right do they then in return use the poisonous drug to injure the Chinese people? Even though the barbarians may not necessarily intend to do us harm, yet in coveting profit to an extreme, they have no regard for injuring others. Let us ask, where is your conscience? I have heard that the smoking of opium is very strictly forbidden by your country; that is because the harm caused by opium is clearly understood. Since it is not permitted to do harm to your own country, then even less should you let it be passed on to the harm of other countries—how much less to China! Of all that China exports to foreign countries, there is not a single thing which is not beneficial to people; they are of benefit when eaten, or of benefit when used, or of benefit when resold: all are beneficial. Is there a single article from China which has done any harm to foreign countries? Take tea and rhubarb, for example; the foreign countries cannot get along for a single day without them.

From *International Relations of the Chinese Empire* (Shanghai, 1910), Volume I, pp. 138–144.

If China cuts off these benefits with no sympathy for those who are to suffer, then what can the barbarians rely upon to keep themselves alive? Moreover the woolens, camlets, and longells [i.e., textiles] of foreign countries cannot be woven unless they obtain Chinese silk. If China, again, cuts off this beneficial export, what profit can the barbarians expect to make? As for other foodstuffs, beginning with candy, ginger, cinnamon, and so forth, and articles for use, beginning with silk, satin, chinaware, and so on, all the things that must be had by foreign countries are innumerable. On the other hand, articles coming from the outside to China can only be used as toys. We can take them or get along without them. Since they are not needed by China, what difficulty would there be if we closed the frontier and stopped the trade? Nevertheless our Celestial Court lets tea, silk, and other goods be shipped without limit and circulated everywhere without begrudging it in the slightest. This is for no other reason but to share the benefit with the people of the whole world.

The goods from China carried away by your country not only supply your own consumption and use, but also can be divided up and sold to other countries, producing a triple profit. Even if you do not sell opium, you still have this threefold profit. How can you bear to go further, selling products injurious to others in order to fulfill your insatiable desire? . . .

We have further learned that in London, the capital of your honorable rule, and in Scotland (Ssu-ko-lan), Ireland (Ai-lun), and other places, originally no opium has been produced. Only in several places of India under your control such as Bengal, Madras, Bombay, Patna, Benares, and Malwa has opium been planted from hill to hill, and ponds have been opened for its manufacture. For months and years work is continued in order to accumulate the poison. The obnoxious odor ascends, irritating Heaven and frightening the spirits. Indeed you, O King, can eradicate the opium plant in these places, hoe over the fields entirely, and sow in its stead the five grains [i.e., millet, barley, wheat, etc.]. Anyone who dares again attempt to plant and manufacture opium should be severely punished. This will really be a great, benevolent government policy that will increase the common weal and get rid of evil. For this, Heaven must support you and the spirits must bring you good fortune, prolonging your old age and extending your descendants. All will depend on this act. . . .

Now we have set up regulations governing the Chinese people. He who sells opium shall receive the death penalty and he who smokes it also the death penalty. Now consider this: if the barbarians do not bring opium, then how can the Chinese people resell it, and how can they smoke it? The fact is that the wicked barbarians beguile the Chinese people into a death trap. How then can we grant life only to these barbarians? He who takes the life of even one person still has to atone for it with his own life; yet is the harm done by opium limited to the taking of one life only? Therefore in the new regulations, in regard to those barbarians who bring opium to China, the penalty is fixed at decapitation or strangulation. This is what is called getting rid of a harmful thing on behalf of mankind.

Moreover we have found that in the middle of the second month of this year [April 9] Consul [Superintendent] Elliot of your nation, because the opium prohibition law was very stern and severe, petitioned for an extension of the time limit. He requested a limit of five months for India and its adjacent harbors and related territories, and ten months for England proper, after which they would act in conformity with the new regulations. Now we, the commissioner and others, have memorialized and have received the extraordinary Celestial grace of His Majesty the Emperor, who has redoubled his consideration and compassion. All those who within the period of the coming one year (from England) or six months (from India) bring opium to China by mistake, but who voluntarily confess and completely surrender their opium, shall be exempt from their punishment. After this limit of time, if there are still those who bring opium to China then they will plainly have committed a willful violation and shall at once be executed according to law, with absolutely no clemency or pardon. This may be called the height of kindness and the perfection of justice.

Our Celestial Dynasty rules over and supervises the myriad states, and surely possesses unfathomable spiritual dignity. Yet the Emperor cannot bear to execute people without having first tried to reform them by instruction. Therefore he especially promulgates these fixed regulations. The barbarian merchants of your country, if they wish to do business for a prolonged period, are required to obey our statutes respectfully and to cut off permanently the source of opium. They must by no means try to test the effectiveness of the law with their lives. May you, O King, check your wicked and sift out your vicious people before they come to China, in order to guarantee the peace of your nation, to show further the sincerity of your politeness and submissiveness, and to let the two countries enjoy together the blessings of peace. How fortunate, how fortunate indeed! After receiving this dispatch will you immediately give us a prompt reply regarding the details and circumstances of your cutting off the opium traffic. Be sure not to put this off. The above is what has to be communicated. [Vermilion endorsement:] This is appropriately worded and quite comprehensive (*Te-t'i chou-tao*).

39

The English and the Opium Trade

This selection, written by a contemporary Chinese scholar, is an historical account of the issues, events and personalities involved in the opium trade, one of the contentious issues that would eventually lead to the Opium War (1839–1842) and China's first defeat. In the words of one western historian, these events for the West constituted "imperialism begun in a pipe dream."

Discussion Questions

1. How was the opium trade conducted, and how did the trade change between the reign of Qianlong and the beginning of the war in 1839? What were the reasons for these changes?
2. What did the Chinese offer as solutions to the problems caused by the opium trade? Do you see similarities in the Chinese recommendations, and those of Americans today? Were any of the Chinese proposals successful, and if not, why not?
3. What response did the Westerners make to the attempts by the Chinese government to eradicate opium? What do you think of the Western position, and is it in any way similar to the views of those countries involved in the present drug trade? What underlying attitudes, even principles, motivated the Western response?
4. The writer calls the Chinese view of opium "hypocritical." Why, and would you agree? Is this view similar to our contemporary attitude towards drugs?
5. Do you think Commissioner Lin's policies were the only ones available to the Chinese at the time? Was Lin a hero or a fool? Did Captain Elliot, who controlled the British trade in China, handle his role effectively?

Before the eighteenth century England produced no major product marketable in China, and for the most part her ships carried silver rather than goods to China. Economists at that time, whether Chinese or foreign, appreciated the fact that a steady drain of gold and silver was detrimental to a nation's economy, and each nation sought to increase exports, thereby increasing the inflow of gold and silver. After many years in the China trade the British discovered that opium was an extremely lucrative item; thus the British East India Company encouraged the cultivation of opium in India while controlling its transport to China. During the first few years of the Ch'ien-lung Emperor's reign (1736–1795) the Chinese imported only about four hundred chests annually (each chest was about a hundred *chin*; a *chin* is about a kilo). The Ch'ien-lung Emperor had forbidden Chinese merchants to sell opium, but his efforts came to nought. By the time of the Chia-ch'ing Emperor (1796–1820) the import of opium had increased to almost four thousand chests a year. Finally, the Chia-ch'ing Emperor prohibited further imports, but because of corruption among the official class, the enforcement of inspection and prohibition proved to be extremely difficult. The opium trade continued to expand.

The Tao-kuang Emperor was more concerned than all his predecessors over the opium problem. He proved the most determined to suppress its use, and upon ascending the throne, he issued ordinances strictly prohibiting opium smoking. But opium imports increased faster than ever before. During the first year of the Tao-kuang Emperor's reign (1821) the amount of opium coming into China was still quite low, only five thousand chests, but by 1850 it had jumped to over thirty thousand chests (worth about eighteen million Chinese *yuan*). The result was that Chinese silver was rapidly drained away in return for opium which was of no benefit to her whatsoever. The whole country regarded this as a calamity, but officials in Kwangtung felt that the prohibition on opium was utterly impractical in view of the fact that the opium trade was in the interest of those who gave the orders to suppress it. This group suggested instead that the tax on foreign opium be increased, and that local production in China be stepped up simultaneously to compete with the foreign opium trade, thus rendering it no longer profitable for foreign merchants to bring opium from India and thereby halting importation.

By the fourteenth year of the Tao-kuang Emperor's reign (1834) the advocates of this policy were in ascendancy, but no one except Hsu Nai-chi dared publicly speak in its favor. In the eighteenth year of the Tao-kuang Emperor's reign (1838) Huang Chueh-tzu memorialized the Emperor, clamoring angrily for prohibition and advocating summarily stamping out all opium smoking. He claimed that if no one smoked opium, no one would buy opium, and he suggested that those who smoked opium might be cured by capital punishment.

From *Imperial China* by Franz Schurmann and Orville Schell, copyright 1967 by Franz Schurmann and Orville Schell. Used by permission of Random House, Inc.

After Huang Chueh-tzu's memorial had reached the Emperor, the Emperor asked that each provincial governor present his view on the subject. Although no one came forward and directly opposed Huang Chueh-tzu, they felt that his policy was obviously too extreme, maintaining that opium smokers harmed only themselves while the merchants who dealt in opium harmed many. Were not the merchants' crimes much graver than the addicts? They concluded that since Canton was the main port of entry and sale of opium, outlawing its use should begin there.

Lin Tse-hsu, Viceroy for Hunan and Hupei, agreed with Huang Chueh-tzu's proposal and advised that all measures be taken to enforce them. The Tao-kuang Emperor decided that the prohibition of the sale and use of opium ought to be enforced with greater severity; thus he sent Lin Tse-hsu to Canton as his High Commissioner to look into the problem. Lin, a Fukienese and one of the most renowned and capable officials in political circles of his time, and greatly respected by the scholar-official class, was a tremendously self-confident and arrogant man. He had no real experience handling "barbarians," but he recklessly announced that, "I am intimately acquainted with the wily ways of the barbarian from my sojourn in Fukien."

Actually, people at that time were rather hypocritical about the whole opium problem. They admitted in private correspondence to the difficulties of suppressing opium, but in their official memorials they toed the line with ceremonious ostentation. This sort of lack of candor was a great problem among the scholar-official class.

In reality, opium suppression was an extremely complicated and difficult problem, and it would have been no easier without foreign interference. But how much more difficult it was during the Tao-kuang reign, when the English were totally unwilling to allow us to carry out the policy of suppression. Opium was not only commercially very profitable then, it also constituted the greater part of the revenues earned by the Indian government, and in view of this, the English were uneasy about our policy of trying to close the country to free trade. They were eager to settle matters once and for all, and had we given them the slightest pretext over the opium problem, they would not have hesitated to deal with us by force of arms.

We call the war that followed the Opium War; the English call it the Trade War. Both sides had their own reasons. In regard to the opium problem—we tried to get rid of the curse altogether, while the English hoped to maintain the situation as it was; we were the ones who wished to alter the status quo. In regard to the trade problem—the English sought new opportunities and freedom, and it was we who wished to maintain the status quo. Under these circumstances, war was unavoidable.

Clash Between East and West

On March 10 of the nineteenth year of the Tao-kuang Emperor's reign (1839), Lin Tse-hsu arrived at Canton. He spent a week pondering the situation and settling himself before he made his first move. He then issued a proclamation to all foreigners, saying that it was not right to harm others for the sake of one's own profit: "How dare you bring your country's vile opium into China, cheating and harming our people?"

Lin made two demands of the foreigners: first, he asked that they take all the unsold opium and "hand it all over to Chinese officials"; second, he asked that the foreigners pledge not to import any more opium into China. If they continued, said Lin, "the opium will be confiscated and those involved will be decapitated." Unfortunately, the foreigners did not understand that Lin meant business, thinking that he was just another ordinary official who, as a matter of course, had issued a pious proclamation as a formality at the beginning of his term of office. But after all, they thought, would not Lin be willing to sell out like all the other officials after they got around to settling the price of the squeeze and, would not trade then be able to continue as usual? They did not realize that Lin was not this sort of man. Lin said, "If the opium trade does not cease, I, the Imperial High Commissioner, will not leave my post. I will persevere in this matter until the end."

By the end of March the foreigners were still unwilling to hand over their opium stocks. Lin Tse-hsu then issued an order forbidding any movement to and from Canton, and sent troops to encircle the thirteen foreign factories (foreign trading establishments). He ordered all Chinese to leave the factories and he later forbade anyone at all from entering or leaving. In short, Lin turned the thirteen factories into foreign prisons and prohibited the sale of foodstuffs to the inmates.

At that time there were roughly three hundred and fifty foreigners inside the thirteen factories, among whom was the English Superintendent of Trade, Captain Charles Elliot. Naturally, those inside did suffer a certain amount of privation—they had to do chores, like boil their own water, wash their own dishes, and do their own housework—but there was enough food, since the foreigners had previously stored up a large quantity and were also being clandestinely supplied.

Captain Elliot had originally hoped to compromise, but Lin stood firmly to his two demands. At that time the English, unfortunately, happened to have only two small gunboats in Chinese waters, and the troops on board had no chance of landing at Canton. Captain Elliot had no means by which to protest, and to yield was his only alternative. But the way in which he chose to yield is

worth our attention: instead of simply ordering the English merchants to hand over their opium to Lin, he ordered them to hand the opium over to him; in his capacity as Superintendent of Trade, he gave each merchant a receipt, and by one quick maneuver all British opium became the property of the British crown.

Captain Elliot then handed over 20,280 chests of opium to the Chinese. This was a great victory for Lin, who, with one toss of the net, had trapped a million *chin* of opium, The Tao-kuang Emperor was indeed pleased, and he commended Lin, saying, "Your great loyalty to the throne and your unbounded love of your country are unequaled and unmatched by any within or without the Empire."

But still the foreigners did not quite believe that Lin was genuinely determined to suppress the opium trade, and they thought that he must be in some way profiting. They soon learned otherwise.

At Hu-men, on the Pearl River Delta, Lin ordered two huge pools to be dug in the sandy banks. He later wrote:

First I had a series of trenches dug and then I dug ditches to connect them. After this was completed, I had water diverted into the trenches through the ditches. Then I had salt sprinkled on the pools. Finally, I had the unprocessed opium thrown into the pools and added lime to boil the opium. The opium was thereby turned into ashes and completely destroyed. The nauseating odor was more than we could bear. When the tide finally receded we opened the trenches and let the residue flow away. We then used brushes to clean the bottom of the pools so that nothing remained. The process took twenty-three days. Every bit of opium was completely destroyed. Each day civilian and military officials were there to supervise. Even the foreigners came to watch and to record the events in detail. They lavishly praised the Commissioner's integrity.

Meanwhile Captain Elliot had made a thorough report to London and was quietly awaiting further orders. After his apparent success, Lin was greatly relieved. The Emperor was so pleased that he offered Lin a new position—Viceroy to Kwangtung and Kwangsi—but Lin humbly turned down the offer, claiming that "although all the opium in the factories had been completely destroyed, there is still the possibility that more may be smuggled in." Lin wanted to do the job thoroughly, and thus subsequently demanded that all foreign merchants sign a bond committing themselves thenceforth to observe the Chinese regulations prohibiting opium trade. Captain Elliot refused to sign thereby stirring up the simmering conflict once again. But by this time Lin was swelled with new confidence, and claimed that the English power was nowhere near as menacing as in fact it was. In addition, he believed that the English were utterly dependent on the Chinese since they needed Chinese *tea* and *rhubarb!* He thought that if he simply cut off their supply of tea and rhubarb he could bring about their ruination.

The forts at Hu-men were repaired and overhauled. Lin also took a huge iron chain and stretched it across the entrance of Hu-men harbor as a blockade.

That winter Chinese junks clashed on numerous occasions with British ships in the waters around Canton. Each time Lin memorialized the Emperor claiming smashing victories, putting the whole country in a very optimistic mood.

When the British government finally received Elliot's letter, they dispatched Admiral George Elliot as plenipotentiary in charge of an expeditionary force to China.

40

A Letter to Parliament

While many Chinese officials were sending memorials to their emperor over the question of the opium trade, their counterparts in England were also busy. The following letter, composed by one of the editors of this book, is suggested as typical of the kinds of appeals English businessmen made because of their grievances with the way trade was being conducted in China. As you read it, compare the issues considered important here with those highlighted by the Chinese memorials to the emperor.

Discussion Questions

1. What were the key issues in the opium trade, from the perspectives of a member of Parliament and one participating in the trade? Do you think his views were generally representative of the English position?

2. What underlying values and assumptions are presented in the letter? Do you think Cooke has a particular agenda?

3. How do the issues as defined by this English writer compare with those put forth by the Chinese memorialists? What aspects of each arguments over the opium trade would you support?

Mr. Harold Blackstone, Esq.
House of Commons
City of Westminster, England

City of Bristol
January 16, 1832

Dear Sir;

As the Member of Parliament representing our district, I think it is important that I bring to your attention a number of facts relative to our trade with China.

For many years, Cooke and Sons, Ltd., has had a very profitable trade at Canton. We usually bought raw cotton in India and sold it to the Hong merchants at Canton. In exchange we bought tea, silk and porcelain for sale in England and Holland where they were very popular among the carriage trade. As a supporter of your call for free trade, I must point out that it does not exist in China and that is working to the detriment of our company's financial structure. Our grievances about the Canton trade include:

1. The Chinese Hong merchants, appointed by the Imperial Court to control the trade at Canton, are extortionate in their demands for tariffs on our cotton and various excise taxes on the goods we buy. Since they have a monopoly on all trade with China, there is no way to lower their prices through increased competition. It is obvious that additional ports need to be opened to overcome this difficulty and to facilitate greater trade by all Western nations.

2. The Hong merchants have regularly borrowed considerable sums from us to purchase Chinese goods for the next year's trade. Unfortunately much of this money is still owed and there is no legal machinery to recover what is due us. Whenever we forward entreaties to Chinese government officials for redress, the Hoppo (the Hong

board leader) refuses to send them to the proper authorities.

3. Our representatives at Canton are subject to severe restrictions—they cannot leave the precincts of the factories and may not even bring their families to Canton with them. Also they are not permitted to live at Canton year round and must retire to Macau from March through October.

4. The Chinese legal system leaves us at a considerable disadvantage. We are treated like ordinary Chinese subjects and since 1820 have no right of appeal. Chinese law permits arbitrary arrest, and even torture, which is not permissible in England. A few of our sailors have been involved in some regrettable incidents with Chinese civilians and we have been coerced into turning suspects over to the Chinese under pain of losing our trading rights. In one case a sailor was forced to confess to killing a Chinese and was executed without our having any representatives at the trial.

5. Since there is no British ambassador at the Imperial Court in Peking, we have no regular process to deal with all the above abuses of His Majesty's subjects. We are often called 'barbarians' and dealers in 'foreign mud' (opium) and are usually treated in a very condescending manner we are unused to in Western countries.

I hope you will report our position to the Prime Minister and the Foreign Minister so that the situation can be improved to our nation's general benefit.

Your Humble Servant,

Robert Cooke

41

Beatable Barbarians

This selection provides another example of Chinese culture-centrism. As the introduction to the readings suggests, the Chinese knew neither themselves nor their opponents, and, as you read, consider the reasons for their lack of knowledge.

Discussion Questions

1. What is this writer's view of the English? Where do you think he gets his information, and what are the biggest mistakes he makes in his assessments of the English?

2. How does this selection compare with others written by Chinese on their view of the Westerners? If you had been the Chinese emperor, how would you have reacted to this memorial?

3. What does this selection reveal about Chinese values compared with Western values?

Beatable Barbarians

The English barbarians are an insignificant and detestable race, trusting entirely to their strong ships and large guns; but the immense distance they have traversed will render the arrival of seasonable supplies impossible, and their soldiers, after a single defeat, being deprived of provisions, will become dispirited and lost. Though it is very true that their guns are destructive, still in the attack of our harbors they will be too elevated, and their aim moreover rendered unsteady by the waves; while we in our forts, with larger pieces, can more steadily return the fire. Notwithstanding the riches of their government, the people are poor, and unable to contribute to the expenses of an army at such a distance. Granted that their vessels are their homes, and that in them they defy wind and weather, still they require a great draft of water; and, since our coasts are beset with shoals, they will certainly, without the aid of native pilots, run ashore, without approaching very closely. Though waterproof, their ships are not fireproof, and we may therefore easily burn them. The crews will not be able to withstand the ravages of our climate, and surely waste away by degrees; and to fight on shore, their soldiers possess not sufficient activity. Without, therefore, despising the enemy, we have no cause to fear them. While guarding the approaches to the interior, and removing to the coast the largest guns, to give their ships a terrific reception, we should at the same time keep vessels filled with brushwood, oil, saltpeter, and sulphur, in readiness to let them drive, under the direction of our marine, with wind and tide against their shipping. When once on fire, we may open our batteries upon them, display the celestial terror, and exterminate them without the loss of a single life.

From "A Censor's Memorial on the English Barbarians," in Sir John Francis Davis, *China During the War and Since the Peace*, 2 vols., London, 1852, pp. 11–13.

42

Treaties of Nanjing and Wang-hea

Key provisions of the treaties ending the Opium War are presented in this selection. The Treaty of Nanjing was the first of four treaties that were signed with China by the Western nations, ending formal hostilities. As if these assaults to China's sovereignty were not enough, two years later, the Treaty of Wang-hea, signed by the United States and China, provided additional humiliation to a China humbled by their loss, and, for that reason, they have been called the "unequal treaties." These treaties also established a pattern in the West's dealing with other nations in Asia and throughout the world, where similar negotiations led to the establishment of a relationship favorable to the West's interests. In addition to the economic and territorial provisions of the treaties, the sections dealing with diplomatic conduct between nations, which contains the concept of "most favored nation," is also important. Article XXI of the Treaty of Wang-hea introduced the right of extraterritoriality, or the right for foreigners to be governed by western judicial standards.

Discussion Questions

1. Based on the reasons that the Opium War was fought, how successful were the victors in achieving their objectives in these treaties? What price did the Chinese have to pay for defeat?
2. Do you think the treaties were fair to China? Given the earlier arguments of Qianlong and Commissioner Lin, with which provisions would the Chinese find most difficult to comply? Which of the provisions was most injurious to China's view of itself? Which was most injurious to the West's view of itself?
3. If you were a member of the Chinese government at this time (1840s), what course of action would you now recommend to your emperor?

Treaty of Nanjing, 1842

Victoria, by the Grace of God, Queen of the United Kingdom of Great Britain and Ireland, Defender of the Faith, etc., etc., etc. To all and Singular to whom these Presents shall come. Greetings! Whereas a Treaty between Us and Our Good Brother the Emperor of China, was concluded and signed, in the English and Chinese Languages, on board Our Ship the *Cornwallis*, at Nanjing, on the Twenty-ninth day of August, in the Year of Our Lord One Thousand Eight Hundred and Forty-two, by the Plenipotentiaries of Us and of Our said Good Brother, duly and respectively authorized for that purpose; which Treaty is hereunto annexed in Original:—

ARTICLE I.

There shall henceforward be Peace and Friendship between Her Majesty the Queen of the United Kingdom of Great Britain and Ireland, and His Majesty the Emperor of China, and between their respective Subjects, who shall enjoy full security and protection for their persons and property within the Dominions of the other.

ARTICLE II.

His Majesty the Emperor of China agrees, that British Subjects, with their families and establishments, shall be allowed to reside, for the purpose of carrying on their Mercantile pursuits, without molestation or restraint at the Cities and Towns of Canton, Amoy, Foochow-fu, Ningpo, and Shanghai. . . .

ARTICLE III.

It being obviously necessary and desirable, that British Subjects should have some Port whereat they may careen and refit their ships, when required, and keep Stores for that purpose, His Majesty the Emperor of China cedes to Her Majesty the Queen of Great Britain, etc., the Island of Hongkong. . . .

ARTICLE IV.

The Emperor of China agrees to pay the sum of Six Millions of Dollars as the value of Opium which was delivered up at Canton in the month of March 1839, as a Ransom for the lives of Her Britannic Majesty's Superintendent and Subjects, who had been imprisoned and threatened with death by the Chinese High Officers.

ARTICLE VI.

The Government of Her Britannic Majesty having been obliged to send out an Expedition to demand and obtain redress for the violent and unjust Proceedings of the Chinese High Authorities towards Her Britannic Majesty's Officers and Subjects, the Emperor of China agrees to pay the sum of Twelve Millions of Dollars on account of the Expenses incurred. . . .

From the Treaty of Nanjing, Vol. I, pp. 351–356, and "The Most-Favored Nation Clause: Article VIII, Treaty of the Bogue, p. 393, in *China: Treaties, Conventions, Etc., Between China and Foreign States*, published at the Statistical Department of the Inspectorate General of Customs, 2 vols., 1917.

ARTICLE XII.

On the assent of the Emperor of China to this Treaty being received and the discharge of the first instalment of money, Her Britannic Majesty's Forces will retire from Nanjing and the Grand Canal, and will no longer molest or stop the Trade of China. The Military Post at Chinhai will also be withdrawn, but the Islands of Koolangsoo and that of Chusan will continue to be held by Her Majesty's Forces until the money payments, and the arrangements for opening the Ports to British Merchants be completed.

Treaty of Wang-Hea, 1844

ARTICLE I.

There shall be a perfect, permanent, and universal peace and a sincere and cordial amity between the United States of America on the one part, and the Ta-Tsing Empire on the other part, and between their people respectively, without exception of persons or places.

ARTICLE II.

Citizens of the United States resorting to China for the purpose of commerce will pay duties of import and export prescribed by the Tariff which is fixed by and made a part of this Treaty. They shall in no case be subject to other or higher duties than are or shall be required of the people of any other nation whatever. . . . If the Chinese Government desire to modify in any respect the said Tariff, such modifications shall be made only in consultation with Consuls or other functionaries thereto duly authorised in behalf of the United States, and with consent thereof. And if additional advantages or privileges of whatever description be conceded hereafter by China to any other nation, the United States and the citizens thereof shall be entitled thereupon to a complete, equal, and impartial participation in the same.

ARTICLE III.

The citizens of the United States are permitted to frequent the five ports of Quangchow, Amoy, Fuchow, Ningpo, and Shanghai, and to reside with their families and trade there, and to proceed at pleasure with their vessels and merchandise to or from any Foreign port and either of the said five ports, and from either of said five ports to any other of them; but the said vessels shall not unlawfully enter the other ports of China, nor carry on a clandestine and fraudulent trade along the coasts thereof; and any vessel belonging to a citizen of the United States which violates this provision shall, with her cargo, be subject to confiscation to the Chinese Government.

ARTICLE XIX.

All citizens of the United States in China peaceably attending to their affairs, being placed on a common footing of amity and goodwill with subjects of China, shall receive and enjoy, for themselves and everything appertaining to them, the special protection of the local authorities of Government, who shall defend them from all insult or injury of any sort on the part of the Chinese.

If their dwellings or their property be threatened or attacked by mobs, incendiaries, or other violent or lawless persons, the local officers, on requisition of the Consul, will immediately despatch a military force to disperse the rioters, and will apprehend the guilty individuals and punish them with the utmost rigour of the law.

ARTICLE XXI.

Subjects of China who may be guilty of any criminal act towards citizens of the United States shall be arrested and punished by the Chinese authorities according to the laws of China, and citizens of the United States who may commit any crime in China shall be subject to be tried and punished only by the Consul or other public functionary of the United States thereto authorised according to the laws of the United States; and in order to the prevention of all controversy and disaffection, justice shall be equitably and impartially administered on both sides.

43

China and the West Evaluate Each Other after the Opium War

This selection examines some of the conclusions reached by the Chinese and the Europeans at the end of the Opium War in the nineteenth century.

The Chinese Concluded That:

1. Westerners were now arrogantly, often ignorantly, contemptuous of them. Popular British attitudes are summed up in this verse (from a Punch cartoon, 1858):
    "With their little pig-eyes and the large pigtails,
    And their diet of rats, dogs, slugs and snails,
    All seem to be game in the frying-pan
    Of that nasty feeder John Chinaman.
    Sing lie-tea, my sly John Chinaman,
    No fightee, my coward John Chinaman.
    John Bull has a chance, let him if he can,
    Somewhat open the eyes of John Chinaman."
    (However, after the Opium Wars, scurrilous Chinese posters called the British "dogs, pigs, and beasts.")

2. The Westerners based their feelings of superiority on their advanced technological, industrial and military resources—railways, steamships, modern weaponry. Westerners also felt morally and spiritually superior as enlightened Christians compared to the "heathen Chinee."

3. Their lucky tiger caps and ancient cannons were no defence against Western weapons.

Gunpowder could blow up cities as well as make pretty fireworks. "Learn the techniques of the barbarians in order to control them," counselled some.

4. They themselves disagreed in their reactions to the West. Wrote one progressive, Feng, member of China's "self-strengthening movement," "Eventually we must consider manufacturing and industrializing and using weapons ourselves. . . . Only thus will we be able to pacify the Empire: only thus can we play a leading role on the globe." Asked the Court Tutor, "Why is it necessary to learn from barbarians? Moreover they are our enemies. . . . How can we forget this enmity and humiliation one single day?"

5. Some Westerners wanted Chinamen's souls and minds rather than their land and money, and this dangerous missionary activity led to social disruption. This was because most Chinese were disinterested in and hostile to Christian doctrine and some missionaries were contemptuous of the Chinese. Wrote one: "China consists of 360 millions of human beings huddled together under the sway of one despotic monarch, influenced by

From Pat Barr, *Foreign Devils: Westerners in the Far East*, copyright © 1970 by Penguin Books Ltd., Harmondsworth, England, pp. 84–85. Reprinted with permission.

the same delusive philosophy and bowing down to the same absurd superstitions."

6. Foreign ways of eating and dressing were most uncomfortable and hideous. A Chinaman visiting Australia wrote to his family back home: "These remarkable people [Australians] like clothes that imprison them. Their thick coats fit tightly around their arms and body, narrow trousers restrict the movement of their knees, tough leather pinches their feet and hats unyielding in shape grip their heads. Their movements nevertheless are quick and abrupt; what they do without the restraint of their garments I dare not imagine; perhaps their cramping clothes are a necessary check to their fury, instituted by their sages." (But other Western products he envied, such as messages "borne on mysterious airwaves" and "a trumpet" that will "preserve a man's voice for generations.")

The Westerners Concluded That:

1. The easiest, quickest way to "open" the nations of the Far East to trade was by force of arms and if diplomatic demands were backed by gunboats, the Orientals gave in. Some Westerners didn't like the morality of this. They were told it was for the Orientals' own good that the superior benefits of Western civilization should be taken to them.

2. The Orientals lacked a number of so-called indispensables to modern living. Wrote one merchant of China in 1860: "There are no carriages, horses nor fine harnesses; no pictures worth more than a few shillings; no well-laid breakfast or dinner tables; no newspapers, postmen, railways, tramways, carpets, table-cloths, writing desks, gas lamps, matches or even respectable candles; no house-games, cigars, wine, beer, clean linen, washstands; or, in short, any article of luxury." (But there was a much greater gulf between the living standards of East and West in the nineteenth century than there had

been in the sixteenth and seventeenth centuries.)

3. In spite of all they "lacked," many Orientals did not clamor for Western things. They did not like them, could not afford them and considered buying and selling a very lowly occupation.

4. In China, particularly, the forces of reaction were very strong. The Chinese tore up the first rail-lines that were laid because they "disturbed the spirits of the earth"; they cut down telegraph wires that "disturbed the spirits of the air." (The Chinese understood that "new" did not necessarily equal "good.")

5. The Oriental countries possessed their own rich literatures, sophisticated systems of moral philosophy and social organization. (But though most Westerners knew this much, few really appreciated Oriental culture. Most Westerners lived in the treaty ports where they created little bits of Europe round themselves and kept the Orient out. Those Orientals who wanted to understand foreign ways flocked to these ports that acted as bridgeheads and focal points of Western penetration.)

6. Some Oriental customs were definitely backward-looking and ruthless—for instance the subjugation of women and the binding of women's feet in China so that they tottered like cripples. (But the Chinese considered that the tight-corseting of the Victorian woman's waist and hips was just as barbarous.) Westerners were also shocked at the habit of killing unwanted female babies; they overlooked the lingering distress inflicted on young children in the mines and factories of their homelands.

7. There were even greater differences between the Chinese and Japanese. China was a much more difficult case for Western treatment. Japan was everybody's favorite Asian nation at the end of the nineteenth century. The twentieth century brought grave second thoughts.

44

The Reform Movement in China, 1898—Chang Chih-tung

A critical issue for the Chinese since their defeat in the Opium War in 1842 and the disastrous Taiping Rebellion, finally suppressed in 1864, was how to regain their loss of sovereignty and reestablish the stability they had once enjoyed. While most of those responsible for leading China preferred to continue the Confucian-oriented policies of the past, there were some officials who, in the 1870's, advocated reform in the form of a "self-strengthening" movement. With the slogan, "Learn the superior technology of the barbarian, in order to control him," the T'ung Chih Restoration led to new plans for a modern army and navy, industrialization and changes within the diplomatic corps, but the changes were slow for lack of government support. The "Hundred Days of Reform" would sprout in 1898, after China's shocking defeat in the Sino-Japanese War, with decrees issued by the dozens. The following selection presents a case for change in the form of a memorial written to Emperor Kuang Hse, a nephew of the Empress Dowager Cixi, the real power in China at the time. His essay was translated and published in English as *China's Only Hope*. Though the writer was one of China's leading officials at the time, and his memorial was praised by the emperor himself as a model of classical Chinese scholarship, few of the suggestions were adopted due to the opposition from the Empress, other conservative officials and the coming of the Boxer Rebellion. As you read, consider why, given all of the humiliations that China had suffered, there would not have been a greater impetus for change at this time.

Discussion Questions

1. In one of his statements, the writer suggests, "Know what is important." What was that and do you think the suggestions he made would have saved China further humiliation? What additional proposals would you have made?
2. When he refers to the parable of Confucius, what do you think his purpose and his intended audience were?
3. What aspects of Western values and institutions does the writer admire and how does he suggest China make use of them? What is his opinion of China? Of its values?

In no period of China's history has there arisen an emergency like the present. It is a time of change, and His Imperial Highness, the Emperor of China, has accepted the situation by altering somewhat the system of civil and military examinations and by establishing schools. . . . The Conservatives are evidently off their food from inability to swallow, whilst Liberals are like a flock of sheep who have arrived at a road of many forks and do not know which to follow. The former do not understand what international intercourse means, the latter are ignorant of what is radical in Chinese affairs. The Conservatives fail to see the utility of modern military methods and the benefits of successful change, while the Progressionists, zealous without knowledge, look with contempt upon our widespread doctrines of Confucius. Thus those who cling to the order of things heartily despise those who even propose any innovation, and they in turn cordially detest the Conservatives with all the ardor of their liberal convictions. It thus falls out that those who really wish to learn are in doubt as to which course to pursue, and in the meantime error creeps in, the enemy invades our coast, and, consequently, there is no defence and no peace.

The present condition of things is not due to outside nations, but to China herself. It has ever been true that the number of our able men has been proportioned to the good qualities of the government, and that morals are gauged by the conduct of the schools. In view of many facts, and with the hope of relieving our country from her present embarrassments, We, the Viceroy of the Liang Hu, have prepared this work especially for the Chinese

From Chang Chih-tung, *China's Only Hope: An Appeal*, trans. by Samuel I. Woodbridge, New York, 1900, pp. 19–21, 25, 26.

under our jurisdiction, and generally for our countrymen in the other provinces. . . .

The corollaries of these Twenty Chapters may be briefly Comprehended in Five Objects of Knowledge.

1. Know the shame of not being like Japan, Turkey, Siam, and Cuba.
2. Know the fear that we will become India, Annam, Burmah, Korea, Egypt, and Poland.
3. Know that if we do not change our customs we cannot reform our methods, and if we do not reform our methods we cannot utilize the modern implements of war, etc.
4. Know what is important. The study of the old is not urgent; the call for men of attainments in useful knowledge is pressing. Foreign education is of different kinds. Western handicraft is not in demand, but a knowledge of the methods of foreign governments is a consummation devoutly to be wished.
5. Know what is radical. When abroad, do not forget your own native country; when you see strange customs, do not forget your parents; and let not much wisdom and ingenuity make you forgot the holy sages.

It will be seen then that the purport of what we have written accords well with the Doctrine of the Mean. Long ago, when the kingdom of Lu was in a weak condition, Duke Ai (B. C. 550) inquired of Confucius about government. He replied: "To he fond of learning is the next thing to knowledge. To be up and doing comes near to perfection. Know what shame is, and you will not be far from heroism." Finally the sage said: "If these principles can be carried out, although one may be stupid, yet he will become clever; although weak, he will attain to strength." These maxims were spoken in the time of Lu. How much more urgent are they now when China has become great, with her almost limitless territory and her teeming population of four hundred millions!. . . .

Chapter 1. United Hearts

How circumscribed would be the responsibility of one graduate, the altruism of one official, or the duty of a single individual! But if by one determined purpose the heart's of *all* the graduates, the officials, and the men of China were united, our country world rest upon a great rock and we could defy the world to overthrow us. To attain this object it is necessary first that every man should fulfill his duty to his parents and elders. The country would then be at peace. And if every Chinese would but exercise his wisdom and courage the Empire would become strong. . . . .

We would here state that there are now three things necessary to be done in order to save China from revolution. The first is to *maintain the reigning dynasty*; the second is to *conserve the Holy Religion*; and the third is to *protect the Chinese race*. These are inseparably connected; in fact they constitute one. . . .

Under the present circumstances there is nothing for it but to arouse ourselves to the situation. Let us display our loyalty and love and embrace every opportunity to become wealthy and strong; let our first object be the veneration of the Imperial Court which vouchsafes its protection to the Commonwealth, and let those who hold the reins of government consider the general good. . . .

Chapter III. The Three Moral Obligations

The Sovereign is the head of the Subject, the Father is the head of the Son, and the Husband is the head of the Wife. These tenets have been handed down from the sages, and as Heaven does not change, so they never change. They constitute the first of the Five Relations and the mainspring of every act. . . . Know then, that the obligation of subject to sovereign is incompatible with republicanism. . . .

Now, we have examined somewhat into the methods of Western Governments. They have their Lords and Commons, their Senates and Representatives, which hold their prerogatives in State matters. But we have noticed that the Sovereign, or the President, retains the power of dissolving these assemblies; and in case one assembly does not suit him he exercises this power, dismisses the obnoxious body and convenes another. A Constitutional Government with a Sovereign, and a Republic are about the same. In the West the intercourse of Sovereign, Ministers, and People is easy, the rules of deportment meagre, and the needs of the people are communicated to the sovereign with rapid facility; but the bearing or dignity of the Western Prince is not to be compared with that of the Chinese Emperor. Western people, however, love their sovereigns more than the Chinese do theirs, and, although they may leave home and live abroad thousands of miles from their native land they do not disobey their country's laws or defraud their rulers. . . . It is a mistake, then, to suppose that Western countries do not maintain the doctrine of the Relation of Subject to Sovereign. . . .

Chapter IV. The Recognition of Class

The highest degree of culture was reached in the Chow (B. C. 1122–255) Dynasty. Then began the decline about which Confucius grieved. The Dynasties following had no powerful neighbors to strive against, but heaped up large treasures of literary lore at the expense of power. This accumulation produced the hollowness of forms, and this, in turn begat weakness.

Not so all the countries of Europe. These were opened up at a late period in history, fresh and vigorous. Surrounded by strong neighbors, they were always in circum-

stances of desperate competition, stripped for a fight and ever striving to escape destruction. Continual apprehension produced determination, and determination begat strength. Of all countries China alone has for these fifty years proved herself almost irreclaimably stupid and not awake. Many of the officials and people are proud and indolent. They contentedly rest in the belief that the old order of things will suffice for those dangerous times, and in the end become the easy prey of outsiders. . . .

Chapter IX. Cast Out the Poison

The Custom's Returns for the past few years give the value of our imports at 80,000,000 Taels, and the exports at 50,000,000 Taels. The balance of *thirty million Taels* represents what has been consumed in smoking the pernicious opium pipe!. Assuredly it is not foreign intercourse that is ruining China, but his dreadful poison. Oh, the grief and desolation it has wrought to our people! . . . Opium has spread with frightful rapidity and heart-rending results through the provinces. Millions upon millions have been struck down by the plague. To-day it is running like wildfire. In its swift, deadly course it is spreading devastation everywhere, wrecking the minds and eating away the strength of its victims. The ruin of the mind is the most woeful of its many deleterious effects. . . .

Therefore we say, bring learning to the front in order to remedy the opium evil! . . . All the countries of the world recoil with disgust at the idea of smoking this vile, ill-smelling, poisonous stuff. Only our Chinese people love to sleep and eat with the deadly drug, and in the deadly drug we are self-steeped, seeking poverty, imbecility, death, destruction. . . .

45

Japan Evaluates the West

These two selections highlight some of the conclusions reached by the Japanese after their initial encounter with the "barbarians," and then, on the eve of the Meiji Restoration.

The Japanese Concluded That:

1 Some barbarians behaved violently and aggressively like pirates.
2 The barbarians had cultural values and intellectual standards of their own. In some fields, barbarian knowledge was even ahead of theirs. (Few admitted this.)
3 The European barbarians were all Christians, but they believed in different varieties of Christianity. It was easy to make use of these religious differences.
4 There was quite a lot to learn from the barbarians—how to build large ships, how to navigate, make maps and more efficient guns. Also, the barbarians had interesting ideas about science, mathematics and medicine.
5 The barbarians were ill-mannered and very dirty. They seldom washed and generally used their fingers to eat food and they were amazed at the cleanliness of the Japanese.
6 A careful distinction should be made between those foreigners who came to preach and those who traded. Some barbarians (the Dutch for example) were ready to ignore all religious

considerations for the sake of a profitable monopoly of trade.

The Japanese Concluded That:

1 Westerners were now arrogantly, often ignorantly, contemptuous of *them*.
2 Westerners based their feelings of superiority on their advanced technological, industrial and military resources—railways, steamships, modern weaponry. They also felt morally and spiritually superior as enlightened Christians compared to the heathen Japanese.
3 They themselves disagreed in their reactions to the West.
4 Some Westerners sought their souls and minds rather than their land and money, and that this dangerous missionary activity led to social disruption.
5 The most effective way to maintain their national identity in the face of the expanding Western nations was to adopt Western techniques. The sooner they seemed 'civilized' in Western eyes, the sooner they

From Pat Barr, *Foreign Devils: Westerners in the Far East*, copyright © 1970 by Penguin Books Ltd., Harmondsworth, England, p. 44. Reprinted with permission.

could deal with foreigners on equal diplomatic and economic terms.

6   They needed, none the less, to understand the basic political and moral ideas of Western civilization as well as its outward forms. Building railways and steamships was not enough. This idea, explained by Fukuzawa Yukichi, was difficult and was not fully grasped at first.

7   Democratic forms of government brought new problems and violent new divisions in the country. Several forms of over-rapid 'modernization' caused disruption and unhappiness.

8   This very over-enthusiasm sometimes made them laughing stocks in Western eyes.

Foreigners jeered at Japanese men who wore top hats with flowing silk robes, or ate beefsteaks with chopsticks. The Japanese were afraid of ridicule. The government, when ordering all coolies to remain fully clothed even when labouring hard, warned, '*You must not be laughed at by foreigners.*'

9   As Fukuzawa pointed out, Westerners didn't always live up to their Christian morals. Foreign traders often cheated (so did Japanese); many 'Christian gentleman' had affairs with Japanese women.

10   In some fields—engineering, medicine, military tactics, shipbuilding—'West Was Best.' (The Japanese were more honest about this than most Chinese.)

46

Japan: The Charter Oath of the Five Articles

The Charter Oath of 1868 was a statement of general principles meant to appeal to the broadest possible support for the Meiji Restoration. Its vagueness left room for adjustment in a rapidly changing situation and attempted to alienate as few people and groups as possible.

Discussion Questions

1. Why do you think the Oath called for the wide establishment of deliberative assemblies?
2. What elements in the Oath advocate change and what elements might appeal to more conservative interests in Japanese society?

By this oath we set up as our aim the establishment of the national weal on a broad basis and the framing of a constitution and laws.

1. Deliberative assemblies shall be widely established and all matters decided by public discussion.
2. All classes, high and low, shall unite in vigorously carrying out the administration of affairs of state.
3. The common people, no less than the civil and military officials, shall each be allowed to pursue his own calling so that there may be no discontent.
4. Evil customs of the past shall be broken off and everything based upon the just laws of Nature.
5. Knowledge shall be sought throughout the world so as to strengthen the foundations of imperial rule.

From *Sources of Japanese Tradition* by William Theodore de Bary. Copyright © 1980 by Columbia University Press. Reprinted with permission of the publisher.

47

Japan: Overenthusiasm
for Westernization

Many Japanese became enthusiastic about the Westernization of their country by the 1880's, often acting as if they wished to have no part of their past. Copying the dress, manners and social relations of Westerners became very popular in some quarters. In the following case, one Robun Kanagaki uses eating beef (which had been forbidden by Buddhist law) as an occasion to praise many other aspects of Western culture.

Discussion Questions

1. What justification does Kanagaki give for violating traditional Japanese Buddhist customs?

2. What does he admire about the West and what does he think is the secret of their progress?

A man about thirty-five, rather swarthy it is true, but of clear complexion, thanks apparently to the daily use of soap, which purges all impurities. His hair, not having been cut for some hundred days, is long and flowing, and looks as if it is in the process of being let out altogether, in the foreign style. Naturally enough, he uses that scent called Eau de Cologne to give a sheen to his hair. He wears a padded silken kimono beneath which a calico undergarment is visible. By his side is his

From *Modern Japanese Literature* by Donald Keene, editor, copyright © 1956 by Grove Press, Inc. Used with permission of Grove/Atlantic Monthly Press.

Western-style umbrella, covered in gingham. From time to time he removes from his sleeve with a painfully contrived gesture a cheap watch, and consults the time. As a matter of fact this is merely so much display to impress others, and the chain is only gold-plate. He turns to his neighbor, who is also eating beef, and speaks:

Excuse me, but beef is certainly a most delicious thing, isn't it? Once you get accustomed to its taste, you can never go back to deer or wild boar again. I wonder why we in Japan haven't eaten such a clean thing before? For over 1620—or is it 1630—years people in the West have been eating huge quantities of beef. Before then, I understand, beef and mutton were considered the king's exclusive property, and none ever entered the mouth of a commoner, unless he happened to be something on the order of a daimyo's chief retainer. We really should be grateful that even people like ourselves can now eat beef, thanks to the fact that Japan is steadily becoming a truly civilized country. Of course, there are some unenlightened boors who cling to their barbaric superstitions and say that eating meat defiles you so much that you can't pray any more before Buddha and the gods. Such nonsense shows they simply don't understand natural philosophy. Savages like that should be made to read Fukuzawa's article on eating beef. In the West they're free of superstitions. There it's the custom to do everything scientifically, and that's why they've invented amazing things like the steamship and the steam engine. Did you know that they engrave the plates for printing newspapers with telegraphic needles? And that they bring down wind from the sky with balloons? Aren't they wonderful inventions! Of course, there are good reasons behind these inventions. If you look at a map of the world you'll see some countries marked "tropical," which means that's where the sun shines closest. The people in those countries are all burnt black by the sun. The king of that part of the world tried all kinds of schemes before he hit on what is called a balloon. That's a big round bag they fill with air high up in the sky. They bring the bag down and open it, causing the cooling air inside the bag to spread out all over the country. That's a great invention. On the other hand, in Russia, which is a cold country where the snow falls even in summer and the ice is so thick that people can't move, they invented the steam engine. You've got to admire them for it. I understand that they modeled the steam engine after the flaming chariot of hell, but anyway, what they do is to load a crowd of people on a wagon and light a fire in a pipe underneath. They keep feeding the fire inside the pipe with coal, so that the people riding on top can travel a great distance completely oblivious to the cold. Those people in the West can think up inventions like that, one after the other. . . . You say you must be going? Well, good-bye. Waitress! Another small bottle of sake. And some pickled onions to go with it!

48

Japan: The Imperial Rescript on Education

During the Meiji period the leaders understood the importance of education. The establishment of public schools was a high priority and by 1905, 95% of the children were in schools. These schools were meant to instill values as well as skills. A concerted effort was made to inculcate values of nationalism, loyalty to the emperor and respect for authority. An important part of this was the Imperial Rescript on Education which was issued in 1890 and was dutifully read in the schools on a regular basis.

Discussion Questions

1. What view of Japan is presented in the Rescript?

2. What personal qualities are advocated in the document?

3. What is the purpose of education as seen here?

4. Do you think the Rescript encourages independence and initiative in students?

Know ye, Our Subjects!

Our Imperial Ancestors have founded Our Empire on a basis broad and everlasting and have deeply and firmly implanted virtue; Our subjects, ever united in loyalty and filial piety, have from generation to generation illustrated the beauty thereof. This is the glory of the fundamental character of Our Empire, and herein also lies the source of Our education. Ye, Our subjects, be filial to your parents, affectionate to your brothers and sisters; as husbands and wives be harmonious, as friends true; bear yourselves in modesty and moderation; extend your benevolence to all; pursue learning and cultivate arts, and thereby develop your intellectual faculties and perfect your moral powers; furthermore, advance the public good and promote common interests; always respect the Constitution and observe the laws; should any emergency arise, offer yourselves courageously to the State; and thus guard and maintain the prosperity of Our Imperial Throne, coeval with heaven and earth. So shall ye not only be Our good and faithful subjects, but render illustrious the best traditions of your forefathers.

The way here set forth is indeed the teaching bequeathed by Our Imperial Ancestors, to be observed alike by Their Descendants and subjects, infallible for all ages and true in all places. It is Our wish to lay it to heart in all reverence, in common with you. Our subjects, that we may all thus attain to the same virtue.

The 30th day of the 10th month of the 23rd year Meiji.

49

Japan Observes the West

The Japanese policy of isolation under the Tokugawa vanished with the appearance of Commodore Perry's ships in 1853 and 1854. Subsequently the Japanese were forced to submit to a series of "unequal treaties" similar to those imposed on China. Since no Japanese wanted to become another China or India, the samurai responsible for the overthrow of the shogun in 1868 determined that Japan should be able to stand up to the Western powers on equal terms. Yukichi Fukuzawa (1834–1901), who had made several trips the the United States and Europe, supported Western learning so this could be brought about. (Later in life he became a fervent nationalist and promoter of Japanese expansion.)

The following selection is from his *Autobiography* in which he recalls his impressions of the West and his views on education.

Discussion Questions

1. In what ways does Fukuzawa show his pride in Japan's accomplishments?

2. What aspects of American and British life surprised him? Did he seem to think Japan was superior or just different?

3. What does he think Japan should learn from the West?

4. In the past Japan had been an ardent admirer of Chinese civilization, from which Japan had borrowed much; does Fukuzawa still seem to have that admiration?

I am willing to admit my pride in this accomplishment for Japan. The facts are these: It was not until the sixth year of Kaei (1853) that a steamship was seen for the first time; it was only in the second year of Ansei (1855) that we began to study navigation from the Dutch in Nagasaki; by 1860, the science was sufficiently understood to enable us to sail a ship across the Pacific. This means that about seven years after the first sight of a steamship, after only about five years of practice, the Japanese people made a trans-Pacific crossing without help from foreign experts. I think we can without undue pride boast before the world of this courage and skill. . . .

As I consider all the other peoples of the Orient as they exist today, I feel convinced that there is no other nation which has the ability or the courage to navigate a steamship across the Pacific after a period of five years of experience in navigation and engineering. Not only in the Orient would this feat stand as an act of unprecedented skill and daring. Even Peter the Great of Russia, who went to Holland to study navigation, with all his attainments could not have equalled this feat of the Japanese. Without doubt, the famous emperor was a man of genius, but his people did not respond to his leadership in the practice of science as did our Japanese in this great adventure.

As soon as our ship came into the port of San Francisco, we were greeted by many important personages who came on board from all over the country. Along the shores thousands of people were lined up to see the strange newcomers.

* * *

Our hosts in San Francisco were very considerate in showing us examples of modern industry. There was as yet no railway laid to the city, nor was there any electric light in use. But the telegraph system and also Galvani's electroplating were already in use. Then we were taken to a sugar refinery and had the principle of the operation explained to us quite minutely. I am sure that our hosts thought they were showing us something entirely new, namely looking for our surprise at each new device of engineering. But on the contrary, there was really nothing new, at least to me. I knew the principle of the telegraphy even if I had not seen the actual machine before; I knew that sugar was bleached by straining the solution with bone-black, and that in boiling down the solution, the vacuum was used to better effect than heat. I had been studying nothing else but such scientific principles ever since I had entered Ogata's school.

Rather, I was surprised by entirely different things in American life. First of all, there seemed to be an enormous waste of iron everywhere. In garbage piles, on the seashores—everywhere—I found lying old oil tins, empty cans, and broken tools. This was remarkable to us, for in Yedo, after a fire, there would appear a swarm of people looking for nails in the ashes.

Then too, I was surprised at the high cost of daily commodities in California. We had to pay a half-dollar for a bottle of oysters, and there were only twenty or thirty in the bottle at that. In Japan the price of so many would be only a cent or two.

Things social, political, and economic proved most inexplicable. One day, on a sudden thought, I asked a gentleman where the descendants of George Washington might be. He replied, "I think there is a woman who is directly descended from Washington. I don't know where she is now, but I think I have heard she is married." His answer was so very casual that it shocked me.

Of course, I knew that America was a republic with a new president every four years, but I could not help feeling that the family of Washington would be revered above all other families. My reasoning was based on the reverence in Japan for the founders of the great lines of rulers—like that for Ieyasu of the Tokugawa family of Shoguns, really deified in the popular mind. So I remember the astonishment I felt at receiving this indifferent answer about the Washington family. As for scientific inventions and industrial machinery, there was no great novelty in them for me. It was rather in matters of life and social custom and ways of thinking that I found myself at a loss in America. . . .

Before we sailed, the interpreter, Nakahama, and I each bought a copy of Webster's dictionary. This, I know, was the very first importation of Webster's into Japan. Once I had secured this valuable work, I felt no disappointment on leaving the new world and returning home again.

* * *

When I asked a gentleman [in England] what the "election law" was and what kind of a bureau the Parliament really was, he simply replied with a smile, meaning I suppose that no intelligent person was expected to ask such a question. But these were the things most difficult of all for me to understand. In this connection, I learned that there were bands of men called political parties—the Liberals and the Conservatives—who were always fighting against each other in the government.

For some time it was beyond my comprehension to understand what they were fighting for, and what was meant, anyway, by "fighting" in peace time. "This man and that man are enemies in the House," they would tell me. But these "enemies" were to be seen at the same table, eating and drinking with each other. I felt as if I could not make much out of this. It took me a long time, with some tedious thinking, before I could gather a general notion of these separate mysterious facts. In some of the more complicated matters, I might achieve an understanding five or ten days after they were explained to me. But all in all, I learned much from this initial tour of Europe.

* * *

In my interpretation of education, I try to be guided by the laws of nature and I try to coordinate all the physical actions of human beings by the very simple laws of "number and reason." In spiritual or moral training, I regard the human being as the most sacred and responsible of all orders, unable in reason to do anything base. Therefore, in self-respect, a man cannot change his sense of humanity, his justice, his loyalty or anything belonging to his manhood even when driven by circumstances to do so. In short, my creed is that a man should find his faith in independence and self-respect.

From my own observations in both Occidental and Oriental civilizations, I find that each has certain strong points and weak points bound up in its moral teachings and scientific theories. But when I compare the two in a general way as to wealth, armament, and the greatest happiness for the greatest number, I have to put the Orient below the Occident. Granted that a nation's destiny depends upon the education of its people, there must be some fundamental differences in the education of Western and Eastern peoples.

In the education of the East, so often saturated with Confucian teaching, I find two things lacking; that is to say, a lack of studies in number and reason in material culture, and a lack of the idea of independence in spiritual culture. But in the West I think I see why their statesmen are successful in managing their national affairs, and the businessmen in theirs, and the people generally ardent in their patriotism and happy in their family circles.

I regret that in our country I have to acknowledge that people are not formed on these two principles, though I believe no one can escape the laws of number and reason, nor can anyone depend on anything but the doctrine of independence as long as nations are to exist and mankind is to thrive. Japan could not assert herself among the great nations of the world without full recognition and practice of these two principles. And I reasoned that Chinese philosophy as the root of education was responsible for our obvious shortcomings.

With this as the fundamental theory of education, I began and, though it was impos-

sible to institute specialized courses because of lack of funds, I did what I could in organizing the instructions on the principles of number and reason. And I took every opportunity in public speech, in writing, and in casual conversations, to advocate my doctrine of independence. Also I tried in many ways to demonstrate the theory in my actual life. During my endeavor I came to believe less than ever in the old Chinese teachings. . . .

The true reason of my opposing the Chinese teaching with such vigor is my belief that in this age of transition, if this retrogressive doctrine remains at all in our young men's minds, the new civilization cannot give its full benefit to this country. In my determination to save our coming generation, I was prepared even to face single-handed the Chinese scholars of the country as a whole.

Gradually the new education was showing its results among the younger generation; yet men of middle age or past, who held responsible positions, were for the most part uninformed as to the true spirit of Western culture, and whenever they had to make decisions, they turned invariably to their Chinese sources for guidance. And so, again and again I had to rise up and denounce the all-important Chinese influence before this weighty opposition. It was not altogether a safe road for my reckless spirit to follow.

50

Communitarian vs. Individualistic Capitalism

Capitalism is the economic system most closely associated with the modern West, its key ideas having been first articulated by Adam Smith in his 1776 *The Wealth of Nations*, and serving as impetus and a rationale for the Industrial Revolution in England. The natural laws of the economy that Smith developed, those of supply and demand, the "invisible hand" of the market, and free trade, to name a few, have served to explain and to justify the activities of generations of individual entrepreneurs, organizations and governments. Though Smith or Karl Marx, the founder of socialism, never used the term in any systematic way, it nevertheless emerged by the early 20th century to refer to an entire economic system, or ideology, characterized by the control of the means of production (personal and corporate property) by a distinct group of private individuals (Marx called them the bourgeoisie or the capitalists), whose actions also influence both the labor force and the consumer. While few dispute the origins of capitalism, or its influence in the Industrial Revolution, there have been some, including the author of the following selection, the contemporary economist Lester Thurow, who question whether there is only one variety of capitalism. As you read, consider his distinction between communitarian and individualistic capitalism, and his assertion that these types derive from their respective historical traditions.

Discussion Questions

1. What does Thurow mean by communitarian capitalism? Individualistic capitalism? What evidence does he use to support his arguments, and do you think he presents an accurate characterization of the process of industrialization in Britain, America, Germany and Japan?

2. How has history influenced the type of capitalism presently used by the "I's" of America and Great Britain, as opposed to "Das Volk" and "Japan, Inc.?" Do you agree with his views? How do you think Adam Smith or Karl Marx would answer this question?

3. Should there be only one type of capitalism? If so, which one seems the most productive or the most reflective of 21st century values and economic realities?

I n March 1990 the two biggest business groups in the world, Japan's Mitsubishi and Germany's Daimler Benz-Deutsch Bank, held a secret meeting in Singapore to talk about a global alliance. Among other things, both were interested in discussing how to expand their market share in civilian aircraft production.

From an American perspective, everything about that Singapore meeting was highly illegal, violating both antitrust and banking laws. In the US, banks cannot own industrial firms and businesses cannot sit down behind closed doors to plan joint strategies. Those doing so get thrown in jail for extended periods of time. Yet today Americans cannot force the rest of the world to play the economic game as they think it should be played. The game will be played under international, not American, rules.

With economic competition between communism and capitalism over, this other competition . . . between two different forms of capitalism . . . has quickly taken over the economic playing field. Using a distinction first made by Harvard's George C. Lodge, the individualistic, Anglo-Saxon, British-American form of capitalism is going to face off against the communitarian German and Japanese variants of capitalism: The "I" of America or the United Kingdom versus "Das Volk" and "Japan Inc." The essential difference between the two is the relative stress placed on communitarian and individualistic values as the best route to economic success.

Shareholders and Stakeholders

America and Britain champion individualistic values: the brilliant entrepreneur, Nobel Prize winners, large wage differentials, individual responsibility for skills, easy-to-fire-easy-to-quit, profit maximization, hostile mergers and takeovers. Their hero is the Lone Ranger.

From Lester Thurow, "Communitarian vs. Individualistic Capitalism," in *New Perspectives Quarterly*, Vol. 9, No. 1 (Winter 1992) pp. 41–45. Reprinted by permission of *New Perspectives Quarterly*, Los Angeles.

In contrast, Germany and Japan trumpet communitarian values: business groups, social responsibility for skills, team work, firm loyalty, growth-promoting industry and government strategies. Anglo-Saxon firms are profit maximizers; Japanese and German business firms play a game best termed "strategic conquest." Americans believe in "consumer economics"; Japanese believe in "producer economics."

In the Anglo-Saxon variant of capitalism, the individual is supposed to have a personal economic strategy for success, while the business firm is to have an economic strategy reflecting the wishes of its individual shareholders. Since shareholders want income to maximize their lifetime consumption, their firms must be profit maximizers. For the profit-maximizing firm, customer and employee relations are merely a means of achieving higher profits for the shareholders. Using this formula, lower wages equal higher profits . . . and wages are to be beaten down where possible. When not needed, employees are to be laid off. For their part, workers in the Anglo-Saxon system are expected to change employers whenever opportunities exist to earn higher wages elsewhere.

Whereas in Anglo-Saxon firms the shareholder is the only stakeholder, in Japanese business firms employees are seen as the No. 1 stakeholder, customers No. 2, and the shareholders a distant No. 3, whose dividend pay-outs are low. Because employees are the prime stakeholders, higher employee wages are a central goal of the firm in Japan. The firm can be seen as a "value-added maximizer" rather than as a "profit maximizer." Profits will be sacrificed to maintain either wages or employment.

Workers in the communitarian system join a company team and are then considered successful as part of that team. The key decision in an individual's personal strategy is to join the "right" team.

In the United States or Great Britain, employee turnover rates are viewed positively. Firms are getting rid of unneeded labor when they fire workers, and individuals are moving to higher wage opportunities when they quit. Job switching, voluntary or involuntary, is almost a synonym for efficiency. In both Germany and Japan job switching is far less prevalent. In fact, many Japanese firms still refer to voluntary quits as "treason."

Coalesce for Success

Beyond personal and firm strategies, communitarian capitalists believe in having strategies at two additional levels. Business groups such as Japan's Mitsui Group or Germany's Deutsche Bank Group are expected to have a collective strategy in which companies are financially interlocked and work together to strengthen each other's activities. At the top of the pyramid of Japanese business groups are the major *zaibatsu* (Mitsui group, 23 member firms; Mitsubishi group, 28 member firms; Sanwa group, 39 member firms; Dai-Ichi Kangyo group, 45 member firms). The members of each group will own a controlling block of shares in each of the firms in the group. In addition, each member firm will in turn have a group of smaller customers and suppliers, the *keiretsu*, grouped around it. Hitachi has 688 firms in its family; Toyota has 175 primary members and 4,000 secondary members.

Similar patterns exist in Germany. The Deutsche Bank directly owns 10 percent or more of the shares in 70 companies: It owns 28 percent of Germany's largest company Daimler-Benz; 10 percent of Europe's largest reinsurance company Munich Rai; 25 percent of Europe's largest department store chain, Karstady; 30 percent of Germany's largest construction company, Philipp Holzmann; and 21 percent of Europe's largest sugar producer, Sudzucker. Through its trust department, Deutsche Bank indirectly controls many more shares that don't have to be publicly disclosed.

When the Arabs threatened to buy a controlling interest in Mercedes Benz a few years ago, the Deutsche Bank intervened on behalf of the German economy to buy a controlling interest. Now the bank protects the managers of Mercedes Benz from the raids of the financial Vikings: it frees the managers from the tyranny of the stock market, with its emphasis on quarterly profits, and it helps plan corporate strategies and raise the money to carry out these strategies. But it also fires the managers if Mercedes Benz slips in the auto market and prevents the managers from engaging in self-serving activities such as poison pills or golden parachutes, which do not enhance the company's long-term prospects.

Government's Role in Economic Growth

Both Europe and Japan believe that government has a role to play in economic growth. An example of this philosophy put into practice is the pan-European project called Airbus Industries, a civilian aircraft manufacturer owned by the British, French, German and Spanish governments, designed to break the American monopoly and get Europe back into civilian aircraft manufacturing. Today it is a success, with 20 percent of the aircraft market and announced plans to double production and capture one-third of the worldwide market by the mid-1990s.

Airbus' penetration into the aircraft manufacturing industry has severely affected US manufacturers. In 1990 Boeing's market share of new orders dropped to 45 percent . . . the first time in decades it had been below 50 percent. McDonnell Douglas' market share has been reduced from 30 percent to 15 percent. In this particular industry, a greater European share can only mean a smaller mar-

ket share for Boeing and the demise of McDonnell Douglas.

The Europeans now have a number of pan-European strategic efforts underway to catch up with America and Japan. Each is designed to help European firms compete in some major industry. European governments spend from 5 1/2 percent (Italy) to 1 3/4 percent (Britain) of the GNP aiding industry. If the US had spent what Germany spends (2 1/2 percent of GNP), $140 billion would have gone to help US industries in 1991. In Spain, where the economy grew more rapidly than any other in Europe in the 1980s, government-owned firms produced at least half of the GDP. In France and Italy, the state sector accounts for one-third of the GNP.

"Social Market" vs. "Market" Economy

Germany, the dominant European economic power, sees itself as having a "social market" economy and not just a "market" economy. State and federal governments in Germany own more shares in more industries . . . airlines, autos, steel, chemicals, electric power, transportation . . . than any non-communist country on the face of the globe. Public investments such as Airbus Industries are not controversial political issues. Privatization is not sweeping Germany as it did Great Britain.

In Germany, government is believed to have an important role to play in insuring that everyone has the skills necessary to participate in the market. Its socially financed apprenticeship system is the envy of the world. Social welfare policies are seen as a necessary part of a market economy. Unfettered capitalism is believed to generate levels of income inequality that are unacceptable.

The US, by contrast, sees social welfare programs as a regrettable necessity brought about by people who will not provide for their own old age, unemployment or ill health. Continual public discussions remind everyone that the higher taxes required to pay for social welfare systems reduce work incentives for those paying taxes and that social welfare benefits undercut work incentives for those that get them. In the ideal Anglo-Saxon market economy social welfare policies would not be necessary.

Administrative Guidance

In Japan, industry representatives working with the Ministry of International Trade and Industry present "visions" as to where the economy should be going. In the past these visions served as guides to the allocation of scarce foreign exchange or capital flows. Today what the Japanese know as "administrative guidance" is a way of life, and it is used to aim R&D funding at key industries.

An example of this can be found in the Japanese strategy toward semiconductor chips, which was similar to Europe's Airbus plan in that it was lengthy, expensive and eventually successful in breaking the dominance of American firms. The government-financed "very-large-integrated-circuit-chip" research project was just part of a much larger effort, where a combination of patience, large investments and American mistakes (a reluctance to expand capacity during cyclical downturns) paid off in the end.

The idea of administrative guidance could not be more foreign to the minds of American officials. According to the politically correct language of the Bush administration, the US government has no role in investment funding and a "legitimate" R&D role only in "pre-competitive, generic, enabling technologies." These rules are sometimes violated in practice, but the principle is clear: Governments should protect private property rights, then get out of the way and let individuals do their thing. Capitalism will spontaneously combust.

History as Destiny

These different conceptions of capitalism flow from very different histories. In the formative years of British capitalism during the 19th century, Great Britain did not have to play "catch up" with anyone. As the initiator of the industrial revolution, Great Britain was the most powerful country in the world.

The US similarly had a head start in its industrial revolution. Protected by two great oceans, the US did not feel militarily threatened by Britain's early economic lead. In the last half of the 19th century, when it was moving faster than Great Britain, Americans could see that they were going to have to catch up without deliberate government efforts to throw more coal into the American economic steam engines.

On the other hand, 19th-century Germany had to catch up with Great Britain if it was not to be overrun in the wars of Europe. The rulers of German states were expected by their subjects to take an active part in fostering the economic growth of their territories. To have its rightful place at the European table, Prussia had to have a modern industrial economy. German capitalism needed help to catch up.

The Japanese system similarly did not occur by accident. Admiral Perry arrived in the mid-1800s and with a few cannon balls forced Japan to begin trading with the rest of the world. But the mid-19th century was the height of colonialism. If Japan did not quickly develop, it would become a colony of the British, French, Dutch, Germans or Americans. Economic development was part of national defense . . . perhaps a more important part than the army itself, for a modern army could not be built without a modern economy.

In both Germany and Japan, economic strategies were important elements of military strategies for remaining independent and becoming powerful. Governments pushed actively to insure that the economic combustion took place. They had to up the intensity of that combustion so that the economic gaps, and hence military gaps, between themselves and their potential enemies could be cut in the shortest possible time. Under these circumstances, it was not surprising that firms were organized along military lines or that the line between public and private disappeared. Government and industry had to work together to design the national economic strategies necessary for national independence. In a very real sense, business firms became the front line of national defense.

American history is very different. Government's first significant economic act . . . the Interstate Commerce Commission . . . was enacted to prevent the railroads from using their monopoly power to set freight rates that would rip off everyone else. A few decades later, its second significant act . . . the antitrust laws . . . was to prevent Mr. Rockefeller from using his control over the supply of lighting oil to extract everyone else's income. The third major source of government economic activity flowed from the collapse of capitalism in the 1930s, when government had to pick up the resultant mess.

As a result adversarial relations and deep suspicions of each other's motives are deeply embedded in American history. While very different histories have led to very different systems, today those very different systems face off in the same world economy.

Let me suggest that the military metaphors now so widely used should be replaced with the language of football. Despite the desire to win, football has a cooperative as well as a competitive element. Everyone has to agree on the rules of the game, the referees, and how to split the proceeds. One can want to win yet remain friends both during and after the game. But what the rest of the world knows as football is known as soccer in America. What Americans like about American football . . . frequent time-outs, lots of huddles, and unlimited substitutions . . . are not present in world football. It has no time-outs, no huddles and very limited substitutions. It is a faster game.

51

Some Reflections on Japanese Imperialism

In the words of one Japanese diplomat on the eve of Japan's imperial age, it was necessary for Japan to be a "guest at the table" rather than "food on the plate." To that end Japan became an imperialist power with its acquisition of Taiwan after the Sino-Japanese War of 1894–1895. As the author of this reading suggests, that was rather late in the history of imperialism. While the European powers had several centuries of colonial activity under their belts, both Japan and the United States were newcomers in the late 19th century, and thus, offer interesting parallels.

Discussion Questions

1. How does the author characterize Japanese imperialism, and how was it different from the imperialism of the Western powers, including the United States?
2. What motivated Japanese imperialism and were its motivations essentially similar or different from those of the other imperialist powers?
3. To what degree was racism a factor in Japan's imperialism, or in the way Japan's actions were viewed at the time, or by historians today?
4. What does the author mean when he says that "the swashbuckling, sword-carrying colonist suddenly looked to the West like an artifact in a museum?" Might Japan's imperialism be considered "too much, too late?"
5. Would you say that Japanese imperialism was successful, or as successful as that of the United States or the European powers?

Some Reflections of Japanese Imperialism

Japan's imperial experience was different from that of the West in several fundamental respects: it was late in world time; it involved the colonization of contiguous territory; it involved the location of industry and an infrastructure of communications and transportation in the colonies, bringing industry to the labor and raw materials, rather than vice-versa; finally, it was accomplished by a country that always saw itself as disadvantaged and threatened by more advanced countries. Japan was "weak and puny," Professor Eto says, and this Japanese self-perception affected their colonial enterprise throughout. All of these characteristics made themselves felt most strongly in Korea, the closest and perhaps strategically the most important of Japan's possessions.

Japan entered upon colonization late in world colonial development, in the context of a globe with hundreds of years of colonial experience and where, as King Leopold said three years before the Meiji Restoration, "the world has been pretty well pillaged already." With most of the good colonial territories already spoken for, and with Western powers knocking at her door, Japan had little space for maneuver. Furthermore, for several decades Japan faced the possibility of becoming a dependency, perhaps even a colony, of one of the Western powers. With imperial attention mostly focused on China and its market of supposedly vast dimensions, however, Japan got what E. H. Norman called a "breathing space" within which to mobilize its resources and to resist the West. Her success was manifest in victories over China and Russia within the decade 1895 to 1905, but that should not blind us to Japan's perception of her position as poised between autonomy and dependence in a highly competitive world system, nor to the very real threats posed by the West. While the British and the Americans marveled at Japanese industrial and military prowess at the turn of the century, the Kaiser sent his famous "yellow peril" mural to the Tsar, and the French worried about Japanese skills being tied to a vast pool of Chinese labor, posing a dire threat to the West. In such circumstances the Japanese were hardly prone to worry about the sensitivities of Taiwanese or Koreans, but rather saw them as resources to be deployed in a global struggle; and, of course, Japan never lacked for Westerners (including socialists like Sydney and Beatrice Webb, and hardy Americans like Theodore Roosevelt) who were quick to justify Japanese aggression.

The relative lateness of this endeavor imparted several characteristics to it: first, a post-haste, anticipatory quality to colonial planning; second, an extraordinary interest in and mimicking of previous colonial experience; third, a rather quick anachronism to the whole enterprise; and last, the simple fact that Japan had little choice but to colonize its contiguous neighbors.

Many have spoken of Japan's defensive reform and industrialization after 1868, and so it was with Japan's imperial expansion: aggressive to Taiwanese and Koreans, it looked defensive to Japanese planners in a predatory world. And, like reform at home, the colonial effort included an aspect which was anticipatory, preconceived and planned. The characteristic figure in this architectonic endeavor was therefore not an adventurous Cecil Rhodes type, but an administrator and planner like Goto Shimpei. Ever watchful of the previous behavior of the west, colonial planners would both mimic the West and seek to avoid its errors. When one has a real model to follow, one can both copy and and anticipate future developments. Thus, Japanese bureaucrats intervened at home with social schemes designed to nip in the bud the agitation of a newborn working class, and intervened abroad to steam off pressure in the colonies by giving certain moderates a voice (while always mindful not to go too far as, in Japanese eyes, the British had in India). Thus, whether it was Ito Hirobumi discovering the secret of the German state, a colonial administrator studying French policies of assimilation, or an architect designing a railroad station in the classic style for Seoul or Harbin, Japanese behavior mirrored the European experience.

There was also something anachronistic about Japanese imperialism, perhaps not in the seizure of Taiwan, but certainly by 1910 in the annexation of Korea and *a fortiori* in 1931 with the invasion of Manchuria. Japan since the 1880's has always seemed in some vague way to be about twenty years behind European and American developments, and therefore to be persisting in the lathered pursuit of things of which the West was tiring. By 1910 strong anti-imperialist movements had developed in England and America, and shortly thereafter Woodrow Wilson not only called for self-determination in the colonies but pursued an American neo-imperialism that envisioned organizing great spaces in the world for free trade and competition, thereby branding the unilateral possession of colonial territory as outmoded or immoral, or both. The enlightened powers, Wilson thought, should follow the League of Nations mandate system, holding colonies in trust. For this reason, some at the time, like Syngman Rhee, urged that Korea become a mandate under the United States.

Another great power, Russia, emerged from World War I with an equally potent idea: self-determination and national revolution for colonial peoples. Whether it was Lenin or Wilson, both had the effect of changing the rules of the game for latecomers like Japan. The swashbuckling, sword-carrying colonist suddenly looked to the West like an artifact in a museum. Within Japan pressure from liberals and socialists was also manifest, and in Korea socialist and communist groups soon emerged after the 1919 independence uprisings. For Japan this unanticipated anti-imperialism was a nasty shock. Just as it marched out to join the "progressive" nations with its newly acquired accoutrement of colonies, the established colonial powers changed the rules and condemned Japan for pursuing the backward ideas of the nineteenth century. These and other pressures combined to produce under Hara Kei a reform movement in the colonies, but also, and more importantly, I think, a dogged determination to hold onto the Japanese sphere, irrespective of events in the West.

In order to acquire colonies in the first place, Japan had to maximize its comparative advantages by seeking territory close to home. The West, always stretched a bit in East Asia, could be thwarted in the near reaches of Japan. Thus, unlike virtually any other colonial power, Japan colonized countries that nearly touched its borders (the Nan'yo was clearly the exception, of course).

This then made feasible a tight, integral linking of the colonial territories to the metropole. Contiguity could also facilitate the settling of colonial migrants, especially an insular, homogenous people who abhor distance from the homeland.

It also made possible extraordinarily rapid exchange-time in market relations. Japan wasted no time in enhancing this possibility through laying railroads, opening ports and making heavy investments in communications sectors. Contiguity maximized control close to home, so that anti-colonial resisters had to flee abroad; what guerrillas existed (or subsisted) within the Japanese sphere by the 1930's did so in remote regions, such as the wild Sino-Korean border areas. The rest fled into central China, to the Soviet Union, or gave up the struggle entirely. The difference with, say, France in Vietnam, is obvious. Japan's lateral expansion also meant that the military, in the form of a land army resident in the colony, was the preferable coercive force—not a navy or a tiny cadre of colonial ministers a la England. Edward Chen documents the uses of this military force in Taiwan and Korea, and Mark Peattie notes the appropriateness of Hannah Arendt's continental expansion formulation for the case of Japan. One of Arendt's points, additionally, was that empires that expand by using armies to annex contiguous territory and to control foreign populations tend to be more repressive.

Unfortunately for Japan, her nearby territories were not like those in Africa, thinly populated by tribes and possessing little or no claim to recognized nation-state territorial status. Places like Taiwan were heavily populated, and places like Korea were both heavily populated *and* well-recognized for having a unitary states stretching back more than a milennium. Japan could not claim that it had carved a new nation out of the wilderness; instead it had to destroy the Yi Dynasty, which had stood for five hundred years, and put an end to an ancient nation rather than begin to forge a new one. Thus Japan's attempt at legitimizing the colonial enterprise in Korea always struck Koreans as absurd. Koreans had nothing for which to thank them and the liquidation of Korean sovereignty for which to hate them, along with their Korean collaborators. Japan's colonization of Korea therefore is much more comparable to, say, the historical relationship between England and Ireland, or Germany and Poland, than it is to European colonization in Africa or Southeast Asia. Korea's political, economic and social level was not so far from Japan's as to justify a civilizing colonial mission. Japan colonized a state, not a people, *substituting* for a state that had long considered itself superior (in the Confucian way of looking at things) to the "island barbarians" from Japan.

A political force that lacks in authority and legitimacy uses coercion, and Japan was no different. Yet in Korea the colonial power emphasized not only military and police forms of control, but also the development of the peninsula under strong state auspices. This was particularly true after the depression, when Japan utilized a "mighty trio" of state organization, central banks and *zaibatsu* conglomerates to industrialize Korea and parts of Manchuria. The colonial state in Korea bulked much larger in the economy than in Taiwan, as shown by figures on government capital formation in the Mizoguchi and Yamamoto article; much like its role in the decades after Meiji, the state substituted for an absent or at most incipient entrepreneurial class. David Landes writes that, in Japan,

> It was the State that conceived modernization as a goal and industrialization as a means, that gave birth to the new economy in haste and pushed it unrelentingly as an ambitious mother her child prodigy. And though the child grew and developed its

own resources, it never overcame the deformity imposed by this forced nurture.

The deformations were even more marked when such a role for the state was imposed on Korea, a state that stood above and apart from a society that had not yet reached Japan's level of social, political and economic development. Thus a highly articulated, disciplined, penetrating colonial bureaucracy substituted both for the traditional Yi Dynasty and for indigenous groups and classes that under "normal" conditions would have accomplished Korean development themselves. When a foreign bureaucracy replaces an in-

digenous one, or when foreign entrepreneurs run roughshod over indigenous enterprise, or when colonial education replaces Confucian teaching, the act of substitution rather than creation makes colonization that much more difficult to justify in the eyes of the colonized.

The colonial state replaced an old weak state, held society at bay, so to speak. This experience goes a long way toward explaining the subsequent (post-1945) pronounced centralization of both North and South Korea, and it has certainly provided a model for state-directed development in the South since 1961.

52

Macauley's Minute on Education

Perhaps the most important single act of British policy in India was the decision in 1835 to support education in the English language and curriculum. In the 18th century the East India Company had been cautious not to disturb traditional Indian society and culture and therefore sponsored Persian, Arabic and Sanskritic studies—this was known as the Orientalist approach. But in the early 19th century, as the Company became the paramount power in India, both the British and some Indians such as Ram Mohun Roy, who had a good knowledge of Western as well as Eastern learning, pressed for a new educational system that would allow Indians to get jobs in the new government. The British were slow to respond, but in 1834 Thomas Babington Macauley became president of the Committee on Public Instruction in India and broke the deadlock between the Orientalists and the Anglicists in favor of the latter.

The introduction of English education had deep and lasting significance for India. One result was the creation of a new class of Indians who could act as intermediaries between the British and the Indian population they ruled. Another was the spread of European values throughout India which challenged Indians to rethink their own past and either reject, accept or compromise with what the West represented. In addition, the English language acted to provide a common tongue in a country traditionally divided by caste, region, culture and numerous languages. Indian Muslims, by contrast, tended to be alienated by the new education since it did not include Koranic studies which they considered a prerequisite to any further education.

The following selection comes from Macaulay's famous Minute on Education in which he argued for the Anglicist position in 1835.

Discussion Questions

1. Do you think Macauley was in a position to pass judgment on "Oriental" studies?

2. Why did he think English education was so superior to that already being offered?

3. What kind of Indians did he wish to create and what role did he see them playing?

4. How do you think such "Macaulay-type" Indians would be received by the British and the Indians?

We have to educate a people who cannot at present be educated by means of their mother-tongue. We must teach them some foreign language. The claims of our own language it is hardly necessary to recapitulate. It stands preeminent even among the languages of the West. It abounds with works of imagination not inferior to the noblest which Greece has bequeathed to us; with models of every species of eloquence; with historical compositions, which, considered merely as narratives, have seldom been surpassed, and which, considered as vehicles of ethical and political instruction, have never been equaled; with just and lively representations of human life and human nature; with the most profound speculations on metaphysics, morals, government, jurisprudence, and trade; with full and correct information respecting every experimental science which tends to preserve the health, to increase the comfort, or to expand the intellect of man. Whoever knows that language has ready access to all the vast intellectual wealth, which all the wisest nations of the earth have created and hoarded in the course of ninety generations. It may safely be said that the literature now extant in that language is of far greater value than all the literature which three hundred years ago was extant in all the languages of the world together.

The question now before us is simply whether, when it is in our power to teach this language, we shall teach languages in which, by universal confession, there are no books on any subject which deserve to be compared to our own; whether, when we can teach European science, we shall teach systems which, by universal confession, whenever they differ from those of Europe, differ for the worse; and whether, when we can patronize sound philosophy and true history, we shall countenance, at the public expense, medical doctrines which would disgrace an English farrier, astronomy which would move laughter in girls at an English boarding school, history abounding with kings thirty feet high and reigns thirty thousand years long, and geography, made up of seas of treacle and seas of butter.

To sum up what I have said, I think it clear that we are not fettered by the Act of Parliament of 1813; that we are not fettered by any pledge expressed or implied; that we are free to employ our funds as we choose; that we ought to employ them in teaching what is best worth knowing; that English is better worth knowing than Sanscrit or Arabic; that the natives are desirous to be taught English, and are not desirous to be taught Sanscrit or Arabic; that neither as the languages of law, nor as the languages of religion, have the Sanscrit and Arabic any peculiar claim to our engagement; that it is possible to make natives of this country thoroughly good English scholars; and that to this end our efforts ought to be directed.

In one point I fully agree with the gentlemen to whose general views I am opposed. I feel with them, that it is impossible for us, with our limited means, to attempt to educate the body of the people. We must at present do our best to form a class who may be interpreters between us and the millions whom we govern; a class of persons, Indian in blood and color, but English in taste, in opinions, in morals, and in intellect. To that class we may leave it to refine the vernacular dialects of the country, to enrich those dialects with terms of science borrowed from the Western nomenclature, and to render them by degrees fit vehicles for conveying knowledge to the great mass of the population.

53

India and the West

Swami Vivekananda (1863–1902) was originally planning to study law in Britain and return to India to achieve success as many in his generation had. But his interviews with the mystic and spiritual teacher Sri Ramakrishna turned his life around and he gave up worldly pursuits to become an ascetic; twelve years later he became a missionary of Vedantic Hinduism to the world. In 1893 he addressed the First World Parliament of Religions in Chicago and spent four years lecturing in America and England. He returned home a national hero and, although he died at 39, deeply impressed his fellow Indians with the greatness of Hinduism and gave them a new-found sense of pride and confidence in their own culture. His interest in helping the masses of the population was very influential on Gandhi, who gladly recognized his debt to Vivekananda. Both Vivekananda and Gandhi believed India could achieve greatness by living up to her own high ideals.

The following selection is from a speech given by Vivekananda in New York in which he evaluates and compares East and West.

Discussion Questions

1. Why did Vivekananda believe that the world of his day needed a spiritual "adjustment?"

2. What does he think is wrong with the idea of progress as the West defined it?

3. What can the Occident and the Orient learn from each other?

Whenever virtue subsides and vice prevails, I come down to help mankind," declares Krishna, in the *Bhagavad-Gita*. Whenever this world of ours, on account of growth, on account of added circumstances, requires a new adjustment, a wave of power comes, and as man is acting on two planes, the spiritual and the material, waves of adjustment come on both planes. On the one side, of the adjustment on the material plane, Europe has mainly been the basis during modern times, and of the adjustment on the other, the spiritual plane, Asia has been the basis throughout the history of the world. Today, man requires one more adjustment on the spiritual plane; today when material ideas are at the height of their glory and power, today when man is likely to forget his divine nature, through his growing dependence on matter, and is likely to be reduced to a mere money-making machine, an adjustment is necessary; the voice has spoken, and the power is coming to drive away the clouds of gathering materialism. The power has been set in motion which, at no distant date, will bring unto mankind once more the memory of its real nature, and again the place from which this power will start will be Asia. This world of ours is on the plan of the division of labor. It is vain to say that one man shall possess everything. Yet how childish we are! The baby in its ignorance thinks that its doll is the only possession that is to be coveted in this whole universe. So a nation which is great in the possession of material power thinks that that is all that is to be coveted, that that is all that is meant by progress, that that is all that is meant by civilization, and if there are other nations which do not care for possession, and do not possess that power, they are not fit to live, their whole existence is useless! On the other hand, another nation may think that mere material civilization is utterly useless. From the Orient came the voice which once told the world, that if a man possesses everything that is under the sun and does not possess spirituality, what avails it? This is the Oriental type; the other is the Occidental type.

Each of these types has its grandeur, each has its glory. The present adjustment will be the harmonizing, the mingling of these two ideals. To the Oriental, the world of spirit is as real as to the Occidental is the world of senses. In the spiritual, the Oriental finds everything he wants or hopes for; in it he finds all that makes life real to him. To the Occidental he is a dreamer; to the Oriental, the Occidental is a dreamer, playing with ephemeral toys, and he laughs to think that grown-up men and women should make so much of a handful of matter which they will have to leave sooner or later. Each calls the other a dreamer. But the Oriental ideal is as necessary for the progress of the human race as is the Occidental, and I think it is more necessary. Machines never made mankind happy, and never will make. He who is trying to make us believe this, will claim that happiness is in the machine, but it is always in the mind. The man alone who is the lord of his mind can become happy, and none else.

And what, after all, is power of machinery? Why should a man who can send a current of electricity through a wire be called a very great man, and very intelligent man? Does not Nature do a million times more than that every moment? Why not then fall down and worship Nature? What avails it if you have power over the whole of the world, if you have mastered every atom in the universe? That will not make you happy unless you have the power of happiness in yourself, until you have conquered yourself. Man is born to conquer Nature, it is true, but the Occidental means by "Nature" only the physical or external Nature. It is true that external Nature is majestic, with its mountains, and oceans, and rivers, and with the infinite powers and varieties. Yet there is a more majestic internal Nature of man, higher than the sun, moon, and the stars, higher than this earth of ours, higher than the physical universe, transcending these little lives of ours; and it affords another field of study. There the Orientals excel, just as the Occidentals excel in the other. Therefore it is fitting that, whenever there is a spiritual adjustment, it should come from the Orient. It is also fitting that when the Oriental wants to learn about machine-making, he should sit at the feet of the Occidental and learn from him. When the Occident wants to learn about the spirit, about God, about the soul, about the meaning and the my of this universe, he must sit at the feet of the Orient to learn.

54

The Case for India

In 1930 Will Durant went to India to do research for the first volume of *The Story of Civilization*. While there he was shocked by what he saw and decided to write a book presenting the Indian side of the growing debate with England over Indian independence.

   The selections below illustrate how he thought England had worked to India's disadvantage, especially in the 19th century.

Discussion Questions

1. Why did Durant blame England for India's condition as he himself observed it?

2. Do you think his evidence supports his assertion that India's poverty was caused by British imperialism?

3. By what techniques does Durant say that England deprived India of its native wealth?

4. How was India transformed into "a purely agricultural country?"

5. Durant supports the "economic drain theory of empire." What do you think that is, according to the reading?

A Note to the Reader*

I went to India to help myself visualize a people whose cultural history I had been studying for The Story of Civilization. I did not expect to be attracted by the Hindus, or that I should be swept into a passionate interest in Indian politics. I merely hoped to add a little to my material, to look with my own eyes upon certain works of art, and then to return to my historical studies, forgetting this contemporary world.

But I saw such things in India has made me feel that study and writing were frivolous things in the presence of a people—one–fifth of the human race—suffering poverty and oppression bitterer than any to be found elsewhere on the earth. I was horrified. I had not thought it possible that any government could allow its subjects to sink to such misery.

I came away resolved to study living India as well the India with the brilliant past; to learn more of this unique Revolution that fought with suffering, accepted but never returned; to read the Gandhi of today as well as the Buddha of long ago.

And the more I read the more I was filled with astonishment and indignation at the apparently conscious and deliberate bleeding of India by England throughout a hundred and fifty years. I began to feel that I had come upon the greatest crime in all history.

And so I ask the reader's permission to abandon for a while my researches into the past, so that I may stand up and say a word for India. I know how weak words are in the face of guns and blood; how irrelevant mere truth and decency appear beside the might of empires and gold. But if even one Hindu, fighting for freedom far off there on the other side of the globe, shall hear this call of mine and be a trifle comforted, then these months of work on this little book will seem sweet to me. For I know of nothing in the world that I would rather do today than to be of help to India.

Will Durant
October 1, 1930.

With a government responsible to England, not to India, it is natural that the power of taxation should be freely used. Though before the coming of the English the land was private property, the Government made itself the sole owner of the soil and charged for it a land tax or rental now equal to one–fifth of the produce. In many cases in the past this land tax has amounted to half the gross produce, in some cases to more than the entire gross produce; in general it is two to three times as high as under pre–English rule. The Government has the exclusive right to manufacture salt, and adds to its sale–price a tax amounting to one–half a cent per pound.

A member of parliament, Cathcart Wilson, says: "The percentage of taxes in India, as related to the gross produce, is more than that

---

* Note. This book has been written without the knowledge or co–operation in any form, of any Hindu, or of any person acting for India.

of any other country." Until recently the rate was twice as high as in England, three times as high as in Scotland. Herbert Spencer protested against "the pitiless taxation which wrings from the poor Indian ryots nearly half the product of their soil." Another Englishman, the late H.M. Hyndman, after detailing the proof that taxation in India was far heavier than in any other country, though its population is poorer, entitled his book *The Bankruptcy of India*. Sir William Hunter, former member of the Viceroy's Council, said in 1875: "The government assessment does not leave enough food to the cultivator to support himself and his family throughout the year."

The result is a pitiful crushing of the Hindu spirit, a stifling of its pride and growth, a stunting of genius that once flourished in every city of the land. Have we felt that the Hindu character is degraded, that it lacks virility and initiative? But what people could have retained these qualities under such ruthless alien rule? "Subjection to a foreign yoke," says Professor Ross, "is one of potent causes of the decay of nations." Said Charles Francis Adams before the American Historical Association in 1901: "There is not an instance in all recorded history . . . where a so–called inferior race or community has been elevated in its character, or made self–sustaining, or self-governing, or even put on the way to that result through a condition of dependency or tutelage. I might, without much danger, assert that the condition of dependency, even for communities of the same race and blood, always exercises an emasculating and deteriorating influence. I would undertake, if called upon, to show that this rule is invariable." "The foreign system under which India is governed today." says Gandhi, "has reduced India to pauperism and emasculation. We have lost self–confidence."

The British charge the Hindu with lack of manliness; but it is the British who have driven it out of him by the accident of superior guns and the policy of merciless rule. If there is rebellion in India to–day let every true Briton be glad; for it means that India is not quite dead, that the spirit of liberty is risen again, and that the Hindu can be a man after all.

The economic condition of India is the inevitable corollary of its political exploitation.

Even the casual traveler perceives the decay of agriculture (which absorbs 85% of the people), and the destitution of the peasant. He sees the Hindu ryot in the rice–fields, wading almost naked in the mud of a foreign tyrant's land; his loin-cloth is all the finery that he has. In 1915 the Statistical Department of Bengal, the most prosperous of India's provinces, calculated the average wage of the able–bodied agricultural laborer to be $3.60 per month. His hut is of branches often open at the sides, and loosely roofed with straw; or it is a square of dried mud adorned with a cot of dried mud, and covered with mud and sticks and leaves. The entire house and furnishings of a family of six including all their clothing, are worth $10. The peasant cannot afford newspapers or books, entertainment, tobacco, or drink. Almost half his earnings go to the Government and if he cannot pay the tax, his holding, which may have been in his family for centuries, is confiscated by the State.

If he is fortunate he escapes from the over-taxed land and takes refuge in the cities. Provided there are not too many other applicants, he may get work in Delhi the capital of India, carrying away the white master's excrement; sanitary facilities are unnecessary when slaves are cheap. Or he can go to the factory, and become, if he is very lucky, one of the 1,409,000 "hands" of India. He will find difficulty in getting a place, for 33% of the factory workers are women, and 8% are children. In the mines 34% of the employees are women, of whom one–half work underground; 16% of the miners are children. In the cotton mills of Bombay the heat is exhausting, and the lungs are soon destroyed by the fluff–laden air; men work there until they reach a subsistence wage, and then their health breaks down. More than half the factories use their employees fifty–four hours a week. The average wage of the factory workers is sixty to seventy cents a day; though allowance must be made for the inferior skill and strength of the Hindu as compared with the European or American laborer long trained in the ways of machines. In Bombay, in 1922, despite the factory acts of that year, the average wage of the cotton workers was 33 cents. In that same year the profit of the owners of those mills was 125%. This was an "off-year"; in better years, the owners said, the profits were 200%. The work–man's home is like his wage; usually it consists of one room, shared by the family with various animals; Zimand found one room with thirty tenants. Such is the industrial revolution that a British government has allowed to develop under its control, despite the example of enlightened legislation in America and England.

The people flock to the factories because the land cannot support them; and the land cannot support them because it is overtaxed, because it is overpopulated, and because the domestic industries with which the peasants formerly eked out in winter their gleanings from the summer fields, have been destroyed by the British control of Indian tariffs and trade. For of old the handicrafts of India were known throughout the world; it was *manufactured*—i.e., hand–made—goods which European merchants brought from India to sell to the West. In 1680, says the British historian Orme, the manufacture of cotton was almost universal in India, and the busy spinning–wheels enabled the women to round out the earnings of their men.

But the English in India objected to this competition of domestic industry with their mills at home; they resolved that India should be reduced to a purely agricultural country, and be forced in consequence to become a vast market for British machine–made goods. The Directors of the East India Company gave orders that the production of raw silk should be encouraged, and the manufacture of silk fabrics discouraged; that silk–winders should be compelled to work in the Company's factories, and be prohibited, under severe penalties, from working outside. Parliament discussed ways and means of replacing Hindu by British industries. A tariff of 70–80% was placed upon Hindu textiles imported into free–trade England, while India was compelled, by foreign control of her government, to admit English textiles almost duty free. Lest Indian industries should nevertheless continue somehow to exist, an excise tax was placed on the manufacture of cotton goods in India. As a British historian puts it:

> It is a melancholy instance of the wrong done to India by the country on which she has become dependent. . . . Had India been independent, she would have retaliated, would have imposed prohibitive duties upon British goods, and would thus have preserved her own productive industry from annihilation. This act of self–defense was not permitted her; she was at the mercy of the stranger. British goods were forced upon her without paying any duty, and the foreign manufacturer employed the arm of political injustice to keep down and ultimately strangle a competitor with whom he could not have contended on equal terms.

And another Englishman wrote:

> We have done everything possible to impoverish still further the miserable beings subject to the cruel selfishness of English commerce. . . . Under the pretense of free trade, England has compelled the Hindus to receive the products of the steam–looms of Lancashire, Yorkshire, Glasgow, etc., at merely nominal duties; while the hand–wrought manufactures of Bengal and Behar, beautiful in fabric and durable in wear, have heavy and almost prohibitive duties imposed on their importation into England.

The result was that Manchester and Paisley flourished, and Indian industries declined; a country well on its way to prosperity was forcibly arrested in its development and compelled to be only a rural hinterland for industrial England. The mineral wealth abounding in India's soil was not explored, for no competition with England was to be allowed. The millions of skilled artisans whom Indian handicrafts had maintained were added to the hundreds of millions who sought support from the land. "India," says Kohn, "was transformed into a purely agricultural country, and her people lived perpetually on the verge of starvation" The vast population which might have been comfortably supported by a combination of tillage and industry, became too great for the arid soil; and India was reduced to such penury that to–day nothing is left of her men, her women and her children but empty stomachs and fleshless bones.

To this ruining of the land with taxation, this ruining of industry with tariffs, and this ruining of commerce with foreign control, add the drainage of millions upon millions of dollars from India year after year—and the attempt to explain Indian poverty as the result of her superstitions becomes a dastardly deception practised upon a world too busy to be well informed. This drain having been denied, it is only necessary to state the facts, and to introduce them with a quotation from a document privately addressed by the British government in India to the Parliament of England.

> Great Britain, in addition to the tribute which she makes India pay her through the customs, derives benefits from the savings of the service of the three presidencies (the provinces of Calcutta, Madras and Bombay) being spent in England instead of in India; and in addition to these savings, which probably amount to $500,000,000, she derives benefit from the fortunes realized by the European mercantile community, which are all remitted to England.

This is a general statement; let us fill it in.

Consider first the drain on India through trade. Not merely is this carried in British ships; far worse than that, there is an astounding surplus of exports over imports. In 1927, e.g., imports were $651,600,000, exports

were $892,800,000; the excess of exports, $241,200,000. Where goes the money that pays for this excess? But it is the officials, the merchants and the manufacturers (most of whom are British) who take the great bulk of this profit, and return it to their countries in one form or another. As an East Indian merchant said in a Parliamentary report in 1853, when this process of bleeding was on a comparatively modest scale: "Generally up to 1847, the imports were about $30,000,000 and the exports about $47,500,000. The difference is the tribute which the Company received from the country.

Consider, second, the drain through fortunes, dividends and profits made in India and spent abroad. The British come as officials or soldiers or traders; they make their money and return to Great Britain.

Consider, third, the drain through salaries and pensions derived from India and spent abroad. In 1927 Lord Winterton showed, in the House of Commons, that there were then some 7500 retired officials in Great Britain drawing annually $17,500,000 in pensions from the Indian revenue; Ramsay MacDonald put the figure at $20,000,000 a year. When England, which is almost as over–populated as Bengal, sends its sons to India, she requires of them twenty–four years of service, reduced by four years of furloughs; she then retires them for life on a generous pension, paid by the Hindu people. Even during their service these officials send their families or their children to live for the most part in England; and they support them there with funds derived from India.

Almost everything bought by the British in India, except the more perishable foods, is purchased from abroad. A great proportion of the funds appropriated for supplies by the Government of India is spent in England.

As early as 1783 Edmund Burke predicted that the annual drain of Indian resources to England without equivalent return would eventually destroy India. From Plassey to Waterloo, fifty–seven years, the drain of India's wealth to England is computed by Brooks Adams at two–and–a–half to five billion dollars. He adds, what Macaulay suggested long ago, that it was this stolen wealth from India which supplied England with free capital for the development of mechanical inventions, and so made possible the Industrial Revolution.

Though it may seem merely spectacular to juggle such figures, it is highly probable that the total wealth drained from India since 1757, if it had an been left and invested in India, would now amount, at a low rate of interest, to $400,000,000,000. Allow for money reinvested in India, and a sum remains easily equivalent to the difference between the poorest and the richest nations in the world. The same high rate of taxation which has bled India to perhaps a mortal weakness, might have done her no permanent injury if the wealth so taken had all been returned into the economy and circulation of the country; but bodily withdrawn from her as so much of it was, it has acted like a long–continued transfusion of vital blood. "So great an economic drain out of the resources of the land," says Dutt, "would impoverish the most prosperous countries on earth; it has reduced India to a land of famines more frequent, more widespread and more fatal, than any known before in the history of India, or of the world."

Sir Wilfred Scawen Blunt sums it up from the point of view of a true Englishman:

> India's famines have been severer and more frequent, its agricultural poverty has deepened, its rural population has become more hopelessly in debt, their despair more desparate. The system of constantly enhancing the land values (i.e. raising the valuation and assessment) has not been altered. The salt tax . . . still robs the very poor. . . . What was bad twenty–five years ago is worse now. At any rate there is the same drain of India's food to alien mouths. Endemic famines and endemic plagues are facts no official statistics can explain away. . . . Though myself a good Conservative . . . I own to being shocked at the bondage in which the Indian people are held; . . . and I have come to the conclusion that if we go on developing the country at the present rate, the inhabitants, sooner or later, will have to resort to cannibalism, for there will be nothing left for them to eat.

And now, having quoted authorities sufficiently to guard against relying on my own too brief experience, I may be permitted, despite that limitation, to express my own judgment and feeling. I came to India admiring the British, marveling at their imperial capacity for establishing order and peace, and thankful for the security which their policing of the world's waters has given to every traveler. I left India feeling that its awful poverty is an unanswerable indictment of its alien government, that so far from being an excuse for British rule, it is overwhelming evidence that the British ownership of India has been a calamity and a crime. For this is quite unlike the Mohammedan domination: those invaders came to stay, and their descendants call India their home; what they took in taxes and tribute they spent in India, developing its industries and resources, adorning its literature and art. If the British had done likewise, India would to–day be a flourishing nation. But the present plunder has now gone on beyond bearing; year by year it is destroying one of the greatest and gentlest peoples of history.

The terrible thing is that this poverty is not a beginning, it is an end; it is not growing less, it is growing worse; England is not "preparing India for self-government," she is bleeding it to death. "Even as we look on," said another loyal Englishman, H. M. Hyndman, "India is becoming feebler and feebler. The very life–blood of the great multitude under our rule is slowly, yet ever faster ebbing away."

Any man who sees this crime, and does not speak out, is a coward. Any Englishman or any American, seeing it and not revolted by it, does not deserve his country or his name.

55

Xhosa Freedom Fighters

Among the most vigorous resisters to the expansion of the Dutch and British in South Africa, the Bantu-speaking Xhosa stand out. They were the first to clash with the whites and proved more than capable of holding their own against the Dutch in the last decades of the 18th century. An influential Xhosa spiritual leader and warrior named Makana proclaimed that his mission was to annihilate all white men and in 1819, after a number of attacks by the whites, led his army into the Cape Colony (which had come under British control in 1795.) They were repulsed and the British pushed them back in a brutal fashion, murdering and plundering as they went. To make peace, Makana turned himself over to the British; he was imprisoned for life. To secure his release, several prominent Xhosa offered themselves in exchange for Makana. The following selection is a speech made by one of them at a parley with the British. (The British refused to make peace or release Makana, who died in 1820 while trying to escape.)

Discussion Questions

1. How did the Xhosa justify their resistance to the Europeans?
2. Were the Xhosa united in their efforts?
3. Do the Xhosa appear to have been peace-loving people?

The war, British chiefs, is an unjust one. You are striving to extirpate a people whom you forced to take up arms.

When our fathers and the fathers of the Boers first settled in the Suurveld [an area west of the Fish River], they dwelt together

Roux, Edward. *Time Longer Than Rope.* Reprinted by permission of The University of Wisconsin Press.

in peace. Their flocks grazed on the same hills: there herdsmen smoked together out of the same pipes; they were brothers . . . until the herds of the Xhosas increased so as to make the hearts of the Boers sore. What those covetous men could not get from our fathers for old buttons, they took by force. Our fathers were *men*; they loved their cattle; their wives and children lived upon milk; they fought for their property. They began to hate the colonists who coveted their all, and aimed at their destruction.

Now, their kraals and our fathers' kraals were separate. The Boers made commandos on our fathers. Our fathers drove them out of the Suurveld; and we dwelt there because we had conquered it. There we were circumcised; there we married wives; and there our children were born. The white men hated us, but could not drive us away. When there was war we plundered you. When there was peace some of our bad people stole; but our chiefs forbade it. Your treacherous friend, Gaika [the Xhosa chief who was an ally of the British] always had peace with you; yet, when his people stole, he shared in the plunder. Have your patrols ever found cattle taken in time of peace, runaway slaves or deserters, in the kraals of our chiefs? Have they ever gone into Gaika's country without finding such cattle, such slaves, such deserters, in Gaika's kraals? But he was your friend; and you wished to possess the Suurveld. You came at last like locusts [in attack of 1818]. We stood; we could do no more. You said, "Go over the Fish River . . . that is all we want." We yielded and came here.

We lived in peace. Some of our bad people stole, perhaps; but the nation was quiet . . .

the chiefs were quiet. Gaika stole . . . his chiefs stole . . . his people stole. You sent him copper; you sent him beads; you sent him horses, on which he rode to steal more. To us you sent only commandos.

We quarreled with Gaika about grass . . . no business of yours. You sent a commando . . . you took our last cow . . . you left only a few calves, which died for want, along with our children. . . . You gave half of what you took to Gaika; half you kept yourselves. Without milk . . . our corn destroyed . . . we saw our wives and children perish . . . we saw that we must ourselves perish, we followed, therefore, the tracks of our cattle into the Colony. We plundered and we fought for our lives. We found you weak; we destroyed your soldiers. We saw that we were strong; we attacked your headquarters, Grahamstown . . . and if we had succeeded, our right was good, for you began the war. We failed . . . and you are here.

We wish for peace; we wish to rest in our huts; we wish to get milk for our children; our wives wish to till the land. But your troops cover the plains, and swarm in the thickets, where they cannot distinguish the man from the woman and shoot all.

You want us to submit to Gaika. That man's face is fair to you, but his heart is false. Leave him to himself. Make peace with us. Let him fight for himself . . . and we shall not call on you for help. Set Makana at liberty; and Islambi, Dushani, Kongo and the rest will come to make peace with ou at any time we fix. But if you will still make war, you may indeed kill the last man of us . . . but Gaika shall not rule over the followers of those who think him a woman.

56

"Things Fall Apart"

If asked which groups were most active in the European imperialism of Africa, most would identify business interests and traders, and, perhaps, government officials. Few would readily mention missionaries, whose connections to either business activities or government policy seem distant. However, the missionary played an important role in colonizing efforts throughout the world, and a study of the way they perceived their role, the policies they helped to implement, the assumptions that guided their actions, and their interaction with both business and political institutions allows us to explore the cultural impact of imperialism. For just as there were profound political and economic changes resulting from the imperial policies of the European powers, there were equally startling cultural and social transformations that influenced traditional cultures. Likewise the interactions between the missionaries and the peoples among whom they worked, provide us with a personal window into the process of colonization, and give us an opportunity to explore the various responses of those who were the missionaries' intended converts. The following selection is from a widely acclaimed novel, *Things Fall Apart*, by Chinua Achebe, set around the year 1900, whose main character, Okonkwo, is faced with the coming of the missionaries and its ramifications within his own family. Though a fictional account, the selection highlights the interactions between the missionaries and the Africans, and reveals the turmoil created by this new force in their presence.

Discussion Questions

1. What was the initial reaction of most of the Africans to the missionaries? Why did some of the Africans change their minds about the Europeans, and why did others refuse to change?

2. What assumptions guided the missionaries in their work? Was there any attempt to understand African culture and religion?

3. Would you consider the missionary to be as much of an imperialist as a merchant or government official?

4. Why do you think Okonkwo acted as he did? What do you think happened to him as a result?

5. If you were an African living at that time, what would your response to the missionaries have been?

The missionaries spent their first four or five nights in the marketplace, and went into the village in the morning to preach the gospel. They asked who the king of the village was, but the villagers told them that there was no king. "We have men of high title and the chief priests and the elders," they said.

It was not very easy getting the men of high title and the elders together after the excitement of the first day. But the missionaries persevered, and in the end they were received by the rulers of Mbanta. They asked for a plot of land to build their church.

Every clan and village had its "evil forest." In it were buried all those who died of the really evil diseases, like leprosy and smallpox. It was also the dumping ground for the potent fetishes of great medicine men when they died. An "evil forest" was, there-fore, alive with sinister forces and powers of darkness. It was such a forest that the rulers of Mbanta gave to the missionaries. They did not really want them in their clan, and so they made them that offer which nobody in his right senses would accept.

"They want a piece of land to build their shrine," said Uchendu to his peers when they consulted among themselves. "We shall give them a piece of land." He paused, and there was a murmur of surprise and disagreement. "Let us give them a portion of the Evil Forest. They boast about victory over death. Let us give them a real battlefield in which to show their victory." They laughed and agreed, and sent for the missionaries, whom they had asked to leave them for a while so that they might "whisper together." They offered them as much of the Evil Forest as they cared to take. And to their greatest amazement the missionaries thanked them and burst into song.

"They do not understand," said some of the elders. "But they will understand when they go to their plot of land tomorrow morning." And they dispersed.

The next morning the crazy men actually began to clear a part of the forest and to build their house. The inhabitants of Mbanta expected them all to be dead within four days. The first day passed and the second and third and fourth, and none of them died. Everyone was puzzled. And then it became known that the white man's fetish had unbelievable power. It was said that he wore glasses on his eyes so that he could see and talk to evil spirits. Not long after, he won his first three converts.

Although Nwoye had been attracted to the new faith from the very first day, he kept it secret. He dared not go too near the missionaries for fear of his father. But whenever they came to preach in the open marketplace or the village playground, Nwoye was there. And he was already beginning to know some of the simple stories they told.

"We have now built a church," said Mr. Kiaga, the interpreter, who was now in charge of the infant congregation. The white man had gone back to Umuofia, where he built his headquarters and from where he paid regular visits to Mr. Kiaga's congregation at Mbanta.

"We have now built a church," said Mr. Kiaga, "and we want you all to come in every seventh day to worship the true God."

On the following Sunday, Nwoye passed and repassed the little red-earth and thatch building without summoning enough courage to enter. He heard the voice of singing and although it came from a handful of men it was loud and confident. Their church stood on a circular clearing that looked like the open mouth of the Evil Forest. Was it waiting to

snap its teeth together? After passing and re-passing by the church, Nwoye returned home.

It was well known among the people of Mbanta that their gods and ancestors were sometimes long-suffering and would deliberately allow a man to go on defying them. But even in such cases they set their limit at seven market weeks or twenty-eight days. Beyond that limit no man was suffered to go. And so excitement mounted in the village as the seventh week approached since the impudent missionaries built their church in the Evil Forest. The villagers were so certain about the doom that awaited these men that one or two converts thought it wise to suspend their allegiance to the new faith.

At last the day came by which all the missionaries should have died. But they were still alive, building a new red-earth and thatch house for their teacher, Mr. Kiaga. That week they won a handful more converts. And for the first time they had a woman. Her name was Nneka, the wife of Amadi, who was a prosperous farmer. She was very heavy with child.

Nneka had had four previous pregnancies and childbirths. But each time she had borne twins, and they had been immediately thrown away. Her husband and his family were already becoming highly critical of such a woman and were not unduly perturbed when they found she had fled to join the Christians. It was a good riddance.

One morning Okonkwo's cousin, Amikwu, was passing by the church on his way from the neighboring village, when he saw Nwoye among the Christians. He was greatly surprised, and when he got home he went straight to Okonkwo's hut and told him what he had seen. The women began to talk excitedly, but Okonkwo sat unmoved.

It was late afternoon before Nwoye returned. He went into the *obi* and saluted his father, but he did not answer. Nwoye turned round to walk into the inner compound when his father, suddenly overcome with fury, sprang to his feet and gripped him by the neck.

"Where have you been?" he stammered.

Nwoye struggled to free himself from the choking grip.

"Answer me," roared Okonkwo, "before I kill you!" He seized a heavy stick that lay on the dwarf wall and hit him two or three savage blows.

"Answer me!" he roared again. Nwoye stood looking at him and did not say a word. The women were screaming outside, afraid to go in.

"Leave that boy at once!" said a voice in the outer compound. It was Okonkwo's uncle, Uchendu. "Are you mad?"

Okonkwo did not answer. But he left hold of Nwoye, who walked away and never returned.

He went back to the church and told Mr. Kiaga that he had decided to go to Umuofia where the white missionary had set up a school to teach young Christians to read and write.

Mr. Kiaga's joy was very great. "Blessed is he who forsakes his father and his mother for my sake," he intoned. "Those that hear my words are my father and my mother."

Nwoye did not fully understand. But he was happy to leave his father. He would return later to his mother and his brothers and sisters and convert them to the new faith.

As Okonkwo sat in his hut that night, gazing into a log fire, he thought over the matter. A sudden fury rose within him and he felt a strong desire to take up his machete, go to the church and wipe out the entire vile and miscreant gang. But on further thought he told himself that Nwoye was not worth fighting for. Why, he cried in his heart, should he, Okonkwo, of all people, be cursed with such a son? He saw clearly in it the finger of his personal god or *chi*. For how else could he explain his great misfortune and exile and now his despicable son's behavior? Now that he had time to think of it, his son's crime stood out in its stark enormity. To abandon the gods of one's father and go about with a lot of effeminate men clucking like old hens was the very depth of abomination. Suppose when he died all his male children decided to follow Nwoye's steps and abandon their ancestors? Okonkwo felt a cold shudder run through him at the terrible prospects, like the prospect of annihilation. He saw himself and his fathers crowding round their ancestral shrine waiting in vain for worship and sacrifice and finding nothing but ashes of bygone days, and his children the while praying to the white man's god. If such a thing were ever to happen, he, Okonkwo, would wipe them off the face of the earth.

Okonkwo was popularly called the "Roaring Flame." As he looked into the log fire he recalled the name. He was a flaming fire. How then could he have begotten a son like Nwoye, degenerate and effeminate? Perhaps he was not his son. No! he could not be. His wife had played him false. He would teach her! But Nwoye resembled his grandfather, Unoka, who was Okonkwo's father. He pushed the thought out of his mind. He, Okonkwo, was called a flaming fire. How could he have begotten a woman for a son? At Nwoye's age Okonkwo had already become famous throughout Umuofia for his wrestling and his fearlessness.

He sighed heavily, and as if in sympathy the smoldering log also sighed. And immediately Okonkwo's eyes were opened and he saw the whole matter clearly. Living fire begets cold, impotent ash. He sighed again, deeply.

The young church in Mbanta had a few crises early in its life. At first the clan had assumed that it would not survive. But it had gone on living and gradually becoming stronger. The clan was worried, but not overmuch. If a gang of *efulefu* decided to live in the Evil Forest it was their own affair. When one came to think of it, the Evil Forest was a fit home for such undesirable people. It was true they were rescuing twins from the bush, but they never brought them into the village. As far as the villagers were concerned, the twins still remained where they had been thrown away. Surely the earth goddess would not visit the sins of the missionaries on the innocent villagers?

But on one occasion the missionaries had tried to overstep the bounds. Three converts had gone into the village and boasted openly that all the gods were dead and impotent and that they were prepared to defy them by burning all their shrines.

"Go and burn your mothers' genitals," said one of the priests. The men were seized and beaten until they streamed with blood. After that nothing happened for a long time between the church and the clan.

But stories were already gaining ground that the white man had not only brought a religion but also a government. It was said that they had built a place of judgment in Umuofia to protect the followers of their religion. It was even said that they had hanged one man who killed a missionary.

"Does the white man understand our custom about land?"

"How can he when he does not even speak our tongue? But he says that our customs are bad; and our own brothers who have taken up his religion also say that our customs are bad. How do you think we can fight when our own brothers have turned against us? The white man is very clever. He came quietly and peaceably with his religion. We were amused at his foolishness and allowed him to stay. Now he has won our brothers, and our clan can no longer act like one. He has put a knife on the things that held us together and we have fallen apart."

There were many men and women in Umuofia who did not feel as strongly as Okonkwo about the new dispensation. The white man had indeed brought a lunatic religion, but he had also built a trading store and for the first time palm-oil and kernel became things of great price, and much money flowed into Umuofia.

And even in the matter of religion there was a glowing feeling that there might be something in it after all, something vaguely akin to method in the overwhelming madness.

This growing feeling was due to Mr. Brown, the white missionary, who was very firm in restraining his flock from provoking the wrath of the clan. Mr. Brown learned a good deal about the religion of the clan and he came to the conclusion that a frontal attack on it would not succeed. And so he built a school and a little hospital in Umuofia. He went from family to family begging people to send their children to his school. But at first they only sent their slaves or sometimes their lazy children. Mr. Brown begged and argued and prophesied. He said that the leaders of the land in the future would be men and women who had learned to read and write. If Umuofia failed to send her children to the school, strangers would come from other places to rule them. They could already see that happening in the Native Court, where the D.C. was surrounded by strangers who spoke his tongue. Most of these strangers came from the distant town of Umuru on the bank of the Great River where the white man first went.

In the end Mr. Brown's arguments began to have an effect. More people came to learn in his school, and he encouraged them with gifts of singlets and towels. They were not all young, these people who came to learn. Some of them were thirty years old or more. They worked on their farms in the morning and went to school in the afternoon. And it was not long before the people began to say that the white man's medicine was quick in working. Mr. Brown's school produced quick results. A few months in it were enough to make one a court messenger or even a court clerk. Those who stayed longer became teachers; and from Umuofia laborers went forth into the Lord's vineyard. New churches were established in the surrounding villages and a few schools with them. From the very beginning religion and education went hand in hand.

Okika sprang to his feet and also saluted his clansmen four times. Then he began to speak:

"You all know why we are here, when we ought to be building our barns or mending our huts, when we should be putting our compounds in order. My father used to say to me: 'Whenever you see a toad jumping in broad daylight, then know that something is after its life.' When I saw you all pouring into this meeting from all the quarters of our clan so early in the morning, I knew that something was after our life." He paused for a brief moment and then began again:

"All our gods are weeping. Idemili is weeping, Ogwugwu is weeping, Agbala is weeping, and all the others. Our dead fathers are weeping because of the shameful sacrilege they are suffering and the abomination we have all seen with our eyes." He stopped again to steady his trembling voice.

"This is a great gathering. No clan can boast of greater numbers or greater valor. But are we all here? I ask you: Are all the sons of Umuofia with us here?" A deep murmur swept through the crowd.

"They are not," he said. "They have broken the clan and gone their several ways. We who are here this morning have remained true to our fathers, but our brothers have deserted us and joined a stranger to soil their father-land. If we fight the stranger we shall hit our brothers and perhaps shed the blood of a clansman. But we must do it. Our fathers never dreamed of such a thing, they never killed their brothers. But a white man never came to them. So we must do what our fathers would never have done. Eneke the bird was asked why he was always on the wing and he replied: 'Men have learned to shoot without missing their mark and I have learned to fly without perching on a twig.' We must root out this evil. And if our brothers take the side of evil must root them out too. And we must do it now. We must bale this water now that it is only ankle-deep. . . .

At this point there was a sudden stir in the crowd and every eye was turned in one direction. There was a sharp bend in the road that led from the marketplace to the white man's court, and to the stream beyond it. And so no one had seen the approach of the five court messengers until they had come round the bend, a few paces from the edge of the crowd. Okonkwo was sitting at the edge.

"What do you want here?"

"The white man whose power you know too well has ordered this meeting to stop."

In a flash Okonkwo drew his machete. The messenger crouched to avoid the blow. It was useless. Okonkwo's machete descended twice and the man's head lay beside his uniformed body.

The waiting backcloth jumped into tumultuous life and the meeting was stopped. Okonkwo stood looking at the dead man. He knew that Umuofia would not go to war. He knew because they had let the other messengers escape. They had broken into tumult instead of action. He discerned fright in that tumult. He heard voices asking: "Why did he do it?"

He wiped his machete on the sand and went away.

57

The Dual Mandate in Africa

Sir F.D. Lugard, a famous British colonial soldier and governor, offers a justification of colonization in Africa and sees it as a two-way process.

Discussion Questions

1. What does Lugard mean by the "dual mandate?"

2. What are the major contributions of Europe to Africa, as he sees them?

3. What does Lugard mean when he says that "their very discontent is a measure of their progress?

4. Are Lugard's arguments convincing?

The Dual Mandate

In accepting responsibility for the control of these new lands, England obeyed the tradition of her race. British Africa was acquired not by groups of financiers, nor yet . . . by the efforts of her statesmen, but in spite of them. It was the instinct of the British democracy which compelled us to take our share. . . .

The fundamental character of British official policy in West Africa, [a Labour leader] says, has primarily been influenced by a desire to promote the welfare and advancement of the native races. England, he points out, led the way in the suppression of the overseas slave trade, paying enormous sums in compensation to slave-owners . . . and in patrolling the seas [to intercept slave ships]. She [took up] the cause of Congo reform, and of the indentured labor [labor bound to colonists by contract] in Portuguese West Africa. The extension of British control in the Gold Coast hinterland was (he adds) to . . . [protect] the natives, and in southern Nigeria to suppress war and human sacrifice. . . .

Let it be admitted at the outset that European brains, capital, and energy have not been, and never will be, expended in developing the resources of Africa from motives of pure philanthropy; that Europe is in Africa for the mutual benefit of her own industrial classes, and of the native races in their progress to a higher plane; that the benefit can be made reciprocal, and that it is the aim and desire of civilized administration to fulfill this dual mandate.

By railways and roads, by reclamation of swamps and irrigation of deserts, and by a system of fair trade and competition, we have added to the prosperity and wealth of these lands, and [have] checked famine and disease. We have put an end to the awful misery of the slave trade and intertribal war, to human sacrifice, and the ordeals of the witch doctor. Where these things survive, they are severely suppressed. We are endeavoring to teach the native races to conduct their own affairs with justice and humanity, and to educate them alike in letters and in industry.

When I recall the state of Uganda at the time I made the treaty in 1890 which brought it under British control, or the state of Nigeria ten years later, and contrast them with the conditions of today [late 1920's], I feel the British effort—apart from benefits to British trade—has not been in vain. In Uganda a triangular civil war was raging: Protestants, Roman Catholics, and Muslims—representing the rival political factions of British, French, and Arabs—were murdering each other. Only a short time previously, triumphant paganism had burned Christians at the stake. . . . Today there is an ordered government with its own native parliament. Liberty and justice have replaced chaos, bloodshed, and war. The wealth of the country steadily increases. . . .

In Nigeria in 1902 slave-raiding armies of 10,000 or 15,000 men laid waste the country, and wiped out its population annually in the quest for slaves. Hundreds of square miles of rich will-watered land were depopulated. . . .

From Sir F. D. Lugard, *The Dual Mandate in British Tropical Africa*, copyright © 1929 by William Blackwood & Sons, Ltd., London, pp. 616–619. Reprinted with permission of Pillans & Wilson, Edinburgh.

Nowhere was there security for life and property. Today the native emirs [(chiefs) compete] with each other in the progress of their schools; the native courts administer justice and themselves have liberated over 50,000 slaves. The . . . emirs are keenly interested in such questions as afforestation, artesian well-boring, and vaccination. The native prisons have been pronounced by the medical authority to be a model for government to imitate; the leper settlement in Bornu under purely native control is the most successful I know of.

I refer to these two countries because I happen to have personally witnessed their condition prior to the advent of British control, but similar results may be seen in every other British dependency in tropical Africa.

As Roman imperialism laid the foundations of modern civilization, and led the wild barbarians of [the British Isles] along the path of progress, so in Africa today we are repaying the debt, and bringing to the dark places of the earth—the abode of barbarism and cruelty—the torch of culture and progress, while ministering to the material needs of our own civilization. In this task the nations of Europe have pledged themselves to cooperation. . . . Towards the common goal each will advance by the methods most consonant with [suited to] its national genius. British methods have not perhaps in all cases produced ideal results, but I am profoundly convinced that there can be no question but that British rule has promoted the happiness and welfare of the primitive races. Let those who question it examine the results impartially. If there is unrest, and a desire for independence, as in India and Egypt, it is because we have taught the value of liberty and freedom, which for centuries these peoples had not known. Their very discontent is a measure of their progress.

We hold these countries because it is the genius of our race to colonize, to trade, and to govern. The task in which England is engaged in the tropics . . . has become part of her tradition, and she has ever given of her best in the cause of liberty and civilization. There will always be those who cry aloud that the task is being badly done, that it does not need doing, that we can get more profit by leaving others to do it, that it brings evil to subject races and breeds profiteers at home. These were not the principles which prompted our forefathers, and secured for us the place we hold in the world today in trust for those who shall come after us.

58

The Berlin Act, 1885

The Berlin West Africa Conference of 1884–5 gave international recognition to an already existing situation. Since 1880 the great powers had become increasingly suspicious of each others' designs on Africa, even though individually they had little interest in the continent. Fear of another power or powers gaining ascendency there impelled the powers to make adversarial claims. The European powers rushed to make treaties with various African rulers to lay claim to territory. Bismarck of Germany, who had said that "for Germany to acquire colonies would be like a poverty-stricken Polish nobleman providing himself with silks and sables, when he needed shirts," dropped his opposition to colonial ventures when Britain occupied Egypt in 1882. In 1884 he convened a conference in Berlin to set down rules to formalize the chaotic "scramble."

Every major power in Europe, plus the United States and the Ottoman Empire, attended and the formal act was promulgated in early 1885. The Act included the following provisions.

Discussion Questions

1. What clauses in the act were indicative of European imperialistic sentiments?

2. How did the powers expect to regularize the process of acquiring territories?

The Berlin Act, 1885

Article VI

Provisions Relative to Protection of the Natives, of Missionaries and Travellers, as well as Relative to Religious Liberty

Preservation and Improvement of Native Tribes; Slavery, and the Slave Trade

All the powers exercising sovereign rights or influence in the aforesaid territories bind themselves to watch over the preservation of the native tribes, and to care for the improvement of the conditions of their moral and material well-being, and to help in suppressing slavery, and especially the slave trade.

Religious and Other Institutions. Civilization of Natives

They shall, without distinction of creed or nation, protect and favour all religious, scientific, or charitable institutions, and undertakings created and organized for the above ends, or which aim at instructing the natives and bringing home to them the blessings of civilization.

Protection of Missionaries, Scientists, and Explorers

Christian missionaries, scientists, and explorers, with their followers, property, and collections, shall likewise be the objects of especial protection.

Religious Toleration

Freedom of conscience and religious toleration are expressly guaranteed to the natives, no less than to subjects and to foreigners.

Notification of Acquisitions and Protectorates on Coasts of African Continent

Article XXXIV

Any power which henceforth takes possession of a tract of land on the coasts of the African continent outside of its present possessions, or which, hitherto without such possessions, shall acquire them, as well as the Power which assumes a Protectorate there, shall accompany the respective act with a notification thereof, addressed to the other Signatory Powers of the present Act, in order to enable them, if need be, to make good any claims of their own.

Extracts from the General Appendices. Cited in Raymond Leslie Buell, *The Native Problem in Africa* (New York: The Macmillan Co., 1928) II, pp. 891–907.

59

Imperialism in Africa—Gain or Loss?

Noted contemporary historian Basil Davidson provides a view of the impact of imperialism in Africa, highlighting the cultural changes that resulted. As you read, consider Davidson's reminders that the process of imperialism was full of contradictions, and compare his comments with those of Coleman (No. 101).

Discussion Questions

1. What were Africa's strengths and weaknesses, according to Davidson? How did Africa's strengths become its weaknesses?

2. What is the "power gap" that Davidson mentions? What are the two "mythologies" of imperialism in Africa that need correcting, and do you agree with him?

3. What does Davidson identify as the gains that Africans reaped from imperialism? What losses does he list? Were there more gains than losses? Do you agree with his assessment?

4. How do Davidson's conclusions with respect to the impact of imperialism in Africa compare with Coleman's?

How one measures the African balance of loss and gain through this gruelling episode of European colonial rule will depend, no doubt, upon who one is. Most Africans, or at any rate those not privileged in belonging to an élite . . . have probably seen in it little but loss for their continent. Most Europeans, even when thinking not solely of their own interests, have claimed for it little but gain. A just balance will in any case vary from one territory to another and even from one colonial power to another. Besides, it was nothing if not a contradictory process, . . . and individual judgements will accordingly vary about the weight or value to be placed on one side or the other of the scales.

The matter becomes even more elusive in the sphere of moral judgements. Could there ever be a moral justification for invading and expropriating the territory and possessions of other peoples? The Victorians generally thought there could, provided always that the invading and expropriating were done outside Europe. Adhering to a vulgarized Darwinism, they held themselves so far superior in the human scale to these "tribes without the law," these "fluttered folk and wild," as to be in duty bound to save such benighted populations from the darkness in which they were supposedly plunged. It appeared to Richard Burton, perhaps the most successful propagator of such views, that it must be "egregious nonsense" to question the natural and inherent superiority of Europeans over Africans: "everyone who has studied the natural history of man," he opined in his usual tone of declamation, the hectoring tone of a man who has travelled much but understood little, "must have the same opinion." Yet there were others, less insensitive and self-regarding, who also believed in the moral imperatives of colonial rule; and not a few of these others were men deserving of respect.

Today we can look at these things a little more objectively. Nobody now will care to argue in Burton's tone, or nobody at any rate who is likely to be worth hearing. Even gentler views of the same kind will be hard to sustain in the light of the colonial record. Among Africans there was disillusionment almost from the first. While the diviners of the Luo may have instructed their people to accept and aid these "red strangers" from the sea as beings of a marvellous benevolence, closer acquaintance brought a different view, and the twilight of those particular gods was as swift as the African dusk itself. Even before "full occupation" had been assured, there were movements of protest against European rule: among the Luo, for example, as early as 1913. Then it was that Onyango Dunde relayed to his followers a message from their god Mumbo, pronouncing that "all Europeans are your enemies, but the time is shortly coming when they will all disappear from our country."

Yet the Victorians had a point. However confusedly, they saw that Africans really were in a different, an earlier, phase of sociopolitical growth; and the best of them wished to make it possible for this phase to be followed, as painlessly as might be, by an advance into the technology and attitudes of the industrial world. There was, very clearly, a great need for the "modern" reconstruction of African life and thought: not, as we may easily agree today, because the industrial world was inherently capable of offering more happiness than the old world of rural subsistence, but because the old world of rural subsistence could not possibly withstand the strains of exposure to the consequences of technological change in the rest of the world. That old world must either transform itself, or collapse in helpless ruin. Africans, in short, could no longer defend themselves on the basis of their old traditions and modes of organization. The "power gap" between Africa and the industrially advanced nations, those that had begun to reduce Africa to an underlying dependence during the slave trade, had by now become disastrously wide.

This gap had appeared long before. When Affonso of Kongo, back at the beginning of the sixteenth century, had vainly pressed the king of Portugal to send him shipwrights, or at least to sell him a ship for ocean-going travel, he was only expressing the inability of African society to adapt itself to the needs of building ships and sailing them. . . . The further self-defence and self-realization of Africa required, in brief, a closing of the technological power gap in ways that could only result from new social attitudes and structures.

On one side of the balance, then, there was this need for a creative revolutionary break with the long unfolding of African Iron Age society. The need was not a new one. It had been there from as far back as the time when modern engineering took its rise in western Europe. It had steadily widened. And now, with the direct confrontation of European colonial presence, it became an urgent need. This is another way of saying that there had

been nothing in the prolonged Afro-European contact of pre-colonial times that was able, much less aimed, at producing any such crucial transformation. These chapters have suggested several reasons why this was so.

One of them lay in the dynamic strength of African systems of self-rule which had enabled mankind to populate and master the continent by methods and ideologies native to itself. Those systems had only begun to exhaust their social value when the general crisis of the nineteenth century moved over their horizon. They had revealed themselves capable of an almost infinitely subtle adaptability to shifting circumstances and challenges. . . . Little had come from outside that could have seemed in any way socially preferable.

Not surprisingly: for what had come from outside was often the worst that outside civilization could offer. Islam made an exception. The value that large numbers of Africans found in Islam, whether for the overleaping of ethnic conflicts, for the development of new techniques of trade and credit, or the organization of new forms of self-rule, suggests that Islam, on the whole, was often a factor of constructive transformation. "On the whole," however; there were many exceptions. Islam also led to forms of oligarchical despotism which had not existed before, to the introduction of slave labour and to the extension of the overland slave trade. And it did all this without "breaking the mould" of Iron Age continuity: without breaking it, that is, either because the Muslim powers of North Africa and the Middle East lacked the necessary know-how, or because Islam in Africa, in order to succeed, had to naturalize itself to African attitudes and beliefs. Early Christianity in Africa, aside from the special cases of Christian Nubia and Ethiopia, made no such concessions, and failed almost everywhere to achieve more than a fleeting and eventually insignificant impact, as anyone may see who cares to read the Papal records.

For the rest, what came from outside arrived in the guise of settlers of a persistent rapacity and arrogance, whether in the manner of the Portuguese along the Zambezi or of the Boers in the far south, or of traders, plying the Atlantic trade, whose capacity to transfer cultural progress was always, to put it mildly, minimal. None of these could help towards any constructive transformation, towards any far-reaching change, such as could move African society from its pre-industrial subsistence base to one which could absorb the early possibilities of modern technological progress.

Even the European settlers along the Zambezi brought nothing new except firearms and an often gross ambition for personal wealth and power. Far from helping to transform the structures of African life, they merely degraded these structures, or else themselves became adapted to African modes. . . . Standing outside the moralities of Africa and Europe alike, such settler groups became little more than armed bandits. . . ."

The Boers were different, for they were often skilled and laborious farmers, producing wealth by their own work as well as purloining it from the Africans whom they enslaved. Yet the Boers were just as incapable of transmitting any of the technological progress of western Europe, for they knew nothing of it. Fastened within their own pre-industrial ideology, they behaved according to the teachings of a religion which was set in its principles and practices against anything that was not of an extreme conservatism, and they had accordingly nothing useful to give Africa. Only much later, when faced themselves with a violent challenge from Europe in the shape of the Anglo-Boer War of 1899, did a few of them begin to understand that they, too, might have to move with the times. When they did so move, however,

their old conservatism simply acquired a new form, and the outcome for Africans was even worse than before.

If the Atlantic trade produced some changes among coastal peoples who engaged in it, these were changes which remained within the pre-industrial mould. The peoples of the Niger Delta, of the Guinea Coast and Senegambia, proved well able to adapt their social structures to the handling of a vast and various trade with Europeans. These adaptations were often ingenious. Yet they, too, could produce no decisive shift towards technological advance. Not a single one of these peoples, for example, ever embarked upon ocean trading on their own account until the latter part of the nineteenth century; and then, of course, it was too late: the mounting pressures of European monopoly saw to that. King Ja Ja of Opobo, the shrewdest of those who tried it, ended his career in British imperial captivity.

If one asks, all the same, just why it was that these coastal peoples, faced as they were for so many years with the clear evidence of technological superiority on the European side, still failed to learn its lessons and launch some kind of technological revolution of their own, one is brought back again to the nature of the systems within which they lived. To the strength of these systems; but also to their weakness. They were strong because they were the product of centuries of successful trial and error by which men had worked out ways of living in the tropics and the forests, in the grasslands and the mountains of this often harsh continent. These systems were, if you like, the outcome of a long period of natural selection of a social kind: they enclosed men within frameworks of spiritual and moral behaviour, collective duty and individual responsibility, that rested on traditions of inherently sufficient power and persuasion.

It is easy to forget the self-confidence that was undoubtedly engendered by these tried and tempered modes of life, although the resilience and durability of African cultural attitudes repeatedly remind one of it even in the changed world of today. . . . The systems were strong, in other words, because within the limits of the world they knew they worked manifestly better than anything that was offered them in exchange. They worked better not only at a material level but also in terms of spiritual, moral and socially constructive behaviour.

These traditional systems were weak for at least two large reasons. First, and above all, because they were the victims of their own success. They might be flexible in day-to-day adjustment. Towards all questions of structural change they showed a fundamental hostility. They were conservative by the strictest definition. They were the result, after all, of long years of careful experiment which had had to balance one danger of disintegration or failure against another, and often in circumstances of great ecological difficulty. Having reached stability, structures such as these were bound to induce an extreme distrust of far-reaching change. Although the outcome of a great deal of daring experiment in the past, they had reached a self-perpetuating level where further large experiment seemed not only unwise, but also, given the spiritual sanctions that helped to stay them up, positively wrong.

Secondly, these systems were very numerous. Pre-colonial Africa lived within a multitude of petty frontiers; exceptions such as the wide empires of the Sudan, Guinea, Central Africa, only prove the rule. Underlying unities of culture there might certainly be; seldom or never did they lead to unities of action. This was the political weakness of Africa in face of the slave trade, and afterwards of the slave trade's natural successor, colonial invasion. Individual kings and merchants might perceive the damage of the slave trade. They could never prevent it, or turn it to more than local or immediate profit, because they could never achieve unity with rivals and competitors; and the same was to be true of the European imperialist challenge. Africans, in sum, did not build their own ships and sail the ocean seas (except for the Swahili of the East Coast, who sometimes did), or otherwise embark on revolutionary technical experiment, because they saw no sufficient reason and interest in doing so, or, when European pressure taught them differently, because they lacked the social power to command or invent the necessary means. They needed a structural revolution in the content as well as in the form of their societies; and the circumstances in which this could take place were not yet present. . . .

The gains of colonial rule can be argued: to say that they were part of a deliberate process and could not have been achieved by other means, is to mistake the nature of the experience, as well as to ignore the losses.

There would seem, in fact, to be two mythologies at work. One of these reflects a wish to believe that only a period of foreign rule could bring Africa fully into the modern world. The other, opposing the first, is that all the ills and troubles of the continent today are due to its colonial heritage. Muting the emotional overtones, and standing as far as one may outside apologetics, we should be able to recognize that truth lies somewhere between these extremes. The colonial experience was undoubtedly heavy in its consequences. Most of these consequences were bad for Africans. But the total experience was dialectical by nature. The ills of Africa today derive partly from the colonial heritage, but also partly from Africa's still existing need for profound structural transformation. This need must have been present in any case, colonial period or not.

Seen from this standpoint, and eschewing moral aspects of the matter, it is the negative sides of the experience that seem likely to command the judgement of history. Even when considered from the relatively narrow aspect of a reduction in the number of self-governing units, in the quantity of frontiers, it cannot be said that the central result of colonial rule was to reconstruct Africa on modern lines, on the lines that were necessary to Africa's reconstruction from the Iron Age limits of the past. If there was virtue in a simple reduction—supposing, of course, what cannot be supposed in the light of the evidence: that the reduction was made with a view to African benefit and not to imperialist convenience—there was little or none in the way it was achieved. Vast areas such as the Congo Basin were casually clamped within a single system of colonial rule, while others were fragmented, as in western Africa, into a scatter of little colonies for which a viable independence was never even considered to be possible, much less desirable.

Viewed from other aspects, the answer appears to be the same. What the central consequence of colonial rule proved to be was not the modern reconstruction of Africa, but the far-reaching dismantlement and ruin of the societies and structures which the invaders had found.

Nobody need doubt that by 1900 the greater part of Africa most urgently required a renovation in terms of industrial science, mechanical production and new social relationships. But it was not the colonial system that provided or ever could provide this renovation. Potent to destroy, the bearers of the white man's burden proved helpless to rebuild, and the troubles of post-colonial Africa after the 1960s were to confirm this point with a weary insistence. All that was achieved, in general, was a deepening of that very large crisis of change and transformation which much of Africa had already entered before the invaders came on the scene. The invaders could and did widen this crisis. They proved unable to resolve it. Nor, for the most part, did they try to resolve it.

Of course there is more to be said than this. There is scarcely a single chapter in the colonial experience that does not have its inner contradictions. To see only the destructive essence, the undermining of Iron Age society, would be to ignore a number of lesser consequences, of side-effects, that were not negative, or at any rate not purely so. While the impact and value of these varied with the nature of the metropolitan society from which the rulers came, they were present even in colonies, such as those of Portugal, that were governed by an attitude almost pre-industrial or even pre-capitalist. Though wastefully and planlessly, with reluctance or contempt, the colonial rulers nonetheless opened a few new doors to the outside world. They helped to overcome the comparative isolation of the past. Their paternalist yet persevering Christian missionary endeavour and self-sacrifice—all this being very much akin to the comparable Christian effort among the British working classes of the nineteenth century—became a powerful influence in awakening a minority of Africans to their true situation and in preparing for a different future.

Even in this educational field, however, the balance of gain was not a simple one. There was public education, true enough; but throughout the colonial period this was never more than sparsely available, even at an elementary level, and was couched most clearly in the concepts and prejudices of the educators. Even if it may have been rare that French history books taught Africans that their ancestors were Gauls, the spirit of the teaching was exactly in that vein: it taught African inferiority and European superiority. For the greater part, moreover, it was designed to do no more than provide a little primitive literacy and counting for hewers of woods and drawers of water. It ranged from a relatively high percentage of children at primary schools, after 1945, in the British and French territories and in the Belgian Congo, to the pathetic levels of the Portuguese "civilizing effort" in Angola and Mozambique, where less than 1 per cent of African populations ever saw the inside of a school, no matter how rudimentary, before the wars of resistance began in 1961.

So far as secondary education is concerned, there is no exaggeration in saying that the whole of tropical Africa possessed only a handful of secondary schools up to the time of political independence in the late 1950s. Some of the characteristic examples must make painful reading for Europeans who have wished to believe in the reality of "trusteeship." After forty years of British administration in Tanganyika, a population not far short of 10 million people was able to enroll exactly 318 pupils in the class of standard 12 (the last in the four-year secondary course), while the number of school-certificates, permitting pupils to carry on with their studies, was 245. Taking the three British East African territories together—Kenya, Tanganyika and Uganda—the official figures show that populations totalling some 24 million people were able to achieve, after several decades of "trusteeship," fewer than 2,000 school-certificates every year: fewer than one, that is, for every 12,000 people. In West Africa the position was generally rather better; elsewhere, it was often much worse. After thirty-three years of Crown Colony rule in Southern Rhodesia, official figures for 1958 showed that 12,158 African children entered school at the bottom of the scale, in sub-standard A, while the number who got through to the top, standard 12, totalled exactly 13; and this, one may note, for an African population of approximately 3 million.

For the majority, then, colonial education either had no meaning, because it did not touch them, or none that was useful as an instrument of cultural enlightenment. Mass participation in anti-colonial struggles of one kind or another was a continuous feature of colonial life, but little of it owed anything to the influence of what was learned at school. The great revolts rested on their own traditions of political independence. The anti-colonial prophets, whether of African religion or separatist Christianity, founded their Messianic teachings upon ideas that lay outside the paternalist lessons of the schools. . . .

Most of the elites were content to accept the values of their masters. They tended to live double lives, in their "European" guise and in their "native" guise—and to prefer the first to the second, since the first carried with it not only comfort but also a certain prestige. This often meant a clear break between the colonial and native milieu, and a corresponding incapacity of the elites to use the education they possessed for the task of transforming African dependence into independence. An African leader has summarized all this. Colonial education, he points out, "was not designed to prepare young people for the service of their own country; instead, it was motivated by a desire to inculcate the values of the colonial society and to train individuals for the service of the colonial state. . . . This meant that colonial education induced attitudes of human inequality, and in practice underpinned the domination of the weak by the strong, especially in the economic field." It was education for the *status quo*, but a strictly colonial *status quo*. For even where a better understanding of the world helped to undermine the authority of the colonial regime, it also undermined the authority of all those Africans who stood for traditional methods and therefore, in the circumstances, for continued subjection, technological inferiority and poverty of social power. . . .

These are among the reasons why the colonial conquest was unique, and why it must be judged as such. Many African empires had arisen in the past, many innovating regimes, many strong reformers. Yet these had remained within their Iron Age framework even though, as the nineteenth century wore on, some of them were beginning to escape from it. Many outside influences and even a few outside invasions had arrived in previous centuries. But these had never been sufficiently large or long-enduring, or launched from a sufficiently different social system, to resist more or less rapid absorption into the adaptive patterns of indigenous African life. With colonialism it was altogether different. After that, Africa could never again be the same. The patterns of indigenous life simply could not contain, much less absorb, these eruptive methods and technologies; they wrecked the old framework beyond hope of repair. In this destructive and preparatory sense the colonial experience may be said to have performed a considerable transformation, however blind and painful. By 1945 the whole complex structure of Iron Age society, so greatly out of step as it was with the world from which the conquerors came, had suffered a collapse so fatal that it could never be put together again. . . .

Just as the industrial revolution had swept away the confining bonds of pre-industrial society in Britain a century and more earlier, and had done this in a comparably planless, violent and blindly painful way, so too did the colonial hurricane level to the ground every great polity it found, shaking them to their very roots, and leaving in its wake the need not only for new structures, but for structures of an altogether different and expansive type.

Yet there remained, one may repeat, a profound difference between the consequences of the industrial revolution in Europe and those of the colonial system in Africa. The first destroyed but also, after its fashion, mightily rebuilt afresh; the second, having gone far to ruin what it found, could only leave for Africans the task of making a new society. No such new society came into being during the colonial period. Little was left behind but an utter impoverishment of the old society, a chaos of ideas and social relationships. Nothing could be less true than the oft-repeated statement, heard so often during the last years of the colonial period, that "we have at least prepared these peoples for their own emancipation." When the principal colonial powers eventually withdrew, everything of basic social meaning remained to be renewed or built afresh. . . .

60

The African Roots of the War

In 1967 when the Reverend Martin Luther King, Jr. spoke in opposition to the Vietnam War, he was criticized for being unpatriotic and for abandoning his first priority, civil rights. Yet Dr. King argued that there were important connections between American foreign policy, and its domestic policy. Race played an important role in each, with the war against communism fought disproportionately by African-Americans, many of whom were deprived of their civil and economic rights at home. In fact, King was not the first African-American leader to speak on the internal as well as the external causes for war and discrimination. In 1915, the noted American scholar, W. E. B. du Bois, published this article in the *Atlantic Monthly*. In his cry to recognize Africa as the "Land of the Twentieth Century," he also pointed to the devastation that had resulted from the "desperate struggle for Africa" which led to imperial rivalry and had culminated in World War I. In particular, du Bois noted the role that race, or what he called the "Color Line," had played in both imperialism and in war, believing that race would be the paramount issue for the Twentieth Century. Though we are now in the 21st century, his words of warning, as well as his suggestions for remedying conflict, present an important message.

Discussion Questions

1. How does du Bois explain the paradox that Western societies' desire to spread democracy while at the same time being responsible for the exploitation caused by imperialism and racism?

2. Why does the author refer to Africa as hiding "the roots . . . of war today . . . and war tomorrow?"

3. How did the imperialism of the late 19th century lead to World War I?

4. What does race, or the "Color Line," as du Bois puts it, have to do with internal economic problems as well as international ones? Is race still an important factor in world events?

The African Roots of the War

I

"Semper novi quid ex Africa," cried the Roman proconsul; and he voiced the verdict of forty centuries. Yet there are those who would write world history and leave out this most marvelous of continents. Particularly today most men assume that Africa lies far afield from the centres of our burning social problems, and especially from our present problem of World War.

Yet in a very real sense Africa is a prime cause of this terrible overturning of civilization which we have lived to see; and these words seek to show how in the Dark Continent are hidden the roots, not simply of war today but of the menace of wars tomorrow.

Always Africa is giving us something new or some metempsychosis of a world-old thing. On its black bosom arose one of the earliest, if not the earliest, of self-protecting civilizations, and grew so mightily that it still furnishes superlatives to thinking and speaking men. Out of its darker and more remote forest fastnesses, came, if we may credit many recent scientists, the first welding of iron, and we know that agriculture and trade flourished there when Europe was a wilderness.

Nearly every human empire that has arisen in the world, material and spiritual, has found some of its greatest crises on this continent of Africa, from Greece to Great Britain. As Mommsen says, "It was through Africa that Christianity became the religion of the world." In Africa the last flood of Germanic invasions spent itself within hearing of the last gasp of Byzantium, and it was again through Africa that Islam came to play its great role of conqueror and civilizer.

With the Renaissance and the widened world of modern thought, Africa came no less suddenly with her new old gift. Shakespeare's Ancient Pistol cries,—

"A fourtre for the world, and worldings base!

I speak of Africa, and golden joys."

He echoes a legend of gold from the days of Punt and Ophir to those of Ghana, the Gold Coast, and the Rand. This thought had sent the world's greed scurrying down the hot, mysterious coasts of Africa to the Good Hope of gain, until for the first time a real world-commerce was born, albeit it started as a commerce mainly in the bodies and souls of men.

So much for the past; and now today: the Berlin Conference to apportion the rising riches of Africa among the white peoples met on the fifteenth day of November, 1884. Eleven days earlier, three Germans left Zanzibar (whither they had gone secretly disguised as mechanics), and before the Berlin Conference had finished its deliberations they had annexed to Germany an area over half as large again as the whole German Empire in Europe. Only in its dramatic suddenness was this undisguised robbery of the land of seven million natives different from the methods by which Great Britain and France got four million square miles each, Portugal three quarters of a million, and Italy and Spain smaller but substantial areas.

The methods by which this continent has been stolen have been contemptible and dishonest beyond expression. Lying treaties, rivers of rum, murder, assassination, mutilation, rape, and torture have marked the progress of Englishman, German, Frenchman, and Belgian on the dark continent. The only way in which the world has been able to endure the horrible tale is by deliberately stopping its ears and changing the subject of conversation while the deviltry went on.

It all began, singularly enough, like the present war, with Belgium. Many of us remember Stanley's great solution of the puzzle of Central Africa when he traced the mighty Congo sixteen hundred miles from Nyangwe to the sea. Suddenly the world knew that here lay the key to the riches of Central Africa. It stirred uneasily, but Leopold of Belgium was first on his feet, and the result was the Congo Free State—God save the mark! But the Congo Free State, with all its magniloquent heralding of Peace, Christianity, and Commerce, degenerating into murder, mutilation and downright robbery, differed only in degree and concentration from the tale of all Africa in this rape of a continent already furiously mangled by the slave trade. That sinister traffic, on which the British Empire and the American Republic were largely built, cost black Africa no less than 100,000,000 souls, the wreckage of its political and social life, and left the continent in precisely that state of helplessness which invites aggression and exploitation. "Color" became in the world's thought synonymous with inferiority, "Negro" lost its capitalization, and Africa was another name for bestiality and barbarism.

Thus the world began to invest in color prejudice. The "Color Line" began to pay dividends. For indeed, while the exploration of the valley of the Congo was the occasion of the scramble for Africa, the cause lay deeper. The Franco-Prussian War turned the eyes of those who sought power and dominion away from Europe. Already England was in Africa, cleaning away the debris of the slave trade and half consciously groping toward the new Imperialism. France, humiliated and impoverished, looked toward a new northern African empire sweeping from the Atlantic to the Red Sea. More slowly Germany began to see the dawning of a new day, and, shut out from America by the Monroe Doctrine, looked to Asia and Africa for colonies. Portugal sought anew to make good her claim to her ancient African realm; and thus a continent where Europe claimed but a tenth of the land in 1875, was in twenty-five more years practically absorbed.

II

Why was this? What was the new call for dominion? It must have been strong, for consider a moment the desperate flames of war that have shot up in Africa in new call for dominion? It must have been strong, for consider a moment the desperate flames of war that have shot up in Africa in the last quarter of a century: France and England at Fashoda, Italy at Adua, Italy and Turkey in Tripoli,

England and Portuagal at Delagoa Bay, England, Germany, and the Dutch in South Africa, France and Spain in Morocco, Germany and France in Agadir, and the world at Algeciras.

The answer to this riddle we shall find in the economic changes in Europe. Remember what the nineteenth and twentieth centuries have meant to organized industry in European civilization. Slowly the divine right of the few to determine economic income and distribute the goods and services of the world has been questioned and curtailed. We called the process Revolution in the eighteenth century, advancing Democracy in the nineteenth, and Socialization of Wealth in the twentieth. But whatever we call it, the movement is the same: the dipping of more and grimier hands into the wealth-bag of the nation, until today only the ultra stubborn fail to see that democracy in determining income is the next inevitable step to Democracy in political power.

With the waning of the possibility of the Big Fortune, gathered by starvation wage and boundless exploitation of one's weaker and poorer fellows at home, arose more magnificently the dream of exploitation abroad. Always, of course, the individual merchant had at his own risk and in his own way tapped the riches of foreign lands. Later, special trading monopolies had entered the field and founded empires overseas. Soon, however, the mass of merchants at home demanded a share in this golden stream; and finally, in the twentieth century, the laborer at home is demanding and beginning to receive a part of his share.

The theory of this new democratic despotism has not been clearly formulated. Most philosophers see the ship of state launched on the broad, irresistible tide of democracy, with only delaying eddies here and there; others, looking closer, are more disturbed. Are we, they ask, reverting to aristocracy and despotism—the rule of might? They cry out and then rub their eyes, for surely they cannot fail to see strengthening democracy all about them?

It is this paradox which has confounded philanthropists, curiously betrayed the Socialists, and reconciled the Imperialists, and captains of industry to any amount of "Democracy." It is this paradox which allows in America the most rapid advance of democracy to go hand in hand in its very centres with increased aristocracy and hatred toward darker races, and which excuses and defends an inhumanity that does not shrink from the public burning of human beings.

Yet the paradox is easily explained: the white workingman has been asked to share the spoil of exploiting "chinks and niggers." It is no longer simply the merchant prince, or the aristocratic monopoly, or even the employing class, that is exploiting the world: it is the nation; a new democratic nation composed of united capital and labor. The laborers are not yet getting, to be sure, as large a share as they want or will get, and there are still at the bottom large and restless excluded classes. But the laborer's equity is recognized, and his just share is a matter of time, intelligence and skillful negotiation.

Such nations it is that rule the modern world. Their national bond is no mere sentimental patriotism, loyalty, or ancestor-worship. It is increased wealth, power, and luxury for all classes on a scale the world never saw before. Never before was the average citizen of England, France, and Germany so rich, with such splendid prospects of greater riches.

Whence comes this new wealth and on what does its accumulation depend? It comes primarily from the darker nations of the world—Asia and Africa, South and Central America, the West Indies and the islands of the South Seas. There are still, we well believe, many parts of white countries like Russia and North America, not to mention Europe itself, where the older exploitation still holds. But the knell has sounded faint and far, even there. In the lands of darker folk, however, no knell has sounded. Chinese, East Indians, Negroes, and South American Indians, are by common consent for governance by white folk and economic subjection to them. To the furtherance of this highly profitable economic dictum has been brought every available resource of science and religion. Thus arises the astonishing doctrine of the natural inferiority of most men to the few, and the interpretation of "Christian brotherhood" as meaning anything that one of the "brothers" may at any time want it to mean.

Like all world-schemes, however, this one is not quite complete. First, of all, yellow Japan has apparently escaped the cordon of this color bar. This is disconcerting and dangerous to white hegemony. If, of course, Japan would join heart and soul with the whites against the rest of the yellows, browns, and blacks, well and good. There are even good-natured attempts to prove the Japanese "Aryan," provided they act "white." But blood is thick, and there are signs that Japan does not dream of a world governed mainly by white men. This is the "Yellow Peril," and it may be necessary, as the German Emperor and many white Americans think, to start a world-crusade against this presumptuous nation which demands "white" treatment.

Then, too, the Chinese have recently shown unexpected signs of independence and autonomy, which may possibly make it necessary to take them into account a few decades hence. As a result, the problem in Asia has resolved itself into a race for "spheres" of economic "influence," each provided with a more or less "open door" for business opportunity. This reduces the danger of open clash between European nations, and gives the yellow folk such chance for desperate unarmed resistance as was shown by China's repulse of the Six Nations of Bankers. There

is still hope among some whites that conservative North China and the radical South may in time come to blows and allow actual white dominion.

One thing, however, is certain: Africa is prostrate. There at least are few signs of self-consciousness that need at present be heeded. To be sure, Abyssinia must be wheedled, and in America and the West Indies Negroes have attempted futile steps toward freedom; but such steps have been pretty effectually stopped (save through the breech of "miscegenation"), although the ten million Negroes in the United States need, to many men's minds, careful watching and ruthless repression.

III

Thus the European mind has worked, and worked the more feverishly because Africa is the Land of the Twentieth Century. The world knows something of the gold and diamonds of South Africa, the cocoa of Angola and Nigeria, the rubber and ivory of the Congo, and the palm oil of the West Coast. But does the ordinary citizen realize the extraordinary economic advances of Africa and, too, of black Africa, in recent years? E. T. Morel, who knows his Africa better than most white men, has shown us how the export of palm oil from West Africa has grown from 283 tons in 1800, to 80,000 tons in 1913, which together with by-products is worth to-day $60,000,000 annually. He shows how native Gold Coast labor, unsupervised, has come to head the cocoa-producing countries of the world with an export of 89,000,000 pounds (weight *not* money) annually. He shows how the cotton crop of Uganda has risen from 3000 bales in 1909 to 50,000 bales in 1914; and he says that France and Belgium are no more remarkable in the cultivation of their land than the Negro province of Kano. The trade of Abyssinia amounts to only

$10,000,000 a year, but it is its infinite possibility of growth that is making the nations crowd to Addis Abba. All these things are but beginnings; "but tropical Africa and its peoples are being brought more irrevocably each year into the vortex of the economic influences that sway the western world." There can be no doubt of the economic possibilities of Africa in the near future. There are not only the well-known and traditional products, but boundless chances in a hundred different directions, and above all, there is a throng of human beings who, could they once be reduced to the docility and steadiness of Chinese coolies or of seventeenth and eighteenth century European laborers, would furnish to their masters a spoil exceeding the gold-haunted dreams of the most modern of Imperialists.

This, then, is the real secret of that desperate struggle for Africa which began in 1877 and is now culminating. Economic dominion outside Africa has, of course, played its part, and we were on the verge of the partition of Asia when Asiatic shrewdness warded it off. America was saved from direct political dominion by the Monroe Doctrine. Thus, more and more, the Imperialists have concentrated on Africa.

The greater the concentration the more deadly the rivalry. From Fashoda to Agadir, repeatedly the spark has been applied to the European magazine and a general conflagration narrowly averted. We speak of the Balkans as the storm-centre of Europe and the cause of war, but this is mere habit. The Balkans are convenient for occasions, but the ownership of materials and men in the darker world is the real prize that is seeing the nations of Europe at each other's throats today.

The present world war is, then, the result of jealousies engendered by the recent rise of armed national associations of labor and capital whose aim is the exploitation of the wealth of the world mainly outside the European circle of nations. These associations, grown jealous and suspicious at the division of the spoils of trade-empire, are fighting to enlarge their respective shares; they look for expansion, not in Europe but in Asia, and particularly in Africa. "We want no inch of French territory," said Germany to England, but Germany was "unable to give" similar assurances as to France in Africa.

The difficulties of this imperial movement are internal as well as external. Successful aggression in economic expansion calls for a close union between capital and labor at home. Now the rising demands of the white laborer, not simply for wages but for conditions of work and a voice in the conduct of industry, make industrial peace difficult. The workingmen have been appeased by all sorts of essays in state socialism, on the one hand, and on the other hand by public threats of competition by colored labor. By threatening to send English capital to China and Mexico, by threatening to hire Negro laborers in America, as well as by old-age pensions and accident insurance, we gain industrial peace at home at the mightier cost of war abroad.

In addition to these national war-engendering jealousies there is a more subtle movement arising from the attempt to unite labor and capital in world-wide freebooting. Democracy in economic organization, while an acknowledged ideal, is today working itself out by admitting to a share in the spoils of capital only the aristocracy of labor—the more intelligent and shrewder and cannier workingmen. The ignorant, unskilled, and restless still form a large, threatening, and, to a growing extent, revolutionary group in advanced countries.

The resultant jealousies and bitter hatreds tend continually to fester along the color line. We must fight the Chinese, the laborer argues, or the Chinese will take our bread and butter. We must keep Negroes in their places, or Negroes will take our jobs. All over the world there leaps to articulate speech and ready action that singular assumption that if white men do not throttle colored men, then China, India, and Africa will do to Europe what Europe had done and seeks to do to them.

On the other hand, in the minds of yellow, brown, and black men the brutal truth is clearing: the black or colored man is being more and more confined to these parts of the world where life for climatic, historical, economic, and political reasons is most difficult to live and most easily dominated by Europe for Europe's gain.

IV

What, then, are we to do, who desire peace and the civilization of all men? Hitherto the peace movement has confined itself chiefly to figures about the cost of war and platitudes on humanity. What do nations care about the cost of war, if by spending a few hundred millions in steel and gunpowder they can gain a thousand millions in diamonds and cocoa? How can love of humanity appeal as a motive to nations whose love of luxury is built on the inhuman exploitation of human beings, and who, especially in recent years, have been taught to regard these human beings, as inhuman? I appealed to the last meeting of peace societies in St. Louis, saying, "Should you not discuss racial prejudice as a prime cause of war?" The secretary was sorry but was unwilling to introduce controversial matters!

We, then, who want peace, must remove the real causes of war. We have extended gradually our conception of democracy beyond our social class to all social classes in our nation; we have gone further and extended our democratic ideals not simply to all classes of our own nation, but to those of other nations of our blood and lineage—to what we call "European" civilization. If we want real peace and lasting culture, however,

we must go further. We must extend the democratic ideal to the yellow, brown, and black peoples.

To say this, is to evoke on the faces of modern men a look of blank hopelessness. Impossible! we are told, and for some many reasons,—scientific, social and what not,—that argument is useless. But let us not conclude too quickly. Suppose we have to choose between this unspeakably inhuman outrage on decency and intelligence and religion which we call the World War and the attempt to treat black men as human, sentient, responsible beings? We have sold them as cattle. We are working them as beasts of burden. We shall not drive war from this world until we treat them as free and equal citizens in a world-democracy of all races and nations. Impossible? Democracy is a method of doing the impossible. It is the only method yet discovered of making the education and development of all men a matter of all men's desperate desire. It is putting firearms in the hands of a child with the object of compelling the child's neighbors to teach him, not only the real and legitimate uses of a dangerous tool but the uses of himself in all things. Are there other and less costly ways of accomplishing this? There may be in some better world. But for a world just emerging from the rough chains of an almost universal poverty, and faced by the temptation of luxury and indulgence through the enslaving of defenseless men, there is but one adequate method of salvation—the giving of democratic weapons of self-defense to the defenseless.

Nor need we quibble over those ideas,—wealth, education, and political power,—soil which we have so forested with claim and counterclaim that we see nothing for the woods.

What the primitive peoples of Africa and the world need and must have if war is to be abolished is perfectly clear:—

First: land. Today Africa is being enslaved by the theft of her land and natural resources. A century ago black men owned all but a morsel of South Africa. The Dutch and English came, and today 1,250,000 whites own 264,000,000 acres, leaving only 21,000,000 acres for 45,000,000 natives. Finally, to make assurance doubly sure, the Union of South Africa has refused natives even the right to *buy* land. This is a deliberate attempt to force the Negroes to work on farms and in mines and kitchens for low wages. All over Africa has gone this shameless monopolizing of land and natural resources to force poverty on the masses and reduce them to the "dumb-driven-cattle" stage of labor activity.

Secondly: we must train native races in modern civilization. This can be done. Modern methods of educating children, honestly and effectively applied, would make modern, civilized nations out of the vast majority of human beings on earth today. This we have seldom tried. For the most part Europe is straining every nerve to make over yellow, brown, and black men into docile beasts of burden, and only an irrepressible few are allowed to escape and seek (usually abroad) the education of modern men.

Lastly, the principle of home rule must extend to groups, nations, and races. The ruling of one people for another people's whim or gain must stop. This kind of despotism has been in later days more and more skillfully disguised. But the brute fact remains: the white man is ruling black Africa for the white man's gain, and just as far as possible he is doing the same to colored races elsewhere. Can such a situation bring peace? Will any amount of European concord or disarmament settle this injustice?

Political power today is but the weapon to force economic power. Tomorrow, it may give us spiritual vision and artistic sensibility. Today, it gives us or tries to give us bread and butter, and those classes or nations or races who are without it starve, and starvation is the weapon of the white world to reduce them to slavery.

We are calling for European concord today; but at the utmost European concord will mean satisfaction with, or acquiescence in, a given division of the spoils of world-dominion. After all, European disarmament cannot go below the necessity of defending the aggressions of the white against the blacks and browns and yellows. From this will arise three perpetual dangers of war. First, renewed jealously at any division of colonies or spheres of influence agreed upon, if at any future time the present division comes to seem unfair. Who cared for Africa in the early nineteenth century? Let England have the scraps left from the golden feast of the slave trade. But in the twentieth century? The end was war. These scraps looked too tempting to Germany. Secondly: war will come from the revolutionary revolt of the lowest workers. The greater the international jealousies, the greater the corresponding costs of armament and the more difficult to fulfill the promises of industrial democracy in advanced countries. Finally, the colored peoples will not always submit passively to foreign domination. To some this is a lightly tossed truism. When a people deserve liberty they fight for it and get it, say such philosophers; thus making war a regular, necessary step to liberty. Colored people are familiar with this complacent judgment. They endure the contemptuous treatment meted out by whites to those not "strong" enough to be free. These nations and races, composing as they do a vast majority of humanity, are going to endure this treatment just as long as they must and not a moment longer. Then they are going to fight and the War of the Color Line will outdo in savage inhumanity any war this world has yet seen. For colored folk have much to remember and they will not forget.

But is this inevitable? Must we sit helpless before this awful prospect? While we are planning, as a result of the present holocaust, the disarmament of Europe and a European international world-police, must the rest of the world be left naked to the inevitable horror of war, especially when we know that it is directly in this outer circle of races, and not in the inner European household, that the real causes of present European fighting are to be found?

Our duty is clear. Racial slander must go. Racial prejudice will follow. Steadfast faith in humanity must come. The domination of one people by another without the other's consent, be the subject black or white, must stop. The doctrine of forcible economic expansion over subject peoples must go. Religious hypocrisy must stop. "Blood-thirsty" Mwanga of Uganda killed an English bishop because he feared that his coming meant English domination. It did mean English domination, and the world and the bishop knew it, and yet the world was "horrified"! Such missionary hypocrisy must go. With clean hands and honest hearts we must front high Heaven and beg peace in our time.

In this great work who can help us? In the Orient, the awakened Japanese and the awakening leaders of New China; In India and Egypt, the young men trained in Europe and European ideals, who now form the stuff that Revolution is born of. But in Africa? Who better than the twenty-five million grandchildren of the European slave trade, spread through the Americas, and now writhing desperately for freedom and a place in the world? And of these millions first of all the ten million black folk of the United States, now a problem, then a world-salvation.

Twenty centuries before Christ a great cloud swept over sea and settled on Africa, darkening and well-nigh blotting out the culture of the land of Egypt. For half a thousand years it rested there until a black woman, Queen Nefertari, "the most venerated figure in Egyptian history," rose to the throne of the Pharoahs and redeemed the world and her people. Twenty centuries after Christ, black Africa, prostrate, raped, and shamed, lies at the feet of the conquering Philistines of Europe. Beyond the awful sea a black woman is weeping and waiting with her sons on her breast. What shall the end be? The world-old and fearful things. War and Wealth, Murder and Luxury? Or shall it be a new thing—a new peace and new democracy of all races: a great humanity of equal men? "Semper novi quid ex Africa!"

61

The Social History of the Machine Gun—World War I

World War I was not only the first world war but also the first total war, involving civilians far-removed from the battlefields in a direct and significant way. In fact, there were more civilian casualties than combatant, a reflection of the stalemated military situation that developed early in August, 1914, at the Battle of the Marne. Each side tried, through any means possible, to destroy the other side's ability to wage war—the classic elements of a war of attrition. Thus, the symbols of World War I came to be the trench, no-man's land, barbed wire, and, above all, the machine gun. Yet this was not the scenario envisioned by the statesmen of the day, who were surprised by the very start of the war itself, nor the military leaders, whose contempt for technology and whose plans for the conduct of the war are highlighted in this selection. Most agreed with a British historian of the period who argued that modern weapons, if needed at all, would have a beneficial and deterrent effect on any future war in that "if any man could invent a means of destruction, by which two nations going to war with each other would see large armies destroyed . . . in a single campaign they would both hesitate at entering upon another. . . . In this sense the greatest destroyer is the greatest philanthropist." The reality of World War I destroyed this and many other illusions—about modern technology and modern warfare.

Discussion Questions

1. How did 19th century military leaders view war? What role did technology play in their definition of war, and why?

2. What do you see as the basic contradiction between the military's notions of war and the reality of the industrialized societies of which the military was a part? Why you think 19th century leaders were so wrong in their assessment of war, technology and human beings?

3. How did the role of the soldier change with World War I?

4. What lessons from this examination of the role of technology in World War I could we apply to our present situation? Does this selection reveal anything about the human potential for self-destruction?

(There was) a decided hardening of the arteries . . . in the general staffs, evidenced in their reluctance to consider technological innovations; how utterly averse they were to changes in material was discovered to their great chagrin by industrialists like Colt, Krupp and Whitworth, and the military inventor and officer Werner Siemens grew so disgusted with the Prussian service that he gave it up to go into industry. . . . Especially in the first half of the nineteenth century . . . the officer remained a romantic in the industrial age.

A. Vagts, *History of Militarism*

General Manteuffel gave a very clear example of this contempt for all things technical when he attacked the whole notion of schools "where often enough haughty teachers, as a rule full of hostility to war and the better classes, proud of their fancied scholarship, in brutal ways kill the feeling of honour and, saturated with the destructive tendencies of the time, almost exclusively rationalist, educate for everything else but character."

But there was more to the officers' attitude than a mere inability to comprehend technological progress. Because of their aristocratic origins many of the officers were, as Vagts put it, romantics in an industrial age. Their social isolation limited them to a conception of war as it had existed in a previous century. They still believed in the glorious cavalry charge and, above all, the supremacy of man as opposed to mere machines. Certainly they acknowledged that soldiers got killed by fire-arms, but they were never prepared to admit that advances in technology had reached such a level that the staunchest assault by the best of troops could be brought to nothing by modern weapons.

Certain thinkers did see that this was so. Engels, for example, stated flatly that:

> Force is not mere act of will but calls for very real conditions before it starts to work, in particular tools, of which the perfect one overcomes the imperfect ones; that furthermore these tools must be produced, which means at the same time that the producer of more perfect tools, vulgo arms, beats the producer of more imperfect ones.

But the officers of the nineteenth century completely missed this point about the increasing dominance of the tools of war. For them war still was an act of will. Military memories and traditions had been formed in a pre–industrial age when the final bayonet or cavalry charge might be decisive. For them, in the last analysis, man was the master of the battlefield. In the military hierarchies of Europe the traditional ideas lived on, and the whole period up to 1918 and even beyond is dominated by this basic contradiction. In a stimulating study of the fictional treatment of war at this time, I. F. Clarke is drawn to just this conclusion:

> The great paradox running through the whole of this production of imaginary wars between 1871 and 1914 was the total failure of army and navy writers to guess what would happen when the major industrial nations decided to fight it out.

In Prussia, Heros von Borcke took pains to examine many corpses and found so few stabbing wounds that he concluded that" bayonet fights rarely if ever occur, and exist only in the imagination." After spending twelve years examining the nature of modern warfare the Polish banker, Ivan Bloch, came to the conclusion that:

> War will become a kind of stalemate. . . . Everybody will be entrenched. It will be a great war of entrenchments. The spade would be as indispensable to the soldier as his rifle. . . . It will of necessity partake of the character of siege operations. . . . There will be increased slaughter . . . on so terrible a scale as to render it impossible to get

troops to push the battle to a decisive issue. They will try to, thinking that they are fighting under the old conditions, and they will learn such a lesson that they will abandon the attempt for ever.

But such warnings fell on deaf ears. The average officer was simply not receptive to any ideas that might force him to change his comfortable habits.

The most bizarre reflection of the contradiction between the old modes of thought and the new weapons was the grim determination with which military establishments clung on to their cavalry regiments. Thus the British Cavalry Training Manual of 1907: "It must be accepted as a principle that the rifle, effective as it is, cannot replace the effect produced by the speed of the horse, the magnetism of the charge, and the terror of cold steel." Luckily for the Germans, in the First World War, they used machine guns, pill boxes and barbed wire that seem to have been immune to such awesome tactics. That it took the British generals so long to get this through their heads is partly explained by the fact that nearly all of them were cavalry men. Thus Haig, in 1904, attacked a writer who "sneers at the effect produced by sword and lance in modern war; surely he forgets that it is not the weapons carried but the moral factor of an apparently irresistible force, coming on at highest speed in spite of rifle fire, which affects the nerves and aim of the . . . rifleman."

It is thus hardly surprising that the general military reaction to the machine gun was something less than enthusiastic. There was some support from seemingly important quarters, but in fact such proponents of automatic weapons tended to be isolated individuals or to come from groups unable to make much impact on the orthodox military establishment. In 1882, Lord Charles Beresford asserted that: "In my opinion, machine guns, if properly worked, could decide the fate of a campaign, and would be equally useful ashore or afloat." Beresford was actually a Navy man, and he, and others, had all gained their reputations in the many colonial wars that Britain waged in the nineteenth century. Though this made them popular figures with the general public it, in fact, reduced their influence within the military hierarchy. For, in the last analysis, the majority of soldiers regarded such imperialist expeditions as mere sideshows, and concentrated their thoughts upon the possibility of a future war in Europe. So the machine gun became associated with colonial expeditions and the slaughter of natives, and was thus by definition regarded as being totally inappropriate to the conditions of regular European warfare.

The most tragic aspect of the High Commands' blindness to the power of automatic weapons was their chronic inability to recognise exactly what it meant to face up to an enemy equipped with such weapons. For all power had now passed to the defensive and the main reason for this was the presence of the machine guns. As one writer has put is: "It was as simple as this: three men and a machine gun can stop a battalion of heroes." The essential tragedy of the First World War is that the British commanders did not grasp this basic fact over three years.

The war on the ground had congealed almost immediately. The first trench warfare took place in September 1914 as the Germans on the Chemin des Dames Ridge, on the Aisne, dug in to block the Allied advance. By October 1914 one officer was able to write that: "The foremost infantry of both armies are now too securely entrenched, 200 to 400 yards apart, for attacks to have much chance of success save at prohibitive price." These were the conditions that prevailed for the next three years and more. The power of the defence, and particularly the machine gun, had rendered almost nil the chances of a successful frontal attack.

One of the first British offensives took place at Neuve Chapelle, in March 1915. The offensive was doomed to failure from the first because it was carried out with insufficient men and equipment. It had been intended that the French and the British should share the burden but Sir John French had tired of ceaseless French demands for aid in other sectors, and in a fit of pique decided to mount the attack with his own forces. The events of the first day made abundantly clear the characteristics of the new style of warfare. The actual infantry assault was preceded by a concentrated artillery barrage, intended to knock out the front line defences. When it stopped the British were to move forward. The experiences of one unit, the 2nd Scottish Rifles, in this battle have been meticulously studied, and are typical of the day's events:

> Ferrers was first out from 'B' Company, his monocle in his eye and his sword in his hand. As the guns stopped firing there was a moment of silence. Then the guns started again, firing behind the German lines. . . . Almost at the same moment came another noise, the whip and crack of the enemy machine guns opening up with deadly effect. From the intensity of their fire, and its accuracy, it was clear that the shelling had not been as effective as expected. . . . As the attack progressed the German positions which did most damage were two machine gun posts in front of the Middlesex. Not only did they virtually wipe out the 2nd Middlesex with frontal fire, but they caused many of the losses in the 2nd Scottish Rifles with deadly enfilade, or flanking fire.

In other words, two machine guns, a dozen Germans at most, brought to a halt two battalions of British infantry, or something over 1,500 men. Similar experiences were recorded all down the line of attack, and as the Germans pushed more men and machine guns into the threatened sector the attack swiftly fizzled out.

But the Allied High Command drew no lessons from this reverse. It was merely felt that the next time all that was needed was more shells, more men, and possibly just a little more offensive spirit. In September, at the Battle of Loos, exactly the same thing happened again. But still no one thought to question the British tactics. Instead they got rid of the commander–in–chief. At the end of the year French was replaced by Haig.

Through bitter experience the machine taught that man himself was no longer master of the battlefield. The individual counted for nothing, all that mattered now was the machinery of war. If a machine gun could wipe out a whole battalion of men in three minutes, where was the relevance of the old concepts of heroism, glory and fair play between gentlemen? Lloyd George said that almost eighty per cent of the First World War casualties were caused by machine guns. In a way in which death was dealt out to so many with such mechanical casualness how could the old traditional modes of thought survive? The First World War was an event of crucial significance in the history of Western culture, a four–year trauma in which men tried to hold on to their old self–confidence in the face of horrors that would have been literally unimaginable two or three years earlier.

The confusion manifested itself in many ways. Some tried to cling on to the old modes of thought. In this respect the praise for the German machine–gunners achieves a new significance. In it one sees a desperate attempt to create new heroes in a war in which heroism was in fact irrelevant. Men tried to forget the weapons themselves, the mere machines that killed so unerringly and so indiscriminately, and remember only the men that pressed the trigger. Thus death could be made a little more acceptable.

Even those who retained their humanity and sensitivity also showed signs of the spiritual confusion that overtook those on the Western Front. Nowhere is this more clearly evidenced than in the work of the First World War poets. A poem of Siegfried Sassoon's, *The Redeemer*, shows this as well as any one poem can. Sassoon tells how he saw an English soldier struggling along with a load of planks, and in the darkness imagined for a moment that he was Christ on his cross. The last verse reads:

He faced me, reeling in his weariness,
Shouldering his load of planks, so hard to bear.
I say that he was Christ, who wrought to bless
All groping things with freedom bright as air,
And with his mercy washed and made them fair.
Then the flame sank, and all grew black as pitch,
While we began to struggle along the ditch;
And someone flung his burden in the muck,
Mumbling: 'O Christ Almighty, now I'm stuck!'

The intentionally pathetic ending clearly reveals Sassoon's feeling that, try as he might to rekindle some belief in the old religious and ethical sureties of the days before the war, a new reality has been born in which such beliefs count for nothing besides the facts of the mud, the darkness and the heavy load. One critic has put the whole thing very well:

The poets of World War I made it clear that man could no longer depend on his personal courage or strength for victory or even survival; mechanisation, the increased size of armies, the intensification of operations, the scientific efficiency of long–distance weapons destroyed the very elements of human individuality: courage, hope, enterprise, and a sense of the heroic possibilities in moral and physical conflict.

62

World War I: War of Attrition

Field Marshall Sir Douglas Haig:

"In the stage of the wearing-out struggle losses will necessarily be heavy on both sides, for in it the price of victory is paid. If the opposing forces are approximately equal in numbers, in courage, in morale and in equipment, there is no way of avoiding payment of the price or of eliminating this phase of the struggle.

In former battles this stage of the conflict has rarely lasted more than a few days, and has often been completed in a few hours. When armies of millions are engaged, with the resources of great empires behind them, it will inevitably be long. It will include violent crises of fighting which, when viewed separately and apart from the general perspective, will appear individually as great indecisive battles. To this stage belong the great engagements of 1916 and 1917 which wore down the strength of the German armies."

General Erich von Falkenhayn on Verdun:

"We can probably do enough for our purposes with limited resources. Within our reach behind the French sector of the Western Front there are objectives for which the French General Staff would be compelled to throw in every man they have. If they do so the forces of France will bleed to death—as there can be no question of voluntary withdrawal—whether we reach our goal or not."

World War I: Battlefield Statistics

Battle of Verdun (1915):

Artillery used by both sides: ca. 2,000 guns
In four months of battle, over 24,000,000
    shells had been fired by both sides
This was equivalent to 1,000 shells for each
    square meter of the battlefield

Battle of the Somme (1916):

27,768,076 rounds were fired in 153 days
    of battle by the British
This was equivalent to 181,491 rounds/day
    or 3,951 tons/day
which required 13 trains/day to transport

Battle of Arras (1917):

The Canadian Corps used 377 heavy guns
    on a front of four miles
(1 heavy for every 20 yards of front)
            plus
1 field gun for every 10 yards of front
2,687,653 rounds were fired in the prelimi-
    nary bombardment
4,261,500 rounds were fired during the
    most intensive fighting

Third Battle of Ypres (1917):

4,283,550 rounds were fired in the prelimi-
    nary bombardment

World War I: Casualties

Personnel:

65,000,000 mobilized
10,000,000 soldiers died in battle
20,000,000 soldiers wounded
7,000,000 permanently disabled
20,000,000 civilians killed
Battle of Verdun: 750,000 killed and wounded
Battle of the Somme: 1,200,000 killed and wounded
One-half of all French males, 20–32 years old, killed

Four Empires Destroyed:

1. The German Empire
2. The Austrian Empire
3. The Russian Empire
4. The Ottoman Empire

Adapted from John Terraine, *White Heat: The New Warfare, 1914–1918,* Sidgwick & Jackson, London, 1982.

World War I: The Cost
(Carnegie Foundation Estimate)
$400,000,000,000 (1914 dollars)

This amount could:

1. Give every family in the British Isles, Belgium, Russia,
   the U.S., Germany, Canada and Australia a $2500
   house, $1000 worth of furniture and a $500 five-acre lot,

   and

2. Provide a $5,000,000 library and a $10,000,000 university to every community of over 20,000 people,

   and

3. Create a fund to pay from interest alone 125,000 teachers
   and 125,000 nurses,

   and

4. Purchase every piece of property and all the wealth of
   both England and France.

63

War in the Trenches

Eric Maria Remarque's *All Quiet on the Western Front* is the most famous
example of the genre of war novels that were written in the 1920's. The purpose
of these books was to bring home to the civilians what it was like to be in the
trenches during the war. Remarque presents his novel as a memoir by a certain
Paul Baumer, an eighteen-year-old German soldier who finds himself thrown
into the abyss of war for the first time, like almost all of the soldiers in World
War I.

Discussion Questions

1. How does Remarque describe the changes that men went through when they
   made the transition from civilian to soldier?

2. What was fighting in the trenches like?

3. What grand and noble objectives do the soldiers seem to be fighting for? If
   you knew about the conditions of trench warfare, would you volunteer?

4. When men kill each other in war is it murder?

5. What had happened to all the great advances of Western civilization for those
   who fought in the trenches? When Baumer says, "The Bushmen are primitive
   and naturally so, but we are primitive in an artificial sense," what does he
   mean?

"Surely Himmelstoss was a very different fellow as a postman," say I, after Albert's disappointment has subsided.

"Then how does it come that he's such a bully as a drill-sergeant?"

The question revives Kropp, more particularly as he hears there's no more beer in the canteen. "It's not only Himmelstoss, there are lots of them. As sure as they get a stripe or a star they become different, as though they'd swallowed concrete."

"That's the uniform," I suggest.

"Roughly speaking it is," says Kat, and prepares long speech; "but the root of the matter lies elsewhere. For instance, if you train a dog to eat potatoes and afterwards put a piece of meat in front of him, he'll snap at it, it's his nature. And if you give a man a little bit of authority he behaves just the same way, he snaps at it too. The things are precisely the same. In himself **man is essentially a beast**, only he butters it over like a slice of bread with a little decorum. The army is based on that; one man must always have power over the other. The mischief is merely that each one has much too much power. A non-com. can torment a private, a lieutenant a non-com., a captain a lieutenant, until he goes mad. And because they know they can, they all soon acquire the habit more or less. Take a simple case: we are marching-back from the parade-ground dog-tired. Then comes the order to sing. We are glad enough to be able to trail arms but we sing spiritlessly. At once the company is turned about and has to do another hour's drill as punishment. On the march back the order to sing is given again, and once more we start. Now what's the use of all that? It's simply that the company commander's head has been turned by having so much power. And nobody blames him. On the contrary, he is praised for being strict. That, of course, is only a trifling instance, but it holds also in very different affairs. Now I ask you: Let a man be whatever you like in peace-time, what occupation is there in which he can behave like that without getting a crack on the nose? He can only do that in the army. It goes to the heads of them all, you see. And the more insignificant a man has been in civil life the worse it takes him."

. . .

From the earth, from the air, sustaining forces pour into us—mostly from the earth. To no man does the earth mean so much as to the soldier. When he presses himself down upon her long and powerfully, when he buries his face and his limbs deep in her from the fear of death by shell-fire, then she is his only friend, his brother, his mother; he stifles his terror and his cries in her silence and her security; she shelters him and gives him a new lease of ten seconds of life, receives him again and often for ever.

Earth!—Earth!—Earth!

Earth with thy folds, and hollows and holes, into which a man may fling himself and crouch down! In the spasm of terror, under the hailing of annihilation, in the bellowing death of die explosions, O Earth, thou grantest us the great resisting surge of new-won life. Our being, almost utterly carried

---

away by the fury of the storm, streams back through our hands from thee, and we, thy redeemed ones, bury ourselves in thee, and through the long minutes in a mute agony of hope bite into thee with our lips! . . .

We trudge onward in single file through the trenches and shell-holes and come again to the zone of mist. Katczinsky is restive, that's a bad sign.

"What's up, Kat?" says Kropp.

"I wish I were back home." Home—he means the huts.

"It won't last much longer, Kat."

He is nervous. "I don't know, I don't know—"

We come to the communication-trench and then the open fields. The little wood reappears; we know every foot of ground here. There's the cemetery with mounds and the black crosses.

That moment it breaks out behind us, swells, roars, and thunders. We duck down— a cloud of flame shoots up a hundred yards ahead of us.

The next minute under a second explosion part of the wood rises slowly in the air, three or four trees sail up and then crash to pieces. The shells begin to hiss safety-valves— heavy fire—

"Take cover!" yells somebody, "Cover!"

The fields are flat, the wood is too distant and dangerous—the only cover is the grave-yard and the mounds. We stumble across in the dark and as though spirited away every man lies glued behind a mound.

Not a moment too soon. The dark goes mad. It heaves and raves. Darknesses blacker than the night rush on us with giant strides, over us and away. The flames of the explo-sions light up the graveyard.

There is no escape anywhere. By the light of the shells—I try to get a view of the fields. They are a surging sea, daggers of flame from the explosions leap up like fountains. It is impossible for anyone to break through it.

The wood vanishes, it is pounded, crushed, torn to pieces. We must stay here in the graveyard.

The earth bursts before us. It rains clods. I feel a smack. My sleeve is torn away by a splinter. I shut my fist. No pain. Still that does not reassure me: wounds don't hurt till afterwards. I feel the arm all over. It is grazed but sound. Now a crack on the skull, I begin to lose consciousness. Like lightning the thought comes to me: Don't faint, sink down in the black broth and immediately come up to the top again. A splinter slashes into my helmet, but has travelled so far that it does not go through. I wipe the mud out of my eyes. A hole is torn up in front of me. Shells hardly ever land in the same hole twice, I'll get into it. With one bound I fling myself down and lie on the earth as flat as a fish; there it whistles again, quickly I crouch to-gether, claw for cover, feel something on the left, shove in beside it, it gives way, I groan, the earth leaps, the blast thunders in my ears, I creep under the yielding thing, cover myself with it, draw it over me, it is wood, cloth, cover, cover, miserable cover against the whizzing splinters.

I open my eyes—my fingers grasp a sleeve, an arm. A wounded man? I yell to him—no answer—a dead man. My hand gropes farther, splinters of wood—now I re-member again that we are lying in the grave-yard.

But the shelling is stronger than every-thing. It wipes out the sensibilities, I merely crawl still deeper into the coffin, it should protect me, and especially as Death himself lies in it too.

Before me gapes the shell-hole. I grasp it with my eyes as with fists. With one leap I must be in it. There, I get a smack in the face, a hand clamps on to my shoulder—has the dead man waked up?—The hand shakes me, I turn my head, in the second of light I stare into the face of Katczinsky, he has his mouth wide open and is yelling. I hear nothing, he rattles me, comes nearer, in a momentary lull his voice reaches me: "Gas-Gaas-Gaaas—Pass it on."

I grab for my gas-mask. Some distance from me there lies someone. I think of nothing but this: That fellow there must know: Gaaas-Gaaas—

I call, I lean toward him, I swipe at him with the satchel, he doesn't see—once again, again—he merely ducks—it's a recruit—I look at Kat desperately, he has his mask ready—I pull out mine too, my helmet falls to one side, it slips over my face, I reach the man, his satchel is on the side nearest me, I seize the mask, pull it over his head, he understands, I let go and with a jump drop back into the shell-hole.

The dull thud of the gas—shells mingles with the crash of the high explosives. A bell sounds between the explosions, gongs, and metal clappers warning everyone—Gas—Gas—Gaas.

Someone plumps down behind me, another. I wipe the goggles of my mask clear of the moist breath. It is *Kat, Kropp*, and someone else. All four of us lie there in heavy, watchful suspense and breathe as lightly as possible.

These first minutes with the mask decide between life and death: is it tightly woven? I remember the awful sights in the hospital: the gas patients who in day-long suffocation cough their burnt lungs up in clots.

Cautiously, the mouth applied to the valve, I breath.

The gas still creeps over the ground and sinks into all hollows. Like a big, soft jelly-fish it floats into our shellhole and lolls there obscenely. I nudge Kat, it is better to crawl out and lie on top than to stay here where the gas collects most. But we don't get as far as that; a second bombardment begins. It is no longer as though the shells roared, it is the earth itself raging.

With a crash something black bears down on us. It lands close beside us; a coffin thrown up.

I see Kat move and I crawl across. The coffin has hit the fourth man in our hole on his out-stretched arm. He tries to tear off his gas-mask with the other hand. Kropp seizes him just in time, twists the hand sharply behind his back and holds it fast. . . .

We have become wild beasts. We do not fight, we defend ourselves against annihilation. It is not against men that we fling our bombs, what do we know of men in this moment when Death with hands and helmets is hunting us down—now, for the first time in three days we can see his face, now, for the first time in three days we can oppose him; we feel a mad anger. No longer do we lie helpless, waiting on the scaffold, we can destroy and kill, to save ourselves, to save ourselves and be revenged.

We crouch behind every corner, behind every barrier of barbed wire, and hurl heaps of explosives at the feet of the advancing enemy before we run. The blast of the hand-grenades impinges powerfully on our arms and legs; crouching like cats we run on, overwhelmed by this wave that bears us along, that fills us with ferocity, turning us into thugs, into murderers, into God only knows what devils; this wave that multiplies our strength with fear and madness and greed of life, seeking and fighting for nothing but our deliverance. If your own father came with them you would not hesitate to fling a bomb into him. . . .

It is nearly noon. The sun blazes hotly, the sweat stings in our eyes, we wipe it off on our sleeves, and often blood with it. At last we reach a trench that is in a somewhat better condition. It is manned and ready for the counter-attack, it receives us. Our guns open up in full blast and cut off the enemy attack.

The lines behind us stop. They can advance no farther. The attack is crushed by our artillery. We watch. The fire lifts a hundred yards and we break forward. Beside me a lance-corporal has his head torn off. He runs a few steps more while the blood spouts from his neck like a fountain.

It does not come quite to hand-to-hand fighting; they are driven back. We arrive once again at our shattered trench and pass on beyond it.

Oh, this turning back again! We reach the shelter of the reserves and yearn to creep in and disappear; but instead we must turn round and plunge again into the horror. If we were not automata at that moment we would continue lying there, exhausted, and without will. But we are swept forward again, powerless, madly savage and raging; we will kill, for they are still our mortal enemies; their rifles and bombs are aimed against us, and if we don't destroy them, they will destroy us.

The brown earth, the torn, blasted earth, with a greasy shine under the sun's rays; the earth is the background of this restless, gloomy world of automatons, our gasping is the scratching of a quill, our lips are dry, our heads are debauched with stupor—thus we stagger forward, and into our pierced and shattered souls bores the torturing image of the brown earth with the greasy sun and the convulsed and dead soldiers, who lie there—it can't be helped—who cry and clutch at our legs as we spring away over them.

We have lost all feeling for one another. We can hardly control ourselves when our hunted glance lights on the form of some other man. We are insensible, dead men, who through some trick, some dreadful magic, are still able to run and to kill. . . .

One morning two butterflies play in front of our trench. They are brimstone-butterflies, with red spots on their yellow wings. What can they be looking for here? There is not a plant nor a flower for miles. They settle on the teeth of a skull. The birds too are just as carefree, they have long since accustomed

themselves to the war. Every morning larks ascend from No Man's Land. A year ago we watched them nesting; the young ones grew up too.

We have a spell from the rats in the trench. They are in No Man's Land-we know what for. They grow fat; when we see one we have a crack at it. . . .

We see men living with their skulls blown open; we see soldiers run with their two feet cut off, they stagger on their splintered stumps into the next shell-hole; a lance-corporal crawls a mile and half on his hands dragging his smashed knee after him; another goes to the dressing-station and over his clasped hands bulge his intestines; we see men without mouths, without jaws, without faces; we find one man who has held the artery of his arm in his teeth for two hours in order not to bleed to death. The sun goes down, night comes, the shells whine, life is at an end.

Still the little piece of convulsed earth in which we lie is held. We have yielded no more than a few hundred yards of it as a prize to the enemy. But on every yard there lies a dead man.

* * *

A man cannot realize that above such shattered bodies there are still human faces in which life goes its daily round. And this is only one hospital, one single station; there are hundreds of thousands in Germany, hundreds of thousands in France, hundreds of thousands in Russia. How senseless is everything that can ever be written, done, or thought, when such things are possible. It must all be lies and of no account when the culture of a thousand years could not prevent this stream of blood being poured out, these torture-chambers in their hundreds of thousands. A hospital alone shows what war is.

I am young, I am twenty years old; yet I know nothing of life but despair, death, fear, and fatuous superficiality cast over an abyss of sorrow. I see how peoples are set against one another, and in silence, unknowingly, foolishly, obediently, innocently slay one another. I see that the keenest brains of the world invent weapons and words to make it yet more refined and enduring. And all men of my age, here and over there, throughout the whole world, see these things; all my generation is experiencing these things with me. What would our fathers do if we suddenly stood up and came before them and proffered our account? What do they expect of us if a time ever comes when the war is over? Through the years our business has been killing; it was our first calling in life. Our knowledge of life is limited to death. What will happen afterwards? And what shall come out of us?

* * *

Here, on the borders of death, life follows an amazingly simple course, it is limited to what is most necessary, all else lies buried in gloomy sleep;—in that lies our primitiveness and our survival. We more subtly differentiated we must long since have gone mad, have deserted, or have fallen. As in a polar expedition, every expression of life must serve only the preservation of existence, and is absolutely focussed on that. All else is banished because it would consume energies unnecessarily. That is the only way to save ourselves. In the quiet hours when the puzzling reflection of former days, like a blurred mirror, projects beyond me the figure of my present existence, I often sit over against myself, as before a stranger, and wonder how the unnameable active principle that calls itself Life has adapted itself even to this form. All other expressions lie in a winter sleep, life is simply one continual watch against the menace of death; it has

transformed us into unthinking animals in order to give us the weapon of instinct—it has reinforced us with dullness, so that we do not go to pieces before the horror, which would overwhelm us if we had clear, conscious thought—it has awakened in us the sense of comradeship, so that we escape the abyss of solitude—it has lent us the indifference of wild creatures, so that in spite of all we perceive the positive in every moment, and store it up as a reserve against the onslaught of nothingness. Thus we live a closed, hard existence of the utmost superficiality, and rarely does an incident strike out a spark. But then unexpectedly a flame of grievous and terrible yearning flares up.

Those are the dangerous moments. They show us that the adjustment is only artificial, that it is not simple rest, but sharpest struggle for rest. In the outward form of our life we are hardly distinguishable from Bushmen; but whereas the latter can be so always, because they are so truly, and at best may develop further by exertion of their spiritual forces, with us it is the reverse; our inner forces are not exerted toward regeneration, but toward degeneration. The Bushmen are primitive and naturally so, but we are primitive in an artificial sense, and by virtue of the utmost effort.

And at night, waking out of a dream, overwhelmed and bewitched by the crowding face; a man perceives with alarm how slight is the support, how thin the boundary that divides him from the darkness. We are little flames poorly sheltered by frail walls against the storm of dissolution and madness, in which we flicker and sometimes almost go out. Then the muffled roar of the battle becomes a ring that encircles us, we creep in upon ourselves, and with big eyes stare into the night. Our only comfort is the steady breathing of our comrades asleep, and thus we wait for the morning. . . .

64

Japan at Versailles

Japan's role in the twentieth century has been a study in contrasts. Her victory over the Russians in 1905 inspired nationalists all over the world, and by World War I, Japan was in a position to demand full equality with the Western powers. However, as these readings suggest, Japan's perspective on her rights in Asia, on her relationship with the West, and her role in the Wilsonian world order, reflect potential contradictions that would lead Japan, the friend in the early twentieth century, to become Japan the foe by the 1930's.

1. What values and interests seemed to be motivating the Japanese leaders at Versailles? Were these interests markedly different from those influencing the other leaders?

2. What were Japan's main goals at Versailles? How did these differ from the aims of other countries? What potential conflicts do you see?

3. What was Japan's position towards China, and what inconsistencies do you find in her position as compared with other Japanese aims at Versailles?

Japanese Aims at the Paris Peace Conference

The Peace Conference had its origins in the idealism of American President Woodrow Wilson. The year before the war had ended Wilson had set forth in his State of the Union Message his famous Fourteen Points. Among the more important of these were the abolition of secret treaties, freedom of the seas, reduction of armaments, and specific proposals based on the self-determination of various countries. Yet another noteworthy feature was his proposal for the "establishment of a League of Nations with the aim of guaranteeing the political and territorial sovereignty of all nations, large and small alike."

Japan at the time was in the reign of the Emperor Taisho, the successor of the Emperor Meiji. The press was free, and championship of the people's rights was such that this period would later be known as that of "Taisho democracy." Government during the Meiji era had for the most part been under the strict control of the elder statesmen who had played key roles in the Meiji Restoration. However, in the Taisho era a system of government by two major parties was well on the way to establishment. The right to vote still depended upon the amount of taxes paid, but general elections were already in the cards.

The Japanese press was unanimous in its support of Wilson's proposals, and welcomed them as advancing the cause of humanity. However, the response of experienced members of the Foreign Ministry was somewhat more complex. In a word, they were perplexed. These men were accustomed to living by the rules of the jungle of international relations, where might was right and clandestine plotting indispensable. Never before had the "ideals" that Wilson proposed been put forth as fundamental principles of international polities. While they felt they could not openly oppose Wilson's idealism, neither could they speak out with any enthusiasm in favor of it. Their hands were tied, and they feared the results would be most disadvantageous to their own country. Would this idealism ultimately become the guiding principle of the post-World War I world? Could they be assured it did not conceal a trap that would hinder the further progress of Japan?

One of the delegates to the Paris Peace Conference was Konoe Fumimaro, the eldest son of a family that for a thousand years had been closer than any other to the imperial household, and future prime minister, relinquishing his position to Tojo right before the start of World War II. He was a fair-skinned young man, only twenty-seven years old in 1919, and this philosophically-minded member of the delegation had only shortly before published an essay, "Against a Peace to the Advantage of England and America," in which he challenged openly the "ideals" of Wilson's Fourteen Points. He sharply criticized Japan's leaders for being deceived by the flowery rhetoric of English and American politicians and for endorsing the ideals of the League of Nations without noting the "egoism of England and America" that lay beneath them. Konoe saw the war in Europe as

From Hoye Murakami, *Japan: The Years of Trial, 1919–52,* copyright © 1982 by Hyoe Murakami, pp. 11–26. Reprinted with permission from Kodansha International USA, New York.

a struggle between the established powers and the as yet unestablished powers. Those nations that stood to profit most from the League and the other Fourteen Points were England and America. Japan, therefore, should, at the very least, make its participation in an alliance for peace contingent upon the following two conditions: the rejection of economic imperialism and the abolition of discrimination between the white and yellow races.

Japan, Konoe maintained, had the right to act in its own best interests. This was not to say that Japan could simply ignore other nations, but that it should see their egoism, backed by military and economic power, for what it was. And Japan should resist it for the sake of its own right to exist, which was equally defensible on the grounds of justice and humanity. To the leaders of Japan, who, since the opening of the country, had pursued a foreign policy based entirely upon learning from the West and cooperating with the West—often to their own humiliation—this was an entirely new concept. It seemed a dangerous proposition, excessively direct and naive.

However, there was one Chinese who was deeply impressed by the Konoe article. This was Sun Yat-sen, now known as the father of the Chinese revolution. When Sun saw Konoe he praised his article and predicted that "the Paris Peace Conference would decide the fate not only of Japan but of all the peoples of East Asia." Recalling the Russo-Japanese War, Sun said, "I was in Paris when I heard of Japan's victory. On the way home an Arab I met at the Suez Canal asked me if I was Japanese. I told him I was, and he said to me, 'I've seen a constant stream of wounded Russian soldiers coming through the canal lately, on their way home. That's real proof that an Asian nation can defeat Russia. And when I realized that, I was happier than if my own country had won that

war.' As a fellow Asian, masquerading as a Japanese, I myself had never felt as confident as I did then."

Japan's victory in the Russo-Japanese War of 1904–1905 had been a beacon of rebellion to the people of the world who for the past three hundred years had been ruled by the West. It had aroused a desire for independence among the oppressed peoples of the world, especially in Asia. Sun Yat-sen went on to say, "Yes, until thirty years ago there wasn't a single country in Asia that was entirely independent. But now that Japan has become one of the five great powers it stands at a parting of the ways. Will it participate in the division of Asia, will it act as an agent of the enslavement of Asia; or will it lead the one billion people of Asia and fight by their side? It is unfortunate," he concluded, "that at this crucial time there is neither a true politician nor a true diplomat to be found in Japan." Konoe agreed completely.

Japan's greatest concerns at the Paris Peace Conference were, first, the inclusion of a clause in the Covenant of the League of Nations abolishing racial discrimination, and, second, the guarantee of its rights to the Shantung Peninsula in China, which had been taken from Germany in the war. Japan first acquired rights in China after the Sino-Japanese War of 1894–95, and had entered World War I after an agreement with England, America and France that Japan would receive German concessions in China, to be returned to China at some point in the future. Japanese leaders were still angered by the treatment they had gotten from Germany, Russia and France after the Sino-Japanese War, those countries arguing that Japan's possession of special rights was a threat to peace in Asia. Japan submitted to their pressure, yet immediately thereafter, those three countries, as "rewards" for their intercession, carved out territories for themselves in China. This humiliation had left an indelible impression on the minds of all Japanese, from the nation's leaders down to the humble farmer.

If these interests were to be returned to China in the near future, Wilson argued, would it not be as well to relinquish them at the conference itself? But Japan was insistent for reasons of national dignity and interest. There was a feeling among the Japanese that they were being manipulated and meddled with by the larger powers. If these interests had to be returned to China, and returned shortly, at that, Japan felt that there should be direct negotiations with China, and it wanted to hold the winning card in these negotiations.

Relations between Japan and China were extremely complex. Virtually every Japanese felt himself to be in league with the Chinese in their determination to prevent European aggression. To this end the modernization and unification of China were essential. The Sino-Japanese War in no way diminished this desire. In 1900 Japan for the first time joined forces with the Western nations in armed intervention in China; yet even then the idea of cooperation between Japan and China remained a strong current in the ideas and activities of the ordinary citizen. Many Chinese students had come to study in Japan while many Japanese military men had been involved as advisers in the modernization of China's armed forces. While Japan advanced steadily toward becoming a well-ordered modern nation, China was left behind, as disordered as ever, an insignificant state that fell prey to the European powers. Seeing this, Japan's hopes gave way to irritation, while throughout the nation contempt for the Chinese came to prevail. Japan came to feel that, if it was China's fate to be divided up among the great powers, then Japan, its neighbor, who had defended China against the encroachment of Russia, has a right to its fair share of the spoils.

World War I changed the world in two major ways. First, it gave birth to the Soviet Union, the first of the new states to be founded on the principles of communism. At the time, this suggested that armed intervention by the once-powerful Russia would diminish, but eventually the great powers came to fear that the new ideas would infiltrate their own nations and lead to revolution. Japan, although powerful, was nonetheless still unsettled internally by the process of development. As a near neighbor of Russia, it was one of the nations that felt its influence most strongly.

Secondly, there was the rise of America. America had had, until then, little power to influence international politics, but as a result of World War I it had become the richest nation in the world and the financial backer of the European nations. It not only became a formidable military power, but also acquired a powerful voice in world politics. Insofar as America often based policies upon ideals, often admittedly, to its own advantage, it had a different style of diplomacy from that of the European powers.

Europe and America had divided up the world and grown rich on its abundant resources and population. America, with much of its own vast continent still to develop, had in the name of the Monroe Doctrine barred Japanese immigrants from every country within its sphere of influence except Brazil.

Japan had two possible paths of action before it. It could stand up for justice and humanity, to which end it would have to resign itself to sacrificing its special interests in China. It might even have to run the risk of becoming a weak nation. Or, on the other hand, it could adhere to nineteenth-century principles of power, and, with the greatest caution, make its way in the world as a rival of the great powers.

Anti-Asian Discrimination and the Racial Equality Clause

As the structure of the League of Nations began to take shape under the guidance of England and America, the Japanese government, like Konoe, sensed the danger of racial bias working to Japan's disadvantage. Anti-Asian discrimination in America was great. The many Asian immigrants who endured the arduous Pacific crossing to work in the mining industries and to build the railroads that helped fuel the American industrial revolution, were now being discriminated against in many ways. In San Francisco in October 1906, the Board of Education gave as its reason for excluding Japanese children from public schools the fact that they were "vicious, immoral, of an age and maturity too advanced for safe association with the younger American children." Discrimination against the Japanese on the West Coast was, as with the Chinese, based upon resentment of cheap labor and cultural differences, but with an additional element. As one might expect in a situation that had arisen shortly after the Russo-Japanese War, the anti-Japanese leaders on the coast covertly feared the West Coast would be "occupied" by Japan. Thus, the anti-Japanese movement was both politically motivated and well-organized.

In April of 1906, the great San Francisco earthquake occurred, and the Japanese people sent contributions totaling $245,000, more than half the amount collected throughout the world. When immediately thereafter the immigration problem arose, it was hardly surprising that the Japanese felt that America was "ungrateful." President Roosevelt, who had been upset with earlier laws discriminating against Asians, continued to voice his displeasure at Western legislators' attempts to restrict Japanese immigration, but at the same time negotiated a gentleman's agreement with the Japanese government to send no more immigrants. (In 1924 national immigration restrictions would be enacted that prohibited Japanese and Chinese immigrants from coming to the U.S.). Further demonstrations of anti-Asian sentiment would lead to a California law prohibiting Japanese from owning real estate and limiting their right to rent land to three years. Wilson, president at the time, appealed to Californians to rescind their laws, but to no avail.

England's delegate, too, felt that since equality of member nations was the fundamental spirit of the League of Nations, Japan's proposal of a racial-equality clause could hardly be denied. However, he opposed the proposal on account of the rigid opposition of the Commonwealth prime ministers, in particular Australian Prime Minister William M. Hughes. Behind-the-scenes negotiations dragged on from the end of January until April. Makino tried every possible tactic: he repeatedly sought the support and cooperation of English and American delegates; he spoke with Henry W. Steed, the chief correspondent of the *Times*, who alerted public opinion in England through his writings; he attempted to persuade Hughes to reconsider his position. All the British Commonwealth leaders tried to persuade Hughes to change his mind, but Hughes, who feared defeat in domestic elections, threatened to withdraw his delegation and refuse to sign the treaty if Japan's proposal was included in any form whatever. South Africa's Prime Minister Louis Botha told Makino, "Strictly between ourselves, I think he is mad."

Japanese had long been working in northern Australia, planting sugar cane and gathering pearls. The first act of the newly established Commonwealth Council in 1901 was to prohibit the entry of Asians. The new immigration laws required a dictation test given in a European language, which all but completely excluded immigrants from Japan. On the other hand, illiterate Europeans could be excused from the examination at the discretion of immigration officials. Australia's Attorney General Alfred Deakin said of the law, "If restrictions were to be based on race, we would provoke the antagonism of Japan, as one of the civilized nations of the world, and we would not attain our objective." He then went on to say, "The Japanese are extremely enterprising and energetic, and moreover the standard of living they are accustomed to is low. As competitors they are the most dangerous of the Asians, and we must make every effort to keep them out. In short, we exclude the Japanese not because they are an inferior race, but because they are a superior one."

The committee that was to make the decision concerning Japan's proposal of a clause in the covenant calling for equal treatment of nations was convened on the evening of April 11. Wilson was the chairman and there were sixteen other members. The vote was divided as follows: eleven in favor, i.e., two votes each from Japan, France, and Italy, and one vote each from Greece, China, Serbia, Portugal, and Czechoslovakia; and five opposed, i.e., England, America, Poland, Brazil, and Romania. Makino had been advised in advance that because England was opposed America would join it.

Wilson declared as chairman that "since the committee could not reach a unanimous decision, the proposal cannot be adopted." Makino protested that most matters at the conference had been decided by majority vote and was supported in this by several others. However, Wilson dismissed this objection, saying, "I raised this matter on the understanding that such an important matter required the unanimous agreement of the committee, or that at least there be no opposition."

In this way Japan's racial-equality proposal was defeated. News of Japan's frustration in Paris, as well as the exclusion of the Japanese from the Pacific Coast, was reported in detail in Japan. A succession of protest meetings was held, but their efforts were thwarted by the fact that Japan's delegation in Paris could do nothing as long as England and America opposed them. The only way left open to them was to state clearly Japan's intentions for the future.

Due to Wilson's idealism it was expected that he would support the Japanese clause for racial equality at the Paris Peace Conference, and, in principle, he did. It was the English, particularly concerned over anti-Asian feeling in Australia, who persuaded Wilson to drop his support for the clause. The Japanese delegates protested that "if it is to be a principle of the League of Nations that certain peoples are not to be given just and equal treatment, this will strike those peoples as odd, and in the future, will undermine their faith in the very principles of justice and equality that are supposed to regulate relations between member nations." The Paris press was unanimous in its sharp criticism of the League rejections. One paper pointed out that "it was outrageous that although a clause recognizing America's Monroe Doctrine was included, the equal treatment amendment sought by Japan was rejected."

65

The Impact of World War I—
The Age of Anxiety

"What shall I think tomorrow?"

George Grosz, 1920

Psychology

Freud—Death Wish—Aggression Instinctual

"Men are not gentle friendly creatures, but are naturally aggressive; no man can trust another man. Man to man is a wolf."

Civilization and Its Discontents

Pavlov—Behavioral Conditioning

Art

"The Lost Generation"

Alienation, Cubism, Surrealism, Futurism, Dadaism

Religion

Concept of Original Sin Reemerges

"Civilization is a disease which is almost invariably fatal, unless its course is checked in time . . . If so-called civilized nations show any protracted vitality, it is because they are only civilized at the top. Ancient civilizations were destroyed by imported barbarians. We breed our own."

Dean of St. Paul's Cathedral,
"The Idea of Progress"

Science

There Are No Absolute Truths

Heisenberg—The Uncertainty Theory

Einstein—The Theory of Relativity

Curie—The Sub-Atomic (Nuclear) World

Eugenics—The science of race

Anthropology

Cultural Relativism

History

"You are a product of your conditioning."

Philosophy

Nietzsche—Western Civilization Is Decadent

"Disintegration characterizes this time, and thus, uncertainty. Nothing stands firmly on its feet or on a hard faith in itself, one lives for tomorrow as the day after tomorrow is dubious. Everything on our way is slippery and dangerous, and the ice that still supports us has become thin: all of us feel the warm, uncanny breath of the thawing wind: where we still walk, soon no one will be able to walk."

The Will to Power

William James—Pragmatism

Sartre, Camus—Existentialism

"Existence precedes essence"

"Man is condemned to be free"

Political Ideology

Totalitarianism

Lenin—Communism

Mussolini, Hitler—Fascism

66

Lenin and Communism

In his book *State and Revolution*, written in 1917, Vladimir Lenin (1870–1924) discusses what will happen when revolution replaces the bourgeois capitalist system with a "dictatorship of the proletariat."

Discussion Questions

1. What is the link between the dictatorship of the proletariat and democracy?

2. How does communism "render the state absolutely unnecessary?" How do you think Lenin is defining the term "state?"

3. Do you agree that democracy means equality?

4. What do you think Lenin means when he implies that democracy is more a means than an end?

5. Why do you think that in Russia the dictatorship of the "proletariat" never did disappear under communism?

The dictatorship of the proletariat—*i.e.*, the organisation of the vanguard of the oppressed as the ruling class for the purpose of crushing the oppressors—cannot produce merely an expansion of democracy. *Together* with an immense expansion of democracy which *for the first time* becomes democracy for the poor, democracy for the people, and not democracy for the rich folk, the dictatorship of the proletariat produces a series of restrictions of liberty in the case of the oppressors, the exploiters, the capitalists. We must crush them in order to free humanity from wage-slavery; their resistance must be broken by force; it is clear that where there is suppression there is also violence, there is no liberty, no democracy.

Engels expressed this splendidly in his letter to Bebel when he said, as the reader will remember, that "as long as the proletariat still *needs* the state, it needs it not in the interests of freedom, but for the purpose of crushing its antagonists; and as soon as it becomes possible to speak of freedom, then the state, as such, ceases to exist." . . .

Only Communism renders the state absolutely unnecessary, for there is *no one* to be suppressed—"no one" in the sense of a *class,* in the sense of a systematic struggle with a definite section of the population. We are not Utopians, and we do not in the least deny the possibility and inevitability of excesses on the part of *individual persons,* nor the need to suppress *such* excesses. But, in the first place, no special machinery, no special apparatus of repression is needed for this; this will be done by the armed people itself, as simply and as readily as any crowd of civilised people, even in modern society, parts a pair of combatants or does not allow a woman to be outraged. And, secondly, we know that the fundamental social cause of excesses which consists in violating the rules of social life is the exploitation of the masses, their want and their poverty. With the removal of this chief cause, excesses will inevitably begin to "wither away." We do not know how quickly and in what succession, but we know that they will wither away. With their withering away, the state will also wither away. . . .

Democracy means equality. The great significance of the struggle of the proletariat for equality, and the significance of equality as a slogan, are apparent, if we correctly interpret it as meaning the abolition of *classes.* But democracy means only *formal* equality. Immediately after the attainment of equality for all members of society *in respect* of the ownership of the means of production, that is, of equality of labour and equality of wages, there will inevitably arise before humanity the question of going further from formal equality to real equality, *i.e.*, to realising the rule, "From each according to his ability; to each according to his needs." By what stages, by means of what practical measures humanity will proceed to this higher aim—this we do not and cannot know. But it is important to realise how infinitely mendacious is the usual bourgeois presentation of Socialism as something lifeless petrified, fixed once for all, whereas in reality, it is *only* with Socialism that there will commence a rapid, genuine, real mass advance, in which first the *majority* and then the whole of the population will take part—an advance in all domains of social and individual life.

Democracy is a form of the state—one of its varieties. Consequently, like every state, it consists in organised, systematic application of force against human beings. This on the one hand. On the other hand, however, it signifies the formal recognition of the equality of all citizens, the equal right of all to determine the structure and administration of the state. This, in turn, is connected with the fact that, at a certain stage in the development of democracy, it first rallies the proletariat as a revolutionary class against capitalism, and gives it an opportunity to crush, to smash to bits, to wipe off the face of the earth the bourgeois state machinery—even its republican variety: the standing army, the police, and bureaucracy; then it substitutes for all this a *more* democratic, but still a state machinery in the shape of armed masses of workers, which becomes transformed into universal participation of the people in the militia. . . .

[Eventually] the whole of society will have become one office and one factory, with equal work and equal pay.

But this "factory" discipline, which the proletariat will extend to the whole of society after the defeat of the capitalists and the overthrow of the exploiters, is by no means our ideal, or our final aim. It is but a *foothold* necessary for the radical cleansing of society of all the hideousness and foulness of capitalist exploitation, *in order to advance further.*

From the moment when all members of society, or even only the overwhelming majority, have learned how to govern the state *themselves,* have taken this business into their own hands, have "established" control over the insignificant minority of capitalists, over the gentry with capitalist leanings, and the workers thoroughly demoralised by capitalism—from this moment the need for any government begins to disappear. The more complete the democracy, the nearer the moment when it begins to be unnecessary. The more democratic the "state" consisting of armed workers, which is "no longer a state in the proper sense of the word," the more rapidly does every state begin to wither away.

For when *all* have learned to manage, and independently are actually managing by themselves social production, keeping accounts, controlling the idlers, the gentlefolk, the swindlers and similar "guardians of capitalist traditions," then the escape from this national accounting and control will inevitably become so increasingly difficult, such a rare exception, and will probably be accompanied by such swift and severe punishment (for the armed workers are men of practical life, not sentimental intellectuals, and they will scarcely allow any one to trifle with them), that very soon the *necessity* of observing the simple, fundamental rules of everyday social life in common will have become a *habit.*

The door will then be wide open for the transition from the first phase of Communist society to its higher phase, and along with it to the complete withering away of the state.

67

The God That Failed

Arthur Koestler (1905–1983) was a Hungarian-born writer on many twentieth-century themes from science to politics. In *The God That Failed*, which was published in 1949, Koestler was one of six authors who explained why they found communism appealing in the 1920's and why they later became disillusioned with the movement. The following is a selection from his contribution to that book.

Discussion Questions

1. How did World War I affect the way Koestler thought about the direction of Western civilization?

2. Do you find his explanation of why he found communism appealing convincing?

3. Is it legitimate to say that he had gone through what amounts to a religious conversion experience?

The bourgeois family will vanish as a matter of course with the vanishing of Capital. . . . The bourgeois claptrap about the family and education, about the haloed correlation of parent and child, becomes all the more disgusting the more, by the action of modern industry, all family ties among the proletarians are torn asunder. . . .

Thus the "Communist Manifesto." Every page of Marx, and even more of Engels, brought a new revelation, and an intellectual delight which I had only experienced once before, at my first contact with Freud. Torn from its context, the above passage sounds ridiculous; as part of a closed system which made social philosophy fall into a lucid and comprehensive pattern, the demonstration of the historical relativity of institutions and ideals—of family, class, patriotism, bourgeois morality, sexual taboos—had the intoxicating effect of a sudden liberation from the rusty chains with which a pre-1914 middle-class childhood had cluttered one's mind. Today, when Marxist philosophy has degenerated into a Byzantine cult and virtually every single tenet of the Marxist program has become twisted round into its opposite, it is difficult to recapture that mood of emotional fervor and intellectual bliss.

I was ripe to be converted, as a result of my personal case history; thousands of other members of the intellegentsia and the middle classes of my generation were ripe for it by virtue of other personal case-histories; but, however much these differed from case to case, they had a common denominator: the rapid disintegration of moral values, of the pre-1914 pattern of life in postwar Europe, and the simultaneous lure of the new revelation which had come from the East.

The new star of Bethlehem had risen in the East; and for a modest sum, Intourist was prepared to allow you a short and well-focused glimpse of the Promised Land.

I began for the first time to read Marx, Engels and Lenin in earnest. By the time I had finished with *Feuerbach* and *State and Revolution*, something had clicked in my brain which shook me like a mental explosion. To say that one had "seen the light" is a poor description of the mental rapture which only the convert knows (regardless of what faith he has been converted to). The new light seems to pour from all directions across the skull; the whole universe falls into pattern like the stray pieces of a jigsaw puzzle assembled by magic at one stroke. There is now an answer to every question, doubts and conflicts are a matter of the tortured past—a past already remote, when one had lived in dismal ignorance in the tasteless, colorless world of those who *don't know.* Nothing henceforth can disturb the convert's inner peace and serenity—except the occasional fear of losing faith again, losing thereby what alone makes life worth living, and falling back into the outer darkness, where there is wailing and gnashing of teeth.

68

Mussolini: What Is Fascism?

Benito Mussolini (1883–1945) came to power in Italy in 1922 as the leader of a new movement called Fascism (so named from the *fasces*, a bundle of sticks which was a symbol of unified power in ancient Rome—*e pluribus unum*).

The following is an article written by Mussolini for the Italian Encyclopedia in 1932.

Discussion Questions

1. Earlier in his career, Mussolini had been a socialist. What reasons does he give for turning against it?

2. What key ideas of the Enlightenment does he reject? Why?

3. Was Mussolini correct in arguing that fascism "is the characteristic doctrine of our time"?

4. What is meant by calling fascism nationalist and statist?

Benito Mussolini: What Is Fascism, 1932

Fascism, the more it considers and observes the future and the development of humanity quite apart from political considerations of the moment, believes neither in the possibility nor the utility of perpetual peace. It thus repudiates the doctrine of Pacifism—born of a renunciation of the struggle and an act of cowardice in the face of sacrifice. War alone brings up to its highest tension all human energy and puts the stamp of nobility upon the peoples who have courage to meet it. All other trials are substitutes, which never really put men into the position where they have to make the great decision—the alternative of life or death. . . .

. . . The Fascist accepts life and loves it, knowing nothing of and despising suicide: he rather conceives of life as duty and struggle and conquest, but above all for others—those who are at hand and those who are far distant, contemporaries, and those who will come after . . .

. . . Fascism [is] the complete opposite of...Marxian Socialism, the materialist conception of history of human civilization can be explained simply through the conflict of interests among the various social groups and by the change and development in the means and instruments of production. . . . Fascism, now and always, believes in holiness and in heroism; that is to say, in actions influenced by no economic motive, direct or indirect. And if the economic conception of history be denied, according to which theory men are no more than puppets, carried to and fro by the waves of chance, while the real directing forces are quite out of their control, it follows that the existence of an unchangeable and unchanging class-war is also denied—the natural progeny of the economic conception of history. And above all Fascism denies that class-war can be the preponderant force in the transformation of society. . . .

After Socialism, Fascism combats the whole complex system of democratic ideology, and repudiates it, whether in its theoretical premises or in its practical application. Fascism denies that the majority, by the simple fact that it is a majority, can direct human society; it denies that numbers alone can govern by means of a periodical consultation, and it affirms the immutable, beneficial, and fruitful inequality of mankind, which can never be permanently leveled through the mere operation of a mechanical process such as universal suffrage. . . .

. . . Fascism denies, in democracy, the absur[d] conventional untruth of political equality dressed out in the garb of collective irresponsibility, and the myth of "happiness" and indefinite progress. . . .

. . . Given that the nineteenth century was the century of Socialism, of Liberalism, and of Democracy, it does not necessarily follow that the twentieth century must also be a century of Socialism, Liberalism and Democracy: political doctrines pass, but humanity remains, and it may rather be expected that this will be a century of authority . . . a century of Fascism. For if the nineteenth century was a century of individualism it may be expected that this will be the century of collectivism and hence the century of the State. . . .

The foundation of Fascism is the conception of the State, its character, its duty, and its aim. Fascism conceives of the State as an absolute, in comparison with which all individuals or groups are relative, only to be conceived of in their relation to the State. The conception of the Liberal State is not that of a directing force, guiding the play and development, both material and spiritual, of a collective body, but merely a force limited to the function of recording results: on the other hand, the Fascist State is itself conscious and has itself a will and a personality—thus it may be called the "ethic" State. . . .

. . . The Fascist State organizes the nation, but leaves a sufficient margin of liberty to the individual; the latter is deprived of all useless and possibly harmful freedom, but retains what is essential; the deciding power in this question cannot be the individual, but the State alone. . . .

. . . For Fascism, the growth of empire, that is to say the expansion of the nation, is an essential manifestation of vitality, and its opposite a sign of decadence. Peoples which are rising, or rising again after a period of decadence, are always imperialist; and renunciation is a sign of decay and of death. Fascism is the doctrine best adapted to represent the tendencies and the aspirations of a peo-

ple, like the people of Italy, who are rising again after many centuries of abasement and foreign servitude. But empire demands discipline, the coordination of all forces and a deeply felt sense of duty and sacrifice: this fact explains many aspects of the practical working of the regime, the character of many forces in the State, and the necessarily severe measures which must be taken against those who would oppose this spontaneous and inevitable movement of Italy in the twentieth century, and would oppose it by recalling the outworn ideology of the nineteenth century—repudiated wheresoever there has been the courage to undertake great experiments of social and political transformation; for never before has the nation stood more in need of authority, of direction and order. If every age has its own characteristic doctrine, there are a thousand signs which point to Fascism as the characteristic doctrine of our time. For if a doctrine must be a living thing, this is proved by the fact that Fascism has created a living faith; and that this faith is very powerful in the minds of men is demonstrated by those who have suffered and died for it.

69

Hitler and Nazism

Adolf Hitler started writing his autobiography *Mein Kampf (My Struggle)* while he was in Landsberg prison after his abortive coup (putsch) in Munich in 1923. It was published in two volumes in 1925 and 1927.

Discussion Questions

1. Comparing Hitler's racism to that of H.S. Chamberlain, is there anything new?
2. What is a "folkish state" and what is its purpose?
3. What are some specific ways in which Hitler's ideas are antithetical to democracy?

Adolf Hitler: Mein Kampf

Just as little as Nature desires a mating between weaker individuals and stronger ones, far less she desires the mixing of a higher race with lower one, as in this case her entire work of higher breeding, which has perhaps taken hundreds of thousands of years, would tumble at one blow.

Historical experience offers countless proofs of this. It shows with terrible clarity that with any mixing of the blood of the Aryan with lower races the result was the end of the culture-bearer.

* *

Thus the highest purpose of the folkish State is the care for the preservation of those racial primal elements which, supplying culture, create the beauty and dignity of a higher humanity. . . .

The folkish State, through this realization, has to direct its entire education primarily not at pumping in mere knowledge, but at the breeding of absolutely healthy bodies. Of secondary importance is the training of the mental abilities. But here again first of all the development of the character, especially the promotion of will power and determination, connected with education for joyfully assuming responsibility, and only as the last thing, scientific schooling.

Thereby the folkish State has to start from the presumption that a man, though scientifically little educated but physically healthy, who has a sound, firm character, filled with joyful determination and will power, is of greater value to the national community than an ingenious weakling.

* *

A view of life which, by rejecting the democratic mass idea, endeavors to give this world to the best people, that means to the most superior men, has logically to obey the same aristocratic principle also within this people and has to guarantee leadership and highest influence within the respective people to the best heads. With this it does not build up on the idea of the majority, but on that of the personality.

* *

After my joining the German Workers' Party, I immediately took over the management of the propaganda. . . . Propaganda had to precede far in advance of the organization and to win for the latter the human material to be utilized. . . .

The psyche of the great masses is not receptive to half measures or weakness.

Like a woman, whose psychic feeling is influenced less by abstract reasoning than by undefinable, sentimental longing for complementary strength, who will submit to the strong man rather than dominate the weakling, thus the masses love the ruler rather than the suppliant, and inwardly they are far more satisfied by a doctrine which tolerates no rival than by the grant of liberal freedom; they often feel at a loss what to do with it, and even easily feel themselves deserted. . . .

The great masses' receptive ability is only very limited, their understanding is small, but their forgetfulness is great. As a consequence of these facts, all effective propaganda has to limit itself only to a very few points and to use them like slogans until even the very last man is able to imagine what is intended by such a word.

70

The Hitler Myth

The following article by Ian Kershaw attempts to explain the extraordinary hold Hitler had on the German people, including his opponents, after he came to power in 1933.

Discussion Questions

1. Does Kershaw make a convincing distinction between Hitler's personality and his popular image? Is he implying that Hitler was a "phony?"

2. How was Hitler's popular image the product of certain elements in Germany's past?

3. How did non-Nazis see Hitler?

4. How did Hitler win over the masses of the German people after he was named chancellor in 1933?

5. What does Kershaw say were the seven bases of the "Hitler Myth?" Was Hitler the creation of political image-makers like more recent leaders?

6. What happened when Hitler himself succumbed to the "Hitler Myth?"

7. What lessons for all democratic societies can be learned from Hitler's political career?

For almost a decade after 1933, Hitler enjoyed a remarkable degree of popularity among the great majority of the German people. However dramatic and spectacular his political career, concentration on Hitler's character and personality—in some respects bizarre, in others downright mediocre and wholly unpleasant—can nevertheless do little to explain the magnetism of his popular appeal. Nor can his extraordinary impact on the German people in these years be accounted for satisfactorily by seeing in Hitler's personal Weltanschauung (notably in his obsessions with the "Jewish Question" and with Lebensraum) a mirror image of the motivation of Nazism's mass following. Recent research has done much to qualify such assumptions, suggesting too that even deep into the period of the dictatorship itself Hitler's own ideological fixations had more of a symbolic than concrete meaning for most Nazi supporters.

What seems necessary, therefore, is an examination not of Hitler's personality, but of his popular image—how the German people saw their leader: the "Hitler Myth." The "Hitler Myth" was a double-sided phenomenon. On the one hand, it was a masterly achievement in image-building by the exponents of the new techniques of propaganda, building upon notions of "heroic" leadership widespread in right-wing circles long before Hitler's rise to prominence. On the other hand, it has to be seen as a reflection of "mentalities," value-systems, and socio-political structures which conditioned the acceptance of a "Superman" image of political leadership. Both the active manufacture of Hitler's public image and the receptivity to it by the German people need, therefore, to be explored.

Images of "heroic" leadership were already gaining ground in populist-nationalist circles of the German Right in the late nineteenth century. Their inclusion as a growing force in the political culture of the Right in Kaiser's Germany (and there are parallels in prefascist Italy, which later gave rise to the cult of the Duce) was largely shaped by three interlinked factors: the social and political disruption accompanying a simultaneous transition to nation-state, constitutional government (if strongly authoritarian in character), and industrialised society; the deep fragmentation of the political system (reflecting fundamental social cleavages); and, not least, the spread of a chauvinistic-imperialist ideology clamouring for a rightful "place in the sun" for Germany, a "have-not" nation.

Growing disappointment on the populist Right with Wilhelm II promoted notions of a "People's Kaiser" who, embodying strength and vitality, would crush Germany's internal enemies and, at the expense of inferior peoples, would provide the new nation with greatness and would win an empire for "a people without living space."

The extreme glorification of military values before and especially during the First World War, and the Right's shock and trauma at defeat, revolution, and the victory of the hated Social Democrats, promoted the exten-

---

From Ian Kershaw, "The Hitler Myth," copyright © November 1985 by History Today, Ltd., London. Reprinted by permission.

sion and partial transformation of "heroic" leadership images in the 1920s. Following the abdication of the Kaiser and the end of the old political order, ideal leadership was envisaged as being embodied in a man from the people whose qualities would reflect struggle, conflict, the values of the trenches. Hard, ruthless, resolute, uncompromising, and radical, he would destroy the old privilege- and class-ridden society and bring about a new beginning, uniting the people in an ethnically pure and socially harmonious "national community." The extreme fragmentation of Weimar politics kept such visions alive on the nationalist and völkisch Right. And by the early 1930s, perceptions of the total failure of Weimar democracy and mortal crisis of the entire political system allowed the image to move from the wings of politics to centre stage. By then, one man in particular was making a claim—accepted by increasing numbers of people—that he alone could re-awaken Germany and restore the country's greatness. This was Adolf Hitler, the leader of the Nazis.

Within the Nazi Party, the beginnings of a personality cult around Hitler go back to 1922–3, when some party members were already comparing him with Napoleon or describing him as Germany's Mussolini. Of course, Hitler only gradually established an unchallengeable authority within the party, initially having to contend with some powerful factions of opposition. And although his own concept of leadership was already becoming more "heroic" in the year before his *Putsch* attempt, it was only during imprisonment following its failure that he came to believe that he himself was Germany's pre-destined great leader. During the following years in which the Nazis were little more than a minor irritant in German politics, the "Hitler Myth" was consciously built up within the Movement as a device to integrate the party, to fend off leadership challenges,

and to win new members. The introduction in 1926 of a compulsory *"Heil Hitler"* fascist-style greeting and salute among party members was an outward sign of their bonds with their leader. Pseudo-religious imagery and fanciful rhetoric so ludicrous that it even occasionally embarrassed Hitler became commonplace in references to the leader in party publications.

Before 1930, the nascent *Führer* cult around Hitler found an echo among at most a few hundred thousand followers. But with the Nazi Party's breakthrough in the 1930 election (which brought it 18.3 per cent of the vote), the *Führer* cult ceased to be merely the property of a fanatical fringe party. The potential was there for its massive extension, as more and more Germans saw in Nazism—symbolised by its leader—the only hope for a way out of gathering crisis. Those now surging to join the Nazi party were often already willing victims of the "Hitler Myth." Not untypical was the new party member who wrote that after hearing Hitler speak for the first time, "there was only one thing for me, either to win with Adolf Hitler or to die for him. The personality of the *Führer* had me totally in its spell." Even for the vast majority of the German people who did not share such sentiments, there was the growing feeling—encouraged by Hitler's profile even in the non-Nazi press—that Hitler was not just another politician, that he was a party leader extraordinary, a man towards whom one could not remain neutral. He polarised feelings between bitter hatred and ecstatic devotion, but he could no longer be ignored, or shrugged off as a political nonentity.

For the thirteen million Germans who voted Nazi in 1932, Hitler symbolised—chameleon-like—the various facets of Nazism which they found appealing. In his public portrayal, he was a man of the people, his humble origins emphasising the rejection of privilege and the sterile old order in favour of a new, vigorous, upwardly-mobile society built upon strength, merit, and achievement. He was seen as strong, uncompromising, ruthless. He embodied the triumph of true Germanic virtues—courage, manliness, integrity, loyalty, devotion to the cause—over the effete decadence, corruption, and effeminate weakness of Weimar society. Above all, he represented "struggle"—as the title of his book *Mein Kampf* advertised: struggle of the "little man" against society's "big battalions," and mortal struggle against Germany's powerful internal and external enemies to assure the nation's future. More prosaically, for the many still less convinced, he headed a huge mass movement which, given the weak and divided Weimar parties, seemed to offer the only way out of all-embracing crisis.

Still, not one German in two cast a vote for Hitler's party in the March election of 1933—held five weeks after Hitler had been appointed Chancellor in an atmosphere of national euphoria coupled with terroristic repression of the Left. Most Germans remained either hostile to, or unconvinced by, their new "people's Chancellor," as the Nazi press dubbed him. Within the diehard ranks of the persecuted socialist and Communist Left, of course, the hatred of Hitler and all he stood for—which in many respects was accurately foreseen—was implacable. In Catholic quarters, deep suspicions lingered about the anti-Christian tendencies of Nazism—though there was already a growing readiness to distance Hitler himself from the "dangerous elements" in his movement. And bourgeois circles continued to see in Hitler the social upstart and vulgar demagogue, mouthpiece of the hysterical masses, the head of a party containing some wild and threatening elements—but a man, with all his faults, who could have his uses for a time. Attitudes towards Hitler in early 1933 varied greatly, therefore, and were often heatedly negative.

Three factors at least have to be taken into account in explaining how, nevertheless, the *Führer* cult could, within a strikingly short time, extend its hold to wide sections of the population, and eventually to the overwhelming majority of Germans. Of crucial significance was the widespread feeling that the Weimar political system and leadership was utterly bankrupt. In such conditions, the image of a dynamic, energetic, "youthful" leader offering a derisive change of direction and backed by an army of fanatical followers was not altogether unattractive. Many with grave doubts were prepared to give Hitler a chance. And compared with the pathetic helplessness of his predecessors as Chancellor, the apparent drive and tempo of government activity in the months after he took office seemed impressive.

Secondly, the gross underestimation of Hitler again paved the way for at first reluctant or condescending and then wholehearted, enthusiasm for the way he apparently mastered within such a short time the internal political situation which had seemed beyond the capabilities of an upstart rabble-rouser. Thirdly, and most importantly, Hitler embodied an already well-established, extensive ideological consensus which also embraced most of those, except the Left, who had still not given him their vote in March 1933. Its chief elements were virulent anti-Marxism and the perceived need for a powerful counter to the forces of the Left; deep hostility towards the failed democratic system and a belief that strong, authoritarian leadership was necessary for any recovery; and a widespread feeling, even extending to parts of the Left, that Germany had been badly wronged at Versailles, and was threatened by enemies on all sides. This preexisting wide consensus offered the potential for strong support for a national leader who could appear to offer absolute commitment, personal sacrifice, and selfless striving in the cause of inner unity and outward strength.

By 1933, Nazi propaganda had been highly successful in establishing "charismatic authority" as the organisational premise of the Nazi Party, and then in portraying Hitler to Nazi sympathisers as not just another party leader, but as *the* Leader for whom the nation had been waiting—a man of incomparably different stature to contemptible party politicians. The most important propaganda step now remained to be taken: the conversion, for the "majority of the majority" that had still not supported Hitler in March 1933, of his image from that of leader of the Nazi Movement to that of national leader.

Given the fact that Nazi propaganda now enjoyed a virtual monopoly within Germany, and that those taking a less than favourable view of Hitler's qualities were now incarcerated or silenced by fear and repression, the scene was set for the rapid establishment by the end of 1934 of the full-blown *Führer* cult of an almost deified national leader. No doubt many Germans found the extremes of the now omnipresent Hitler cult nauseating. But they were for the most part coming to accept that Hitler was no ordinary head of government. Above all, one could not ignore his "achievements": "order" had been restored; unemployment was falling rapidly; the economy was picking up strongly; Germany was beginning to stand up for itself again in the world. The record seemed to speak for itself.

By 1935, Hitler could be hailed in the Nazi press—and there was by now hardly any other press to speak of inside Germany—as the "Symbol of the Nation" who, having struggled as an "ordinary worker" to establish Germany's "social freedom," had now, as a one-time ordinary "Front soldier," re-established Germany's "national freedom"—a reference to the recent reassertion of German military sovereignty. The message being con-

veyed was that people and nation found their identity, their "incarnation," as it was put, in the person of the *Führer*. To this weight placed upon Hitler's "achievements," Goebbels added the pathos of the human qualities of the *Führer*: his simplicity and modesty, toil and endeavour for his people, mastery of all problems facing the nation, toughness and severity, unshakable determination though flexibility of method in the pursuit of far-sighted goals. With all this went the intense loneliness and sadness of a man who had sacrificed all personal happiness and private life for his people. This extraordinary catalogue of personal virtues—making the "human" Hitler almost inhuman in the degree of his perfection was set alongside the political genius of the *Führer* as a human counterpart to the image of the lofty, distant statesman. It amounted to almost a mirror of contemporary bourgeois values—characteristics with which almost everyone could find some point of association.

Difficult though it is to evaluate, evidence of the receptivity to this image—drawn both from sources from within the regime and those hostile to the Nazi system—lends strong support to Goebbels' claim in 1941 that the creation of the "Hitler Myth" had been his greatest propaganda achievement. The powerfully integrative force of Hitler's massive popularity seems undeniable. Goebbels might have added, however, that the way had been paved for him by the constant exposure to rabid chauvinist-imperialist values pumped into the population for decades by a stridently nationalist press (excepting the publications of the Left) and by a variety of forms of "socialisation" in schools, the bourgeois youth movement, the army, and an entire panoply of "patriotic" clubs, leagues, and associations.

Of course, the political culture was far from a unitary one, and not all Germans were affected. As is well known, the socialist subculture remained relatively immune. Those schooled in the traditions of the Socialist and Communist parties continued throughout the Third Reich to be the least susceptible to the appeal of the "Hitler Myth." To a lesser extent, the Catholic subculture was also resistant to the full extremes of the *Führer* cult, though strong traditions of authoritarianism and especially endemic anti-Marxism allowed for substantial inroads. Clearly, therefore, Hitler's popularity was far from complete, the *Führer* cult far from uniform in its impact. However, detailed examination of an extensive mass of sources relating to the formation of popular opinion and attitudes in the Third Reich suggests at least seven significant bases of the "Hitler Myth" which can be singled out.

Firstly, Hitler was seen as the embodiment of strong and, where necessary, ruthless enforcement of "law and order"—the representative of "popular justice," the voice of the "healthy sentiment of the people." An example can be seen in the great gains in popularity which accrued to him in spring 1933 as a result of the brutal Nazi onslaught on the Left, "clearing away" the Socialist and Communist "enemies of the state." Even more spectacular as an illustration is the extraordinary boost to Hitler's popularity following the ruthless massacre of members of his own Movement—the leaders of the highly unpopular SA—in June 1934. In reality, the purge of the SA leadership served to crush a destabilising element in the regime and further the power-political ambitions of the army and the SS. But none of this was reflected in Hitler's image following the purge. As even opponents of the regime acknowledged, Hitler's blood-letting was hugely popular, welcomed as a blow struck for law and order—"popular justice" eradicating corruption and immorality within the Movement. The propagated image of a leader upholding public morality corresponded

closely with commonly-held values and prejudices—for instance, in the condemnation of rowdiness and disorder, venal corruption and homosexuality. In what was a complete inversion of reality, Hitler was seen to be signalling a triumph for values associated with "normality."

Secondly, Hitler was seen as representing the national interest, putting the nation first before any particularist cause and wholly detached from any personal, material, or selfish motives. Crucial to this image was the way, after 1933, in which propaganda succeeded in isolating Hitler from the growing unpopularity of the Nazi Party itself. The wholly positive resonance of the portrayal of Hitler, the national leader, contrasted vividly with the sullied reputation of party functionaries, the "little Hitlers," whose corruption and greed, jumped-up arrogance and highhandedness, pettiness and hypocrisy, were a daily scandal. And whereas the local party officials bore the brunt of extensive and real daily discontent, Hitler's popularity was cushioned by the myth that he was being kept in the dark about the misdeeds of his underlings, was unaware of the just complaints of his people.

Without at least the prospect of an improved living standard, the extent of the effective integration produced by the "Hitler Myth" would have been difficult to achieve. A third, extremely important, component of the perceived *Führer* image was, therefore, that of the architect and creator of Germany's "economic miracle" of the 1930s. Part of the apologetic of the post-war era was, of course, that despite his "mistakes," Hitler had revamped the economy, rid Germany of unemployment, and built the motorways. This is itself testimony to the penetrating and enduring features of this aspect of the contemporary Hitler image. Certainly, by 1939 it was difficult to deny that economic conditions in Germany, for whatever reasons, had improved dramatically since the Depression era. However, more than in any other sphere, perceptions of Hitler's image in the context of economic and social policy were determined by experiences which divided for the most part along class lines.

The working class remained the social grouping least impressed by the "economic miracle" and *relatively* immune to the image of Hitler as the creator of Germany's striking new prosperity. After all, with their own standard of living pinned down to Depression levels in the years 1933–36, most industrial workers saw no particular reason to offer marked signs of gratitude to the *Führer*. Through repression and intimidation, low wages, and longer hours, the "economic miracle," as most realised, was being carried out on their own backs. Nevertheless, as the underground worker resistance was forced to admit, Hitler undoubtedly did gain some popularity among workers for "his" work creation and the economic recovery which "he" had brought about. And in the first years of the Third Reich in particular, the "socialist" aspect of the Hitler image also struck a chord among many of the poorer Germans who were recipients of the "Winter Aid." Even so, on the whole it appears that the image of the economic miracle-worker, the restorer of Germany's prosperity, had its greatest appeal among those sectors of the population who benefited most from the economic boom of the rearmament period: the middle class, who, despite their unceasing grumbling, continued to provide the main base of support for the regime and devotion to Hitler to at least the middle of the war.

Fourthly, in matters affecting established institutions and traditions, Hitler was seen as a "moderate," opposed to the radical and extreme elements in the Movement. An obvious example is the "church struggle." Whenever fundamental institutions or basic traditional props of both major Christian denominations were under attack—as in the Nazi attempt in 1934 to abolish surviving Protestant bishoprics with a firm tradition of independence, or to remove crucifixes, the symbol of Christianity itself, from Catholic schoolrooms in 1936 and again in 1941, Hitler was looked to as the defence against the "wild elements" in the party.

His apparent non-involvement in, or aloofness from, the bitter conflicts, before finally intervening to end the disturbance— put down to party radicals and the "new heathenism" associated above all with Rosenberg—and "restore order," left Hitler's standing among churchgoers relatively unscathed, despite the slump in popularity of the party. Grotesque as it seems, Hitler himself continued to be widely regarded as a God-fearing and deeply religious man. Even church leaders with a reputation for hostility to Nazism were persuaded of his sincerity, belief in God, and acceptance of the role of Christianity and the churches. Their public avowals of obedience to the *Führer* and recognition of his leadership and achievements played no small part in helping to give legitimation to the "Hitler Myth."

Fanatical commitment to uncompromising and ruthless action against the "enemies of the people" was a fifth crucial component of Hitler's image. But he was regarded as condoning only lawful, "rational" action, not the crude violence and public brutalities of the party's distasteful "gutter" elements. No one could have been left in any doubt, for instance, of Hitler's fanatical anti-Semitism and determination to exclude Jews from German society. And at the beginning of his career, anti-Semitism had been a keynote of almost all his speeches and must have been a dominant component of his popular image among early converts to Nazism. However, during the period of the party's major electoral successes, anti-Semitism appears to have featured less prominently in Hitler's public addresses, and was less important as an electoral drawing card than has often been presumed—tending mainly to function as a general touchstone for other propaganda themes.

After 1933, Hitler was extremely careful to avoid public association with the generally unpopular pogrom-type anti-Semitic outrages, particularly of course following the nation-wide "Crystal Night" pogrom in November 1938. In the years when his popularity was soaring to dizzy heights, moreover, Hitler's public pronouncements on the "Jewish Question" were less numerous than might be imagined, and, while certainly hate-filled, were usually couched in abstract generalities in association with western plutocracy or Bolshevism. In these terms, bolstering the passive anti-Semitism already widespread among the German people and lending support to "legal" measures—for the most part popular—excluding Jews from German society and the economy, Hitler's hatred of the Jews was certainly an acceptable component of his popular image, even if it was an element "taken on board" rather than forming a centrally important motivating factor for most Germans. Even during the war, when his vitriolic public onslaughts on the Jews came far more frequently and contained dire allusions to their physical extermination, the signs are that this was not a centrally formative factor shaping attitudes towards Hitler among the German people.

Sixthly, Hitler's public profile in the arena of foreign affairs stood in stark contrast to reality. He was commonly seen here as a fanatical upholder of the nation's just rights to territory "robbed" from Germany in the peace settlement after the First World War, a rebuilder of Germany's strength, and a statesman of genius—to which his astounding run of diplomatic coups seemed to offer ample testimony. Amid the widespread, deep fears of another war, he was also, astonishingly, seen by many as a "man of peace" who "would do everything he could to settle things peacefully" (as one then youthful observer later came to describe her feelings at the time)—a defender of German rights, not a racial-imperialist warmonger working towards a "war of annihilation" and limitless German conquest. Hitler's imposing series of "triumphs without bloodshed" directed at "peace with honour"—tearing up the Versailles settlement, winning back the Saar, restoring "military sovereignty," recovering the Rhineland, uniting Austria with Germany, and bringing the Sudetenland "home into the Reich"—won him support in all sections of the German people and unparalleled popularity, prestige, and acclaim.

Finally, there is Hitler's image, when war came, as the military strategist of genius, outwitting Germany's enemies in an unbelievable run of *Blitzkrieg* victories, culminating in the taking of France within four weeks when a generation earlier four years had not been enough. Even after the war started to turn sour for Germany in the winter of 1941–2, the unpopularity of the party and its despised representatives at home continued for a time to stand in stark contrast to the image of the *Führer*'s devotion to duty in standing with his soldiers at the Front. However, according to Max Weber's model, "charismatic leadership" could not survive lack of success. And indeed, as "his" astonishing run of victories turned gradually but inexorably into calamitous defeat, the tide of Hitler's popularity first waned rather slowly, then ebbed sharply. The decline accelerated decisively following the catastrophe of Stalingrad, a defeat for which Hitler's personal responsibility was widely recognised.

The "Hitler Myth" was now fatally flawed. In the face of defeats, personal losses, misery, and sacrifice, the earlier successes began to be seen in a new light. Hitler was now increasingly blamed for policies which had led to war. His much vaunted strong will, resolution, unshakeable determination, and absolute fanaticism were regarded more and more not as attributes but as the main stumbling blocks to the longed-for peace. With no more successes to proclaim, Hitler was now reluctant even to speak to the German people. The new image put out by Goebbels of Hitler as a latterday Frederick the Great—distant majesty finally triumphant in the face of extreme adversity—symbolised the growing gulf.

Important reserves of popularity remained to the end. Hatred of the Allies prompted by terror bombing campaigns partially benefited Hitler and the regime for a while; some temporary vain hopes were placed in the *Führer*'s promises of new weapons which would accomplish the desired "retaliation"; a short-lived upsurge of support and proclamation of loyalty followed the attempt on his life in July 1944—an indication that a successful coup might have encountered a new version of the "stab-in-the-back" legend; and surprisingly large numbers of prisoners-of-war in the west continued till the end to avow their belief in Hitler. But the potency of the "Hitler Myth" had vanished. Eloquent commentary on this is a report on a remembrance ceremony at the war memorial in the little Bavarian alpine town of Markt Schellenberg on March 11th, 1945:

> When the leader of the *Wehrmacht* unit at the end of his speech for the remembrance called for a *"Sieg-Heil"* for the *Führer,* it was returned neither by the *Wehrmacht* present, nor by the *Volkssturm,* nor by the spectators of the civilian population who had turned up. This silence of the masses had a depressing effect, and probably reflects better than anything the attitudes of the people.

Unquestionably, the adulation of Hitler by millions of Germans who may otherwise have been only marginally committed to the Nazi ideology, or party, was a crucial element of political integration in the Third Reich. Without this mass base of support, the high level of plebiscitary acclamation, which

the regime could repeatedly call upon to legitimise its actions and to take the wind out of the sails of the opposition, is unthinkable. It also enabled the specifically Nazi élite to free itself from dependence upon the support of traditional conservative ruling groups, thereby boosting the autonomy of the "wild men" in the Movement. Without the degree of popular backing which Hitler was able to command, the drive, dynamism, and momentum of Nazi rule could hardly have been sustained.

The *Führer* cult necessarily influenced the relations of the Nazi leadership itself with Hitler, as well as those of the traditional ruling élites. Inevitably, it surrounded Hitler with toadies, flatterers, and sycophants, shielding him from rational criticism or genuine debate, and bolstered increasing detachment from reality. Nor could Hitler himself remain impervious to the extraordinary cult which had been created around him and which came to envelop him. His own person gradually became inseparable from the myth.

Hitler had to live out more and more the constructed image of omnipotence and omniscience. And the more he succumbed to the allure of his own *Führer* cult and came to believe in his own myth, the more his judgement became impaired by faith in his own infallibility and guidance "by providence," enabling him to "go his way with the certainty of a sleepwalker." His room for manoeuvre now became restricted by his own need to protect the "Hitler Myth" and sustain his prestige, aware as he was that if Nazism lost its forward momentum and stagnation set in, Hitler's own popularity and the mass base of the regime's support would be fatally undermined. To this extent, it has been claimed with some justification, that "Hitler well understood his own function, the role which he had to act out as 'Leader' of the Third Reich," that he "transformed himself into a function, the function of *Führer*."

71

Nationalism and Militarism in Japan

After a flourishing democratic movement associated with the Taisho period in the 1920's, the Depression, nationalism in China, communism in the Soviet Union and the rise of fascism in Europe led those advocating a more nationalistic and militaristic direction for Japan to gain prominence. This reading highlights some of the key influences on the radical nationalists in the Japan of the 1930's.

Discussion Questions

1. What traditional Japanese values and institutions influenced the radical nationalists? What contemporary ideas?

2. What was the role Japan was to play in the world? How did the vision of Kita Ikki or Ishiwara Kanji correspond to the reality of world developments?

3. How were the radical nationalists able to gain so much power in Japan?

4. Would you describe the views of the radical nationalists as fascist? What did these groups share with Mussolini's Italy and Hitler's Germany, or other fascist movements? What differences existed?

Central to the consciousness of national identity in Japan was the Shintō myth: that the emperor was a descendant in the direct line of the sun-goddess, Amaterasu; that the people were also of divine descent, though from lesser gods; and that between emperor and people there was a mystical bond, superior to anything of the kind to be found elsewhere in the world. In one sense these ideas were as old as the historical record. In another they derived from modern politics. In order to give Meiji Japan unity and cloak its innovations in legitimate authority, there had been a constant reiteration after 1868—in imperial decrees, in schools, in the training of conscript soldiers—that a subject's duty and loyalty stemmed from this mystique, not from any concept of social contract or popular sovereignty. Around it, too, there clustered other virtues: the preservation of traditional values and behaviour; obligations to the family and community; respect for an inherited culture.

In so far as nationalism ensured a commitment to patriotic aims and a large measure of support for the decisions of the emperor's government, it contributed much to the emergence of orthodox imperialism in the early phase of Japanese expansion. After about 1918, however, it was becoming politically ambivalent. There was still agreement on all sides that Japan must be Great Japan. There was still the same amuletic vocabulary: "the national polity," "the national essence," "the national family." Nevertheless, as Japanese society became more bourgeois, so nationalism became in one of its guises a critique and a lament: that landlords had become absentees, exploiting villagers; that business men were *nouveaux riches*; that politicians were party men, seeking only power; that none of them put nation first. At schools and universities, it was said, the young were being taught to esteem individualism, which was a Western word for selfishness.

In these circumstances, nationalism became critical of contemporary leadership. It demanded a reaffirmation of what used to be and a call to Japanese to go back to it. This involved *inter alia* a return to the same kind of ambitions overseas and the same kind of imperialist policies in pursuit of them as had developed in the Meiji era. Nationalism was also revolutionary, however. It denied the validity of much that had been done in the name of modernization in the past; demanded once again a complete reordering of society, effected by force in the emperor's name; and condemned the whole world order as unjust. It therefore called upon Japanese to carry through to completion the tasks which the Meiji leaders had left half-done, both at home and overseas. The heroes it chose were the "men of spirit" of the 1860s, who had helped to bring the Tokugawa down. Its methods, like theirs, were terrorism and the *coup d'état*. Patriotic assassination, never absent for long from modern Japanese politics, became frequent and respectable again.

The political movement, or perhaps one should call it the political activity, that took shape under these influences after 1930, has been variously described as "ultra-national-ist" and "fascist." There was a strong element of agrarianism in it, reflecting a hostility to urban life and all it stood for. There were strands of socialism and Pan-Asianism. And as those statements imply, there was little coherence or unity. In this context, as in others, the Japanese were prone to form associations and societies, most of them small and clustering round one or two men of personality or charisma. Such groups rarely worked together. Certainly they never comprised a mass organization such as Hitler or Mussolini could command. What is more, their avowed function was not to seize power, but to destroy it. Out of chaos, they believed, would come in some mysterious way a better Japan.*

The most famous of these nationalist revoluntaries was Kita Ikki (1883–1937). Like many Meiji radicals, he came from a fairly well-to-do family. He had links with the Kokuryukai (Amur Society); was much influenced when young by Social Darwinism; and spent several years in China after the 1911 Revolution. The outcome of these experiences was a book entitled *A Plan for the Reorganization of Japan* (*Nihoit kaizō hōan taikō*), which was written in Shanghai in 1919, but not published in Japan until 1923, when it was banned by the police. Its theme was that Japan must be fundamentally reformed in order that it might be fit to give leadership to a resurgent Asia. The reform, Kita argued, would need to be initiated by a *coup d'état*, having as its objects a declaration of martial law and the suspension of parliament. This would remove the established cliques which interposed between the emperor and his people. Thereafter it would

be possible for a reconstituted imperial government to destroy the landed and financial interests of the rich; to institute state controls over the economy in preparation for inevitable war; to carry out land reform, giving legal protection to tenant farmers; to introduce profit-sharing and the eight-hour day into industry; and to implement civil liberties.

Kita made a parallel analysis of the international system and the steps that were needed to correct it. The villains of the piece were Britain, "a multimillionaire standing over the whole world," and Russia, "the great landlord of the northern hemisphere." Between them they had put all Asia in thrall, building empires that stretched from Turkey to Siberia. The countries of Asia could not overturn these empires on their own. Only through Japanese assistance could they do so: "our seven hundred million brothers in China and India have no path to independence other than that offered by our guidance and protection." Japan should accordingly "lift the virtuous banner of an Asian league and take the leadership in a world federation." Indeed, this would also enable it to solve problems of its own. Since its population had doubled in the previous fifty years, "great areas adequate to support a population of at least two hundred and forty or fifty millions will be absolutely necessary a hundred years from now."

The programme of domestic policy which Kita put forward was attractive neither to men who had inherited from the Meiji period a place of prominence in Japanese society, nor to those who opposed them from the standpoint of the proletarian left. However, this was conspicuously not true of what he said about Japanese policy overseas. By way of example one might take, first, the ideas of

---

* There are some thoughtful essays in nationalism and kindred subjects in Maruyama Masao, *Thought and Behaviour in Modern Japanese Politics* (1963). The agrarian theme is considered in Thomas Havens, *Farm and Nation in Modern Japan* (1974). Richard Storry, *The Double Patriots* (1957), examines a wide spectrum of patriotic societies from the Meiji period to the end of the Second World War.

Konoe Fumimaro. Konoe belonged to the Fujiwara line, which made him heir to centuries of office at the imperial court, and was subsequently the Prime Minister by whom Japan's New Order was proclaimed in 1938. He cannot be considered actually or potentially a social revolutionary. Nevertheless, from the time that he first published an article in a nationalist magazine in December 1918, he had been a bitter critic of what he saw as Western self-seeking and dishonesty. The policies pursued by Britain and the United States, ostensibly for the purposes of world stability, were, he argued, attempts by the "haves" to keep out the "have-nots." They served to condemn late comers like Japan "to remain forever subordinate to the advanced nations"; and unless something were done to change this situation—such as offering "equal access to the markets and natural resources of the colonial areas"—Japan would be forced "to destroy the status quo for the sake of self-preservation, just like Germany."* Konoe returned to this theme in another article in 1933, in which he maintained that it was the failure to break Anglo-American control of the international economy that had compelled Japan to move into Manchuria in 1931. . . .

Young (and some not-so-young) officers in the army and navy also found it appealing. They, too, founded patriotic societies to debate its implications, treating Kita Ikki's fiery rhetoric as something akin to policy proposals. Since they took the view, long exemplified by their seniors with respect to Manchuria, that the responsibilities of the military were not confined to carrying out the orders of a civilian government, the *Plan* became for many of them the delineation of a future towards which it was their duty to work. Twice after 1930 there were abortive

coups d'état in Tokyo. In the first, which took place on 15 May 1932, junior officers from a naval air station joined with civilian extremists in attacks on public targets and political figures, including members of the cabinet. The Prime Minister, Inukai Tsuyoshi, was assassinated. However, because no generals or admirals moved to exploit the situation, the coup failed. The second attempt came on 26 February 1936, when troops from the First Division, acting on the orders of their company commanders, occupied the centre of the capital and held it for three days. During that period they killed or wounded several leading politicians—though not on this occasion the Prime Minister, who escaped unrecognized—and distributed pamphlets calling for radical changes in Japanese society. The high command, prompted by the emperor, acted with unexpected firmness. Loyal troops were brought in to surround the rebels. When the latter surrendered, a number of their leaders were quickly tried and executed. So was Kita Ikki, who had been personally involved.

The officers who planned and led those operations had, it seems, been misled by vaguely worded expressions of sympathy from their superiors into believing that men of higher rank would come to their support once a coup had been carried out. That they did not so was partly due to the fact that the most powerful among them were more militarist than revolutionary. That is to say, they put the requirements of military strength before those of social change. Army leadership in particular, was principally concerned with—and divided about—the nature of modern warfare and the manner in which Japan should be made ready for it. Under Ugaki Kazushige, who was War Minister in 1924–7 and again in 1929–30, there had emerged a

---

* The article is summarized in Oka Yoshitake, Konoe Fumimaro (1983), 10–13.

nucleus of able officers on the General Staff who sought above all to give the Japanese army greater striking power through modernization. They later passed under the patronage of Minami Jirō, War Minister during 1931, in whose term of office the attack on Manchuria was carried out. Opposition to Minami developed for a number of reasons: because his military reforms had offended many old-fashioned generals; because he wanted to move cautiously on the mainland until Japan had reached full military preparedness; because he was more willing to restrain than to help the radicals. This opposition coalesced round a new grouping, the Kōdō-ha (Imperial Way Faction), led by Araki Sadao. Araki took over the post of War Minister at the end of 1931. Minami's followers, among whom the most prominent were Nagata Tetsuzan (assassinated in 1935) and Tōjō Hideki, then became part of what was to be called the Control Faction (Tōsci-ha). After 1936 this was the dominant group within the army.

Differences between the two factions were in many respects a matter of emphasis, since both acknowledged a common objective in creating a "purer" and more powerful Japan. The Imperial Way faction gave greater weight to ideology and morale: an emperor-centred polity; anti-communism; cooperation (on Japan's terms) with China; the struggle against Soviet Russia. It was self-consciously Asian. The Control faction wanted a Japan better organized for global warfare: military reform; controls over capital and labour, as well as over the allocation of raw materials, such as would benefit strategic industries; a disciplined civilian population; territorial expansion. It was highly professional. And though there was a great deal of overlap in the slogans and patriotic terminology of the two, it was the Control Faction that played the more important part in reshaping Japanese imperialism. The way in which it did so can best be illustrated by examining the views of Ishiwara Kanji. Graduating from staff college in 1918, Ishiwara served in China in 1920–1 and returned sceptical of that country's capacity to serve as a worthwhile partner to Japan, at least in the shorter term. Subsequent study in Germany from 1922 to 1925 gave him a better knowledge of modern warfare and an awareness of the Japanese army's technical deficiencies. He came home to become an instructor at the staff college in 1926. In the next few years, while teaching there, he won recognition as the army's leading theorist on strategy and military history. His next appointment was to the staff of the Kwantung Army, where he planned the operations undertaken in Manchuria in 1931–2. In 1935 he became head of the tactical section of the General Staff. The main lines of Ishiwara's thought had already taken shape by 1931. Central to it was a belief that Japan, acting through the army, was destined to save the world from Marxism and other corrupting ideologies. This would require a series of wars, first against Russia, then against Britain, finally against the United States, in which Japan would stand as the champion of Asia and the embodiment of Confucian righteousness. The culminating struggle would be a holocaust in which warfare would take on a wholly new dimension—though one foreshadowed in western Europe in 1914–18—bringing into action entire populations and the totality of their resources. Preparing Japan to take part in it had both an internal and an external dimension. At home, it would be necessary not only to ensure stability and unity, but also to institute such controls over society and economy as would guarantee the most effective applications of available strength. Abroad, Asia would have to be brought under Japanese dominance, starting with Manchuria. As Ishiwara saw it, "war can maintain war." Each accrual to Japanese strength would make possible the next; and the process, when complete, would make available the economic resources on which final victory would depend.

By asserting the need to integrate political, military, and economic policy for purposes of "defence," as defined in this way, Ishiwara was doing something more than bring together elements that had existed separately hitherto. He was also identifying the army as the principal actor on the national stage. Thus in so far as his ideas determined Japanese actions in the following decade—there was never unanimity concerning them—he was the prophet of what can appropriately be described as military imperialism. It began in Manchuria.

72

I Am a Patriot

The views of some Japanese, especially those in the armed services, are reflected in this soldier's statement on the eve of World War II.

Discussion Questions

1. How is patriotism defined by this soldier? How would you define patriotism today, and are there important similarities or differences with the Japanese view as presented by the soldier?

2. What constitutes the greatest threat to Japan's survival? How does this soldier's view compare with those of the radical nationalists? How does it compare with the views of other Japanese, such as the party politicians, the big businessmen or the people?

3. Do you think that this soldier's view was representative of the majority of Japanese people prior to World War II? Why or why not?

"I Am a Patriot"—A Japanese Officer Speaks on the Eve of War, 1937

My Creed

I am a patriot.
I believe in Yamato—my country.
It has been rightly said that,
> The valor of a Yamato heart
> When faced with a crisis
> Its mettle proves.

A crisis threatens our national existence. My country has for centuries stood high above other nations and now that Nippon is about to make great strides, light and shadow seem to have appeared—we must stir ourselves to find a way forward in these difficult times.
I believe In my Emperor.
> O that I could die
> Beneath the Emperor's banner,
> Though deserveless of a name.

I am loyal and obedient to the Emperor; he is the symbol of unity and I shall follow him implicitly. By implicit obedience I mean offering my life for the sake of the Emperor; this is not self-sacrifice, but a means of living under his august grace. The Emperor is divine. In the legend of the creation of Nippon the Sun Goddess decreed, "As endless as Heaven and Earth shall the Imperial Throne prosper." The Emperor Meiji wrote in his poem of 1910:
> Should we not preserve in dignity
> This Land of Peace
> Handed down from the Age of the Gods?

Our history shows that through ceaseless efforts successive Emperors have overcome every obstacle, expanded Imperial enterprises and built up a good and beautiful nation.
I believe in my Family.
> Precious are my parents that gave me birth
> So that I might serve His Majesty.

My family is more important than myself—or any other individual. Individualism is a way of thinking that makes me, as a person, all-important. It is an evil western idea.

My Fears and Hopes

My creed then is "My Country, My Emperor, My Family." This creed is in danger. Its enemies are abroad and at home.

Across the Sea of Japan I fear Soviet Russia, now recovering her enormous strength, and I fear that China may try to take Manchuria from us. We must not sacrifice Manchuria, won by Yamato in a costly and bloody struggle. Far to the south, Britain and the United States have much wealth invested in oil, rubber, and other raw materials. As a result Nippon is a "have-not" country. Nippon must challenge the old order by expanding overseas. We must secure an equal distribution of the resources of the world.

At home there have been disastrous happenings in the last twenty years. Party politicians have brought dishonor to Yamato. Their behavior has been scandalous. They take bribes from the big business houses like the rich Mitsui and Mitsubishi. I am con-

302 • *Readings in Global History, Volume 2*

vinced these city financiers have fixed both taxes and prices against the interest of the farmer. Industry and big cities mushroom, and they threaten the traditional Nippon way of life. They have brought to our country that other evil of the Western world—the class war. My honorable father is a landowner and many of the men in my regiment come from sturdy peasant stock. We must preserve the values of the countryside against the destructive influences of the West: big business, trade unions, strikes, political corruption, luxury, dance halls, and low moral standards.

Why We Must Act Now

I stand for *Kodo-ha*, the Imperial Way. The nation is one family united in common loyalty to the Emperor. I shall be ruthless in supporting this. I am in deep sympathy with my fellow junior officers and with organizations like the Dragon Society and the Blood Brotherhood League. The terror of the past few years was right; people must be made to see what is right. I am disappointed that our great effort of February 26 last year was not successful, but at least the army has some control and a strong voice in the government.

I believe things are changing for the better. I am told that it is only ten years since the prestige of the military in Nippon reached its lowest point. After the failure of the Siberian Expedition anyone in uniform was the object of pity or silent ridicule. The army had no tanks, aircraft, or radio equipment. Older officers tell me they practiced with paper models of airplanes stuck on bamboo poles and rattled sticks to imitate machine guns. They had to carry out bayonet exercises barefoot to save their boots. Soldiers' food and fuel were scanty and the barracks infested with vermin.

Now, only ten years later, the army has achieved its rightful place in the making of national decisions. Senior officers will be important members of the government, and I think we have a Prime Minister, Prince Konoye, who sympathizes with our ambitions. Even if the politicians cannot agree, at least there is one man with the right idea. I hear that General Tojo has become Chief of Staff of the Kwantung Army. On his appointment on March 1 this year he sent a telegram to the General Staff in Tokyo which advised an immediate attack into China toward Nanking. I support General Tojo in this, for it is well known that Chiang Kai-shek's Nationalist Government of China in Nanking has just signed a pact with their enemies, the Chinese Communists. This pact can only mean one thing: the Chinese intend moving against our forces in Manchukuo.

It is in the national interest that we protect ourselves before it is too late. I am a patriot.

73

Japan's Declaration of War in 1941

The following selection is an excerpt from Tokutomi Iichiro's *Commentary on the Imperial Declaration of War*. Earlier in his career Tokutomi had been enthusiastic about Christianity and liberalism but gradually became a defender of Japanese civilization and government against the West—a not unusual course among his contemporaries. By the 1930's he had become one of the leading spokesmen for the nationalist point of view. His *Commentary* analyzes the Imperial Rescript declaring war point by point and discusses Japan's role in Asia.

Discussion Questions

1. What does Tokutomi mean by the "Imperial Way?"

2. What does he think makes Japan unique as a nation, especially compared with China and the West?

3. How is Japan to become the "Light of Asia and the world?"

Chapter IV: The Basis of the Imperial Way

The virtue of sincerity is represented by the Mirror, the virtue of love is represented by the Jewels, and the virtue of intelligence is represented by the Sword. . . . The interpretation given by Kitabatake Chikafusa has, indeed, grasped the true meaning. Then, it is not wrong to liken the Three Sacred Treasures to the three virtues of intelligence, love, and courage by saying that the Mirror represents the intelligence which reflects everything, the Jewels, the love which embraces everything, and the Sword, the courage which judges between justice and injustice, honesty and dishonesty.

In any case, the basis of the Imperial Way lies in truth, in sincerity, and in justice. Its range is wide and there is nothing it does not embrace. It expels evil, subjugates injustice, absolutely maintains the tenets of justice, and itself occupies a position which can never be violated. The august virtue of the divine imperial lineage has not a single instance when it did not arise from these three virtues. In other words, they form the national character of Nippon, and, at the same time, the national trait of the people of Nippon. Combining them all, we call it the Imperial Way.

The phrase "The three virtues of intelligence, love, and courage" may sound very much like a common ethical teaching, but when considered realistically, it gives us the reason why our country, under whatever circumstances, has never resorted to arms for the sake of arms alone. . . .

Chapter VIII: The Unique Features of the Nation of Nippon

What we should note first of all is that Nippon is not a country built upon that Western individualism patterned after the insistence on rights, nor a country built with the family as the basis as in China . . . our Nippon is neither a country of individualism nor a country of the family system. In Nippon, the family is valued and good lineage is highly regarded the same as in China. However, in Nippon there is that which goes farther and which is greater than these. There is the Imperial Household. In China, there are families, but there is not the Imperial Household. In Nippon, there are families, but still, above them, there is the Imperial Household. In China, families gather to form a nation, but in Nippon the Imperial Household deigns to rule the land, and on the land the families, the members of which are subjects of the Imperial Household, flourish.

That is why, in China, one speaks first of the family and then next of the nation, but, in Nippon, the nation comes first and next the family. In China, if it is to be asked which is valued higher, the nation or the family, it must be answered that, under whatever circumstances, the family is valued first and next the nation. In the West, the individual is valued first, and next the family, and last the nation. In Nippon, the nation is valued first, then next the family, and last the individual. The order of the West is absolutely reversed in Nippon. . . .

From *Sources of Japanese Tradition* by William Theodore de Bary. Copyright © 1980 by Columbia University Press. Reprinted with permission of the publisher.

Chapter XLVIII: Three Qualifications of the Leader of Greater East Asia

Now that we have risen up in arms, we must accomplish our aim to the last. Herein lies the core of our theory. In Nippon resides a destiny to become the Light of Greater East Asia and to become ultimately the Light of the World. However, in order to become the Light of Greater East Asia, we must have three qualifications. The first is, as mentioned previously, strength. In other words, we must expel Anglo-Saxon influence from East Asia with our strength.

To speak the truth, the various races of East Asia look upon the British and Americans as superior to the Nippon race. They look upon Britain and the United States as more powerful nations than Nippon. Therefore, we must show our real strength before all our fellow-races of East Asia. We must show them an object lesson. It is not a lesson in words. It should be a lesson in facts.

In other words, before we can expel the Anglo-Saxons and make them remove all their traces from East Asia, we must annihilate them. In this way only will the various fellow races of Greater East Asia look upon us as their leader. I believe that the lesson which we must first show to our fellow-races in Greater East Asia is this lesson of cold reality.

The second qualification is benevolence. Nippon must develop the various resources of East Asia and distribute them fairly to all the races within the East Asia Co-Prosperity Sphere to make them share in the benefits. In other words, Nippon should not monopolize the benefits, but should distribute them for the mutual prosperity of Greater East Asia.

We must show to the races of East Asia that the order, tranquillity, peace, happiness, and contentment of East Asia can be gained only by eradicating the evil precedent of the encroachment and extortion of the Anglo-Saxons in East Asia, by effecting the real aim of the co-prosperity of East Asia, and by making Nippon the leader of East Asia.

The third qualification is virtue. East Asia embraces various races. Its religions are different. Moreover, there has practically been no occasion when these have mutually united to work for a combined aim. It was the favorite policy of the Anglo-Saxons to make the various races of East Asia compete and fight each other and make them mutually small and powerless. We must, therefore, console them, bring friendship among them, and make them all live in peace with a boundlessly embracing virtue.

In short, the first is the Grace of the Sacred Sword, the second, the Grace of the Sacred Mirror, and the third, the Grace of the Sacred Jewels. If we should express it in other words, we must have courage, knowledge, and benevolence. If Nippon should lack even one of the above three, it will not be able to become the Light of Asia.

74

The Myth of Pearl Harbours

The 50th anniversary commemoration of the Japanese bombing of Pearl Harbor was covered extensively by the American media. The *Newsweek* edition of November 25, 1991, "Remembering Pearl Harbor," was typical in its casting the attack as "an end of innocence. One December day, 50 years ago, an air attack on a drowsy Hawaiian military complex shocked Americans into the era of total war." The author of this reading presents a different view of the event of Pearl Harbor, placing it in the larger context of issues of war and peace, cause and effect, victory and defeat, and forcing us to rethink the significance of Pearl Harbor, and of war itself.

Discussion Questions

1. What are the myths of Pearl Harbor that the author identifies? What evidence does he use to support his views?
2. Why has Pearl Harbor remained such an emotional flashpoint for Americans? How important do you think it is for the Japanese? Do you think that the Japanese attack was "abnormal," and, if so, what elements do you think were responsible for their behavior?
3. The author makes the point that war and peace are very similar. In what ways does he feel they are similar? Do you agree with his views?
4. What do you think of the author's arguments that "the revival of German militarism in the 1930's owed as much to events in France and Britain as to events in Germany," and that "perhaps owed even more to the force of American opinion which made the United States. . .turn away from Europe." How might his comments reflect the attitudes of nations today, as they confront ethnic conflict and aggression?

Most explanations of wars assume that one nation should be totally or mainly blamed. Indeed the debate about blame usually begins before the first shot is fired; each nation insists that it is merely resisting the threat of the enemy. As the war persists, the debate circles the globe by satellite and short wave. At the end of the war the victor often tries to close the debate by affirming in the peace treaty that the loser caused the war, but that does not close the debate.

The idea that one nation must have caused a war intrinsically satisfies us. It is difficult to examine the outbreak of any war without searching for the warmaker. It is also difficult to resist the conclusion that if one nation started the war it must have caused the war. Moreover in most wars it seems easy to identify the nation which initiated the war. Thus one can suggest that in 1904 Japan initiated the war against Russia, that in 1914 Austria initiated the war against Serbia, and that in 1950 North Korea initiated the war against South Korea.

But when one examines more closely those wars in which the outbreak is clearly assigned to one nation, the clarity often vanishes. If the question is asked—why did they, rather than their enemy, fire the first shot—extenuating circumstances multiply. When Japan attacked Russia in 1904, it was partly in response to the despatch of Russian ships and troops to eastern Asia and the failure of diplomatic negotiations. When the United States attacked Britain in 1812 it was partly in response to many British attacks on neutral American merchant ships; in that sense open warfare had replaced intermittent warfare.

The outbreak of war was usually not the abrupt step which we imagine. Moreover when two nations engaged in warlike acts, and one nation extended the conflict to that stage which is usually called war, that was not necessarily the end of the extension.

All wars arise from a relationship between two or more nations. An international war involving one nation is inconceivable. To argue that one nation alone wanted war and caused war is to assume that its enemy had no alternative but to fight in self defence. But before the war the enemy possessed various alternatives. It could peacefully withdraw its demands or offer concessions; it could enlist a powerful ally, though that would also have involved concessions; or it could launch its own surprise attack. If it rejected these alternatives, and found itself attacked, it could still offer those concessions which it had failed to offer earlier. Alternatively it could refuse to resist military invasion and surrender peacefully—a policy adopted by many small nations and large tribes in the last three centuries. If a nation rejected these alternatives, one can only assume that it preferred war. Wars can only occur when two nations decide that they can gain more by fighting than by negotiating. War can only begin and can only continue with the consent of at least two nations.

The leap from peace to war is usually seen as the most revealing event in the fluctuating relations between nations. The leap from war

---

to peace is equally revealing. If it were logical to insist that one nation should bear the blame for beginning a war, then it would be equally logical to insist that one nation should be praised for ending a war. When a distinguished American professor of anthropology, Raoul Naroll, argued positively in 1969 that "one must conclude that it takes only one nation to make a war," he perhaps did not realize that he was also arguing the corollary that it takes only one nation to end a war. If war is immoral and peace is virtuous the nation which terminates a war should be praised just as the nation which initiates a war should be blamed. This does not happen. The initiators of war receive an avalanche of blame, but the initiators of peace are neither identified nor praised.

Wars end when nations agree that war is an unsatisfactory instrument for solving their dispute; wars begin when nations *agree* that peaceful diplomacy is an unsatisfactory instrument for solving their dispute. Agreement is the essence of the transition from peace to war and from war to peace, for those are merely alternating phases of a relationship between nations. Admittedly the existence of that relationship is not easy to recognize when, as nationals, we have learnt since childhood to concentrate on one nation rather than on the relationship between nations. Moreover the mutual agreement which marks the dramatic turning points in that relationship—the move from peace to war or from war to peace—is not easy to detect because of the intense hostility which especially marks the beginning of the war. That two nations, by going to war, thereby agree to employ violent means of solving their dispute is obscured by the more conspicuous fact that they disagree about the justice of their cause.

War is so devastating, dramatic and cruel that it makes us reject the idea that it has many similarities with peace; and yet our rejection prevents us from understanding more about peace and war. We deplore the visible assertion of military power when it breaks the peace but we praise the quiet assertion of military power when it keeps the peace. We forget that if war is immoral, the prizes of victory—whether territory or reparations or prestige or political power—are also immoral. As the highest prize of victory is enhanced international power, and as that power is often utilized by the victor to protect its own interests throughout the subsequent period of peace, the peace can hardly be called righteous.

The character and conditions of peace, unfortunately, are concealed beneath rhetoric and a façade of morality. Though the methods and morality which initiated a war were virtually the same as those which ended a war, the one was declared immoral and the other was declared moral. Thus the Congress of Vienna, the guardian of international morality in 1815, could pronounce judgement on Napoleon Bonaparte: "as an enemy and a disturber of the tranquillity of the world he has rendered himself liable to public vengeance." The victors likewise hired morality as their servant at the end of the First World War. In the Treaty of Versailles, Germany and her allies were formally condemned as the aggressors. The treaty also called for a special tribunal—consisting of judges appointed by the United States, Great Britain, France, Italy and Japan—to try Kaiser Wilhelm II "for a supreme offence against international morality and the sanctity of treaties." In November 1918 however the German emperor had left his headquarters on the western front and fled to Holland, where the refusal of the government to surrender him put an end to the tribunal. Nevertheless Germany's leaders were forced to agree that the harsh conditions imposed on Germany were a punishment for her aggression and a vindication of international morality. The overseas colonies confiscated from Germany, the German territory which was given to five European neighbors, the reparations extracted, the ships scuttled and regiments disbanded, and the garrisoning of foreign troops on a long strip of German soil—all seemed to be just compensation for what the victors described in the Treaty of Versailles as "the war imposed upon them by the aggression of Germany and her allies." Under the treaty the last foreign troops were to be withdrawn from the Rhineland in 1934 but only if the victors deemed to be adequate "the guarantees against unprovoked aggression by Germany." In fact these were the penalties for defeat, not punishments for aggression. If Germany had won she would have imposed similar or even severer penalties, and imposed them too in the name of international morality.

As the victors at Versailles were the custodians of international morality, and as that morality rested on military superiority, it was vital that they should retain that superiority. They forgot that victory is mostly a wasting asset. They failed as custodians because, as if lulled by their own rhetoric, they continued to assert morality while they neglected armaments. The revival of German militarism in the 1930s owed as much to events in France and Britain as to events in Germany. It perhaps owed even more to the force of American opinion which made the United States—the most powerful of the victors of 1918—turn away from Europe. As Dr A. Berriedale Keith of Edinburgh University argued in 1937: "there can be no doubt of the gravity of the responsibility which thus fell on the United States for the subsequent developments of the European situation." He wrote before that situation had been aggravated by German pressure on Austria and Czechoslovakia and Poland, and before the truth dawned that the custodianship of international morality was quickly passing to Berlin.

In essence the last months of the First World War had established a clear relationship between victors and vanquished, and both sides accepted that relationship. Most Germans must

have disliked that relationship intensely, but they had no alternative but to accept it. Peace reigned so long as the relationship was accepted. What blunted and then confused that relationship was as much the decline or defection of the victors as the rise of two of the vanquished nations, Germany and Russia. In the background to the Second World War the isolationists of Washington were as prominent as the expansionists of Berlin; the defensive appeasers of Whitehall were as influential as the assertive appeasers of the Kremlin; and the opportunists in Paris were as influential as the opportunists in Rome. Nevertheless at the end of the Second World War the tribunals in Nuremberg and Tokyo were adamant that German aggression had caused the war in Europe and Japanese aggression the war in the Pacific. The United Nations endorsed the idea and later applied it to other wars.

The façade of international morality—and the belief that one nation is to blame for war—is almost hypnotic in the last days of peace and first days of war. The beneficiaries of the existing international order emphasize the sanctity of treaties and the solemnity of obligations between nations. Forgetting that some of the treaties most sacred to them had been bonded by armed force, they denounce those who break them with armed force. If the treaties are to be broken, formal notice at least should be given, If war is to begin, an official warning should be given. One advantage of a clear warning is that a last opportunity is offered for the peaceful settlement of disputes. Even more important to the beneficiaries of the existing order, a warning of war eliminates the danger of a surprise military attack. For a surprise attack is usually the weapon of nations which hope to change existing boundaries.

In the twentieth century the nations that began wars with surprise attacks were widely denounced even when the heat and partisanship had waned. The attacks were widely interpreted as evidence that one nation was to blame for the war. Japan has been singled out as the exponent of the aggressive, unannounced war. *The Encyclopedia Britannica* refers to Pearl Harbor as "the sneak Japanese attack." Even *The New Cambridge Modern History,* which has remarkable standards of restraint and an admirable dearth of nationalist bias in its host of authors, remarked on the military advantages which Japan gained at Port Arthur in 1904 and Pearl Harbor in 1941 by the "element of complete surprise without a declaration of war." A trio of professors from North American military academies, writing of the Japanese raid on Pearl Harbor, suggested that a surprise attack, unaccompanied by a declaration of war, was "in line with the practices of total warfare and was in the Japanese military tradition." By total warfare they meant the all-out warfare practiced in the twentieth century and visible in the earlier wars of religion. Another scholar hinted at deeper reasons; he wondered whether there was some ingredient in the national character of the Japanese that favored this mode of starting a war.

Did the famous Japanese attacks take advantage of an unprepared enemy or were they no different from the launching of many other modern wars?

Pearl Harbor, in 1941, was almost a replay of Port Arthur. Months before the Japanese attack, diplomatic negotiations between Tokyo and Washington had almost reached a deadlock. While Japan was planning her attack, America was defensively increasing her forces in the Pacific. As a result of hostile edicts Japanese funds in the United States and American funds in Japan were frozen, thus ending commerce between the two nations. While Japan demanded a free hand in China, the United States demanded that Japan should withdraw her forces from China. Neither government seemed likely to yield. In

these circumstances the war was not surprising.

Nor was the method of attack surprising. In January 1941 the United State ambassador in Tokyo, Joseph C. Grew, had warned that the talk about town pointed, if war should occur, to "a surprise mass attack at Pearl Harbor." At Washington however the Office of Naval Intelligence dismissed the possibility, and at Pearl Harbor the playing of war games suggested that a successful attack was unlikely. And so the base of the Pacific fleet lapsed into the same excessive sense of security which had trapped Port Arthur. For Pearl Harbor was far from any Japanese base, was strongly defended, and in the eyes of its defenders was manned by superior men and weapons. Indeed Pearl Harbor seemed far more capable than Port Arthur of withstanding a sudden attack. The Americans had radar in Hawaii to watch the skies for approaching aircraft, they knew the secret Japanese diplomatic code, and they could even plot the movements of many Japanese warships in the Pacific.

The spectacular way in which Japan began her wars against Russia and the United States raises two questions: why were her opening attacks so successful and why were they so denounced as infamous? The questions are related, for if the attacks had not been successful their "infamy" would have been less obvious. The attacks on the enemy fleets at Port Arthur and Pearl Harbor owed most of their success to the complacency of the enemy. Both naval bases seemed relatively secure in peace and in war, for they were heavily fortified and remote from Japanese ports. As both Russia and the United States had considered themselves to be militarily superior to Japan, and as they were inclined to underestimate the military prowess of Asians, their feeling of security was enhanced. Their sense of security was boldly exploited by Japanese tactics. The incentive to exploit it was also high, for Japan faced nations which, militarily, were more powerful than herself. Above all, the opportunity for surprise at sea was higher than on land, and in the wars of 1904 and 1941 sea power was unusually vital.

Why were the Japanese attacks seen as the symbol of infamy? They were infamous partly because they were so successful. They were also deplored because their success seemed to depend on violating accepted rules of warfare. It is sometimes implied that the wars came as a surprise. In fact both wars came when negotiations had reached a deadlock. War, even to the enemy, had seemed highly likely. Even if Japan had declared war before attacking—even if her declaration of war had arrived, for instance, at seven o'clock on a Hawaiian Sunday morning—her attacks would almost certainly have been successful. Indeed they would have been psychologically more successful, for a prior declaration of war would have deprived the enemies of a morale-boosting excuse for the failure of their defenses. As for the belief that Japan was taking unfair advantage of the enemy by not giving a warning, unfair advantages are a characteristic of war. In every war, it seems, at least one of the nations agrees to fight because it believes it is stronger than the enemy, because it believes that it possesses an "unfair advantage" not merely for the first day but for every day of the war. Likewise in each period of peace larger nations peacefully exercise power in preserving their own interests simply because they possess that "unfair advantage."

Those who believe that the Japanese conduct at Port Arthur and Pearl Harbor was abnormal—and so should be explained perhaps by her national character or military tradition—have one final arrow to shoot. They can argue that it is irrelevant whether Japan gained or lost by her surprise attacks. They can simply argue that Japan knowingly scorned the accepted code of fair play when beginning those wars. One must doubt however the existence of that code.

In 1882 a lieutenant-colonel in the intelligence department of the British war office investigated this reputed code of fair play. John Frederick Maurice, a son of the founder of the Christian Socialist movement, had served in the 1870s in the Ashanti War where he was Lord Wolseley's private secretary and in the Zulu War where he helped to capture the Zulu chieftain Cetywayo. Lord Wolseley once said that Maurice was the bravest man he had ever seen under fire; he was also brave in the face of hostile facts. When a tunnel under the English Channel was planned, and the plans aroused fears in Whitehall that the tunnel might be used for a sudden invasion, Maurice was set to work by Lord Wolseley to decide "whether a country living in peace with all its neighbors has any reason to fear that war may suddenly burst upon it." Rather than theorize about the answer to the question, Maurice turned to the past wars of European and North American countries. He began to read a shelf of historians from Voltaire to Kinglake in the confident belief that he would find few wars which had been initiated without a formal warning or declaration. To his surprise he uncovered more and more. He began to realize that most wars had begun with fighting, not with declarations of war. He found forty-seven such wars in the eighteenth century and another sixty in the period 1800 to 1870, and he would have found even more if he had studied what he called European wars against "savage tribes." He also found that in forty-one of those wars which he studied one power appeared to have high hopes of taking the enemy by surprise. Pearl Harbor thus conformed to an old pattern. The stealth of the Japanese had been foreshadowed many times by France, Prussia, Britain, the United States and all the major powers. In contrast, less than ten wars since 1700 had been preceded by declarations of war, and many of those prior declarations were not designed to warn the enemy; they merely announced that a state of war now existed. To Maurice's knowledge only the French declaration of war against Prussia in 1870 had actually been delivered to the enemy as a warning before the beginning of fighting.

When the Japanese launched torpedoes at Port Arthur in 1904, their refusal to make a prior declaration of war violated neither the rules nor the practices of nations. The attack caused a sensation mainly because it was successful. There were cries that the attack breached the rules of warfare but those rules did not exist.

The shock felt by tens of millions of Americans when the Japanese, without declaring war, attacked Pearl Harbor is still visible in the writings of scores of able political scientists and historians. Again and again they go out of their way to notice or to deplore the way in which the Japanese had launched their wars: many have written their denunciations of Japan during years in which the United States was engaged in wars which were marked by no formal declaration either before or during the war. The contradiction is not surprising; of all subjects international war is one of the most emotional, and we are all infected by its emotion. What is more surprising is the widespread belief in so many circles in so many nations that nearly all wars in recent centuries were only begun after the declaration of war.

The popularity of that belief is illuminating. It seems to imply that war and peace are tight compartments with nothing in common. To employ violence without warning when nations are ostensibly at peace is to break the walls of those compartments. A war, without clear warning, is therefore condemned as the intrusion into peace of the spirit and methods of war. An American specialist in international law, Ellery C. Stowell, discussing in 1908 the new Hague convention of declaring war, made the valuable observation that "we must remember that public opinion has never given up those old ideas of the fair man-to-man fight." War of course is not like a prize fight: it has no clear gong to sound the beginning of the fight, no rules of fair play to prevent one side from employing more soldiers or superior weapons, and no gong that ushers in an era of clear peace. War and peace are not separate compartments. Peace depends on threats and force; often peace is the crystallization of past force. Admittedly the popular belief that war *should* begin only after an explicit warning is humane. It is also dangerous because it rests on a deep misunderstanding of the nature and causes of both peace and war.

Opportunism, and the veiled or open use of force, pervade every phase of the sequence of war and peace. They pervade the start of a war, the continuation of war and the end of a war. They pervade the start of peace, the continuation of peace and the end of peace. War and peace are fluctuating phases of a relationship between nations, and the opportunism pervades the entire relationship. Accordingly the popular contrasts of warmaker and peacemaker, of aggressor and victim, of blame and praise, do not fit this relationship. It seems invalid to argue that one nation caused a war or was responsible for war. All we can say is that one nation initiated or started or opened the war, but that is description, not explanation of the beginning of a war.

All nations, their leaders and those who are led, are not equally opportunist. They are not always incapable of restraint. But until we understand what conduct is normal or attainable on the eve of war or peace, our attempts to blame nations or praise nations will rest on standards that are either irrelevant or unattainable.

75

Japanese Accounts of World War II

The following three selections have been taken from *Japan At War, An Oral History*, which includes a variety of accounts based on interviews conducted within the past few years with Japanese women and men who lived through the war. These individuals were willing to speak on an issue that is still very difficult for many Japanese to confront, World War II, and feelings of discomfort permeate the pages of their accounts. As you read, compare the views expressed here with the conventional view of the Japanese still held by many Americans, and with other selections in the reader.

Discussion Questions

1. How do these various accounts compare with your impressions of Japanese actions and attitudes during the War, and with the conventional accounts presented in American texts and by the media?
2. From these accounts, do you think the Japanese were determined to go to war? Thought they would win? Solidly in favor of their government's actions? Superior fighters? Victims?
3. How do Americans today view World War II? Is this similar or different from the way Japanese view World War II?

"My blood boiled at the news."

Itabashi Koshu

Today Itabashi Koshu is the Head Priest of a Zen Buddhist temple near Kanazawa City. The war ended before he could actually serve in it, but he had entered the naval academy in 1944, prepared to "abandon (his) life for the sake of the nation."

I was in the second year of middle school that day, Pearl Harbor Day. "Well, we really did it!" I thought. The sound of the announcement on the radio still reverberates in my ears. [*He hums a few bars from "The Battleship March," the unofficial navy anthem played on the radio to set the tone for victory announcements.*] "News special, News special," high-pitched and rapid. "Beginning this morning before dawn, war has been joined with the Americans and British." I felt as if my blood boiled and my flesh quivered. The whole nation bubbled over, excited and inspired. "We really did it! Incredible! Wonderful!" That's the way it felt then.

I was brought up in a time when nobody criticized Japan. The war started for me, in the brain of this middle-school student, as something that should happen, something that was natural. Every day, we sent warriors off with cheers of *"Banzai! Banzai!"* War was going on in China. "Withdraw your forces," America ordered Japan. If a prime minister with foresight had ordered a withdrawal, he probably would have been assassinated. Even I knew that withdrawal was impossible! There was the ABCD encirclement—the Americans, British, Chinese, and Dutch. They wouldn't give us a drop of oil.

The Japanese had to take a chance. That was the psychological situation in which we found ourselves. If you bully a person, you should give him room to flee. There is a Japanese proverb that says, "A cornered mouse will bite a cat." America is evil, Britain is wrong, we thought. We didn't know why they were encircling us. In Japan, nobody was calculating whether we would win or not. We simply hit out. Our blood was hot! We fought. Until the very end, no one considered that possibility that Japan could lose. We were like Sergeant Yokoi and Lieutenant Onoda—the men who emerged from the jungles, one in Guam, the other in the Philippines, in the 1970s—who couldn't imagine Japan had been defeated. That's the way the whole country felt. Today's youth can't conceive of such feelings.

I was at the First Middle School in Sendai, the best school in Miyagi prefecture. I never really thought about becoming a military man. I was thinking about being a doctor. But the whole nation was at war, everyone was for the war. You don't feel that you want to preserve your own life in such an atmosphere. I guess I was simpleminded, but I thought if you have to go into the military anyway, better to go someplace good. I didn't think I'd make it, but the naval academy was smart, attractive.

From Haruko Taya Cook and Theodore F. Cook, *Japan At War: An Oral History*, copyright © 1992, The New Press, New York, pp. 77–80, 127–134, 208–213, 387–391, 441–447.

I took the entrance exams in my fifth year of middle school. Until then, only two hundred or three hundred were taken from the whole nation each year, but in our time, two or three thousand were admitted. It was as if they were using a bucket to scoop us up.

There was no sense that you personally might be hit by a bullet. You fought for the sake of the nation, for the sake of justice, whenever or wherever the Imperial Standard led. We didn't even think of the pain of being blown to pieces. The objective of war is always these things. No wars have ever been fought for any other reasons. For "the sake of His Imperial Highness" seemed to embody everything—nation, history, race, and peace. That's why it served to inflame passions and cause everyone to seethe with fervor. For Japan, that was a sacred war. Japan claimed it would unite the eight corners of the world under one roof. If Japan had declared it was fighting only to add territory. I don't believe we ever could have gone as far as Borneo.

"I heard it on the radio."

Yoshida Toshio

He was raised in Sasebo, the great naval base, and Yoshida Toshio "ended up an officer without really thinking much about it." Here is part of his account of hearing about Pearl Harbor.

The Imperial Japanese Army and Navy have opened hostilities with the United States and England in the Western Pacific." I was on my way to my office at the Navy Ministry when I heard that announcement. That was how I learned of war for the first time. I, a full lieutenant in the Intelligence Department, Navy General Staff, assigned to the English Section, didn't even know they were planning it. I got off the train at Shimbashi Station. From a restaurant called the Shimbashitei, a radio was blaring news. I felt like someone had poured cold water on my head.

I knew Japan shouldn't fight a war. I looked at Japan like an outsider. A chill cut right through me. I can feel it now. I ran to the Navy Ministry. Those who had known about Pearl Harbor were all smiles. The people in my section didn't know anything.

Every time I remember that day I am seized with the same feeling of disappointment. In the next couple of days, information about the attack on Pearl Harbor, that afternoon of December 8, came pouring in. Soon everyone knew. "Victory, victory!" Things became raucous with the news. But people like me thought from the beginning that Japan would be completely defeated. I was stunned by this success. Those in the Operations Section told us, "We planned this!" They were swaggering up and down the halls, swinging their shoulders. Full of pride.

I was supposed to be an insider. I was in a section which had to have a critical mode of thinking, which had to try to look into the future. For about seven months just prior to the outbreak of the war I had been in Indonesia, in Surabaja and Batavia, trying to purchase oil. Japan had been cut off by America, so we were trying to get some petroleum from the Dutch East Indies. But Japan's authorities failed in "risk management." You can say that just by looking at that time with what passes for common sense today. The leaders looked only at their pluses and paid no attention to minuses. When looking at weapons systems, they only measured offensive capa-bilities, not defensive requirements. They held that if you attack, the path of opportunity will open up naturally. If you try to defend yourself, you will lose. "Advance, advance" therefore became the only objective. But what would happen when you advanced? What situation would arise? These things were not in their minds. It was almost a philosophy. Manage risks to prevent a collision between countries? Protect your interests by preventing risks? That was not something that they cared about. As in *bushido*, whether you lived or died was not crucial, individual autonomy or independence, *were not* important.

"As long as I don't fight, I'll make it home."

Suzuki Murio

Suzuki Murio is a well-known poet and professor at Osaka University of the Arts. This account is of his experiences as a "bottom-ranked" soldier assigned to a heavy-machine-gun company in China and in the Philippines.

I wasn't the "dedicated solder" you were supposed to be. In fact, three of us were even transferred to a regular infantry unit. Booted out of the machine guns! One was from Waseda University. He soon disappeared somewhere. Escaped. That left two of us, Yamada and me. I'm sure there must have been something in Yamada's background; he was so glum and melancholy. I'm the only one who survived the war.

My "spiritual component" was most deficient! Veteran soldiers taught me the tricks: how to get into hospital, how to wrangle a tour at the training camp, how to get the best jobs. I was thrown into one training camp after another. There were special camps to instill *"Yamato damashii."**Some soldiers who wanted to make the army a career were trained there too, but most assigned didn't want to go

---

* *Yamato damashii* [the spirit of Yamato (Japan)] encompassed the purportedly unique qualities of the Japanese people, invoked to explain the courage and dedication of the Japanese fighting man. Such spiritualism was a key element in military training.

back to their units. After three weeks, if you'd gotten the Yamato Spirit, they'd make you go to the front lines, so we'd urge each other to stay a while longer.

There was one kind of duty, called liaison, where you were a courier, carrying messages between units. You were told where to go, and when you left you asked if a reply was needed. The answer was usually no. You were to just hand over the message and come back. Sometimes you caught a ride on a truck that departed maybe once a week or so. In China, as far as you could see there was nothing. You were completely exposed and there weren't any guards on the truck either, if you were lucky enough to have a truck at all. The weapon you were carrying yourself was your only defense.

If you didn't move along with the main force when you were out in the countryside, there was always the possibility you'd be captured. Everyone was scared of that. We were all exhausted. Usually the road was just a straight stretch connecting hamlet to hamlet, no crossroads at all. Still, I thought, if they were going to jump out and capture me, they would do it whenever they wanted, even out among the fields of sorghum, so I just strolled along, taking my time. I took things as they came, worried about them only if they happened. I still have dreams where I'm walking alone on the continent, and there's never anyone around me.

Battlefields are weird places. Once you left your unit, unless you told them your location, they wouldn't come to pick you up, at least not a lowly soldier like me. As long as the headquarters of your unit was in the district, and you could prove which unit you belonged to, any unit would let you stay and feed you for as long as you liked. But when your unit made a major move to an entirely new area, this wouldn't work anymore. "Your unit's not in Central China, get lost!" was all they'd say. You did have to get back

to your home unit once a month or so. If you were asked what happened to you, it was enough to say "the situation was really bad," or "I got lost." If your goal was to avoid shooting bullets, this was the only way. While roaming around the continent, I learned a lot.

I came down with malaria fairly early, and was put into the malaria ward at a hospital thanks to a deal I worked with a doctor. When I eventually did return to the front, though, I had no choice but to go into action. I was in the ninth company—the last company—in the third battalion of the regiment, and in the third squad of the third platoon. We weren't exactly the best of soldiers, but our casualties were low. I guess we fought well enough. Generally it was said that the casualty ratio in China was one killed to six wounded. A company was roughly one hundred and eighty men, so if thirty were killed, you could say the company had been "wiped out," its combat capability reduced to zero. While I was hiding myself in the hospital, my unit suffered near total annihilation. When the survivors came back, I asked, "What about the commander?" "Died." Practically anyone else—"Dead" was the answer. Twice this happened while I was away from my unit in the two years I was on the China front.

I met all kinds of people. Every unit has people who don't like being soldiers. You can spot them immediately. Slackers were put into all kinds of places for "training," but we'd always hear when they'd finished their stint. It was practically like gangsters coming out of the pen. The news would spread that someone had "come out" on the other side of the Yangtze River, so I'd go down to the Hinoki Unit—that was the embarkation office of the ferry unit that carried troops back and forth across the river, same name no matter where you were—find out who was actually being released, and go meet him when he landed, for a "coming-out party."

One time we started drinking saké at three in the afternoon at one of the bars run by Chinese. They were long and narrow like an eel's bed. My companion's unit was assigned in a big city, where units were under the internal administrative regulations of the army, the same as back in the Homeland. If a soldier went out, he had to be back in barracks by eight in the evening. Suddenly, we realized he'd missed roll call and would already be considered a deserter. We rushed to his base, but the back gate to his barracks was locked. Even the front gate was closed, and a sentry stood there with a rifle, bayonet shining. Then we noticed an automobile marked with a medical officer's blue flag coming. Should we stop it? If professional soldiers who'd just graduated from military medical school were in it, they'd shoot us dead. But we decided to take a chance. Luckily, it only contained the driver, a private first class whose boss was out on the town somewhere. We begged him to take us through the sentry line in return for a case of beer. The car approached the main gate. They opened the barricade to welcome back their doctor. All the sentries lined up. The driver stepped on it and charged past them.

Some Japanese were known to have been captured, some deserted, sometimes we fought among ourselves. Everybody was whipped up to a fever pitch. There were people who bullied others. Weak ones might resist by using their hand grenades. They'd pull the pin and hold it, while everybody flew off in all directions. We all had the tools for murder, but if anybody got killed, the case was just left alone until there was combat. Then the death would then be recorded as died-in-action or missing.

The military is an amalgamation of human beings. Some you can get along with, others you can't. There are a lot of backstabbers.

Sincere men attract sincere men. Easygoing men seem to get together. Birds of a feather.

Shanghai itself wasn't so bad. You got a special pass when you went to Shanghai, like a wooden card you put in your vest pocket, which gave you a little leeway to return after the normal nine-o'clock curfew. I'd ask sentries from my own unit when they were going to be on duty. Sometimes I went out drinking alone in Shanghai and didn't come back until two or three in the morning. Shanghai was the base for the Liberation Army, so you weren't supposed to walk around alone. Even the Japanese Shanghai Naval Landing Force patrolled in pairs, carrying rifles. Even during the day, there were snipers. I borrowed a pistol and took it with me, hidden, the safety catch off. The main streets of Shanghai bustled with crowds, but if you took one step off into an alley you might see five or six corpses no matter which way you looked.

I was often drunk when I got back. Normally, I brought a bottle of whiskey as a gift for the sentry. But when you're drunk, you sometimes think the sentry's one of your own. You just walk up to him, and say, "Hey, I'm back," holding out the bottle to him. Once, I was hauled off to the commander of the guard. He kept berating me: What was I doing out that late. Why was I alone? You should be courtmartialed! "You gave me permission," I kept repeating. In the end all he could do was shout, "Let the bastard in." He kept the whiskey.

Soldiers like me had no idea why we were fighting this war. We were treated as nothing more than consumable goods. The men ordered to fly in the kamikaze planes had only one route open for them. On the continent, at least it was wide open. It all depended on the individual's own character. I thought it would be enough for me if I stayed alive. I wanted to return home, though I didn't particularly strive for that. I didn't have the courage to engage in antimilitary activity, but on that desolate continent I lost the purpose of that war. The feeling grew in me that it was ridiculous to die there, fighting the Communist Eighth Route Army, or the Nationalist Army, or even sometimes finding out that it was the Japanese Army who were shooting at you. There were times I thought I might die at any moment. Tomorrow was far, far away. In that mood, I'd written a haiku in the corner of a military postcard addressed to a friend back in Japan.

> Me tsumureba
> Tani nagare
> Chi no akaki nado.

> When I close my eyes,
> I can see valleys
> Flowing blood red.

But that attracted attention. I was caught in a random mail search and they threatened to send me to the Kempeitai. I was told if I changed the part about "blood red" to "pure blood" [chi no kiyoki] the censor would let it pass. What could I do but agree? I changed it back to red when I published it in my book years later.

If you are in that kind of place for long, you become nihilistic. I think at the basis of such a nihilism is an abiding humanism, though quite different from the nothingness a Buddhist priest asserts is humanism. I still can't see myself connected to any large entity like a country or state. I can't view war macroscopically. I feel I can write about battlefields, but I don't think I can write about war. If you talk about things like the Greater East Asia Co-Prosperity Sphere, that's too grand for me. I can touch only a sphere as large as I can warm with my own body heat.

After the Pearl Harbor attack, from the next day on, things became really strict. I'd often been told, "We're sending you to the Kempei!" If they really had, the Kempei would have half-killed me. There were officers who were always drawing their swords and crying out, "I'll take his head myself!"

Usually military-academy graduates, twenty-four or twenty-five years old. Commanders made out the Spirit of Yamato. If you got stuck in a unit like that, you were really in trouble. Since I wasn't usually at my own unit, I'd take off the first chance I got.

In the Philippines, the enemy showed himself to us. On the Bataan peninsula, my unit was "in reserve." To say it was a "reserve unit" might make it sound easy, but it was like Japanese chess. In shogi a piece you take from the enemy as prisoner may be turned around and placed right back at some crucial spot on the board as your piece. Just so, they dropped us down right in front of the enemy machine guns in the hottest part of the fighting.

By the time we approached the front line, we were already exhausted. "Fall out!" they said, and you'd collapse for five or six minutes. Lie down and try to catch your breath. In the dark you can't see well, but there was a horrible stench. I threw myself down on what turned out to be the belly of a dead horse. Probably from our artillery. Later that night we were given another short rest, but it was such agony to get up once you'd sat down that I tried to sleep standing up. I leaned against something. It smelled terrible and was soft, but I couldn't see it in the dark. I found out it was a breastwork made of corpses. The Americans had piled up native bodies like sandbags. The heads were facing toward us. On the other side there was a firing step. They shot from inside. Our enemy was an allied army of Americans and Filipinos, but the corpses in the wall were all Filipino.

Our main forces kept in close contact with the enemy and pressed them back. Our whole army was advancing toward the sea, since Bataan was a peninsula. But we bogged down because there were pillboxes up in the cliffs above. They had Czech-type machine guns. "Kan! Kan! Kan!" Those air-cooled guns hammered away with bullets as big as rolled hot towels, and we were their target. We were halted in our tracks. It was April 5, 1942. MacArthur was still at Corregidor.

My group of seven didn't know where to go. We thought we'd be best off if we charged to the very bottom of the cliff, where we'd be in the "dead angle," out of the sweep of the machine guns. In the rush I was hit. The person in front of me just wasn't there anymore. Killed instantly. There was one medic assigned to each company of a hundred and eighty men. I had befriended ours and I'd asked him to be sure to save me if I was ever wounded. I often poured extra saké for him. He was with me when they got me, but while he was treating me, orders came from the commander. "Medic, to the front!" Men were being hit up ahead and he had to go forward. I still have thirty bullet fragments in my body. Two of them are as big as the bones of my little finger, lodged in my bones.

But as soon as our main forces had pushed on, enemy soldiers came out of the jungle where they'd been hiding. Our forces couldn't sweep the whole place. I once thought all humans were good by nature, but there we were, left behind on the battlefields, jammed up under that cliff, when a force of maybe sixty or seventy Americans and Filipinos appeared perhaps twenty meters from our position. We had to decide immediately if we would open fire or not. Hamano, the light machine-gunner, and I were the only two who were against shooting. I had to talk the others out of blazing away. I told the men we could probably kill five or six, but stressed that there were sixty or seventy white soldiers and black soldiers. We'd be shot so full of holes we'd look like honeycombs. They glanced in our direction, but kept moving cautiously, passing us by. We were gambling, but we won our bet. They didn't fire either. We didn't shoot, and they didn't announce to anybody that they saw several Japanese over by the cliff. They probably knew the tide was running against them. Maybe they felt, Why die when you've already lost? I guess if you've been long on the battlefield, you know instantly whether the enemy's going to shoot or not. Anyway, that was my philosophy: As long as I don't fight, I'll make it home. I believed in that. Besides, I'd already been shot! I was sent home in June 1942.

A nation has to have great confidence in its own strength to go outside itself. Setting aside any question of motives, in the time of my youth, my physical strength coincided with the strength of my country. There was a strong tide running, and I was swept away in it without any chance to accede or dissent. If you ask me if I have any war responsibility, yes, I believe I do. We walked right into somebody else's country, their home, with our boots on, and we didn't even have visas.

76

The Bombing of Hiroshima

The following selections present recent historical and moral perspectives on the use of atomic weapons in World War II. A summary of the deliberations leading up to the bombing of Hiroshima and Nagasaki are presented in the first reading, with particular attention given to the prevailing attitudes that existed in 1945 towards weapons of mass destruction. Included in the first piece is also a discussion of the alternatives to the use of the bomb, why those alternatives were discarded, and what the advocates of the bomb's use hoped to achieve. The second reading introduces a number of ways to look at the moral issues raised by the introduction of atomic weapons into war, with a reminder that, more than fifty years after the event, the issue raises as many questions as it answers.

Discussion Questions

1. Are Hiroshima and Nagasaki "landmarks on the mental and moral geography of the United States"? What is their meaning to us today? What do you think they will mean to the citizens of the U.S. in 2045?
2. What are the key reasons that the atomic bomb was used in World War II? Do you find Bernstein's arguments convincing? What do you think would have been the "right" decision regarding the use of atomic weapons?
3. Hiroshima and Nagasaki have been called "an end and a beginning." What do you think is meant by this statement, and would you agree after reading these articles?
4. Though Auschwitz and Hiroshima have been compared in another reading, are there similarities between Pearl Harbor and Hiroshima today, as well as historically?

The Atomic Bombings Reconsidered

The Questions America Should Ask

Fifty years ago, during a three-day period in August 1945, the United States dropped two atomic bombs on Japan, killing more than 115,000 people and possibly as many as 250,000, and injuring at least another 100,000. In the aftermath of the war, the bombings raised both ethical and historical questions about why and how they were used. Would they have been used on Germany? Why were cities targeted so that so many civilians would be killed? Were there likely alternative ways to end the war speedily and avoid the Allies' scheduled November 1, 1945, invasion of Kyushu?

Such questions often fail to recognize that, before Hiroshima and Nagasaki, the use of the A-bomb did not raise profound moral issues for policymakers. The weapon was conceived in a race with Germany, and it undoubtedly would have been used against Germany had the bomb been ready much sooner. During the war, the target shifted to Japan. And during World War II's brutal course, civilians in cities had already become targets. The grim Axis bombing record is well known. Masses of noncombatants were also intentionally killed in the later stages of the American air war against Germany; that tactic was developed further in 1945 with the firebombing of Japanese cities. Such mass bombing constituted a transformation of morality, repudiating President Franklin D. Roosevelt's prewar pleas that the warring nations avoid bombing cities to spare civilian

lives. Thus, by 1945, American leaders were not seeking to avoid the use of the A-bomb on Japan. But the evidence from current archival research shows that by pursuing alternative tactics instead, they probably could still have obviated the dreaded invasion and ended the war by November. . . .

By early 1945, World War II—especially in the Pacific—had become virtually total war. The firebombing of Dresden had helped set a precedent for the U.S. air force, supported by the American people, to intentionally kill mass numbers of Japanese citizens. The earlier moral insistence on noncombatant immunity crumbled during the savage war. In Tokyo, during March 9–10, a U.S. air attack killed about 80,000 Japanese civilians. American B-29s dropped napalm on the city's heavily populated areas to produce uncontrollable firestorms. It may even have been easier to conduct this new warfare outside Europe and against Japan because its people seemed like "yellow subhumans" to many rank-and-file American citizens and many of their leaders.

In this new moral context, with mass killings of an enemy's civilians even seeming desirable, the committee agreed to choose "large urban areas of not less than three miles in diameter existing in the larger populated areas" as A-bomb targets. The April 27 discussion focused on four cities: Hiroshima, which, as "the largest untouched target not on the 21st Bomber Command priority list," warranted serious consideration; Yawata, known for its steel industry; Yokohama; and

Tokyo, "a possibility [though] now practically all bombed and burned out and . . . practically rubble with only the palace grounds left standing." They decided that other areas warranted more consideration: Tokyo Bay, Kawasaki, Yokohoma, Nagoya, Osaka, Kobe, Kyoto, Hiroshima, Kure, Yawata, Kokura, Shimonoseki, Yamaguchi, Kumamoto, Fukuoka, Nagasaki, and Sasebo.

The choice of targets would depend partly on how the bomb would do its deadly work— the balance of blast, heat, and radiation. At their second set of meetings, during May 11– 12, physicist J. Robert Oppenheimer, director of the Los Alamos laboratory, stressed that the bomb material itself was lethal enough for perhaps a billion deadly doses and that the weapon would give off lethal radioactivity. The bomb, set to explode in the air, would deposit "a large fraction of either the initial active material or the radioactive products in the immediate vicinity of the target; but the radiation . . . will, of course, have an effect on exposed personnel in the target area." It was unclear, he acknowledged, what would happen to most of the radioactive material: it could stay for hours as a cloud above the place of detonation or, if the bomb exploded during rain or in high humidity and thus caused rain, "most of the active material will be brought down in the vicinity of the target area." Oppenheimer's report left unclear whether a substantial proportion or only a small fraction of the population might die from radiation. So far as the skimpy records reveal, no member of the Target Committee chose to dwell on this matter. They probably assumed that the bomb blast would claim most of its victims before the radiation could do its deadly work.

In considering targets, they discussed the possibility of bombing the emperor's palace in Tokyo and "agreed that we should not recommend it but that any action for this bombing should come from authorities on military policy." They decided to gather information on the effectiveness of using the bomb on the palace.

The Target Committee selected their four top targets: Kyoto, Hiroshima, Yokohama, and Kokura Arsenal, with the implication that Niigata, a city farther away from the air force 509th group's Tinian base, might be held in reserve as a fifth. Kyoto, the ancient former capital and shrine city, with a population of about a million, was the most attractive target to the committee. "From the psychological point of view," the committee minutes note, "there is the advantage that Kyoto is an intellectual center for Japan and [thus] the people there are more apt to appreciate the significance of such a weapon." The implication was that those in Kyoto who survived the A-bombing and saw the horror would be believed elsewhere in Japan.

Of central importance, the group stressed that the bomb should be used as a terror weapon—to produce "the greatest psychological effect against Japan" and to make the world, and the U. S. S. R. in particular, aware that America possessed this new power. The death and destruction would not only intimidate the surviving Japanese into pushing for surrender, but, as a bonus, cow other nations, notably the Soviet Union. In short, America could speed the ending of the war and by the same act help shape the postwar world. . . .

The Agonies of Killing Civilians

During 1945, Stimson found himself presiding, with agony, over an air force that killed hundreds of thousands of Japanese civilians. Usually, he preferred not to face these ugly facts, but sought refuge in the notion that the air force was actually engaged in precision bombing and that somehow this precision bombing was going awry. Caught between an older morality that opposed the intentional killing of noncombatants and a newer one that stressed virtually total war, Stimson could neither fully face the facts nor fully escape them. He was not a hypocrite but a man trapped in ambivalence.

Stimson discussed the problem with Truman on June 6. Stimson stressed that he was worried about the air force's mass bombing, but that it was hard to restrict it. In his diary, Stimson recorded: "I told him I was anxious about this feature of the war for two reasons: first, because I did not want to have the United States get the reputation of outdoing Hitler in atrocities; and second, I was a little fearful that before we could get ready the air force might have Japan so thoroughly bombed out that the new weapon would not have a fair background to show as strength." According to Stimson, Truman "laughed and said he understood."

Unable to reestablish the old morality and wanting the benefits for America of the new, Stimson proved decisive—even obdurate— on a comparatively small matter: removing Kyoto from Groves' target list of cities. It was not that Stimson was trying to save Kyoto's citizens; rather, he was seeking to save its relics, lest the Japanese become embittered and later side with the Soviets. As Stimson explained in his diary entry Of July 24: "The bitterness which would be caused by such a wanton act might make it impossible during the long post-war period to reconcile the Japanese to us in that area rather than to the Russians. It might thus . . . be the means of preventing what our policy demanded, namely, a sympathetic Japan to the United States in case there should be any aggression by Russia in Manchuria."

Truman, backing Stimson on this matter, insisted privately that the A-bombs would be used only on military targets. Apparently the president wished not to recognize the inevitable—that a weapon of such great power would necessarily kill many civilians. At Potsdam on July 25, Truman received glowing reports of the vast destruction achieved by the Alamogordo blast and lavishly recorded the details in his diary: a crater of 1,200 feet in diameter, a steel tower destroyed a half mile away, men knocked over six miles away. "We have discovered," he wrote in his diary, "the most terrible bomb in the history of the world. It may be the fire destruction prophesied." But when he approved the final list of A-bomb targets, with Nagasaki and Kokura substituted for Kyoto, he could write in his diary, "I have told Sec. of War . . . Stimson to use it so that military objectives and soldiers and sailors are the target and not women and children. Even if the Japs are savages, ruthless, merciless, and fanatic . . . [t]he target will be a purely military one." Truman may have been engaging in self-deception to make the mass deaths of civilians acceptable.

Neither Hiroshima nor Nagasaki was a "purely military" target, but the official press releases, cast well before the atomic bombings, glided over this matter. Hiroshima, for example, was described simply as "an important Japanese army base." The press releases were drafted by men who knew that those cities had been chosen partly to dramatize the killing of noncombatants.

On August 10, the day after the Nagasaki bombing, when Truman realized the magnitude of the mass killing and the Japanese offered a conditional surrender requiring continuation of the emperor, the president told his cabinet that he did not want to kill any more women and children. Rejecting demands to drop more atomic bombs on Japan, he hoped not to use them again. After two atomic bombings, the horror of mass death had forcefully hit the president, and he was willing to return partway to the older morality—civilians might be protected from A-bombs. But he continued to sanction the heavy conventional bombing of Japan's cities, with the deadly toll that napalm, incendiaries, and other bombs produced. Between August 10 and August 14—the war's last day on which about 1,000 American planes bombed Japanese cities, some delivering their deadly cargo after Japan announced its surrender—the United States probably killed more than 15,000 Japanese.

The Roads Not Taken

Before August 10, Truman and his associates had not sought to avoid the use of the atomic bomb. As a result, they had easily dismissed the possibility of a noncombat demonstration. Indeed, the post-Hiroshima pleas of Japan's military leaders for a final glorious battle suggest that such a demonstration probably would not have produced a speedy surrender. And American leaders also did not pursue other alternatives: modifying their unconditional surrender demand by guaranteeing the maintenance of the emperor, awaiting the Soviet entry into the war, or simply pursuing heavy conventional bombing of the cities amid the strangling naval blockade.

Truman and Byrnes did not believe that a modification of the unconditional surrender formula would produce a speedy surrender. They thought that guaranteeing to maintain the emperor would prompt an angry backlash from Americans who regarded Hirohito as a war criminal, and feared that this concession might embolden the Japanese militarists to expect more concessions and thus prolong the war. As a result, the president and his secretary of state easily rejected Stimson's pleas for a guarantee of the emperor.

Similarly, most American leaders did not believe that the Soviet entry into the Pacific war would make a decisive difference and greatly speed Japan's surrender. Generally, they believed that the U.S.S.R.'s entry would help end the war—ideally, before the massive invasion of Kyushu. They anticipated Mos-

cow's intervention in mid-August, but the Soviets moved up their schedule to August 8, probably because of the Hiroshima bombing, and the Soviet entry did play an important role in producing Japan's surrender on August 14. Soviet entry without the A-bomb *might* have produced Japan's surrender before November.

The American aim was to avoid, if possible, the November 1 invasion, which would involve about 767,000 troops, at a possible cost of 31,000 casualties in the first 30 days and a total estimated American death toll of about 225,000. And American leaders certainly wanted to avoid the second part of the invasion plan, an assault on the Tokyo plain, scheduled for around March 1, 1946, with an estimated 15,000–21,000 more Americans dead. In the spring and summer of 1945, no American leader believed—as some later falsely claimed—that they planned to use the A-bomb to save half a million Americans. But, given the patriotic calculus of the time, there was no hesitation about using A-bombs to kill many Japanese in order to save the 25,000–46,000 Americans who might otherwise have died in the invasions. Put bluntly, Japanese life—including civilian life—was cheap, and some American leaders, like many rank-and-file citizens, may well have savored the prospect of punishing the Japanese with the A-bomb.

Truman, Byrnes, and the other leaders did not have to be reminded of the danger of a political backlash in America if they did not use the bomb and the invasions became necessary. Even if they had wished to avoid its use—and they did not—the fear of later public outrage spurred by the weeping parents and loved ones of dead American boys might well have forced American leaders to drop the A-bomb on Japan.

No one in official Washington expected that one or two atomic bombs would end the war quickly. They expected to use at least a third, and probably more. And until the day after Nagasaki, there had never been in their thinking a choice between atomic bombs and conventional bombs, but a selection of both—using mass bombing to compel surrender. Atomic bombs and conventional bombs were viewed as supplements to, not substitutes for, one another. Heavy conventional bombing of Japan's cities would probably have killed hundreds of thousands in the next few months, and might have produced the desired surrender before November 1.

Taken together, some of these alternatives—promising to retain the Japanese monarchy, awaiting the Soviets' entry, and even more conventional bombing—very probably could have ended the war before the dreaded invasion. Still, the evidence—to borrow a phrase from F.D. R.—is somewhat "iffy," and no one who looks at the intransigence of the Japanese militarists should have full confidence in those other strategies. But we may well regret that these alternatives were not pursued and that there was not an effort to avoid the use of the first A-bomb—and certainly the second.

Whatever one thinks about the necessity of the first A-bomb, the second—dropped on Nagasaki on August 9—was almost certainly unnecessary. It was used because the original order directed the air force to drop bombs "as made ready' and, even after the Hiroshima bombing, no one in Washington anticipated an imminent Japanese surrender. Evidence now available about developments in the Japanese government—most notably the emperor's then—secret decision shortly before the Nagasaki bombing to seek peace—makes it clear that the second bomb could undoubtedly have been avoided. At least 35,000 Japanese and possibly almost twice that number, as well as several thousand Koreans, died unnecessarily in Nagasaki.

Administration leaders did not seek to avoid the use of the A-bomb. They even believed that its military use might produce a powerful bonus: the intimidation of the Soviets, rendering them, as Byrnes said, "more manageable," especially in Eastern Europe. Although that was not the dominant purpose for using the weapon, it certainly was a strong confirming one. Had Truman and his associates, like the dissenting scientists at Chicago, foreseen that the A-bombing of Japan would make the Soviets intransigent rather than tractable, perhaps American leaders would have questioned their decision. But precisely because American leaders expected that the bombings would also compel the Soviet Union to loosen its policy in Eastern Europe, there was no incentive to question their intention to use the atomic bomb. Even if they had, the decision would probably have been the same. In a powerful sense, the atomic bombings represented the implementation of an assumption—one that Truman comfortably inherited from Roosevelt. Hiroshima was an easy decision for Truman.

The Redefinition of Morality

Only years later, as government archives opened, wartime hatreds faded, and sensibilities changed, would Americans begin seriously to question whether the atomic bombings were necessary, desirable, and moral. Building on the postwar memoirs of Admiral William Leahy and General Dwight D. Eisenhower, among others, doubts began to emerge about the use of the atomic bombs against Japan. As the years passed, Americans learned that the bombs, according to high-level American military estimates in June and July 1945, probably could not have saved a half million American lives in the invasions, as Truman sometimes contended after Nagasaki, but would have saved fewer than 50,000. Americans also came slowly to recognize the barbarity of World War II, especially the mass killings by bombing civilians. It was that redefinition of morality that made Hiroshima and Nagasaki possible and ushered in the atomic age in a frightening way.

That redefinition of morality was a product of World War II, which included such barbarities as Germany's systematic murder of six million Jews and Japan's rape of Nanking. While the worst atrocities were perpetrated by the Axis, all the major nation-states sliced away at the moral code—often to the applause of their leaders and citizens alike. By 1945 there were few moral restraints left in what had become virtually a total war. Even F.D.R.'s prewar concern for sparing enemy civilians had fallen by the wayside. In that new moral climate, any nation that had the A-bomb would probably have used it against enemy peoples. British leaders as well as Joseph Stalin endorsed the act. Germany's and Japan's leaders surely would have used it against cities. America was not morally unique—just technologically exceptional. Only it had the bomb, and so only it used it.

To understand this historical context does not require that American citizens or others should approve of it. But it does require that they recognize that pre- and post-Hiroshima dissent was rare in 1945. Indeed, few then asked why the United States used the atomic bomb on Japan. But had the bomb not been used, many more, including numerous outraged American citizens, would have bitterly asked that question of the Truman administration.

In 1945, most Americans shared the feelings that Truman privately expressed a few days after the Hiroshima and Nagasaki bombings when he justified the weapons' use in a letter to the Federal Council of Churches of Christ. "I was greatly disturbed over the unwarranted attack by the Japanese on Pearl Harbor and their murder of our prisoners of war," the president wrote. "The only language they seem to understand is the one we have been using to bombard them. When you have to deal with a beast you have to treat him as a beast."

The Debate Over Hiroshima

Fifty years later, the question will not be put to rest. What went into the decision to drop the atomic bomb?

The debate is about morality as well as history, but often the history is written as though it settled the morality. Opinions collide, for example, over how many American lives President Harry S. Truman and other high officials thought might be lost if the Allies had invaded Japan. Estimates from American military sources from before August 1945 range from 16,000 to 46,000 deaths, with four times as many wounded.

Writing after the bomb was dropped (on Hiroshima on Aug. 6 and Nagasaki on Aug. 9), Truman said he had feared 500,000 deaths and Secretary of War Henry Stimson said he had envisioned more than one million casualties.

The unstated moral premise in much of this historical fencing is this: the right decision would have been what brought victory with the least loss of life.

* * *

But not everyone agrees that this principle was the essential one. Survey the literature, or simply listen to a dinner conversation where Hiroshima and Nagasaki are considered more compelling topics than Hugh Grant, and at least five basic moral arguments are heard:

All war is wrong. For the pacifist, it does not matter whether killing is done by a bomb, a bayonet or a bow, or whether the victim is a pediatrician or a pilot. The atomic bomb simply made clear on a horrific scale the evil of all war.

Nuclear arms are different. They represent a quantum leap in destructiveness. From the beginning, some scientists and statesmen sensed that to develop and then to use weapons was to sign a pact with the devil. Nothing should be done to diminish the taboo surrounding these weapons or the dread they inspire, not even suggesting that they fall within our normal rules of morality.

Civilians are different. It is immoral to attack, directly and indiscriminately, civilian populations of men, women and children, the young and the old, the healthy and the disabled. This is the principle that condemns terrorism, that declares passengers on a subway or families in a restaurant not fair targets, no matter the justice of the cause. In World War II, first the Germans, then the Allies had already crossed this line, Hiroshima and Nagasaki were massive, single-bomb versions of the fire-bombings of Dresden, Hamburg, Tokyo and scores of smaller Japanese cities. The atomic bomb represented not so much the evil of all war as the evil of total war.

Do the least harm possible. Death, casualties and destruction should be no more than necessary and somehow proportionate to the objective. The distinction between civilian and combatant is not essential in this argument: A life is a life. Less clear is how enemy lives are weighed against one's own, but presumably they are part of the calculation. If dropping the atomic bombs was likely to save lives, not dropping them would have been the immoral deed. This is the principle that fuels the debate between those who defend the bombing and those who maintain it was unnecessary or disproportionate.

War is hell. No nation should go to war except as a last resort, but once in war, morality gives way to efficiency. Minimize one's own losses, whatever it takes. Condemnation of what happens in the heat of battle—indeed, any notion that the reality of war can be squeezed into moral boundaries—is home-front hypocrisy, an effort to prettify the horror with armchair ethics.

After 50 years, does it matter which of these arguments we embrace? Are we doing anything more than still trying to convict or acquit Truman?

Yet the debate matters because nations and civilizations, like individuals, do not live by abstract principles. Moral principles arise from experience; they are tested and revised in the face of new experience, and they must be embodied in experience and the collective memories that result.

Children may learn to be good by heeding the Ten Commandments or the Five Precepts of Buddhism. But long before that, they learn goodness by modeling themselves on parents, teachers, saints and heroes.

Nations, likewise, live by formative events far more than by formal principles. Americans imbibe their fierce attachment to self-determination and redress of rights with their accounts of the Revolution. The principles of nationhood and equality are embodied in the Civil War; appeasement, in Munich; radical evil, in the Holocaust; Western resolve, in the Berlin airlift; adroit crisis diplomacy, in the Cuban missile crisis, and tragic overreaching in Vietnam. These events are landmarks on the mental and moral geography of the United States and of the West in general.

And Hiroshima and Nagasaki?

In 1945, in the midst of the great national sigh of relief that the war was over, only a few public voices denounced the atomic bombings. Polls showed that not only did the vast majority of Americans approve of the bombings, but also that those who questioned them or thought the bomb should have been dropped first on an unpopulated area as a demonstration were outnumbered by those who wished that more atomic bombs could have been dropped on Japan before it had a chance to surrender.

* * *

Many of those protesting voices were religious: the liberal Protestant weekly The Christian Century, theologians like Reinhold and H. Richard Niebuhr, leading Roman Catholic journals like Commonweal and The Catholic World and, somewhat later, America. They spoke in terms of sin, shame, guilt and contrition.

But widespread moral misgivings did not really begin until August 1946, when The New Yorker published John Hersey's understated but excruciatingly detailed account of the human devastation at Hiroshima.

Those misgivings, even a half century later, have never jelled into a consensus, as proved by the inability of the National Air and Space Museum to mount an exhibition that raised serious questions about the bombing. Will the United States ever integrate the bombs of August into its moral self-understanding? Or will they continue to haunt and torment us like ghosts?

77

Auschwitz and Hiroshima

In the following article, William Styron reflects on his own experience in World War II and how he tried to find a perspective to link the Asian and European parts of the conflict.

Discussion Questions

1. What was Styron's personal attitude toward war while it was still being waged? Was he so different from Japanese soldiers, as seen in previous readings?

2. How did his interest in the civil rights movement of the 1960's affect the way he saw the war?

3. What does he think Auschwitz and Hiroshima represent? What do they say about human nature?

4. Why does he say that writers must write "without hope and without despair?"

The Enduring Metaphors of
Auschwitz and Hiroshima

Toward the end of World War II, in the winter of 1945, two momentous events took place simultaneously at distant parts of the earth. It can be safely assumed that none of the participants in either of these grim dramas had the remotest knowledge of the others' existence.

In southern Poland, the army of the Soviet Union had finished evacuating the German concentration camp of Auschwitz. In the Pacific Ocean, 800 miles south of Japan, three United States Marine divisions were commencing the invasion stage of one of the bloodiest campaigns ever fought, the battle for the island of Iwo Jima, which would be of critical importance as a way station for the flight carrying the first atomic bomb.

It might be said that the war in Europe and the Pacific conflict took place on different planets. Most servicemen engaged in the war against the Japanese gave little thought to remote campaigns like the ones in Italy and France. It was a global struggle too vast to comprehend while it was happening. But when it was over and somewhat more comprehensible, we could see that the war left us with, if nothing else, two prodigious and enduring metaphors for human suffering—Auschwitz and Hiroshima. History has carved no sterner monuments to its own propensity for unfathomable evil.

Hiroshima had a profound direct effect on my life; Auschwitz's would come much later. In the summer of 1945 I was a young Marine officer slated to lead my rifle platoon in the invasion of Japan. Most of us were spunky but scared, and we had much to be scared about. The carnage had reached a surreal intensity. Already on Iwo Jima and Okinawa, 17,000 Americans had lost their lives, including many of our friends. It had been predicted that the invasion would produce over half a million American casualties, while perhaps as many as three times that number of Japanese would be killed or wounded, including countless civilians.

Herman Melville wrote, "All wars are boyish, and are fought by boys." I cannot say, from this distance in time, what is more firmly lodged in my memory—the desperate fatalism and sadness that pervaded, beneath our nervous bravado, the days and nights of us young boys, or the joy we felt when we heard of the bomb, of Hiroshima and Nagasaki, and of the thrilling turnaround of our destiny. It was a war we all believed in and I'd wanted to test my manhood; part of me mourned that I never got near the combat zone. But Hiroshima removed from my shoulders an almost tactile burden of insecurity and dread. Later I often used the word ecstatic to describe my reaction. I used it again only a few years ago in, of all places,

Tokyo, when a TV interviewer asked me to express my views about Hiroshima and related matters.

Afterward I had the feeling I'd misspoken badly. But later at a party a Japanese man of my vintage approached me, murmuring a little surreptitiously that he'd seen me on television and wanted to tell me something he'd never told anyone before. He said he'd also been a young infantry officer, the leader of a heavy mortar unit training on Kyushu to repel our invasion, when word came of the bomb and the end of the war. We might have blown each other up, he added, and when I asked him how he'd taken the news he said, "I was ecstatic, like you."

After VJ Day, there was a space of a year or so when it was truly possible to conceive of a world without war. Progenitors of the baby boom, most veterans were diligently amorous. It may be that the gloom descended soon after Winston Churchill's Iron Curtain speech. For me the sense of the future closing down permanently came only six years later, when as a Marine reserve I was called for duty in the Korean War. Back in infantry training, I had nightmarish perception of war as a savage continuum, not a wholesome if often lethal adventure men embarked upon, as in World War II, to strike down the forces of evil, but a perpetual way of life which small oases of peacetime provided intermittent relief. In Asia there was an explosion waiting to happen; America stood ready to light the fuse the French had laid down, and in the next decade the sequel of Vietnam came as no surprise.

In that same decade of the 1960s I became engrossed in the issue of racial conflict in America—especially as it was reflected in history of slavery—and found myself pondering the extent to which race and racial domination played a part in the recent wars. The stunning late-19th-century insight of W.E.B. Du Bois—that the chief problem of

the coming century would be that of race—had swiftly become a self-fulfilling prophecy. Du Bois was speaking of his own African-American people but his prophecy would embrace the globe. If in the First World War nationalistic ambitions largely fueled the conflict, World War II was the incubator of a poisonous and worldwide racism. A poster I recall from the Pacific war was of a buck-toothed and bespectacled rat, with repulsively coiled tail and Japanese army cap; the legend read KNOW YOUR ENEMY.

All Americans fighting in the Pacific were racists. Marines were indoctrinated to regard Japanese soldiers as dangerously rabid animals. The paucity of enemy prisoners taken by our troops was due in part to the Japanese creed of fighting to the last breath, but it was also because of our own policy of extermination, often with an intriguing new weapon, the flamethrower, which roasted our adversaries in their bunkers and burrows. The enemy repaid our racism in kind and generally surpassed us; few people were treated more barbarically than those starving prisoners, many of them European and American but also Asian, who existed amid squalor and privation in the Japanese camps.

When in the mid-1970s I decided to write about another racism—the Nazi racism of total domination—I found that in dealing with the German mind of that period I had to confront certain exquisite paradoxes. Anglo-Saxons, for example, however bitterly abhorred, did not belong among the despised *untermenschen* and were granted a certain provisional respect. A loony relativism at the heart of Hitler's racial policy is demonstrated by the treatment of various POWS. The captured British and American soldiers and airmen were usually confined in a prison where conditions were basically civilized and in fact so comparatively congenial that the farcical image conveyed in "Hogan's Heroes" or "Stalag 17" is not too far off the mark. It was a reputed Nordic identification that prevented all but a small percentage of these prisoners from dying.

In contrast there is the appalling saga of the Soviet prisoners of war, who were, after the Jews, the numerically largest group of victims and whose partial annihilation—over 3 million, or nearly 60 percent of all Soviet POWs—is commentary enough on the Nazis' view of the humanity of the Russians and other Slavs. Which brings me to Auschwitz. I was always struck by the fact that the first executed victims of Auschwitz were not Jews but 600 Soviet POWs. Although the Holocaust was uniquely Jewish, its uniqueness becomes more striking when we can see that it also was ecumenical, but in ways that can only emphasize the peculiar nature of Jewish suffering.

I have been criticized in some quarters for "de-Judaizing" and "universalizing" the Holocaust by creating, in my novel "Sophie's Choice," a heroine who was a Gentile victim of Auschwitz. Such was not my intention; it was rather to show the malign effect of anti-Semitism and its relentless power—power of such breadth, at least in the Nazis' hands, as to be capable of destroying people beyond the focus of its immediate oppression. At Auschwitz, as in the Inferno, Jews occupied the center of hell but the surrounding concentric rings embraced a multitude of other victims.

It would be wrong for them to be forgotten. For years, all of them were largely forgotten, beyond the borders of Jewish remembrance. It wasn't until the late 1970s that the word "Holocaust" fully entered the language; before then, the horror of the camps had a less discernible shape.

As for that other dreadful monolith, it might be said that the sacrifice of its victims represented an object lesson and perhaps a priceless warning, preventing the future use of the weapon that achieved such destruction. If so, the many deaths and the suffering—the same that assured my probable survival and that of my Tokyo comrade in arms, along with legions of others—may be justified, if we who have lived so long afterward are fit to justify such a fathomless event. Certainly the bomb did nothing to eliminate war and aggression, and I am still amazed at the memory of myself, a boy optimist returned home after Hiroshima, firmly convinced—for one brief and intoxicating moment—that the future held out the hope of illimitable peace. Nearly 50 years after that moment the fratricidal horrors and ethnic atrocities that the world has endured, and still endures, remain at the quivering edge of tolerance and are past comprehension. Yet we go on, the earth turns. If you do what I do, you write—as the canny Isak Dinesen said you must do—without hope and without despair.

78

World War II—Major Consequences

1. End of the European Age

2. Rise of the U.S. and the U.S.S.R. to Superpower Status

3. Emergence of the Cold War

4. The Nuclear Age

5. Rise of Nationalism and Independence Movements

6. Rise of Social Movements—Women, Youth, Human Rights, Ethnic, Religious, and Cultural Minorities

7. Internationalism—United Nations, IMF, World Bank

Definition of the Cold War

"A worldwide struggle for power between the United States and the Soviet Union . . . [which led to the creation of a bipolar world.] . . . It never resulted in direct military conflict between the two superpowers, but it did lead to competition on all fronts: ideological, diplomatic, economic, military . . . [and cultural.] Each nation felt besieged by the other."

The West and the World Since 1945

79

Cold War Historiography

	Personal Leadership	Domestic Pressures	International Issues
It Was the Soviets' Cold War	Stalin as paranoid; seized East Europe to shore up power at home. (Adam Elam)	Communist system as requiring a foreign enemy to justify totalitarian rule. (Brzezinski)	Russian and/or Communist bid for Eurasian hegemony forced Western powers into containment. (Kissinger)
It Was the Americans' Cold War	Truman as insecure, ignorant bully; "if only FDR had lived." (Diane Clemens)	"Open door" capitalist imperialism and US military-industrial complex threatened USSR. (Lloyd Gardner)	US came out of WWII with hegemonic power, forced Soviet bloc to resist and defend itself. (Martin Sherwin)
The Deterministic View of the Cold War: It Was Inevitable	Stalin and Truman both scared and suspicious, applied lessons of 1930's and 1940's, and came from opposite backgrounds; agreement impossible. (Robert Divine)	It was the wartime alliance that was the aberration, and after 1945 the cold war between a Wilsonian and Leninist system that dated from 1917 resumed. (Stephen Ambrose)	It was the case of an elephant and a whale; US and USSR posed Asymmetrical threats, each viewed the other as a potential "Nazi Germany," and each feared sneak attack. (Walter McDougall)

Walter McDougall, prepared for a Foreign Policy Research Institute History Institute for Teachers on "The Cold War Revisited." FPRI website: www.fpri.org.

80

Cold War: Churchill and Stalin

Two of the chief protagonists in the Cold War, Churchill and Stalin, are featured in the readings that follow. The Cold War lasted from 1945 to 1989, its name coined by a journalist that sought to describe the quickly emerging hostilities between the democratic nations of Western Europe and the United States, and the communist Soviet Union in the period immediately following World War II. Though these powers had been allies during the war, each sought to ensure that its vision of the world would dominate in the postwar world, while also containing the influence of the other. After 1949, when the Soviet Union detonated its first atomic bomb, no direct military confrontation was possible without bringing about World War III and global annihilation. Irreconcilable ideologies, values, economic and political systems, as well as massive military spending on conventional and nuclear weapons, and "hot spots" like Korea, Cuba, and Vietnam, were part of this period. This set of speeches comes from the early period of the Cold War, where Churchill, in a speech at Westminster College in Fulton, Missouri, in 1946, introduces the now-famous phrase, "Iron Curtain," to refer to the area dominated by the Soviet Union.

Discussion Questions

1. When Churchill states, "But now we all can find any nation, wherever it may dwell, between dusk and dark," to what is he referring? What other challenges to Western nations does he discuss?

2. What does Churchill mean by the "iron curtain," and why does he oppose it? What does he think the Soviet Union wants, if, as he says, they do not desire war?

3. How does Churchill see the role of the United States? The United Nations?

4. Are Churchill's remarks still valid today?

5. What arguments does Stalin present to refute Churchill's position? How does Stalin suggest that communism is growing in influence?

Winston S. Churchill: "Iron Curtain Speech," March 5, 1946

Winston Churchill gave this speech at Westminster College, in Fulton, Missouri, after receiving an honorary degree. With typical oratorical skills, Churchill introduced the phrase "Iron Curtain" to describe the division between Western powers and the area controlled by the Soviet Union. As such the speech marks the onset of the Cold War.

The speech was very long, and here excerpts are presented.

The United States stands at this time at the pinnacle of world power. It is a solemn moment for the American democracy. For with this primacy in power is also joined an awe-inspiring accountability to the future. As you look around you, you must feel not only the sense of duty done, but also you must feel anxiety lest you fall below the level of achievement. Opportunity is here now, clear and shining, for both our countries. To reject it or ignore it or fritter it away will bring upon us all the long reproaches of the aftertime.

It is necessary that constancy of mind, persistency of purpose, and the grand simplicity of decision shall rule and guide the conduct of the English-speaking peoples in peace as they did in war. We must, and I believe we shall, prove ourselves equal to this severe requirement.

I have a strong admiration and regard for the valiant Russian people and for my wartime comrade, Marshal Stalin. There is deep sympathy and goodwill in Britain—and I doubt not here also—toward the peoples of all the Russias and a resolve to persevere through many differences and rebuffs in establishing lasting friendships.

It is my duty, however, to place before you certain facts about the present position in Europe.

From Stettin in the Baltic to Trieste in the Adriatic an iron curtain has descended across the Continent. Behind that line lie all the capitals of the ancient states of Central and Eastern Europe. Warsaw, Berlin, Prague, Vienna, Budapest, Belgrade, Bucharest and Sofia; all these famous cities and the populations around them lie in what I must call the Soviet sphere, and all are subject, in one form or another, not only to Soviet influence but to a very high and in some cases increasing measure of control from Moscow.

The safety of the world, ladies and gentlemen, requires a unity in Europe, from which no nation should be permanently outcast. It is from the quarrels of the strong parent races in Europe that the world wars we have witnessed, or which occurred in former times, have sprung.

Twice the United States has had to send several millions of its young men across the Atlantic to fight the wars. But now we all can find any nation, wherever it may dwell, between dusk and dawn. Surely we should work with conscious purpose for a grand pacification of Europe within the structure of the United Nations and in accordance with our Charter.

In a great number of countries, far from the Russian frontiers and throughout the world, Communist fifth columns are established and work in complete unity and absolute obedience to the directions they receive from the Communist center. Except in the British Commonwealth and in the United States where Communism is in its infancy, the Communist parties or fifth columns constitute a growing challenge and peril to Christian civilization.

The outlook is also anxious in the Far East and especially in Manchuria. The agreement which was made at Yalta, to which I was a party, was extremely favorable to Soviet Russia, but it was made at a time when no one could say that the German war might not extend all through the summer and autumn of 1945 and when the Japanese war was expected by the best judges to last for a further eighteen months from the end of the German war.

I repulse the idea that a new war is inevitable—still more that it is imminent. It is because I am sure that our fortunes are still in our own hands and that we hold the power to save the future, that I feel the duty to speak out now that I have the occasion and the opportunity to do so.

I do not believe that Soviet Russia desires war. What they desire is the fruits of war and the indefinite expansion of their power and doctrines.

But what we have to consider here today while time remains, is the permanent prevention of war and the establishment of conditions of freedom and democracy as rapidly as possible in all countries. Our difficulties and dangers will not be removed by closing our eyes to them. They will not be removed by mere waiting to see what happens; nor will they be removed by a policy of appeasement.

What is needed is a settlement, and the longer this is delayed, the more difficult it will be and the greater our dangers will become.

From what I have seen of our Russian friends and allies during the war, I am convinced that there is nothing they admire so much as strength, and there is nothing for which they have less respect than for weakness, especially military weakness.

For that reason the old doctrine of a balance of power is unsound. We cannot afford, if we can help it, to work on narrow margins, offering temptations to a trial of strength.

Last time I saw it all coming and I cried aloud to my own fellow countrymen and to the world, but no one paid any attention. Up till the year 1933 or even 1935, Germany might have been saved from the awful fate which has overtaken her and we might all have been spared the miseries Hitler let loose upon mankind.

There never was a war in history easier to prevent by timely action than the one which has just desolated such great areas of the globe. It could have been prevented, in my belief, without the firing of a single shot, and Germany might be powerful, prosperous and honored today; but no one would listen and one by one we were all sucked into the awful whirlpool.

We must not let it happen again. This can only be achieved by reaching now, in 1946, a good understanding on all points with Russia under the general authority of the United Nations Organization and by the maintenance of that good understanding through many peaceful years, by the whole strength of the English-speaking world and all its connections.

If the population of the English-speaking Commonwealth be added to that of the United States, with all that such cooperation implies in the air, on the sea, all over the globe, and in science and in industry, and in moral force, there will be no quivering, precarious balance of power to offer its temptation to ambition or adventure. On the contrary there will be an overwhelming assurance of security.

If we adhere faithfully to the Charter of the United Nations and walk forward in sedate and sober strength, seeking no one's land or treasure, seeking to lay no arbitrary control upon the thoughts of men, if all British moral and material forces and convictions are joined with your own in fraternal association, the high roads of the future will be clear, not only for us but for all, not only for our time but for a century to come.

Winston Churchill—March 5, 1946

Joseph Stalin: Reply to Churchill, 1946

. . . In substance, Mr. Churchill now stands in the position of a firebrand of war. And Mr. Churchill is not alone here. He has friends not only in England but also in the United States of America.

In this respect, one is reminded remarkably of Hitler and his friends. Hitler began to set war loose by announcing his racial theory, declaring that only people speaking the German language represent a fully valuable nation. Mr. Churchill begins to set war loose, also by a racial theory, maintaining that only nations speaking the English language are fully valuable nations, called upon to decide the destinies of the entire world.

The German racial theory brought Hitler and his friends to the conclusion that the Germans, as the only fully valuable nation, must rule over other nations. The English racial theory brings Mr. Churchill and his friends to the conclusion that nations speaking the English language, being the only fully valuable nations, should rule over the remaining nations of the world. . . .

As a result of the German invasion, the Soviet Union has irrevocably lost in battles with the Germans, and also during the German occupation and through the expulsion of Soviet citizens to German slave labor camps, about 7,000,000 people. In other words, the Soviet Union has lost in men several times more than Britain and the United States together.

It may be that some quarters are trying to push into oblivion these sacrifices of the Soviet people which insured the liberation of Europe from the Hitlerite yoke.

But the Soviet Union cannot forget them. One can ask therefore, what can be surprising in the fact that the Soviet Union, in a desire to ensure its security for the future, tries to achieve that these countries should have governments whose relations to the Soviet Union are loyal? How can one, without having lost one's reason, qualify these peaceful aspirations of the Soviet Union as "expansionist tendencies" of our Government? . . .

Mr. Churchill wanders around the truth when he speaks of the growth of the influence of the Communist parties in Eastern Europe. . . . The growth of the influence of communism cannot be considered accidental. It is a normal function. The influence of the Communists grew because during the hard years of the mastery of fascism in Europe, Communists showed themselves to be reliable, daring and self-sacrificing fighters against fascist regimes for the liberty of peoples.

Mr. Churchill sometimes recalls in his speeches the common people from small houses, patting them on the shoulder in a lordly manner and pretending to be their friend. But these people are not so simple-minded as it might appear at first sight. Common people, too, have their opinions and their own politics. And they know how to stand up for themselves.

It is they, millions of these common people, who voted Mr. Churchill and his party out in England, giving their votes to the Labor party. It is they, millions of these common people, who isolated reactionaries in Europe, collaborators with fascism, and gave preference to Left democratic parties.

From "Stalin's Reply to Churchill,"
March 14, 1946 (interview with *Pravda*),
The New York Times, p. 4.

81

Vietnamese Declaration of Independence, 1945

The author of this document, Ho Chi Minh, was the leader of the Vietnamese independence movement at the Versailles Conference, where he would present a petition for independence. Ho, who established the Vietnamese Communist Party in 1930 in Paris, would later form the Viet Minh, a coalition of nationalists that would use guerrilla tactics to fight the French, the Japanese, the Americans and the South Vietnamese before Vietnam reunified the country by driving out the Americans and their allies in 1974. When Ho proclaimed the Democratic Republic of Vietnam on September 2, 1945, he consciously modeled his declaration on the American one hoping for U. S. support of its claim to independence. Vietnam had been a colony of France since the 1860s, along with Cambodia and Laos, in what was called French Indochina. The Japanese displaced the French during World War II, which Ho Chi Minh described as another form of imperialism. After the war, there were great hopes from colonized people throughout the world that the European powers would finally relinquish their control, but France, like others, chose to return. American officials ultimately supported the French attempt to reclaim their colony, resulting in the First Indochina War. France would be defeated in 1954, resulting in the division of Vietnam into North and South, and followed by the Second Indochina War, waged by Americans who feared that a communist Vietnam would be the first in a series of "falling dominoes" that would make all of Southeast Asia communist.

Discussion Questions

1. What similarities to the U.S. Declaration of Independence (RGH # 6) can you find? What differences?

2. What are the main charges against the French and the Japanese that Ho makes? Are Ho's claims similar to those of other independence leaders?

3. How does this document reflect Enlightenment principles as well as the ideology of nationalism?

Vietnamese Declaration of Independence, 1945

"All men are created equal. They are endowed by their Creator with certain inalienable rights; among these are Life, Liberty, and the pursuit of Happiness."

This immortal statement was made in the Declaration of Independence of the United States of America in *1776*. In a broader sense, this means: All the peoples on the earth are equal from birth, all the peoples have a right to live, to be happy and free.

The Declaration of the French Revolution made in *1791* on the Rights of Man and the Citizen also states: "All men are born free and with equal rights, and must always remain free and have equal rights."

Those are undeniable truths.

Nevertheless, for more than eighty years, the French imperialists, abusing the standard of Liberty, Equality, and Fraternity, have violated our Fatherland and oppressed our fellow-citizens. They have acted contrary to the ideals of humanity and justice.

In the field of politics, they have deprived our people of every democratic liberty.

They have enforced inhuman laws; they have set up three distinct political regimes in the North, the Center, and the South of Vietnam in order to wreck our national unity and prevent our people from being united.

They have built more prisons than schools. They have mercilessly slain our patriots; they have drowned our uprisings in rivers of blood.

They have fettered public opinion; they have practiced obscurantism against our people.

To weaken our race they have forced us to use opium and alcohol.

In the field of economics, they have fleeced us to the backbone, impoverished our people, and devastated our land.

They have robbed us of our rice fields, our mines, our forests, and our raw materials. They have monopolized the issuing of bank-notes and the export trade.

They have invented numerous unjustifiable taxes and reduced our people, especially our peasantry, to a state of extreme poverty.

They have hampered the prospering of our national bourgeoisie; they have mercilessly exploited our workers.

In the autumn of 1940, when the Japanese Fascists violated Indochina's territory to establish new bases in their fight against the Allies, the French imperialists went down on their bended knees and handed over our country to them.

Thus, from that date, our people were subjected to the double yoke of the French and the Japanese. Their sufferings and miseries increased. The result was that from the end of last year to the beginning of this year, from Quang Tri province to the North of Vietnam, more than two million of our fellow citizens died from starvation. On March 9, the French troops were disarmed by the Japanese. The French colonialists either fled or surrendered showing that not only were they incapable of "protecting" us, but that, in the span of five years, they had twice sold our country to the Japanese.

On several occasions before March 9, the Vietminh League urged the French to ally themselves with it against the Japanese. Instead of agreeing to this proposal, the French colonialists so intensified their terrorist activities against the Vietminh members that before fleeing they massacred a great number of our political prisoners detained at Yen Bay and Caobang.

Notwithstanding all this, our fellow-citizens have always manifested toward the French a tolerant and humane attitude. Even after the Japanese putsch of March 1945, the Vietminh League helped many Frenchmen to cross the frontier, rescued some of them from Japanese jails, and protected French lives and property.

From the autumn of 1940, our country had in fact ceased to be a French colony and had become a Japanese possession.

After the Japanese had surrendered to the Allies, our whole people rose to regain our national sovereignty and to found the Democratic Republic of Vietnam.

The truth is that we have wrested our independence from the Japanese and not from the French.

The French have fled, the Japanese have capitulated, Emperor Bao Dai has abdicated. Our people have broken the chains which for nearly a century have fettered them and have won independence for the Fatherland. Our people at the same time have overthrown the monarchic regime that has reigned supreme for dozens of centuries. In its place has been established the present Democratic Republic.

For these reasons, we, members of the Provisional Government, representing the whole Vietnamese people, declare that from now on we break off all relations of a colonial character with France; we repeal all the international obligation that France has so far subscribed to on behalf of Vietnam and we abolish all the special rights the French have unlawfully acquired in our Fatherland.

The whole Vietnamese people, animated by a common purpose, are determined to fight to the bitter end against any attempt by the French colonialists to reconquer their country.

We are convinced that the Allied nations, which at Tehran and San Francisco have acknowledged the principles of self-determination and equality of nations, will not refuse to acknowledge the independence of Vietnam.

A people who have courageously opposed French domination for more than eight years, a people who have fought side by side with the Allies against the Fascists during these last years, such a people must be free and independent.

For these reasons, we, members of the Provisional Government of the Democratic Republic of Vietnam, solemnly declare to the world that Vietnam has the right to be a free and independent country—and in fact is so already. The entire Vietnamese people are determined to mobilize all their physical and mental strength, to sacrifice their lives and property in order to safeguard their independence and liberty.

Ho Chi Minh, "Declaration of Independence of the Democratic Republic of Vietnam," *Selected Writings* (Hanoi: Foreign Languages Publishing House, 1977), pp. 53–56.

82

"The Short Century—It's Over"

Historians rarely allow themselves to be constrained by the arbitrary dictates of chronology. When it comes to designating eras, ages or even centuries, they often tailor dates to suit actual historical circumstances. In the following article, Professor John Lukacs does just that with the 20th century.

Discussion Questions

1. Why does Lukacs say that the 20th century began in 1914 and ended in 1989, or 1991, rather than 1901 and 2001?

2. What major themes or currents tie the 1914–1989 period together as one age?

3. Can you think of any other historical reasons for using any other dates as the starting and ending points of the 20th century?

The 20th century is now over, and there are two extraordinary matters about this.

First, this was a short century. It lasted 75 years, from 1914 to 1989. Its two principal events were the two world wars. They were the two enormous mountain ranges that dominated its landscape. The Russian Revolution, atom bomb, the end of the colonial empires, the establishment of the communist states, the emergence of two superpowers, the division of Europe and of Germany—all of these were the consequences of the two world wars, in the shadow of which we were living, until now.

The 19th century lasted exactly 99 years, from 1815 to 1914, from the end of Napoleon's wars to the start of the—so-called—First World War. The 18th century lasted 126 years, from 1689 to 1815, from the beginning of the world wars between England and France (of which the American War of Independence was but part) until their end at Waterloo.

Second, we know that the 20th century is over. In 1815, no one knew that this was the end of the Atlantic world wars and the beginning of the Hundred Years' Peace. At that time, everyone, friends as well as enemies of the French Revolution, were concerned with the prospect of great revolutions surfacing again. There were revolutions after 1815, but the entire history of the 19th century was marked by the absence of world wars during 99 years. Its exceptional prosperity and progress were due to that.

In 1689, the very word "century" was hardly known. The "Oxford English Dictionary" notes its first present usage, in English, in 1626. Before that the word meant a Roman military unit of 100 men; then it began to have another meaning, that of 100 years. It marked the beginning of our modern historical consciousness.

We know that the 20th century is over—not merely because of our historical consciousness (which is something different from a wide-spread knowledge of history) but mainly because the confrontation of the two superpowers, the outcome of the Second World War, has died down. The Russians have retreated from Eastern Europe and Germany has been reunited. Outside Europe, even the Korean and the Vietnam wars, the missile crisis in Cuba and other political crises such as Nicaragua were, directly or indirectly, involved with that confrontation.

In 1991, we live in a very different world in which, both the U.S. and the Soviet Union face grave problems with peoples and dictators in the so-called third world. Keep in mind that the ugly events in Lithuania are no exception to this: They involve the political structure of the Soviet Union itself. Even its name, the Union of Soviet Socialist Republics, is becoming an anachronism, as once happened with the Holy Roman Empire.

Keep in mind, too, that no matter when and how the gulf war ends, the so-called Middle East will remain a serious problem both for the U.S. and the Soviet Union. Even in the case of a smashing American political or military victory, its beneficial results will be ephemeral. To think—let alone speak—of a Pax Americana in the Middle East is puerile nonsense.

Not only the configuration of great powers and their alliances but the very structure of political history has changed. Both superpowers have plenty of domestic problems. In the Soviet Union, this has now become frighteningly actual; in the U.S., the internal problems are different but not superficial. The very sovereignty and cohesion of states, the authority and efficacy of the governments are not what they were.

Are we going to see ever larger and larger political units? "Europe" will, at best, become a free-trade economic zone, but a Union of Europe is a mirage. Or are we more likely going to see the break-up of several states into smaller national ones? Are we going to see a large-scale migration of millions of peoples, something that has not happened since the last centuries of the Roman Empire? This is at least possible. The very texture of history is changing before our very eyes.

Are we on the threshold of a new Dark Ages? We must hope not. The main task before us is the rethinking of the word "progress." Like that of "century," the meaning of that word, too, is more recent than we have been accustomed to think. Before the 16th century, that is, before the opening of the so-called modern age (another misnomer, suggesting that this age would last forever) progress simply meant an advance in distance, not in time, without the sense of evolutionary improvement.

Thereafter, the word "progress" began to carry the unquestionable optimistic meaning of endless material and scientific promise, until, during the 20th century, it began to lose some of its shine, because of the increasingly questionable benefits of technology. At the beginning of the 20th century, technology and barbarism seemed to be antitheses. They no longer are. But technology and its threat to the natural environment are only part of the larger problem of progress, a word and an ideal whose more proper and true application is the task of the 21st century that has already begun.

Third World/Developing Nations, 1945–2000

Decolonization, Independence, Revolution, Development

China	India	Africa	Middle East	Latin America
Revolutions 1911—Republican Revolution. —Sun Yatsen, 3 Principles 1919—May 4th Movement 1930–1949—Mao vs. Jiang—Civil War —Long March—1934 —People's Liberation Army —Guerrilla War	Independence: —Modernizers/Traditionalists —Indian National Congress —Partition of Bengal —swaraj—self-rule —Amritsar Massacre —Gandhi and Nehru	Independence (Uhuru) Examples: —Nkrumah-Ghana —Kenyatta-Kenya —Nyerere-Tanzania —Lumumba-Congo	Arab nationalism —Ottoman decline —Arab brotherhood —World War I—created the modern Middle East	Revolutions —Guatemala—1954 —Cuba—1959 —Dom. Rep.—1965 —Jamaica—1977 —Nicaragua—1979 —Mexico—1990's (Chiapas)
Mao Zedong 1949–1976 —People's Republic of China—10/1/49 —rapid industrialization —literacy and social reforms —Sino-Soviet split—1959 —Taiwan and the Nationalists	Satyagraha-Soul Force— —Salt March —Civil disobedience —Nonviolent resistance —Non-cooperation —Social reforms, untouchables —Self-reliance	Strategies in Decolonization— —Nationalist movements —Western-educated leaders —One-party states —Social reforms—education, health, economic development	Arab-Israeli Conflict— —Zionism-Jewish nationalism —1948—State of Israel —Wars—1948, 1956, 1967, 1973. —Intifadas —PLO—Arafat, Hamas —Camp David, Oslo, Wye Accords, Roadmap	Cuba and Castro— —Communism —Anti-Americanism —Bay of Pigs—1961 —Missile Crisis—1962 —Elian—2000 —Embargo
Continuous Revolution—Using ideas to move the masses: —Great Leap Forward —Cultural Revolution—Red Guards	Hindu-Muslim Split— —Jinnah and Pakistan —Partition 1947—Pakistan and India 1971—Bangladesh —Kashmir	Social and Political: —Negritude—African identity —Pan-Africanism —Role of women in development	New States/New Leaders: —Egypt-Nasser (Arab Socialism) —Syria-Assad —Iraq-Hussein (Ba'ath Party) —Jordan-Hussein	Human Rights— —Chile—1973 —Argentina—1977 —El Salvador—1984 —Deseparacidos —Haiti—1990's
Deng Xiaoping 1978–1997 —"To get rich is glorious" —Market totalitarianism —Tiananmen—1989	India after independence— —Nonalignment —1970's—Indira Gandhi —Socialism	South Africa— —Apartheid —African National Congress —Mandela —Majority rule—1994	Political Developments: —Turkey—secular state —Iran-Islamic theocracy—1979 —Saudi Arabia—Wahabism	Economic Development— —Brazil, Chile, Argentina. Mexico— —Colombia. Panama—"narcodemocracies" —NAFTA, Globalization
China Today— —"Fang shou"—relaxation and control —Great power status —Olympics—2008 —Friend or foe? —Impact of globalization	India Today— —Hindu nationalism (BJP) —Nuclear weapons —Economic development —Most populous democracy —Hindu-Muslim conflict —Impact of globalization	Africa Today— —Ethnic conflict —Weak governments —AIDS —Poverty —Economic dependence —Impact of globalization	Middle East Today— —Authoritarian states —Conflict, terrorism —Cultural heterogeneity —Outside intervention —Fundamentalism —Oil and economics	Latin America Today— —Constitutionally weak states —Economic dependence —Drug Trade —Poverty —Democratization —Impact of globalization

Chinese Chronology: 1911–1949

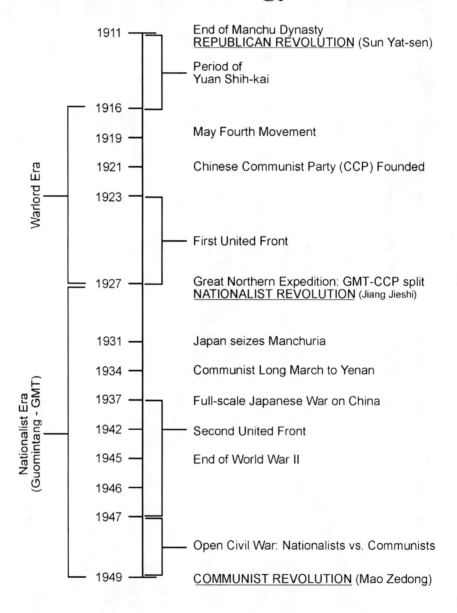

Warlord Era	1911	End of Manchu Dynasty REPUBLICAN REVOLUTION (Sun Yat-sen)
		Period of Yuan Shih-kai
	1916	
	1919	May Fourth Movement
	1921	Chinese Communist Party (CCP) Founded
	1923	
		First United Front
	1927	Great Northern Expedition: GMT-CCP split NATIONALIST REVOLUTION (Jiang Jieshi)
Nationalist Era (Guomintang - GMT)	1931	Japan seizes Manchuria
	1934	Communist Long March to Yenan
	1937	Full-scale Japanese War on China
	1942	Second United Front
	1945	End of World War II
	1946	
	1947	
		Open Civil War: Nationalists vs. Communists
	1949	COMMUNIST REVOLUTION (Mao Zedong)

85

The Peasant Movement in Hunan

In this document, Mao Zedong reported on his investigation of the progress of the communist movement among the peasants of Hunan, his native province, in March of 1927. His emphasis on organizing the peasants of the countryside went against the mainstream of Chinese communists who followed the Marxist-Leninist doctrine that communism must take root among the industrial workers in the cities. In April of 1927 Jiang Jieshi purged the communists in the Guomintang, thus ending the first period of cooperation, or united front, between the right and left within the party. A long period of self-examination among the communists, who had fled to the more remote areas of Jiangsi and Hunan after their expulsion and persecution, eventually led to the adoption of Mao's ideas concerning the importance of the peasantry and a new lease on life for his movement.

Discussion Questions

1. Do you get the impression from Mao's essay that the peasant movement was spontaneous or carefully planned and organized?
2. Who are the objects of the wrath of the peasants? Do they deserve this treatment?
3. How does Mao justify the violence ("going too far") of the peasants?
4. Who are the most revolutionary people?
5. What does he say are the achievements of the peasants?
6. Do you think the peasants believe in "democracy?"

March 1927

The development of the peasant movement in Hunan may be divided roughly into two periods with respect to the counties in the province's central and southern parts where the movement has already made much headway. The first, from January to September of last year, was one of organization. The second period, from last October to January of this year, was one of revolutionary action. The membership of the associations jumped to two million and the masses directly under their leadership increased to ten million.

The main targets of attack by the peasants are the local tyrants, the evil gentry and the lawless landlords, but in passing they also hit out against patriarchal ideas and institutions, against the corrupt officials in the cities and against bad practices and customs in the rural areas.

In a few months the peasants have accomplished what Dr. Sun Yat-sen wanted, but failed to accomplish in the forty years he devoted to the national revolution. Countless thousands of the enslaved—the peasants—are striking down the enemies who battened on their flesh. What the peasants are doing is absolutely right; what they are doing is fine! "It's fine!" is the theory of the peasants and of all other revolutionaries. Every revolutionary comrade should know that the national revolution requires a great change in the countryside. The Revolution of 1911 did not bring about this change, hence its failure. This change is now taking place, and it is an important factor for the completion of the revolution. Every revolutionary comrade must support it, or he will be taking the stand of counter-revolution.

A revolution is an insurrection, an act of violence by which one class overthrows another. A rural revolution is a revolution by which the peasantry overthrows the power of the feudal landlord class. Without using the greatest force, the peasants cannot possibly overthrow the deeprooted authority of the landlords which has lasted for thousands of years. The rural areas need a mighty revolutionary upsurge, for it alone can rouse the people in their millions to become a powerful force. Proper limits have to be exceeded in order to right a wrong, or else the wrong cannot be righted. Those who talk about the peasants "going too far" seem at first sight to be different from those who say "It's terrible!"; but in essence they proceed from the same standpoint and likewise voice a landlord theory that upholds the interests of the privileged classes. Since this theory impedes the rise of the peasant movement and so disrupts the revolution, we must firmly oppose it.

According to the survey of Changsha County, the poor peasants comprise 70 per cent, the middle peasants 20 per cent, and the landlords and the rich peasants 10 per cent of

---

the population in the rural areas. The 70 per cent, the poor peasants, may be sub-divided into two categories, the utterly destitute and the less destitute. The utterly destitute, comprising 20 per cent, are the completely dispossessed, that is, people who have neither land nor money, are without any means of livelihood, and are forced to leave home and become mercenaries or hired laborers or wandering beggars. The less destitute, the other 50 per cent, are the partially dispossessed, that is, people with just a little land or a little money who eat up more than they earn and live in toil and distress the year round, such as the handicraftsmen, the tenant-peasants (not including the rich tenant-peasants) and the semi-owner-peasants. This great mass of poor peasants, or altogether 70 per cent of the rural population, are the backbone of the peasant associations, the vanguard in the overthrow of the feudal forces and the heroes who have performed the great revolutionary task which for long years was left undone. Without the poor peasant class (the "riffraff," as the gentry call them), it would have been impossible to bring about the present revolutionary situation in the countryside, or to overthrow the local tyrants and evil gentry and complete the democratic revolution. The poor peasants, being the most revolutionary group, have gained the leadership of the peasant associations. Leadership by the poor peasants is absolutely necessary. Without the poor peasants there would be no revolution. To deny their role is to deny the revolution. To attack them is to attack the revolution. They have never been wrong on the general direction of the revolution. They have beaten down the local tyrants and evil gentry, big and small, and kept them underfoot.

Most critics of the peasant associations allege that they have done a great many bad things. The peasants' attack on the local tyrants and evil gentry is entirely revolutionary behavior and in no way blameworthy. The peasants have done a great many things, and in order to answer people's criticism we must closely examine all their activities, one by one, to see what they have actually done. I have classified and summed up their activities of the last few months; in all, the peasants under the leadership of the peasant associations have the following great achievements to their credit.

1. Organizing the Peasants into Peasant Associations

This is the first great achievement of the peasants. In counties like Hsiangtan, Hsianghsiang and Hengshan, nearly all the peasants are organized and there is hardly a remote corner where they are not on the move. By the end of January the membership must have reached at least two million. As a family generally enters only one name when joining and has an average of five members, the mass following must be about ten million. This astonishing and accelerating-rate of expansion explains why the local tyrants, evil gentry and corrupt officials have been isolated, why the public has been amazed at how completely the world has changed since the peasant movement, and why a great revolution has been wrought in the countryside. This is the first great achievement of the peasants under the leadership of their associations.

2. Hitting the Landlords Politically

Once the peasants have their organization, the first thing they do is to smash the political prestige and power of the landlord class, and especially of the local tyrants and evil gentry, that is, to pull down landlord authority and build up peasant authority in rural society. This is a most serious and vital struggle. It is the pivotal struggle in the second period, the period of revolutionary action. Without victory in this struggle, no victory is possible in the economic struggle to reduce rent and interest, to secure land and other means of production, and so on.

3. Hitting the Landlords Economically

Prohibition on sending grain out of the area, forcing up grain prices, and hoarding and cornering. This is one of the great events of recent months in the economic struggle of the Hunan peasants. Since last October the poor peasants have prevented the outflow of the grain of the landlords and rich peasants and have banned the forcing up of grain prices and hoarding and cornering. As a result, the poor peasants have fully achieved their objective; the ban on the outflow of grain is watertight, grain prices have fallen considerably, and hoarding and cornering have disappeared.

Prohibition on increasing rents and deposits; agitation for reduced rents and deposits. Last July and August, when the peasant associations were still weak, the landlords, following their long-established practice of maximum exploitation, served notice one after another on their tenants that rents and deposits would be increased. But by October, when the peasant associations had grown considerably in strength and had all come out against the raising of rents and deposits, the landlords dared not breathe another word on the subject. From November onwards, as the peasants have gained ascendancy over the landlords they have taken the further step of agitating for reduced rents and deposits.

Prohibition on canceling tenancies. In July and August of last year there were still many instances of landlords canceling tenancies and re-letting the land. But after October nobody dared cancel a tenancy. Today, the canceling of tenancies and the re-letting of land are quite out of the question.

4. Overthrowing the Feudal Rule of the Local Tyrants and Evil Gentry

The evil gentry who ran these organs were virtual monarchs of the countryside. Comparatively speaking, the peasants were not so much concerned with the president of the Republic, the provincial military governor or the county magistrate; their real "bosses" were these rural monarchs. A mere snort from these people, and the peasants knew they had to watch their step. As a consequence of the present revolt in the countryside the authority of the landlord class has generally been struck down.

5. Overthrowing the Political Power of the County Magistrate and His Bailiffs

In a county where power is in the hands of the local tyrants and evil gentry, the magistrate, whoever he may be, is almost invariably a corrupt official. In a county where the peasants have risen there is clean government, whoever the magistrate.

6. Overthrowing the Clan Authority of the Ancestral Temples and Clan Elders, the Religious Authority of Town and Village Gods, and the Masculine Authority of Husbands

A man in China is usually subjected to the domination of three systems of authority: (1) the state system (authority), ranging from the national, provincial and county government down to that of the township; (2) the clan system (clan authority), ranging from the central ancestral temple and its branch temples down to the head of the household; and (3) the supernatural system (religious authority), ranging from the King of Hell down to the town and village gods belonging to the nether world, and from the Emperor of Heaven down to all the various gods and spirits belonging to the celestial world. As for women, in addition to being dominated by these three systems of authority, they are also dominated by the men (the authority of the husband). These four authorities political, clan, religious and masculine are the embodiment of the whole feudal patriarchal system and ideology, and are the four thick ropes binding the Chinese people, particularly the peasants.

While I was in the countryside, I did some propaganda against superstition among the peasants. I said:

"The gods? Worship them by all means. But if you had only Lord Kuan and the Goddess of Mercy and no peasant association, could you have overthrown the local tyrants and evil gentry? The gods and goddesses are indeed miserable objects. You have worshipped them for centuries, and they have not overthrown a single one of the local tyrants or evil gentry for you! Now you want to have your rent reduced. Let me ask, how will you go about it? Will you believe in the gods or in the peasant association?"

My words made the peasants roar with laughter.

7. Spreading Political Propaganda

The spread of political propaganda throughout the rural areas is entirely an achievement of the Communist Party and the peasant associations. Simple slogans, cartoons and speeches have produced such a widespread and speedy effect among the peasants that every one of them seems to have been through a political school.

8. Peasant Bans and Prohibitions

When the peasant associations, under Communist Party leadership, establish their authority in the countryside, the peasants begin to prohibit or restrict the things they dislike. Gaming, gambling and opium-smoking are the three things that are most strictly forbidden.

Gaming. Where the peasant association is powerful, mahjong, dominoes and card games are completely banned.

The peasant association in the 14th District of Hsianghsiang burned two basketfuls of mahjong sets.

If you go to the countryside, you will find none of these games played; anyone who violates the ban is promptly and strictly punished.

Gambling. Former hardened gamblers are now themselves suppressing gambling; this abuse, too, has been swept away in places where the peasant association is powerful.

Opium-smoking. The prohibition is extremely strict. When the peasant association orders the surrender of opium pipes, no one dares to raise the least objection. In Liling County one of the evil gentry who did not surrender his pipes was arrested and paraded through the villages.

9. Eliminating Banditry

Wherever the peasant associations are powerful, there is not a trace of banditry. Surprisingly enough, in many places even the pilfering of vegetables has disappeared. In other places there are still some pilferers. But in the counties I visited, even including those that were formerly bandit-ridden, there was no trace of bandits.

10. The Movement for Education

In China education has always been the exclusive preserve of the landlords, and the peasants have had no access to it. But the landlords' culture is created by the peasants, for its sole source is the peasants' sweat and blood. In China 90 per cent of the people have had no education, and of these the overwhelming majority are peasants. The moment the power of the landlords was overthrown in the rural areas, the peasants' movement for education began. See how the peasants who hitherto detested the schools are today zealously setting up evening classes!

Now the peasants are enthusiastically establishing evening classes, which they call peasant schools. Some have already been opened, others are being organized, and on the average there is one school per township. The peasants are very enthusiastic about these schools, and regard them, and only them, as their own. The funds for the evening schools come from the "public revenue from superstition," from ancestral temple funds, and from other idle public funds or property.

11. The Cooperative Movement

The peasants really need cooperatives, and especially consumers', marketing and credit co-operatives. When they buy goods, the merchants exploit them; when they sell their farm produce, the merchants cheat them; when they borrow money or rice, they are fleeced by the usurers; and they are eager to find a solution to these three problems.

All the deeds enumerated above have been accomplished by the peasants under the leadership of the peasant associations. Would the reader please think it over and say whether any of them is bad in its fundamental spirit and revolutionary significance? Only the local tyrants and evil gentry, I think, will call them bad.

86

The Communist Political Thesis

In the period after the Long March (1934–5), from their headquarters in Yenan, Mao and the communists engaged in a village-by-village transformation that would gain them the loyalty of many, if not most, Chinese peasants in the northern and central regions of eastern China—areas that were mostly under Japanese control after 1937. In their book *Thunder Out of China*, Theodore H. White and Annalee Jacoby explain the appeal of the communists to the peasants.

Discussion Questions

1. What did the communists do for the peasants?

2. Is it possible to understand the success of the communists over the long run?

3. How did the communists' approach differ from that of the Kuomintang as seen in the U.S. Foreign Service officers' reports?

The entire Communist political thesis could be reduced to a single paragraph: If you take a peasant who has been swindled, beaten, and kicked about for all his waking days and whose father has transmitted to him an emotion of bitterness reaching back for generations—if you take such a peasant, treat him like a man, ask his opinion, let him vote for a local government, let him organize his own police and gendarmes, decide on his own taxes, and vote himself a reduction in rent and interest—if you do all that, the peasant becomes a man who has something to fight for, and he will fight to preserve it against any enemy, Japanese or Chinese. If in addition you present the peasant with an army and a government that help him harvest, teach him to read and write, and fight off the Japanese who raped his wife and tortured his mother, he develops a loyalty to the army and the government and to the party that controls them. He votes for that party, thinks the way that party wants him to think, and in many cases becomes an active participant. . . .

From *Thunder Out of China*, by Theodore H. White and Annalee Jacoby, copyright © 1946, 1961 by William Sloane Associates.

87

U.S. Reports on China

During World War II John S. Service and John Paton Davies, Foreign Service officers for the State Department stationed in Chungking, offered realistic, if pessimistic, accounts of the position of Jiang Jieshi and the Guomintang (GMT). Their analysis was not limited to the situation within Chiang's government but also its prospects for dealing with the communists after the war was over.

Discussion Questions

1. What factors endangered the base of the GMT among the people?

2. How were Chiang and the GMT trying to deal with the problems they faced? Would you agree with Service that their policies were suicidal?

3. Why did Service and Davies seem to think that a communist victory was inevitable? Was there any realistic hope that Chiang could prevail?

4. With this background in mind, what do you think would have been the position of the United States if Chiang had managed to hold out in some region of China? Could the U.S. have guaranteed a GMT victory over the communists?

U.S. Foreign Service Officer Reports

John S. Service and John Paton Davies

June 20, 1944 (Service)

The position of the Kuomintang and the Generalissimo is weaker than it has been for the past ten years.

China faces economic collapse. This is causing disintegration of the army and the government's administrative apparatus. It is one of the chief causes of growing political unrest. The Generalissimo is losing the support of a China which, by unity in the face of violent aggression, found a new and unexpected strength during the first two years of the war with Japan. Internal weaknesses are becoming accentuated and there is taking place a reversal of the process of unification.

1. Morale is low and discouragement widespread. There is a general feeling of hopelessness.

2. The authority of the Central Government is weakening in the areas away from the larger cities. Government mandates and measures of control cannot be enforced and remain ineffective. It is becoming difficult for the Government to collect enough food for its huge army and bureaucracy.

3. The governmental and military structure is being permeated and demoralized from top to bottom by corruption, unprecedented in scale and openness.

4. The intellectual and salaried classes, who have suffered the most heavily from inflation, are in danger of liquidation. The academic groups suffer not only the attrition and demoralization of economic stress; the weight of years of political control and repression is robbing them of the intellectual vigor and leadership they once had.

5. Peasant resentment of the abuses of conscription, tax collection and other arbitrary impositions has been widespread and is growing. The danger is ever-increasing that past sporadic outbreaks of banditry and agrarian unrest may increase in scale and find political motivation. . . .

9. The Kuomintang is losing the respect and support of the people by its school policies and its refusal to heed progressive criticism. It seems unable to revivify itself with fresh blood, and its unchanging leadership shows a growing ossification and loss of a sense of reality. To combat the dissensions and cliquism within the Party, which grow more rather than less acute, the leadership is turning toward the reactionary and unpopular Chen brothers clique.

10. The Generalissimo shows a similar loss of flexibility and a hardening of narrowly conservative views: His growing megalomania and his unfortunate attempts to be "sage" as well as leader—shown, for instance, by "China's Destiny" and his book on econom-

From "U.S. Foreign Service Officer Reports," by John S. Service and John Paton Davies from *United States Relations With China*, with Special Reference to the period 1944–1949. Published by the U.S. Department of State, Washington, D. C., 1949.

ics—have forfeited the respect of many intellectuals, who enjoy in China a position of unique influence. Criticism of his dictatorship is becoming outspoken.

In the face of the grave crisis with which it is confronted the Kuomintang is ceasing to be the unifying and progressive force in Chinese society, the role in which it made its greatest contribution to modern China. . . .

On the internal political front the desire of the Kuomintang leaders to perpetuate their own power overrides all other considerations. The result is the enthronement of reaction.

The Kuomintang continues to ignore the great political drive within the country for democratic reform. The writings of the Generalissimo and the Party press show that they have no real understanding of that term. Constitutionalism remains an empty promise for which the only "preparation" is a halfhearted attempt to establish an unpopular and undemocratic system of local self-government based on collective responsibility and given odium by Japanese utilization in Manchuria and other areas under their control.

Questions basic to the future of democracy such as the form of the Constitution and the composition and election of the National Congress remain the dictation of the Kuomintang. There is no progress toward the fundamental conditions of freedom of expression and recognition of non-Kuomintang groups. Even the educational and political advantages of giving power and democratic character to the existing but impotent Peoples Political Council are ignored.

The Kuomintang shows no intention of relaxing the authoritarian controls on which its present power depends. Far from discarding reducing the paraphernalia of a police state—the multiple and omnipresent secret police organizations, the Gendarmerie, and

so forth—it continues to strengthen them as its last resort for internal security. . . .

These apparently suicidal policies of the Kuomintang have their roots in the composition and nature of the Party.

In view of the above it becomes pertinent to ask *why* the Kuomintang has lost its power of leadership; *why* it neither wishes actively to wage war against Japan itself nor to cooperate whole-heartedly with the American Army in China; and *why* it has ceased to be capable of unifying the country.

The answer to all these questions is to be found in the present composition and nature of the Party. Politically, a classical and definitive American description becomes ever more true; the Kuomintang is a congerie of conservative political cliques interested primarily in the preservation of their own power against all outsiders and in jockeying for position among themselves. Economically, the Kuomintang rests on the narrow base of the rural-gentry-landlords and militarists, the higher ranks of the government bureaucracy, and merchant bankers having intimate connections with the government bureaucrats. This base has actually contracted during the war. The Kuomintang no longer commands, as it once did, the unequivocal support of China's industrialists, who as a group have been much weakened economically, and hence politically, by the Japanese seizure of the coastal cities. . . .

December 9, 1944 (Davies)

. . . The Generalissimo realizes that if he accedes to the Communist terms for a coalition government, they will sooner or later dispossess him and his Kuomintang of power. He will therefore not, unless driven to an extremity, form a genuine coalition government. He will seek to retain his present government, passively wait out the war and conserve his strength, knowing that the Communist issue must eventually be joined.

The Communists, on their part, have no interest in reaching an agreement with the Generalissimo short of a genuine coalition government. They recognize that Chiang's position is crumbling, that they may before long receive substantial Russian support and that if they have patience they will succeed to authority in at least North China. . . .

The Communists would, inevitably, win such a war because the foreign powers, including the United States, which would support the Government, could not feasibly supply enough aid to compensate for the organic weaknesses of the Government.

January 23, 1943 (Service)

. . . Assuming that open hostilities are for the time being averted, the eventual defeat and withdrawal of the Japanese will leave the Kuomintang still confronted with the Communists solidly entrenched in most of North China (East Kansu, North Shensi, Shansi, South Chahar, Hopei, Shantung, North Kiangsu and North Anhwei). In addition the Communists will be in a position to move into the vacuum created by the Japanese withdrawal from Suiyan, Jehol and Manchuria, in all of which areas there is already some Communist activity. In the rest of China they will have the sympathy of elements among the liberals, intellectuals, and students.

. . . There is undoubtedly a strong revulsion in the mind of the average, non-party Chinese to the idea of renewed civil war and the Kuomintang may indeed have difficulty with the loyalty and effectiveness of its conscript troops.

October 9, 1944 (Service)

Just as the Japanese Army cannot crush these militant people now, so also will Kuomintang force fail in the future. With their new arms and organization, knowledge of their own strength, and determination to keep what they have been fighting for, these people—now some 90 million and certain to be many more before the Kuomintang can reach them—will resist oppression. They are not Communists. They do not want separation or independence. But at present they regard the Kuomintang—from their own experience—as oppressors; and the Communists as their leaders and benefactors.

With this great popular base, the Communists likewise cannot be eliminated. Kuomintang attempts to do so by force must mean a complete denial of democracy. This will strengthen the ties of the Communists with the people: a Communist victory will be inevitable. . . .

From the basic fact that the Communists have built up popular support of a magnitude and depth which makes their elimination impossible, *we must draw the conclusion that the Communists will have a certain and important share in China's future . . .* I suggest the future conclusion that unless the Kuomintang goes as far as the Communists in political and economic reform, and otherwise proves itself able to contest this leadership of the people (none of which it yet shows signs of being willing or able to do), the Communists will be the dominant force in China within a comparatively few years.

88

The Foolish Old Man Who Removed the Mountains

During the last months of World War II in the Pacific, Mao Tse-tung (Mao Zedong) wrote the following brief article during a meeting of the Communist Party Congress. In it he explains what had been accomplished and what remained to be done. He also addresses the role of the United States on the scene in China. This article quickly became a classic of Chinese communist literature and was especially popular among the Red Guards during the Cultural Revolution after 1966.

Discussion Questions

1. What spirit do you think Mao was trying to encourage among the Chinese people with the age-old story of the foolish old man?

2. What do you think he meant by the phrase "self-criticism?"

3. Mao alludes to the democratic forces and the reactionary counter-current in the world—what or whom is he referring to?

4. Toward the end of the article he mentions "three major contradictions in the old world;" what are the three contradictions and what is the old world?

June 11, 1945

We have had a very successful congress. We have done three things. First, we have decided on the line of our Party, which is boldly to mobilize the masses and expand the people's forces so that, under the leadership of our Party, they will defeat the Japanese aggressors, liberate the whole people and build a new-democratic China. Second, we have adopted the new, Party Constitution. Third, we have elected the leading body of the Party—the Central Committee. Henceforth our task is to lead the whole membership in carrying out the Party line. Ours has been a congress of victory, a congress of unity. The delegates have made excellent comments on the three reports. Many comrades have undertaken self-criticism; with unity as the objective unity has been achieved through self-criticism. This congress is a model of unity, of self-criticism and of inner-Party democracy.

When the congress closes, many comrades will be leaving for their posts and the various war fronts. Comrades, wherever you go, you should propagate the line of the congress and, through the members of the Party, explain it to the broad masses.

Our aim in propagating the line of the congress is to build up the confidence of the whole Party and the entire people in the certain triumph of the revolution. We must first raise the political consciousness of the van-guard so that, resolute and unafraid of sacrifice, they will surmount every difficulty to win victory. But this is not enough; we must also arouse the political consciousness of the entire people so that they may willingly and gladly fight together with us for victory. We should fire the whole people with the conviction that China belongs not to the reactionaries but to the Chinese people. There is an ancient Chinese fable called "The Foolish Old Man Who Removed the Mountains." It tells of an old man who lived in northern China long, long ago and was known as the Foolish Old Man of North Mountain. His house faced south and beyond his doorway stood the two great peaks, Taihang and Wangwu, obstructing the way. With great determination, he led his sons in digging up these mountains hoe in hand. Another graybeard, known as the Wise Old Man, saw them and said derisively, "How silly of you to do this! It is quite impossible for you few to dig up these two huge mountains." The Foolish Old Man replied, "When I die, my sons will carry on; when they die, there will be my grandsons, and then their sons and grandsons, and so on to infinity. High as they are, the mountains cannot grow any higher and with every bit we dig, they will be that much lower. Why can't we clear them away?" Having refuted the Wise Old Man's wrong view, he went on digging every day, unshaken in his conviction. God was moved by this, and he sent down two angels, who carried the mountains away on their backs. Today, two big mountains lie like a dead weight on the Chinese people. One is imperialism, the other is feudalism. The Chinese Communist Party has long made up its mind to dig them up. We must persevere and work unceasingly, and we, too, will touch God's heart. Our God is none other than the masses of the Chinese people. If they stand up and dig together with us, why can't these two mountains be cleared away?

Yesterday, in a talk with two Americans who were leaving for the United States, I said that the U.S. government was trying to undermine us and this would not be permitted. We oppose the U.S. government's policy of supporting Chiang Kai-shek against the Communists. But we must draw a distinction, firstly, between the people of the United States and their government and, secondly, within the U.S. government between the policy-makers and their subordinates. I said to these two Americans, "Tell the policy-makers in your government that we forbid you Americans to enter the Liberated Areas because your policy is to support Chiang Kai-shek against the Communists, and we have to be on our guard. You can come to the Liberated Areas if your purpose is to fight Japan, but there must first be an agreement. We will not permit you to nose around everywhere. Since Patrick J. Hurley has publicly declared against co-operation with the Chinese Communist Party, why do you still want to come and prowl around in our Liberated Areas?"

The U.S. government's policy of supporting Chiang Kai-shek against the Communists shows the brazenness of the U.S. reactionaries. But all the scheming of the reactionaries, whether Chinese or foreign, to prevent the Chinese people from achieving victory is doomed to failure. The democratic forces are the main current in the world today, while reaction is only a counter-current. The reactionary counter-current is trying to swamp the main current of national independence and people's democracy, but it can never become the main current. Today, there are still three major contradictions in the old world, as Stalin pointed out long ago: first, the contradiction between the proletariat and the bourgeoisie in the imperialist countries; second, the contradiction between the various imperialist powers; and third, the contradiction between the colonial and semicolonial countries and the imperialist metropolitan countries. Not only do these three contradictions continue to exist but they are becoming more acute and widespread. Because of their existence and growth, the time will come when the reactionary anti-Soviet, anti-Communist and anti-democratic counter-current still in existence today will be swept away.

At this moment two congresses are being held in China, the Sixth National Congress of the Kuomintang and the Seventh National Congress of the Communist Party. They have completely different aims: the aim of one is to liquidate the Communist Party and all the other democratic forces in China and thus to plunge China into darkness; the aim of the other is to overthrow Japanese imperialism and its lackeys, the Chinese feudal forces, and build a new-democratic China and thus to lead China to light. These two lines are in conflict with each other. We firmly believe that, led by the Chinese Communist Party and guided by the line of its Seventh Congress, the Chinese people will achieve complete victory, while the Kuomintang's counter-revolutionary line will inevitably fail.

89

The Chinese Cultural Revolution

The rapture that comes when one "truly believes" is captured in this excerpt from *Wild Swans*, whose author, Jung Chang, lived through the tumultuous Great Proletarian Cultural Revolution of the 1960s. Led by the Red Guards, young students and workers who waved Mao Zedong's Little Red Book as a sign of their belief, and urged the banishment of all class enemies and "capitalist roaders," this protest would transform China in many ways. Like the Great Leap Forward almost a decade before, Mao Zedong fired up the Red Guards by using communist ideology to spur them forward, urging them to place the objectives of communism, and of Mao, ahead of family or individual aims or desires. To understand the appeal of Mao and his beliefs, to understand how the author came to tears when thinking how lucky she was to be living at this time, read on.

Discussion Questions

1. Can you imagine yourself ever believing in something as fervently as Jung Chang? Why do you think she was so captivated by Mao?

2. What similarities do the author's statements about her attraction for Mao have in common with Arthur Koestler's enchantment with communism in an earlier text reading?

3. Can you think of any contemporary examples where people feel and act as strongly on their beliefs as did the author of *Wild Swans*? Do you admire such people or do you think they're deluded?

"Father Is Close, Mother Is Close, But Neither Is as Close as Chairman Mao"— The Cult of Mao (1964–1965)

"Chairman Mao," as we always called him, began to impinge directly on my life in 1964, when I was twelve. Having been in retreat for some time after the famine, he was starting his comeback, and in March of the previous year he had issued a call to the whole country, particularly the young, to "learn from Lei Feng."

Lei Feng was a soldier who, we were told, had died at the age of twenty-two in 1962. He had done an awful lot of good deeds—going out of his way to help the elderly, the sick, and the needy. He had donated his savings to disaster relief funds and given up his food rations to comrades in the hospital.

Lei Feng soon began to dominate my life. Every afternoon we left school to "do good deeds like Lei Feng." We went down to the railway station to try to help old ladies with their luggage, as Lei Feng had done. We sometimes had to grab their bundles from them forcibly because some countrywomen thought we were thieves. On rainy days, I stood on the street with an umbrella, anxiously hoping that an old lady would pass by and give me an opportunity to escort her home—as Lei Feng had done. If I saw someone carrying water buckets on a shoulder pole—old houses still did not have running water—I would try unsuccessfully to summon up the courage to offer my help, although I had no idea how heavy a load of water was.

Gradually, during the course of 1964, the emphasis began to shift from boy scoutish good deeds to the cult of Mao. The essence of Lei Feng, the teachers told us, was his "boundless love and devotion to Chairman Mao." Before he took any action, Lei Feng always thought of some words of Mao's. His diary was published and became our moral textbook. On almost every page there was a pledge like: "I must study Chairman Mao's works, heed Chairman Mao's words, follow Chairman Mao's instructions, and be a good soldier of Chairman Mao's." We vowed to follow Lei Feng, and be ready to "go up mountains of knives and down seas of flames," to "have our bodies smashed to powder and our bones crushed to smithereens," to "submit ourselves unquestioningly to the control of the Great Leader"— Mao. The cult of Mao and the cult of Lei Feng were two sides of the same coin: one was the cult of personality; the other, its essential corollary, was the cult of impersonality.

I read my first article by Mao in 1964, at a time when two slogans of Mao's—"Serve the People" and "Never Forget Class Struggle"— dominated our lives. The essence of these two complementary slogans was illustrated in Lei Feng's poem "The Four Seasons," which we all learned by heart

Like spring, I treat my comrades warmly.

Like summer, I am full of ardor for my revolutionary work.

I eliminate my individualism as an autumn gale sweeps away fallen leaves,

And to the class enemy, I am cruel and ruthless like harsh Winter.

In line with this, our teacher said we had to be careful whom we helped on our do-good errands. We must not help "class enemies." But I did not understand who they were, and when I asked, neither the teachers nor my parents were keen to elaborate. One common answer was: "like the baddies in the movies." But I could not see anyone around me who looked like the highly stylized enemy characters in the movie, This posed a big problem. I no longer felt sure about seizing bags from old ladies. I could not possibly ask, "Are you a class enemy?"

We sometimes went to clean the houses in an alley next to our school. In one house there was a young man who used to lounge on a bamboo chair watching us with a cynical smile as we toiled away on his windows. Not only did he not offer to help, he even wheeled his bicycle out of the shed and suggested we clean that for him as well.

"What a pity," he once said, "that you are not the real Lei Feng, and that there are no photographers on hand to take your pictures for the newspapers." (Lei Feng's good deeds were miraculously recorded by an official photographer.) We all hated the lounger with the dirty bicycle. Could he be a class enemy? But we knew he worked at a machinery factory, and workers, we had been repeatedly told, were the best, the leading class in our revolution. I was confused.

One of the things I had been doing was helping to push carts on the streets after school. The carts were often piled high with cement blocks or chunks of sandstone. They were terribly heavy, and every step was an enormous effort for the men who pulled them. Even in cold weather, some would be bare-chested, and shiny beads of sweat trickled down their faces and backs. If the road was even slightly uphill, it was very hard for some of them to keep going. Whenever I saw them, I was attacked by a wave of sadness. Since the campaign to learn from Lei Feng had started, I had stood by a ramp waiting for carts to pass. I would be exhausted after helping to push just one of them. As I left off, the man pulling would give me an almost imperceptible sideways smile, trying not to break his stride and lose momentum.

One day a classmate said to me in a very serious tone of voice that most of the people pulling carts were class enemies who had been assigned to do hard labor. Therefore, she told me, it was wrong to help them. I asked my teacher, since I, in accordance with Chinese tradition, always turned to teachers for authority. But instead of her normal air of confidence, she looked unsettled and said she did not know the answer, which puzzled me. In fact, it was actually true that people pulling carts had often been assigned the job because they had Kuomintang links, or because they were victims of one of the political purges. My teacher obviously did not want to tell me this, but she did ask me to stop helping to push carts. From then on, every time I happened on a cart in the street, I averted my eyes from the bent figure trudging along and quickly walked away with a heavy heart.

To fill us with hatred for class enemies, the schools started regular sessions of "recalling bitterness and reflecting on happiness," at which older people would tell us about the miseries of pre-Communist China. Our generation had been born "under the red flag" in new China, and had no idea what life was like under the Kuomintang. Lei Feng had, we were taught, which was why he could hate the class enemies so deeply and love Chairman Mao with all his heart. When he was seven, his mother was supposed to have hanged herself after being raped by a landlord.

Workers and peasants came to give talks at our school: we heard of childhoods dominated by starvation, freezing winters with no shoes, and premature, painful deaths. They told us how boundlessly grateful they were to Chairman Mao for saving their lives and giving them food and clothing. One speaker was a member of an ethnic group called the Yi, who had a system of slavery until the late 1950s. He had been a slave and showed us scars from appalling beatings under his previous masters. Every time the speakers described the hardships they had endured the packed hall was shaken by sobs. I came out of these sessions feeling devastated at what the Kuomintang had done, and passionately devoted to Mao.

To show us what life without Mao would be like, every now and then the school canteen cooked something called a "bitterness meal," which was supposed to be what poor people had to eat under the Kuomintang. It was composed of strange herbs, and I secretly wondered whether the cooks were playing a practical joke on us—it was truly unspeakable. The first couple of times I vomited.

One day we were taken to an exhibition of "class education" about Tibet: on display were photos of dungeons crawling with scorpions, and horrific instruments of torture, including a tool for scooping out eyes and knives for cutting the tendons in the ankles. A man in a wheelchair who came to our school to give a talk told us he was a former serf from Tibet who had had his ankle tendons severed for some trivial offense. . . .

In spite of all this talk and activity, class enemies for me, and for for much of my generation, remained abstract, unreal shadows. They were a thing of the past, too far away. Mao had not been able to give them an everyday material form. One reason, paradoxically, was that he had smashed the past so thoroughly. However, the expectation of an enemy figure was planted in us.

At the same time, Mao was sowing the seeds for his own deification, and my contemporaries and I were immersed in this crude yet effective indoctrination. It worked partly because Mao adroitly occupied the moral high ground: just as harshness to class enemies was presented as loyalty to the people, so total submission to him was cloaked in a deceptive appeal to be selfless. It was very hard to get behind the rhetoric, particularly when there was no alternative viewpoint from the adult population. In fact, the adults positively colluded in enhancing Mao's cult.

For two thousand years China had an emperor figure who was state power and spiritual authority rolled into one. The religious feelings which people in other parts of the world have toward a god have in China always been directed toward the emperor. My parents, like hundreds of millions of Chinese, were influenced by this tradition.

Mao made himself more godlike by shrouding himself in mystery. He always appeared remote, beyond human approach. He eschewed radio, and there was no television. Few people, except his Court staff, ever had any contact with him. Even his colleagues at the very top only met him in a sort of formal audience. After Yan'an, my father only set eyes on him a few times, and then only at large-scale meetings. My mother only ever saw him once, when he came to Chengdu in 1958 and summoned all officials above Grade 18 to have a group photo taken with him. After the fiasco of the Great Leap Forward, he had disappeared almost completely.

Mao, the emperor, fitted one of the patterns of Chinese history: the leader of a nationwide peasant uprising who swept away a rotten dynasty and became a wise new emperor exercising absolute authority. And, in a sense, Mao could be said to have earned his god-emperor status. He was responsible for ending the civil war and bringing peace and stability, which the Chinese always yearned for—so much that they said "It's better to be a dog in peacetime than a human being in war." It was under Mao that China became a power to be reckoned with in the world, and many Chinese stopped feeling ashamed and humiliated at being Chinese, which meant a tremendous amount to them. In reality, Mao turned China back to the days of the Middle Kingdom and, with the help of the United States, to isolation from the world. He enabled the Chinese to feel good and superior again, by blinding them to the world outside. Nonetheless, national pride was so important to the Chinese that much of the population was genuinely grateful to Mao, and did not find the cult of his personality offensive, certainly not at first. The near total lack of access to information and the systematic feeding of disinformation meant that most Chinese had no way to discriminate between Mao's successes and his failures, or to identify the relative role of Mao and other leaders in the Communists' achievements.

Fear was never absent in the building up of Mao's cult. Many people had been reduced to a state where they did not dare even to think, in case their thoughts came out involuntarily. Even if they did entertain unorthodox ideas, few mentioned them to their children, as they might blurt out something to other children, which could bring disaster to themselves as well as their parents. In the learn-from-Lei Feng years it was hammered into children that our first and only loyalty should be to Mao. A popular song went: "Father is close, Mother is close, but neither is as close as Chairman Mao." We were drilled to think that anyone, including our parents, who was not totally for Mao was our enemy. Many parents encouraged their children to grow up as conformists, as this would be safest for their future.

Self-censorship covered even basic information. I never heard of Yu-lin, or my grandmother's other relatives. Nor was I told about my mother's detention in 1955, or about the famine—in fact, anything that might sow a grain of doubt in me about the regime, or Mao. My parents, like virtually every parent in China, never said anything unorthodox to their children. . . .

I was thirteen in 1965. On the evening of 1 October that year, the sixteenth anniversary of the founding of the People's Republic, there was a big fireworks display on the square in the center of Chengdu. To the north of the square was the gate to an ancient imperial palace, which had recently been restored to its third-century grandeur, when Chengdu was the capital of a kingdom and a prosperous walled city. The gate was very similar to the Gate of Heavenly Peace in Peking, now the entrance to the Forbidden City, except for its color: it had sweeping green-tiled roofs and gray walls. Under the glazed roof of the pavilion stood enormous dark-red pillars. The balustrades were made of white marble. I was standing behind them with my family and the Sichuan dignitaries on a reviewing stand enjoying the festival atmosphere and waiting for the fireworks to begin. Below in the square 50,000 people were singing and dancing. *Bang! Bang!* The signals for the fireworks went off a few yards from where I stood. In an instant, the sky was a garden of spectacular shapes and colors, a sea of wave after wave of brilliance. The music and noise rose from below the imperial gate to join in the sumptuousness. After a while, the sky was clear for a few seconds. Then a sudden explosion brought out a gorgeous blossom, followed by the unfurling of a long, vast, silky hanging. It stretched itself in the middle of the sky, swaying gently in the autumn breeze. In the light over the square, the characters on the hanging were shining: "Long Live Our Great Leader Chairman Mao!" Tears sprang to my eyes. "How lucky, how incredibly lucky I am to be living in the great era of Mao Zedong!" I kept saying to myself. "How can children in the capitalist world go on living without being near Chairman Mao, and without the hope of ever seeing him in person?" I wanted to do something for them, to rescue them from their plight. I made a pledge to myself there and then to work hard to build a stronger China, in order to support a world revolution. I needed to work hard to be entitled to see Chairman Mao, too. That was the purpose of my life.

90

Mao and Gandhi

As nationalists and independence leaders, Mao Zedong and Mohandas Gandhi are compared in this article that originally appeared as a column in the New York Times shortly after the academy-award-winning movie, "Gandhi," was released in 1982.

While India was a British colony, in fact, its "jewel in the crown," China was never directly colonized. Still, both nations faced the impact of imperialism that led to diminished economic, political, and cultural sovereignty. Both countries would see the growth of independence movements that, after World War I, would spawn assertive demands for self-rule. Both Mao and Gandhi fought for and achieved independence for their respective countries at approximately the same time, India in 1947, and China in 1949. Yet their strategies and the ideologies were quite different, as Flora Lewis, the author of this excerpt, describes.

Discussion Questions

1. What similarities did Gandhi and Mao share? Differences?

2. What does the title of the article, "The Force of Dignity," mean? Do you think it's still a valid assertion for those who feel themselves oppressed today?

3. Do you agree with the author that Gandhi's message is a more "winning strategy" for the conflicts in today's world than Mao's?

Mao and Gandhi

Flora Lewis

The temptation in going to see the film "Gandhi" was to look for contrasts with Mao Tse-tung, the impact of the prophet of nonviolence and the revolutionary who preached that "power comes from the barrel of the gun."

Mohandas Gandhi did succeed in wresting independence for the Indian subcontinent with very little bloodshed. He wanted the British to leave of their own choice, and they did. When followers spoiled for a vengeful fight, he commanded them to fight with moral power and the stark display of injustice.

"We've come a long way with the British," he is quoted as saying. "When they leave, we must see them off as friends." So it was. Recently in South Africa, a small group of white and black opponents of apartheid were musing about the efficiency of nonviolence. "It worked in India because of the British," one said mournfully. "It would never have worked with Hitler. It won't work with the Afrikaners."

Not long afterward, in New Delhi, an Indian official expressed the same thoughts. "The British are gentlemen," he said with warmth and admiration.

But India had its civil war all the same, starting the moment of independence. Ten million were killed in a few months, perhaps history's biggest massacre. In the film, a disciple says of the saddened leader as the great day of freedom approaches, "He thinks he has failed." And Gandhi did fail, because he couldn't prevent the violence.

Mao didn't try. On the contrary, he encouraged it. And when his revolution succeeded, he grew impatient. He feared stodgy serenity and reversion to old habits. He called for permanent revolution and turbulence, stirring the Cultural Revolution, in which millions died; and China lost decades that could have been devoted to building and advance.

Both leaders achieved their first aim, with opposite tactics, and both failed to created the society they had envisioned. After all, what emerges is the forces they had in common, the drive that carried them both into history.

It was the demand for dignity. Gandhi expressed it in his person, in his stoicism, in his outraged, youthful cry at South African racism, "But I am a citizen of the British Empire," as in his mature asceticism sharing India's poverty. Mao expressed it in his commanding presence, his perseverance, his will to fight.

It is the demand that still haunts the third world, that makes the victory over colonialism so far short of satisfying now. Gross poverty is a gross indignity. But there are rich people in the newly independent countries, and they are often the most outspoken, the most resentful at what they feel is their plight.

In long independent but undeveloped countries of Latin America, it isn't the peasants and isolated villagers who launch revolution. It is the students, the children of physical comfort and sometimes the workers who come to the cities to find themselves at the bottom of a pecking order that looms visibly, tangibly high above them.

They are insulted, not in their lack of material goods so much as in their deprivation of dignity. They call for justice, madly, as though murdering and destroying were more just. It is a stifling fog.

So the difference between Gandhi and Mao turns out to be that while both understood that the deepest rage is for dignity, for an end to humiliation, contrary to Mao, Gandhi didn't think it was finite. Dignity is one thing human beings can share, portion out endlessly without ever using up the supply so long as the next person's indignity doesn't have to provide it. Mao needed for some to be on top of others.

Violence and nonviolence are tactics. But the sense of individual and collective worth is so demanding that people will die as soon as live for it.

For nearly two generations, the fashion has leaned to a show of force, Mao and Che Guevara-style. Franz Fanon, the North African revolutionary, argued that violence was not only a means but an ennobling goal, and he inspired some of America's black power leaders in the 1960's.

Others understood the essence of Gandhi's message, that the struggle is for dignity. Willingness to use force, however justified at times, is in itself demeaning. In the United States, Martin Luther King knew that, and in Poland it has been the central purpose of Solidarity.

A better sense of this universal human need, which emerges so strongly in Gandhi's life, would make it easier to find ways to deal with conflict in Central America, in Africa, and perhaps even between the superpowers. Good intentions aren't enough, nor is trying to enforce them. Gandhi's insight outlives Mao's.

91

Gandhi: Indian Home Rule

Hind Swaraj (Indian Home Rule) was Gandhi's first complete statement of his social and political ideals. It was written in 1909 in the form of an imagined dialogue between Gandhi [Editor] and a skeptical friend [Reader]. Major themes presented in the excerpts below are the contrast between India and England, the nature of modern civilization and the technique of passive resistance.

Discussion Questions

1. What does Gandhi mean by "civilization?"

2. What does he think are the evils which have grown out of modern civilization? Why does he think it is doomed?

3. Why does Gandhi think that the force of arms is not the best way to achieve home rule?

4. How does he define "passive resistance?" Why does he think it is the only path to follow?

Editor: Let us first consider what state of things is described by the word "civilization." Its true test lies in the fact that people living in it make bodily welfare the object of life. We will take some examples. The people of Europe today live in better-built houses than they did a hundred years ago. This is considered an emblem of civilization, and this is also a matter to promote bodily happiness. Formerly, they wore skins, and used spears as their weapons. Now, they wear long trousers, and, for embellishing their bodies, they wear a variety of clothing, and, instead of spears, they carry with them revolvers containing five or more chambers. If people of a certain country, who have hitherto not been in the habit of wearing much clothing, boots, etc., adopt European clothing, they are supposed to have become civilized out of savagery. Formerly, in Europe, people plowed their lands mainly by manual labor. Now, one man can plow a vast tract by means of steam engines and can thus amass great wealth. This is called a sign of civilization. Formerly, only a few men wrote valuable books. Now, anybody writes and prints anything he likes and poisons people's minds. Formerly, men traveled in wagons. Now, they fly through the air in trains at the rate of four hundred and more miles per day. This is considered the height of civilization. It has been stated that, as men progress, they shall be able to travel in airships and reach any part of the world in a few hours. Men will not need the use of their minds and feet. They will press a button, and they will have their clothing by their side. They will press another button, and they will have their newspaper. A third, and a motor-car will be in waiting for them. They will have a variety of delicately dished up food. Everything will be done by machinery. Formerly, when people wanted to fight with one another, they measured between them their bodily strength; now, it is possible to take away thousands of lives by one man working behind a gun from a hill. This is civilization. Formerly, men worked in the open air only as much as they liked. Now thousands of workmen meet together and for the sake of maintenance work in factories or mines. Their condition is worse than that of beasts. They are obliged to work, at the risk of their lives, at most dangerous occupations, for the sake of millionaires. Formerly, men were made slaves under physical compulsion. Now they are enslaved by temptation of money and of the luxuries that money can buy. There are now diseases of which people never dreamt before, and an army of doctors is engaged in finding out their cures, and so hospitals have increased. This is a test of civilization. Formerly, special messengers were required and much expense was incurred in order to send letters; today, anyone can abuse his fellow by means of a letter for one penny. True, at the same cost, one can send one's thanks also. Formerly, people had two or three meals consisting of home-made bread and vegetables; now, they require something to eat every two hours so that they have hardly leisure for anything else. What more need I say? All this you can ascertain from several authoritative books. These are all true tests of civilization. And if anyone speaks to the contrary, know that he is ignorant. This civilization takes note neither of morality nor of religion. Its votaries calmly state that their business is not to teach religion. Some even consider it to be a superstitious growth. Others put on the cloak of religion, and prate about morality. But, after twenty years' experience, I have come to the conclusion that immorality is often taught in the name of morality. Even a child can understand that in all I have described above there can be no inducement to morality. Civilization seeks to increase bodily comforts, and it fails miserably even in doing so.

This civilization is irreligion, and it has taken such a hold on the people in Europe that those who are in it appear to be half-mad. They lack real physical strength or courage. They keep up their energy by intoxication. They can hardly be happy in solitude. Women, who should be the queens of households, wander in the streets or they slave away in factories. For the sake of a pittance, half a million women in England alone are laboring under trying circumstances in factories or similar institutions. This awful fact is one of the causes of the daily growing suffragette movement.

This civilization is such that one has only to be patient and it will be self-destroyed. According to the teaching of Mahomed this would be considered a Satanic Civilization. Hinduism calls it the Black Age. I cannot give you an adequate conception of it. It is eating into the vitals of the English nation. It must be shunned. Parliaments are really emblems of slavery. If you will sufficiently think over this, you will entertain the same opinion and cease to blame the English. They rather deserve our sympathy. They are a shrewd nation and I therefore believe that they will cast off the evil. They are enterpris-

ing and industrious, and their mode of thought is not inherently immoral. Neither are they bad at heart. I therefore respect them. Civilization is not an incurable disease, but it should never he forgotten that the English people are at present afflicted by it.

Reader: I cannot follow this. There seems little doubt that we shall have to expel the English by force of arms. So long as they are in the country we cannot rest. . . .

Editor: . . . I believe that you want the millions of India to be happy, not that you [merely] want the reins of government in your hands. If that be so, we have to consider only one thing: how can the millions obtain self-rule? You will admit that people under several Indian princes are being ground down. The latter mercilessly crush them. Their tyranny is greater than that of the English, and if you want such tyranny in India, then we shall never agree. My patriotism does not teach me that I am to allow people to be crushed under the heel of Indian princes if only the English retire. If I have power, I should resist the tyranny of Indian princes just as much as that of the English. By patriotism I mean the welfare of the whole people, and if I could secure it at the hands of the English, I should bow down my head to them. If any Englishman dedicated his life to securing the freedom of India, resisting tyranny, and serving the Indians, I should welcome that Englishman as an Indian.

Again [you say that] India can fight . . . only when she has arms. You have not considered this problem at all. The English are splendidly armed; that does not frighten me, but it is clear that, to pit ourselves against them in arms, thousands of Indians must be armed. If such a thing be possible, how many years will it take? Moreover, to arm India on a large scale is to Europeanize it. Then her condition will be just as pitiable as that of Europe. This means, in short, that India must accept European civilization, and if that is what we want, the best thing is that we have among us those who are so well trained in that civilization. We will then fight for a few rights, will get what we can and so pass our days. But the fact is that the Indian nation will not adopt arms, and it is well that it does not.

> Introducing the concept of "soul-force" or "passive resistance," Gandhi argued that it is the only method by which home rule can be regained.

Thousands, indeed tens of thousands, depend for their existence on a very active working of this force. Little quarrels of millions of families in their daily lives disappear before the exercise of this force. Hundreds of nations live in peace. History does not and cannot take note of this fact. History is really a record of every interruption of the even working of the force of love or of the soul. Two brothers quarrel; one of them repents and reawakens the love that was lying dormant in him; the two again begin to live in peace; nobody takes note of this. But if the two brothers, through the intervention of solicitors or some other reason, take up arms or go to law—which is another form of the exhibition of brute force—their doings would be immediately noticed in the press, they would be the talk of their neighbors and would probably go down to history. And what is true of families and communities is true for nations. There is no reason to believe that there is one law for families and another for nations. History, then, is a record of an interruption of the course of nature. Soul-force, being natural, is not noted in history.

Reader: According to what you say, it is plain that instances of this kind of passive resistance are not to be found in history. It is necessary to understand this passive resistance more fully. It will be better, therefore, if you enlarge upon it.

Editor: Passive resistance is a method of securing rights by personal suffering; it is the reverse of resistance by arms. When I refuse to do a thing that is repugnant to my conscience, I use soul-force. For instance, the government of the day has passed a law which is applicable to me. I do not like it. If by using violence I force the government to repeal the law, I am employing what may be termed body-force. If I do not obey the law and accept the penalty for its breach, I use soul-force. It involves sacrifice of self.

Everybody admits that sacrifice of self is infinitely superior to sacrifice of others. Moreover, if this kind of force is used in a cause that is unjust, only the person using it suffers. He does not make others suffer for his mistakes. Men have before now done many things which were subsequently found to have been wrong. No man can claim that he is absolutely in the right or that a particular thing is wrong because he thinks so, but it is wrong for him so long as that is his deliberate judgment. It is therefore meet that he should not do that which he knows to be wrong, and suffer the consequence whatever it may be. This is the key to the use of soul-force.

Reader: You would then disregard laws—this is rank disloyalty. We have always been considered a law-abiding nation. You seem to be going even beyond the extremists. They say that we must obey the laws that have been passed, but that if the laws be bad, we must drive out the lawgivers even by force.

Editor: Whether I go beyond them or whether I do not is a matter of no consequence to either of us. We simply want to find out what is right and to act accordingly. The real meaning of the statement that we are a law-abiding nation is that we are passive resisters. When we do not like certain laws, we do not break the heads of law-givers but we suffer and do not submit to the laws. That we should obey laws whether good or bad is a new-fangled notion. There was no such thing in former days. The people disregarded those laws they did not like and suffered the penalties for their breach. It is contrary to our manhood if we obey laws repugnant to our conscience. Such teaching is opposed to religion and means slavery. If the government were to ask us to go about without any clothing, should we do so? If I were a passive resister, I would say to them that I would have nothing to do with their law. But we have so forgotten ourselves and become so compliant that we do not mind any degrading law.

A man who has realized his manhood, who fears only God, will fear no one else. Man-made laws are not necessarily binding on him. Even the government does not expect any such thing from us. They do not say: "You must do such and such a thing," but they say: "If you do not do it, we will punish you." We are sunk so low that we fancy that it is our duty, and our religion to do what the the law lays down. If man will only realize that it is unmanly to obey laws that are unjust, no man's tyranny will enslave him. This is the key to self-rule or home-rule.

It is a superstition and ungodly thing to believe that an act of a majority binds a minority. Many examples can be given in which acts of majorities will be found to have been wrong and those of minorities to have been right. All reforms owe their origin to the initiation of minorities in opposition to majorities. If among a band of robbers a knowledge of robbing is obligatory, is a pious man to accept the obligation? So long as the superstition that men should obey unjust laws exists, so long will their slavery exist. And a passive resister alone can remove such a superstition.

To use brute-force, to use gunpowder, is contrary to passive resistance, for it means that we want our opponent to do by force that which we desire but he does not. And if such a use of force is justifiable, surely he is entitled to do likewise by us. And so we should

never come to an agreement. We may simply fancy, like the blind horse moving in a circle round a mill, that we are making progress. Those who believe that they are not bound to obey laws which are repugnant to their conscience have only the remedy of passive resistance open to them. Any other must lead to disaster.

Reader: From what you say I deduce that passive resistance is a splendid weapon of the weak, but that when they are strong they may take up arms.

Editor: This is gross ignorance. Passive resistance, that is, soul-force, is matchless. It is superior to the force of arms. How, then, can it be considered only a weapon of the weak? Physical-force men are strangers to the courage that is requisite in a passive resister. Do you believe that a coward can ever disobey a law that he dislikes? Extremists are considered to be advocates of brute force. Why do they, then, talk about obeying laws? I do not blame them. They can say nothing else. When they succeed in driving out the English and they themselves become governors, they will want you and me to obey their laws. And that is a fitting thing for their constitution. But a passive resister will say he will not obey a law that is against his conscience, even though he may be blown to pieces at the mouth of a cannon.

What do you think? Wherein is courage required—in blowing others to pieces from behind a cannon, or with a smiling face to approach a cannon and be blown to pieces? Who is the true warrior—he who keeps death always as a bosom-friend, or he who controls the death of others? Believe me that a man devoid of courage and manhood can never be a passive resister.

This however, I will admit: that even a man weak in body is capable of offering this resistance. One man can offer it just as well as millions. Both men and women can indulge in it. It does not require the training of an army; it needs no jiu-jitsu. Control over the mind is alone necessary, and when that is attained, man is free like the king of the forest and his very glance withers the enemy.

Passive resistance is an all-sided sword, it can be used anyhow; it blesses him who uses it and him against whom it is used. Without drawing a drop of blood it produces far-reaching results. It never rusts and cannot be stolen. Competition between passive resisters does not exhaust. The sword of passive resistance does not require a scabbard. It is strange indeed that you should consider such a weapon to be a weapon merely of the weak.

92

The First Arab Students' Congress, 1938

World War I transformed the Middle East in several ways. The Ottoman Empire, which had controlled much of the Middle East, disintegrated as a consequence of its support of the Central Powers. As a result, much of the territory in the Middle East was up for grabs, and several of the European powers, chief among them the British and the French, were interested in laying claim. In fact, under the terms of the Sykes-Picot agreement, secretly negotiated between the two countries during World War I, a division of Arab lands had already been worked out. However, this agreement conflicted with the promise of independence to Arab leaders as a condition for Arab support of the Entente powers. This much-coveted territory was also the focus of the activities of the Zionists, whose support of the Entente powers had won them support within the British government for a "national homeland" in Palestine. Finally, the League of Nations would establish mandates for the newly-created countries of Palestine, Transjordan, Syria and Iraq. Not too surprisingly, the British and French overlooked earlier promises made to both Arabs and Jews, the French moving into Syria and Iraq, and Britain controlling Palestine and Transjordan. While Egypt and Iraq would win independence during the 1930's, most of the area remained under European control until after World War II, stimulating an Arab nationalism that differed from country to country. In this selection the manifesto of the first congress of Arab student nationalists, held in Paris in 1938, sets forth their demands.

Discussion Questions

1. How do the students define what it means to be an Arab? Is is similar to the way the Jews define what it means to be Jewish? Other ethnic groups, past or present?

2. Are the aims of the Arab nationalists similar to other nationalist groups you've studied? Similar to the Zionists? What differences exist?

3. Why do the Arab students oppose the Jews in Palestine? What is their objection to the Italians and the French? Have any of their demands been met?

Our National Pact

I am an Arab, and I believe that the Arabs constitute one nation. The sacred right of this nation is to be sovereign in her own affairs. Her ardent nationalism drives her to liberate the Arab homeland, to unite all its parts, and to found political, economic, and social institutions more sound and more compatible than the existing ones. The aim of this nationalism is to raise up the standard of living and to increase the material and the spiritual good of the people; it also aspires to share in working for the good of the human collectivity; it strives to realize this by continuous work based on national organization.

I pledge myself to God, that I will strive in this path to my utmost, putting the national interest above any other consideration.

First Principles

The Arabs: All who are Arab in their language, culture, and loyalty, . . . those are the Arabs. The Arab is the individual who belongs to the nation made up of those people. **The Arab Homeland:** It is the land which has been, or is, inhabited by an Arab majority, in the above sense, in Asia and Africa. As such it is a whole which cannot be divided or partitioned. It is a sacred heritage no inch of which may be trifled with. Any compromise

From Sylvia G. Haim, ed., *Arab Nationalism: An Anthology*, copyright © 1962 by The University of California Press, pp. 97–102. Reprinted by permission.

in this respect is invalid and is national treason.

Arab Nationalism: It is the feeling for the necessity of independence and unity which the inhabitants of the Arab lands share. . . . It is based on the unity of the homeland, of language, culture, history, and a sense of the common good.

The Arab Movement: It is the new Arab renaissance which pervades the Arab nation. Its motive force is her glorious past, her remarkable vitality and the awareness of her present and future interests. This movement strives continuously and in an organized manner toward well-defined aims. These aims are to liberate and unite the Arab homeland, to found political, economic, and social organizations more sound than the existing ones, and to attempt afterward to work for the good of the human collectivity and its progress. These aims are to be realized by definite means drawn from the preparedness of the Arabs and their particular situation, as well as from the experience of the West. They will be realized without subscribing to any particular creed of the modern Western ones such as Fascism, Communism, or Democracy.

The Arab National Idea: It is a national idea which proscribes the existence of racial, regional, and communal fanaticisms. It respects the freedom of religious observance, and individual freedoms such as the freedom of opinion, work, and assembly, unless they conflict with the public good. The Arab national idea cannot be contradictory to the good of real racial and religious minorities; it aims rather at treating all sincere patriots on the principle of equality of rights and duties.

Foreign Elements in the Arab Countries

We have said that the Arab countries belong to the Arabs and that benefits therefrom must accrue to them. By Arabs we mean those whom the political report has included under this appellation. As for those elements who are not Arabized and who do not intend to be Arabized but are, rather, intent on putting obstacles in the way of the Arab nation, they are foreign to the Arab nation. The most prominent problem of this kind is that of the Jews in Palestine.

If we looked at the Jews in Palestine from an economic angle we would find that their economy is totally incompatible with the Arab economy. The Jews are attempting to build up a Jewish state in Palestine and to bring into this state great numbers of their kind from all over the world. Palestine is a small country, and they will therefore have to industrialize it so that this large number of inhabitants can find subsistence. And in order to make their industry a success they will have to find markets for their products. For this they depend on the Arab market; their products will therefore flood the Arab countries and compete with Arab industries. This is very harmful to the Arabs.

Moreover, Palestine, placed as it is between the Arab countries in Asia and Africa, occupies an important position in land, sea, and air communications. A foreign state in Palestine will impede these communications and have a harmful effect on commerce. And even if the Jews in Palestine presented no danger other than the economic, this would be enough for us to oppose them and to put an end to their intrigues, so that we may ensure for our country a happy and glorious future.

Among the dangerous alien elements in the Arab countries are the foreign colonies such as the Italians in Tripolitania, the French, and the Frenchified Jews in Tunisia, Algeria, and Morocco. The danger of these elements is akin to that of the Jews in Palestine, even though less prominent and less critical.

93

How the Modern Middle East Map Came to Be Drawn

"A World Still Haunted by Ottoman Ghosts," is the title of a recent article in the *New York Times* by David Fromkin, author of this excerpt from his book, *A Peace to End All Peace.* The Ottoman Empire created by the Turks and eventually ruling over the Arab areas in the Middle East by the 16th century, would collapse in the aftermath of World War I. Though the sultans disappeared, the empire would leave its mark on political, social, economic, and religious institutions, especially in its creation of some two dozen ethnic and national groups that were encouraged to keep a separate identity. The Ottomans were replaced by the British and the French, which, buoyed by the prospect of oil, established their control over the area in the early 1920s. What follows is an account of the key reasons that the Europeans become actively involved in the Middle East, along with the resulting impact to the Arabs living in those areas.

Discussion Questions

1. What were British and French goals in the postwar Middle East, and how successful were they?
2. Would you agree with Fromkin that Enver Pasha deserves the title of "father of the modern Middle East?" What role did Winston Churchill play?
3. What Arab leaders were involved in the decisions to redraw the map of the Middle East?
4. What was the reaction of the Arabs to the changes in their lands resulting from British and French control?
5. What similarities do you see between the expectations and the goals of the British and French after World War I, and those of the "coalition of the willing" today?

How the Modern Middle East Map Came to Be Drawn

David Fromkin

The dictator of Iraq claimed—falsely—
that until 1914 Kuwait had been administered from Iraq, that historically
Kuwait was a part of Iraq, that the
separation of Kuwait from Iraq was an arbitrary decision of Great Britain's after World
War I. The year was 1961; the Iraqi dictator
was Abdul-Karim Qasim; and the dispatch.
of British troops averted a threatened invasion.

*Iraq, claiming that it had never recog-
nized the British-drawn frontier with Kuwait,
demanded full access to the Persian Gulf;
and when Kuwait failed to agree, Iraqi tanks
and infantry attacked Kuwait.* The year was
1973; the Iraqi dictator was Ahmad Hasan
al-Bakr; when other Arab states came to Kuwait's support, a deal was struck, Kuwait
made a payment of money to Iraq, and the
troops withdrew.

August 2, 1990. At 2 A.M. Iraqi forces
swept across the Kuwaiti frontier. Iraq's dictator, Saddam Hussein, declared that the
frontier between Iraq and Kuwait was invalid, a creation of the British after World War
I, and that Kuwait really belonged to Iraq.

It was, of course, true, as one Iraqi dictator
after another claimed that the exact Iraq-Ku-
wait frontier was a line drawn on an empty
map by a British civil servant in the early
1920s. But Kuwait began to emerge as an
independent entity in the early 1700s—two
centuries before Britain invented Iraq. Moreover, most other frontiers between states of
the Middle East were also creations of the
British (or the French). The map of the Arab
Middle East was drawn by the victorious Allies when they took over these lands from the
Ottoman Empire after World War I. By proposing to nullify that map, Saddam Hussein
at a minimum was trying to turn the clock
back by almost a century.

A hundred years ago, when Ottoman governors in Basra were futilely attempting to
assert authority over the autonomous sheik-
dom of Kuwait, most of the Arabic-speaking
Middle East was at least nominally part of the
Ottoman Empire. It had been so for hundreds
of years and would remain so until the end of
World War I.

The Ottomans, a dynasty, not a nationality, were originally a band of Turkish warriors who first galloped onto the stage of history in the 13th century. By the early 20th
century the Ottoman Empire, which once had
stretched to the gates of Vienna, was shrinking rapidly, though it still ruled perhaps 20
million to 25 million people in the Middle
East and elsewhere, comprising perhaps a
dozen or more different nationalities. It was
a ramshackle Muslim empire, held together
by the glue of Islam, and the lot of its non-

Muslim population (perhaps 5 million) was often unhappy and sometimes tragic.

In the year 1900, if you traveled from the United States to the Middle East, you might have landed in Egypt, part of the Ottoman Empire in name but in fact governed by British "advisers." The Egyptian Army was commanded by an English general, and the real ruler of the country was the British Agent and Consul-General—a position to which the crusty Horatio Herbert Kitchener was appointed in 1911.

The center of your social life in all likelihood would have been the British enclave in Cairo, which possessed (wrote one of Lord Kitchener's aides)—all the narrowness and provincialism of an English garrison town: The social schedule of British officials and their families revolved around the balls given at each of the leading hotels in turn, six nights out of seven, and before dark, around the Turf Club and the Sporting Club on the island of El Gezira. Throughout Egypt, Turkish officials, Turkish police and a Turkish army were conspicuous by their absence. Outside British confines you found yourself not in a Turkish-speaking country but in an Arabic-speaking one. Following the advice of the *Baedeker,* you'd likely engage a dragoman—a translator and guide—of whom there were about 90 in Cairo ("all more or less intelligent and able, but scarcely a half of the number are trustworthy").

On leaving Egypt, if you turned north, through the Holy Land and the Levant toward Anatolia, you finally would have encountered the reality of Ottoman government, however corrupt and inefficient, though many cities—Jerusalem (mostly Jewish), Damascus (mostly Arab) and Smyrna, now Izmir (mostly Greek)—were not at all Turkish in character or population.

Heading south by steamer down the Red Sea and around the enormous Arabian Peninsula was a very different matter. Nominally

Ottoman, Arabia was in large part a vast, ungoverned desert wilderness through which roamed bedouin tribes knowing no law but their own. In those days Abdul Aziz ibn Saud, the youthful scion of deposed lords of most of the peninsula, was living in exile, dreaming of a return to reclaim his rights and establish his dominion. In the port towns on the Persian Gulf, ruling sheiks paid lip service to Ottoman rule—but in fact their sheikdoms were protectorates of Great Britain. Not long after you passed Kuwait you reached Basra, in what is now Iraq, up a river formed by the union of the great Tigris and Euphrates.

A muddy, unhealthy port of heterogeneous population, Basra was then the capital of a province, largely Shiite Arab, ruled by an Ottoman governor. Well north of it, celebrated for archaeological sites like Babylon and Nippur, which drew tourists, lay Baghdad, then a heavily Jewish city (along with Jerusalem, one of the two great Jewish cities of Asia). Baghdad was the administrative center of an Ottoman province that was in large part Sunni Arab. Farther north still was a third Ottoman province, with a large population of Kurds. Taken together, the three roughly equaled the present area of Iraq.

Ottoman rule in some parts of the Middle East clearly was more imaginary than real. And even in those portions of the empire that Turkish governors did govern, the population was often too diverse to be governed effectively by a single regime. Yet the hold of the Turkish sultan on the empire's peoples lingered on. Indeed, had World War I not intervened, the Ottoman Empire might well have lasted many decades more.

In its origins, the war that would change the map of the Middle East had nothing to do with that region. How the Ottoman Empire came to be involved in the war at all—and lost it—and how the triumphant Allies found themselves in a position to redesign the Middle Eastern lands the Turks had ruled, is one of the most fascinating stories of the 20th century, rich in consequences that we are still struggling with today.

The story begins with one man, a tiny, vain, strutting man addicted to dramatic gestures and uniforms. He was Enver Pasha, and he mistook himself for a sort of Napoleon. Of modest origins, Enver, as a junior officer in the Ottoman Army, joined the Young Turks, a secret society that was plotting against the Ottoman regime. In 1913, Enver led a Young Turk raiding party that overthrew the government and killed the Minister of War. In 1914, at the age of 31, he became the Ottoman Minister of War himself, married the niece of the sultan and moved into a palace.

As a new political figure Enver scored a major, instant success. The Young Turks for years had urgently sought a European ally that would promise to protect the Ottoman Empire against other European powers. Britain, France and Russia had each been approached and had refused; but on August 1, 1914, just as Germany was about to invade Belgium to begin World War I, Enver wangled a secret treaty with the kaiser pledging to protect the Ottoman domains.

Unaware of Enver's coup, and with war added to the equation, Britain and France began wooing Turkey too, while the Turks played off one side against the other. By autumn the German Army's plan to knock France out of the war in six weeks had failed. Needing help, Germany urged the Ottoman Empire to join the war by attacking Russia.

Though Enver's colleagues in the Turkish government were opposed to war, Enver had a different idea. To him the time seemed ripe: in the first month of the war German armies overwhelmingly turned back a Russian attack on East Prussia, and a collapse of the czar's armies appeared imminent. Seeing a chance to share in the spoils of a likely German victory over Russia, Enver entered into a private conspiracy with the German admiral commanding the powerful warship *Goeben* and its companion vessel, the *Breslau,* which had taken refuge in Turkish waters at the outset of hostilities.

During the last week of October, Enver secretly arranged for the *Goeben* and the *Breslau* to escape into the Black Sea and steam toward Russia. Flying the Ottoman flag, the Germans then opened fire on the Russian coast. Thinking themselves attacked by Turks, the Russians declared war. Russia's allies, Britain and France, thus found themselves at war with the Ottoman Empire too. By needlessly plunging the empire into war, Enver had put everything in the Middle East up for grabs. In that sense, he was the father of the modern Middle East. Had Enver never existed, the Turkish flag might even yet be flying—if only in some confederal way— over Beirut and Damascus, Baghdad and Jerusalem.

Great Britain had propped up the Ottoman Empire for generations as a buffer against Russian expansionism. Now, with Russia as Britain's shaky ally, once the war had been won and the Ottomans overthrown, the Allies would be able to reshape the entire Middle East. It would be one of those magic moments in history when fresh starts beckon and dreams become realities.

"What is to prevent the Jews having Palestine and restoring a real Judaea?" asked H. G. Wells, the British novelist, essayist and prophet of a rational future for mankind. The Greeks, the French and the Italians also had claims to Middle East territory. And naturally, in Cairo, Lord Kitchener's aides soon began to contemplate a future plan for an Arab world to be ruled by Egypt, which in turn would continue to be controlled by themselves.

At the time, the Allies already had their hands full with war against Germany on the Western Front. They resolved not to be distracted by the Middle East until later. The issues and ambitions there were too divisive. Hardly had the Ottoman Empire entered the war, however, when Enver stirred the pot again. He took personal command of the Ottoman Third Army on the Caucasus frontier and, in the dead of winter, launched a foolhardy attack against fortified positions on high ground. His offensive was hopeless, since it was both amateurishly planned and executed, but the czar's generals panicked anyway. The Russian government begged Lord Kitchener (now serving in London as Secretary of State for War) to stage a more or less instant diversionary action. The result was the Allied attack on the Dardanelles, the strait that eventually leads to Constantinople (now Istanbul).

Enver soon lost about 86,000 of his 100,000 men; the few, bloodied survivors straggled back through icy mountain passes. A German observer noted that Enver's army had "suffered a disaster which for rapidity and completeness is without parallel in military history." But nobody in the Russian government or high command bothered to tell the British that mounting a Dardanelles naval attack was no longer necessary. So on the morning of February 19, 1915, British ships fired the opening shots in what became a tragic campaign.

Initially, the British Navy seemed poised to take Constantinople, and Russia panicked again. What if the British, having occupied Constantinople, were to hold onto it? The 50 percent of Russia's export trade flowing through the strait would then do so only with British permission. Czar Nicholas II demanded immediate assurance that Constantinople would be Russia's in the postwar world. Fearing Russia might withdraw from the war, Britain and France agreed. In return, Russia offered to support British and French claims in other parts of the Middle East.

With that in mind, on April 8, 1915, the British Prime Minister appointed a committee to define Britain's postwar goals in the Middle East. It was a committee dominated by Lord Kitchener through his personal representative, 36-year-old Sir Mark Sykes, one of many remarkable characters, including Winston Churchill and T. E. Lawrence, to be involved in the remaking (and remapping) of the Middle East.

A restless soul who had moved from school to school as a child, Sykes left college without graduating, and thereafter never liked to stay long in one spot. A Tory Member of Parliament, before the war he had traveled widely in Asiatic Turkey, publishing accounts of his journeys. Sykes' views tended to be passionate but changeable, and his talent for clever exaggeration sometimes carried over into his politics.

As a traditional Tory he had regarded the sultan's domains as a useful buffer protecting Britain's road to India against Britain's imperial rivals, the czar chief among them. Only 15 months earlier, Sykes was warning the House of Commons that "the disappearance of the Ottoman Empire must be the first step towards the disappearance of our own." Yet between 1915 and 1919, he busily planned the dismantling of the Ottoman Empire.

The Allied attack on the Dardanelles ended with Gallipoli, a disaster told and retold in books and films. Neither that defeat, nor the darkest days of 1916–17, when it looked for a while as though the Allies might lose the war, stopped British planning about how to cut up the Turkish Middle East. Steadily but secretly Sykes worked on. As the fight to overthrow the Ottoman Empire grew more intense, the elements he had to take into account grew more complex.

It was clear that the British needed to maintain control over the Suez Canal, and all the rest of the route to their prized colonial possession, India. They needed to keep the Russians and Germans and Italians and French in check. Especially the French, who had claims on Syria. But with millions of men committed to trench warfare in Europe, they could not drain off forces for the Middle East. Instead, units of the British Indian Army along with other Commonwealth forces attacked in the east in what are now Iraq and Iran, occupying Basra, Baghdad and eventually Mosul. Meanwhile, Allied liaison officers, including notably T. E. Lawrence, began encouraging the smallish group of Arabian tribesmen following Emir (later King) Hussein of the Hejaz, who had rebelled against the Turks, to fight a guerrilla campaign against Turkish forces.

Throughout 1917, in and near the Hejaz area of Arabia, the Arabs attacked the railway line that supported Turkish troops in Medina. The "Arab Revolt" had little military effect on the outcome of the war, yet the fighting brought to the fore, as British clients and potential Arab leaders, not only Hussein of the Hejaz, but two of his sons, Faisal and Abdullah. Both were deadly rivals of Ibn Saud, who by then had become a rising power in Arabia and a client of the British too.

British officials in Cairo deluded themselves and others into believing that the whole of the Arabic-speaking half of the Ottoman Empire might rise up and come over to the Allied side. When the time came, the Arab world did not follow the lead of Hussein, Abdullah and Faisal. But Arab aspirations and British gratitude began to loom large in British, and Arab, plans for the future. Sykes now felt he had to take Arab ambitious into account in his future planning, though he neglected those of Ibn Saud (father of today's Saudi king), who also deserved well of Britain.

By 1917 Sykes was also convinced that it was vital for the British war effort to win Jewish support against Germany, and that pledging support for Zionism could win it. That year his efforts and those of others resulted in the publication of a statement by

Arthur James Balfour, the British Foreign Secretary, expressing Britain's support for the establishment of a Jewish national home in Palestine.

The year 1917 proved to be a turning point. In the wake of its revolution Russia pulled out of the war, but the entrance by the United States on the Allied side insured the Allies a victory—if they could hold on long enough for U.S. troops to arrive in force. In the Middle East, as British India consolidated its hold on areas that are now part of Iraq, Gen. Edmund Allenby's Egyptian-based British army began fighting its way north from Suez to Damascus. Lawrence and a force of Arab raiders captured the Red Sea port of Aqaba (near the point where Israel and Jordan now meet). Then, still other Arabs, with Faisal in command, moved north to harass the Turkish flank.

By October 1918, Allenby had taken Syria and Lebanon, and was poised to invade what is now Turkey. But there was no need to do so, because on October 31 the Ottoman Empire surrendered.

As the Peace Conference convened in Paris, in February 1919, Sykes, who had been rethinking Britain's design for the Middle East, suddenly fell ill and died. At first there was nobody to take his place as the British government's overall Middle East planner. Prime Minister David Lloyd George took personal charge in many Middle East matters. But more and more, as the months went by, Winston Churchill had begun to play a major role, gradually superseding the others.

Accordingly, early that year the ambitious 45-year-old politician was asked by the Prime Minister to serve as both War Minister and Air Minister. ("Of course," Lloyd George wrote Churchill, "there will be but one salary!") Maintaining the peace in the captured—and now occupied—Arab Middle East was among Churchill's new responsibilities.

Cheerful, controversial and belligerent, Churchill was not yet the revered figure who would so inspire his countrymen and the world in 1940. Haunted by the specter of a brilliant father, he had won fame and high office early, but was widely distrusted, in part for having switched political parties. Churchill's foresighted administration of the Admiralty in the summer of 1914 won universal praise, but then the botched Dardanelles campaign, perhaps unfairly, was blamed on him. As a Conservative newspaper put it, "we have watched his brilliant and erratic course in the confident expectation that sooner or later he would make a mess of anything he undertook." In making Churchill minister of both War and Air in 1919, Lloyd George was giving his protégé a try at a political comeback.

By the end of the war, everyone was so used to the bickering among the Allies about who was going to get what in the postwar Middle East that the alternative—nobody taking anything—simply didn't enter into the equation. Churchill was perhaps the only statesman to consider that possibility. He foresaw that many problems would arise from trying to impose a new political design on so troubled a region, and thought it unwise to make the attempt. Churchill argued, in fact, for simply retaining a reformed version of the Ottoman Empire. Nobody took him seriously.

After the war, a British army of a million men, the only cohesive military force in the region, briefly occupied the Middle East. Even as his real work began, however, Churchill was confronted with demands that the army, exhausted from years of war, be demobilized. He understood what meeting those demands meant. Relying on that army, Prime Minister Lloyd George had decided to keep the whole Arab Middle East under British influence; in the words he once used about Palestine: "We shall be there by conquest and shall remain." Now Churchill repeatedly warned that once British troops were withdrawn, Britain would not be able to impose its terms.

Lloyd George had predicted that it would take about a week to agree on the terms of peace to be imposed on the defeated Ottoman Empire. Instead it took nearly two years. By then, in Churchill's words, the British army of occupation had long since "melted away," with the dire consequences he predicted.

In Egypt, demonstrations, strikes and riots broke out. In Arabia, Ibn Saud, though himself a British client, defeated and threatened to destroy Britain's protégé Hussein. In Turkey, the defeated Enver had long since fled the country to find refuge in Berlin. From there he journeyed to Russia, assumed leadership of Bukhara (in what is now the Uzbek Republic of the USSR) in its struggle for independence from Moscow, and was killed in battle against the Red Army of the Soviet Union in 1922. Turkish nationalists under the great Ottoman general Mustafa Kemal (later known as Kemal Ataturk) rebelled against the Allied-imposed treaty and later proclaimed the national state that is modern Turkey.

In Palestine, Arabs rioted against Jews. In what is now Saddam Hussein's Iraq, armed revolts by the tribes, sparked in the first instance by the imposition of taxes, caused thousands of casualties. "How much longer," the outraged London *Times* asked, "are valuable lives to be sacrificed in the vain endeavour to impose upon the Arab population an elaborate and expensive administration which they never asked for and do not want?"

By the end of 1920, Lloyd George's Middle East policy was under attack from all sides. Churchill, who had warned all along that peacetime Britain, in the grip of an economic collapse, had neither the money, the troops, nor the will to coerce the Middle East, was proved right—and placed even more directly in charge. On New Year's Day 1921 he was appointed Colonial Secretary, and soon began to expand his powers, consolidating within his new department responsibility for all Britain's domains in Arabic-speaking Asia.

He assembled his staff by combing the government for its ablest and most experienced officials. The one offbeat appointment was T. E. Lawrence. A young American journalist and promoter named Lowell Thomas, roaming the Middle East in search of a story, had found Lawrence dressed in Arab robes, and proceeded to make him world-famous as "Lawrence of Arabia." A complex personality, Lawrence was chronically insubordinate, but Churchill admired all the wonderful stories he'd heard of Lawrence's wartime exploits.

Seeking to forge a working-consensus among his staff in London and his men in the field, Churchill invited them all to a conference that opened in Cairo on March 12, 1921. During the ten-day session held in the Semiramis Hotel, about 40 experts were in attendance. "Everybody Middle East is here," wrote Lawrence.

Egypt was not on the agenda. Its fate was being settled separately by its new British proconsul, Lord Allenby. In 1922 he established it as an independent kingdom, still largely subject to British control under terms of a unilateral proclamation that neither Egypt's politicians nor its new king, Fuad, accepted.

All Britain's other wartime conquests— the lands now called Israel, the West Bank, Jordan and Iraq—were very much on the agenda, while the fate of Syria and Lebanon, which Britain had also conquered, was on everybody's mind. In the immediate aftermath of the war, it was control of Syria that had caused the most problems, as Lloyd George tried to keep it for Britain by placing it under the rule of Lawrence's comrade-in-

arms, Prince Faisal, son of Hussein. After Syria declared its independence, the French fought back. Occupying all of Syria-Lebanon, they drove Faisal into exile. The French also devised a new frontier for Lebanon that invited eventual disaster, as would become evident in the 1970s and '80s. They refused to see that the Muslim population was deeply hostile to their rule.

Churchill, meanwhile, was confronted by constant Arab disturbances in Palestine. West of the Jordan River, where the Jewish population lived, Arabs fought against Jewish immigration, claiming—wrongly, as the future was to show—that the country was too barren to support more than its existing 600,000 inhabitants. Churchill rejected that view, and dealt with the Arab objections to a Jewish homeland by keeping—though redefining—Britain's commitment to Zionism. As he saw it, there was to be a Jewish homeland in Palestine, but other homelands could exist there as well.

The 75 percent of Palestine east of the Jordan River (Transjordan, as it was called, until it became Jordan in 1950) was lawless. Lacking the troops to police it and wanting to avert additional causes of strife, Churchill decided to forbid Jews from settling there, temporarily at least.

Fittingly while still War and Air Minister, Churchill had devised a strategy for controlling the Middle East with a minimum number of British troops by using an economical combination of airpower and armored cars. But it would take time for the necessary units to be put in place. Meanwhile tribal fighting had to be contained somehow. As the Cairo conference met, news arrived that Abdullah, Faisal's brother, claiming to need "a change of air for his health," had left Arabia with a retinue of bedouin warriors and entered Transjordan. The British feared that Abdullah would attack French Syria and so give the

French an excuse to invade Transjordan, as a first step toward taking over all Palestine.

As a temporary expedient Churchill appointed Abdullah as governor of a Transjordan to be administratively detached from the rest of Palestine. He charged him with keeping order by his prestige and with his own bedouin followers—at least until Britain's aircraft and armored cars were in place. This provisional solution has lasted for seven decades and so have the borders of Transjordan, now ruled over by Abdullah's grandson, Hussein, the Hashemite King of Jordan.

The appointment of Abdullah seemed to accomplish several objectives at once. It went partway toward paying what Lawrence and others told Churchill was Britain's wartime debt to the family of King Hussein, though Hussein himself was beyond help. Too stubborn to accept British advice, he was losing the battle for Arabia to his blood rival, Ibn Saud. Meanwhile Prince Faisal, Britain's preferred Arab ruler, remained in idle exile.

Other chief items on the Cairo agenda were the Ottoman territories running from the Persian Gulf to Turkey along the border of Persia, which make up present-day Iraq. Including what were suspected—but not proved—to be vast oil reserves, at a time when the value of oil was beginning to be understood, these territories had been the scene of the bloodiest postwar Arab uprisings against British rule. They caused so many difficulties of every sort that Churchill flirted with the idea of abandoning them entirely, but Lloyd George would have none of it. If the British left, the Prime Minister warned, in a year or two they might find that they had "handed over to the French and Americans some of the richest oil fields in the world."

As a matter of convenience, the British administered this troubled region as a unit, though it was composed of the three separate Ottoman provinces—Mosul, Baghdad and Basra, with their incompatible Kurdish, Assyrian Christian, Jewish, Sunni Muslim, and Shiite populations. In making it into a country, Churchill and his colleagues found it convenient to continue treating it as a single unit. (One British planner was warned by an American missionary, "You are flying in the face of four millenniums of history . . .") The country was called Iraq—"the well-rooted country"—in order to give it a name that was Arabic. Faisal was placed on the throne by the British, and like his brother Abdullah in Transjordan, he was supposed to keep Iraq quiet until the British were ready to police it with aircraft and armored cars.

One of the leftover problems in 1921 was just how to protect Transjordan's new governor, Abdullah, and Iraq's new king, Faisal, against the fierce warriors of Ibn Saud. In August 1922 Ibn Saud's camel-cavalry forces invading Transjordan were stopped outside Amman by British airplanes and armored cars. Earlier that year, the British forced Ibn Saud to accept a settlement aimed at protecting Iraq. With this in mind, the British drew a frontier line that awarded Iraq a substantial amount of territory claimed by Ibn Saud for Arabia: all the land (in what is now Iraq) west of the Euphrates River, all the way to the Syrian frontier. To compensate Ibn Saud's kingdom (later known as Saudi Arabia) the British transferred to it rights to two-thirds of the territory of Kuwait, which had been essentially independent for about two centuries. These were valuable grazing lands, in which oil might exist too.

It is this frontier line between Iraq, Kuwait and Arabia, drawn by a British civil servant in 1922 to protect Iraq at the expense of Kuwait, that Iraq's Saddam Hussein denounced as invalid when he invaded.

In 1922, Churchill succeeded in mapping out the Arab Middle East along lines suitable to the needs of the British civilian and military administrations. T. E. Lawrence would later brag that he, Churchill and a few others had designed the modern Middle East over dinner. Seventy years later, in the tense deliberations and confrontations of half the world over the same area, the question is whether the peoples of the Middle East are willing or able to continue living with that design.

94

Key Themes of Middle East Politics

The Middle East encompasses some 20 countries situated on the three continents of Europe, Asia, and Africa. Its current importance on the world scene is not new, for it has long been a strategic crossroads where countless cultures have met, exchanged ideas and goods, fought, and coexisted. In the brief article that follows, Adam Garfinkle provides an introduction to some important realities of the Middle Eastern past and present.

Discussion Questions

1. What is the importance of traditional (old) social, political and economic customs on the present day Middle East?

2. How does Garfinkle describe most Middle Eastern political systems, and what role has nationalism played in this process?

3. What kinds of divisions exist within Middle Eastern states, and what impact have these divisions had for political and economic stability?

4. What does Garfinkle mean when he talks about outside intervention in the Middle East in the form of "two overlapping cold wars?" How has the situation changed today?

Key Themes of Middle East Politics

Adam Garfinkle

Scholarly approaches to the study of the modern Middle East vary, but most reputable experts agree on the following basic themes, even if they differ on particulars.

1. Old Civilizations, New States

For the most part, the modern Middle East consists of old societies organized under new states. The Middle East is one of the oldest human habitats on earth, and its ancient civilizations among the most grand and influential. Civilizations in Egypt, Mesopotamia (present day Iraq), ancient Israel, Persia, North Africa, and Anatolia (present day Turkey) gave rise to cultural and social patterns that persist in many ways still today. The rise first of Christianity and then of Islam in the 7th century added other very significant overlays to these ancient legacies. So did the Ottoman Turkish rule of the Middle East, which lasted for 400 years—until the end of World War I.

When the Ottoman Empire ended and European control and influence receded some thirty years later, the landscape revealed mostly recognizable societies, but few if any of those societies were organized in the territorial state of the Western model. (In this respect, the Middle East is more like East Asia as it emerged into the twentieth century, and less like sub-Saharan Africa as it

emerged halfway through the same century.) The borders of the modern Middle East, then, correspond at least roughly to historic frontiers—Yemen is where Yemen was, Egypt is where Egypt was, Iraq is where Babylon/Mesopotamia was, modern Turkey is where the center of Suleyman the Magnificent's empire was, Iran is where the Persia of Cyrus the Great was, the State of Israel is where the kingdoms of David and Solomon were, and so forth.

More important, however, the political systems of most Middle Eastern states are new, arising out of the post-Ottoman period. Not a single state in the region can boast a continuous political regime that predates this century, and the great majority date from after 1946.

What we have then, in most cases, is a relatively recent political system, whose formal structures are mostly borrowed from the West, superimposed upon old and deeply rooted social and political patterns. These patterns, in turn, are rooted in extended family (or clan, or tribe) and communities of faith (sectarian identification). The reason for this has mainly to do with the reaction of local societies over time to life under foreign domination. Today, then, political authority competes with the often conflicting authority that emanates from religious and tribal institutions.

Reprinted by permission of Foreign Policy Research Institute. From handouts prepared for a FPRI Teachers' Workshop on the Middle East. www.fpri.org.

In short, most Middle East states, and particularly the Arab states, exhibit much transparency; formal government structure tends to fold into pre-existing socioeconomic patterns because that is the best, and sometimes the only way short of outright coercion, that the state apparatus can function, or can itself survive. (Israel is the biggest exception to this pattern, Turkey is a partial exception, and Iran is a still lesser one.)

Recent Middle Eastern experience exhibits several patterns, but all come back one way or another to the tension between strong, deeply rooted social authority revolving around extended family (hamula) and religious sectarianism.

Some states, such as Syria, Algeria, Egypt after 1952, and Iraq after July 1958, have tried to accumulate and consolidate power through revolutionary transformations directed from the top down. These political authorities often set themselves up against religious authority and often against the power of the old, aristocratic family networks.

In many cases, Egypt being a good example, accommodation with religious authority rather than repression of it has become the prevalent pattern, with the mammoth state bureaucracy being penetrated by social realities as well as the other way around. In other states, such as Iraq and Syria, a virtual police-state emerged. In virtually none have institutional links developed between state and society to the extent that the majority of people assume the natural, organic social legitimacy of the government.

Other states have taken the more traditional route, trying more patiently to amass state authority by associating themselves with traditional authority patterns. The monarchies of the region, from Morocco to Jordan to Saudi Arabia, are the best examples of such an approach. Some scholars have referred to such states as really only

"families with flags," and, they might have added, with mosques. The evidence thus far suggests that the more traditionally-minded states have fared better in creating social stability, and in maintaining a sense of legitimacy and limited political participation. This is not at all what Western and local regional analysts in the 1950s and 1960s expected or predicted.

Nonetheless, the tension between weak polities and strong societies persists in virtually all Middle Eastern states. Governments naturally appeal to and try to build up local versions of nationalism based around the state (wataniya), but find competing realities and aspirations that are both "too small," (hamula, extended family) and "too large" (qawmiya, Pan-Arabism; or pan-Islamism). Thus, as political sociologists might put it, Middle Eastern—especially Arab—polities have relatively weak cores and strong peripheries.

Correspondingly, the prominence of faith and family as forms of legitimate social authority have made it hard for national political institutions, including political parties, to take root in society. As a result, political pluralism of the sort familiar in the West and elsewhere is very weak in the Middle East, excepting Israel and Turkey, which are functioning democracies. The political mobilization that does occur does so most often according to sectarian or regional tribal affiliation rather than along the lines of a national agenda that cuts across such groupings. Whereas some countries may be only "families with flags," almost all political parties in the region (again, excepting Turkey and Israel) are families or mosque-based groups with "programs" and "banners."

2. Cultural Heterogeneity

The weakness of the Middle Eastern state is also a function of divisions within societies. Not only is the region as a whole diverse, but so are many of the societies within themselves. As to the region as a whole, there are, first of all, cultural divisions along religious lines: between Muslim and Christian (and Jew), and within Islam between Sunni and various heterodox Shi'a groupings. There are also ethnographic/linguistic divisions, between Arab and Persian and Turk, with many smaller demographic groups also of relevance in certain states (for example, Kurds in Iran, Iraq, and Turkey; Berbers and Tuareg in Algeria; Beja/Nubian peoples in the Sudan; Armenians in Lebanon).

There are also divisions between rich states and poor states, between those with dominant traditions of sedentary agriculture and those with traditions of pastoral nomadism of one degree or another, and between, finally, those states that are internally homogeneous and those that are internally heterogeneous—which brings us back to questions of internal political organization, stability, and governmental competency and effectiveness.

In general, all else being equal, the more homogeneous a Middle Eastern state in terms of ethno-linguistic and religious diversity, the easier to govern well and with a benign hand. No Middle Eastern State is completely homogeneous, so we speak in relative terms, but Egypt, Tunisia, and Saudi Arabia are to be counted among the most homogeneous (despite 6 million Christians [Copts] in Egypt and many Shi'a in the al-Hasa province of Saudi Arabia). Syria, Iraq, and Lebanon are among the most heterogeneous, some mainly along sectarian lines (like Syria), and some combinations of ethno-linguistic and sectarian lines (like Iraq).

There are also intermediate cases: Jordan is almost all Sunni Muslim (only 3 percent are Christian and fewer still are Circassian), but it is divided between East Banker and Palestinian identifications; Sudan's Arabs are a relatively homogeneous group but the state includes large numbers of Beja/Nubian peoples who are neither Arab nor Muslim.

These divisions, on the top of weak central state authority, tend to undermine the sense of the state as a single community. They have been the root cause of repression, violence, and even civil war in several countries.

3. Institutional Weaknesses and External Influences

Because of the relative weakness of the state in the Middle East—even those attempting revolution from above and the concomitant bureaucratization of society—many countries in the region have been particularly vulnerable to external influences. These external influences have come in basically two forms: intra-regional and extra-regional.

Over most of the last 40 years, the Middle East has experienced not just one but two overlapping cold wars. Division and conflict among the states of the region (Arab vs. Israel, Arab vs. Iran, and Arab vs. Arab as well) has been the more important of the two. The Yemeni and Lebanese civil wars stand as excellent examples, as do the efforts of the larger regional states (Egypt, Syria, Iraq) to influence political dynamics in Jordan and among the Palestinians.

Nevertheless, the regional cold war drew in the United States and the Soviet Union—and to a lesser extent also Europe, China, Pakistan, and India. Sometimes local states that were locked in protracted regional disputes invited these influences by turning to external powers for weapons, economic aid, and diplomatic support.

Great power conflict that was played out through Middle Eastern proxies sometimes magnified, prolonged, and intensified the violence of local conflicts, but in other cases or at other levels probably helped keep local conflicts from getting out of hand. With the end of the Cold War, the collapse of the Soviet Union and the retreat of Russian power from the region, these dynamics have changed dramatically. In some respects, the considerable success of the Arab-Israeli peace process owes its progress to such changes.

For a bibliography on the Middle East, contact FPRI at 215-732-3774,1 ext. 201, or email ms@fpri.org.

95

The Search for Peace in the Middle East

The following selection presents a succinct, yet balanced view of the long conflict between the Arabs and the Jews. While this pamphlet, first published in 1966, does not include some of the recent developments with regards the Palestinian issue, it does explain the fundamental historical, political, religious and economic grievances of each side in the dispute. As you read, consider those elements that the antagonists have in common, as well as those which divide them.

Discussion Questions

1. Of the claims that each side makes to its right to Palestine, which is most convincing to you and why? Which of the claims seems the least valid? Why?

2. What events, agreements, organizations and personalities would you identify as being the most important in understanding the background of the Arab-Israeli conflict?

3. Have any of the claims mentioned in the selection been addressed, or is no longer in dispute? What additional arguments would you add to each side?

Background

The Jews and the Arabs are ancient and long-suffering peoples, and their sufferings continue. Both have been cruelly dealt with by peoples of other cultures, and both are still subject to manipulation by forces beyond their control. Both are distrustful of other peoples and of each other, as they seek to establish their own identity, their right to respect, freedom and national self-development.

It is one of the great ironies of history that the roots of the present Arab-Jewish struggle should have grown, not in a poisoned soil of ancient mutual animosities, but in the mistreatment each has received at the hands of others. The Jews and the Arabs are Semitic cousins, share cultural traits and traditions, and through long centuries lived in relative peace with one another even during periods when Jews were subject to sustained persecution by the Christian West.

At a time when Europeans tended to confine Jews to money-lending and certain other commercial trades, Jews served as physicians, government officials, philosophers, and scholars in Muslim-controlled societies from Moorish Spain across North Africa to the borders of India. The cultural vitality of the Islamic world, which kept alive Graeco-Roman culture and made fresh advances in mathematics, medicine, science, and philosophy while Christian Europe was struggling through the Dark Ages, was in part attributable to the enlightened policies Islamic rulers followed concerning their able Jewish subjects. Maimonides, the most famous of the medieval Jewish physician-philosophers, was both religious leader of the Jewish community and court physician to Saladin, the Kurdish general who unified a vast expanse of the Muslim world in the twelfth century. In more modern times, many Jews achieved high social, cultural, and financial position in Egypt where they were prominent in the civil service, and some received titles of "Bey" and "Pasha." One of these, Cattaui Pasha, was Minister of Finance to King Fouad less than fifty years ago.

The intensified struggle of Jews and Arabs has come since the end of World War I and most intensely since the end of World War II, as the two peoples, in their own ways, finally sought to put an end to persecution and to their common status as subject peoples—and ran head on into each other.

Zionism, the most dynamic force of nineteenth-century Jewish nationalism, burst upon the world scene just as Arab nationalism was beginning to rise from the dying Turkish Empire. These simultaneously emerging nationalisms, unfortunately, were destined to fight for possession of the same territory in the Holy Land of Palestine.

The nineteenth century, which saw the rapid spread of science, technology, and parliamentary concepts of political freedom over vast areas of the world, also witnessed the rise of the most vicious persecution of the Jews since the Romans drove them from Palestine in A.D. 135. Pogroms in Czarist Russia and in other parts of Eastern Europe in the 1880's raised again the fears which had intermittently assailed the Jews through many centuries of partial assimilation into various European societies. Numerous Jewish groups intensified efforts in Western Europe and America to promote migration away from their tormentors. Some settled in Western Europe, others in Canada and South Africa. The largest groups, by far, came to the United States. About 135,000 Eastern European Jews found new homes in the United States during the 1880's, another 280,000 in the 1890's, and the movement continued into the first part of the twentieth century. Other thousands were caught up in the dream of resettlement as farmers, and Jewish agricultural colonies were planted in Manitoba, Argentina, Australia, and South Africa.

Beginning in the 1860's, there were groups of European Jews who preached the then improbable dream of migration to the Holy Land of Palestine. An imaginative and determined Central European journalist, Theodor Herzl, took up this idea and in 1897, at Basle, Switzerland, challenged the First World Zionist Congress to develop a program for creating a Jewish homeland. He suggested how this should be achieved in a pamphlet entitled *The Jewish State.*

The Zionist movement quickly became a widely debated issue in world Jewry. Some Jewish philanthropists gave it limited support, some intellectual and religious leaders attacked it as both impractical and contrary to the interests of Jewish communities already established in Western countries. The strongest support came from among the Jewish masses seeking to flee from Eastern Europe, even though most of them chose, as the opportunity became available, to migrate to the United States. Around 1903, Herzl began to despair of establishing a homeland in Palestine and seriously raised the question of accepting a British offer to provide lands for

Jewish settlement in the temperate highlands of the new British colonial territories in East Africa. At another time, Argentina was considered. All such proposals were, however, firmly rejected by the rank-and-file of Zionists, in favor of a "return" to the Holy Land.

Throughout the centuries of the Jewish diaspora, a small contingent of Jews had clung tenaciously to the city of Jerusalem. However, by the end of the 1880's, there were estimated to be only about 30,000 to 40,000 Jews in Palestine, or about five per cent of the total population. This was, of course, before political Zionism, as such, began. By the end of World War I, colonies of Jewish settlers, primarily from Russia, had brought the Jewish population of Palestine to approximately 60,000 or about ten per cent of the total.

Initial negotiations for Jewish settlement in Palestine were carried on with the authorities of the Ottoman Empire which had control of Palestine and the adjoining Arab territories. Land for the Jewish newcomers was acquired by purchase from Arab landowners. Peaceful coexistence was stressed by the promoters of the new settlements, and initially there was little difficulty with Arab neighbors. However, certain kinds of friction arose. At the human level, the sale of land sometimes meant that Arab farm workers were turned out without provision for resettlement or absorption into a new society, and this practice produced bitterness, On the broader, political level, it became increasingly clear to the more educated and sophisticated Arabs that these Jewish settlements were eventually going to be welded into some form of political entity to be carved out of Palestine, or that Jewish immigration might reach such a level that the Arabs would become a minority in their homeland. With that realization began the dark fears that produced a growing Arab determination to oppose by any means the Zionist dream.

These apprehensions among the Palestinian Arabs came very much to the fore after the Balfour Declaration was issued by the British Foreign Minister in 1917, and particularly after that document was incorporated into the Versailles peace agreements and the League of Nations Mandates. The Balfour Declaration was simply a one-page letter which Lord Balfour wrote to Lord Rothschild stating that "His Majesty's Government view with favor the establishment in Palestine of a national home for the Jewish people." Coupled with that statement was a gesture of reassurance to the Palestinian Arabs to the effect "that nothing shall be done which may prejudice the civil and religious rights of the existing non-Jewish communities in Palestine." The Arabs, at that time, outnumbered the Jews by almost ten to one. The Balfour Declaration could be interpreted in several ways. Some Zionists saw it as a promise that the Jews of the world would be given all of Palestine and allowed to create there a sovereign state. Others interpreted it as a guarantee of unlimited Jewish immigration, but with no assurance that a Jewish state, as such, would ever be established. For years, bitter debates raged inside and outside Zionist circles over whether full-fledged political statehood was the goal. At various times, some Zionist leaders undertook to calm Arab and other critics by statements denying any ambition to create a Jewish state.

Meanwhile, as was later revealed, the British and the French had in 1916 entered into the secret Sykes-Picot agreement under which these two major powers were to divide between themselves control of much of the Arab world as soon as the Turkish empire could be destroyed. That arrangement was translated into the League of Nations Mandate system under which Britain took over the supervision of Palestine, Trans-Jordan, and Iraq, while France acquired dominance in Lebanon and Syria. As this arrangement was

being worked out, during and immediately after World War I, the British, through Lawrence of Arabia and others, were making promises to Arab nationalists and to individual Arab chieftains that the dreams of Arab national statehood (and of expanded power for particular leaders) would be fulfilled as the Turkish overlords could be driven out. These promises lay at the basis of the British-supported uprisings which culminated in the liberation of Jerusalem, Damascus and other ancient cities long controlled by the Turks.

By the mid-1920's, with British administrators and occupation forces installed in Palestine, a seemingly irreconcilable conflict was emerging. The Holy Land was claimed by a growing group of Jewish newcomers, gathering in from many parts of the world. It was also claimed by the long-settled Arab (Muslim and Christian) majority who took it for granted that they should in time control their own political destiny. Both sides became increasingly concerned to rid the land of British mandatory control and to establish their "rightful" claims on their own.

Competing Claims to Palestine

After the passage of these years, it is still impossible to get agreement on the relative merits of the rival claims to Palestine. Even to try to state what those claims are is to bring down on one's head (as the authors of this statement have discovered) the denunciation of either side, or both. Yet there are two sides to the argument.

The Jews base their claim to the Holy Land on these contentions:

1) Their ancestors controlled Jerusalem and territories to the north and south of that city more than two thousand years ago.
2) In the Scriptures, Jehovah promised this entire land to Abraham and his "seed."

3) The ancient Jewish kingdom was the only independent, indigenous state that area ever had prior to the present day.

4) Though driven out in cruel attacks by the Romans, a remnant of Jews always remained in the Holy land and, for the past century, constituted a majority in the city of Jerusalem.

5) Through all the centuries of the diaspora, Jews maintained their cultural attachment to their ancestral homeland and regularly reaffirmed that attachment through prayers of "next year in Jerusalem."

6) Modern Jewish resettlement in Palestine was on the basis of peaceful purchases of land, with approval of the only legitimate authorities with whom the Zionist leadership could at the time deal: first, the Turkish Sultan and, later, the British mandatory officials.

7) The Palestinian Arabs were late-comers to the area, a migratory people, and never had a Palestinian Arab state.

8) Centuries of persecution, culminating in the holocaust of the Hitler era, drove the Jews to seek and to create a secure national haven as a matter of survival. Such a haven for the Jews could be provided only in Palestine, whereas the Arabs have abundant lands stretching over vast areas in the region which are, or could be, open to the Palestinians.

9) The Jews offered to live at peace with their Arab neighbors either in a shared state or in a partitioned state, but the Arabs refused either solution and, following their own foolhardy resort to violence and subsequent defeats, have forfeited all claim to Palestine.

10) The enormous and effective investment of Jewish labor and capital in developing the land, its agriculture and industry, has established through creative use an indisputable Jewish right.

11) The superior technological and financial resources of the Jews allow them to develop the area, not only for themselves, but also for the Palestinian Arabs and other peoples of the region; it is toward that sort of constructive sharing, not racial aggrandizement, that the humanistic spirit of Zionism is directed.

The Arabs base their claims to Palestine and their opposition to a Jewish state on these contentions:

1) The Arabs as a people have lived on the land of Palestine and had unbroken use of its soil for more than 1,300 years.

2) Accepting the mixing of ethnic strains, which has been going on throughout the Euro-Asian land mass through history, there are no pure races in the Middle East. Among the Arab population there are many who have just as good a claim to descent from the indigenous people of Judea and Samaria from 2,000 years ago—are just as truly among "the seed of Abraham"—as any of the Jews, and have a great deal better ethnic claim than can be put forward by most European Jews with their mixed ancestry.

3) In the course of the assorted empires which ruled over the area, Palestinian Arabs participated, at various levels, in administration of the region, even if there was no specific Palestinian Arab state; even under the Turkish empire there was substantial local self-government on a religious "community" basis.

4) The British promised during World War I that they would assist the Arabs to achieve national identity and independence through the creation of appropriate nation-states. The Palestinian Arabs have as much claim on that assistance as any other people of the Arab world.

5) Following the First World War, self-determination was promised to all the subject peoples ruled by the Central Powers, and that promise applied as much to the Palestinian Arabs as to any other people. This principle was violated when the

promise was given to support the creation of a Jewish homeland in Palestine without consulting the Palestinian Arabs, who were then an overwhelming majority of the people.

6) The Palestinian Arabs, though originally welcoming Jewish settlers when they quietly bought land and moved in, never agreed to become a minority in their own homeland.

7) Although some Arab leaders initially believed that Jewish immigration could be accepted on a basis which would not lead to displacement of the Arabs, from the time of World War I onward Palestinian Arab nationalists argued that the Zionist movement would eventually mean control over Palestine by the Jews and expulsion or subjection of the Arabs.

8) The influx of European Jews has threatened the basic cultural character of Palestine as part of Levantine society. Where Palestinian Arabs and Oriental (or Arabized) Jews have little difficulty adjusting to each other, the Western Jews undermined the hope for any kind of equitable Arab-Jewish partnership.

9) Zionism is another manifestation of Western imperialism. Arabs inevitably must fear the power represented by links between Jewish settlers and the world Zionist movement and the influence of that relationship with and upon Western governments.

10) Continuing Jewish expansionism is proclaimed by some elements in the world Zionist movement and by some political factions in Israel. The Arabs can never accept in their midst a Jewish state which appears to have no fixed conception its territorial boundaries and pursues an aggressive policy trying to stimulate unlimited immigration from all over the world. If successful, that policy would almost certainly create *Lebensraum* demands for the annexation of still more Arab territory.

11) The idea that the Palestinian Arabs should give up their homeland to Jews and move to other Arab lands because there is space for resettlement is rejected as illogical and inhuman; every people has a right to remain on the lands they have long held as their own.

Growth of the Yishuv

Between World War I and World War II, parallel but complete separate and distinct national communities emerged in Palestine: the *Yishuv*, or Jewish community, and the Palestine Arab community. Each had its educational system in which its children were taught to become supporters of the respective national causes. Each developed its political system with its own Arab or Jewish parties; Arab and Jewish social and economic organizations provided for the needs of their respective communities from birth to burial in separate Muslim, Christian or Jewish cemeteries. Arabs and Jews organized security and underground military or paramilitary forces. During this era, the *Yishuv* grew from a few token settlements constituting a mere ten per cent of the population to an effective and strong national community, with nearly a third of the population, but in many respects far stronger than the poorly organized and divided Arab community which opposed its growth.

The Palestinian Arabs did not succeed in their efforts to stop Zionism. Beginning in the 1920's, accelerating in the 1930's and 1940's, the violent struggle of Arab against Jew and Jew against Arab repeatedly broke the calm which the British mandate government tried to maintain. Well warned though the British and the world were by these disorders, no solution to the problem was found. Study commission followed study commission, but the international community paid little attention to what was happening then and gave scant thought to what might happen later.

With Hitler's rise, his assault against Europe and his evil campaign to exterminate the Jews, the flight from Europe became for many European Jews a matter of life or death. Here again, before and after World War II, the Christian West was weighed and found wanting. Instead of opening wide their gates to refugees from Nazi persecution—and perhaps saving millions of lives—the free nations vacillated, took half measures, and waited. In the end, Western Europe and America, plus the Soviet Union, fought and at great cost won a war for their own survival against the Nazi military machine while an estimated six million Jews were murdered. When the fighting ceased, the remnant of continental Jews could, for the most part, think only of getting away from Europe as quickly as possible. With Jewish settlements already well established in Palestine, with a vigorous World Zionist Organization working to assist in resettlement, the movement to Palestine of concentration camp survivors and Jews from other countries grew in size and urgency. The British mandate government tried to impose controls upon that movement but succeeded only partially and in the end abandoned the struggle to administer Palestine, as the flow of immigrants continued and inter-communal violence mounted.

How many of the Jews who went to Palestine in the 1930's and 1940's would have migrated to some other country if they had been given encouragement cannot be known. In any case, the Christian West was able to escape in large measure from its accumulated centuries of anti-Semitic guilt, by cooperating with the dedicated Zionist leadership in helping displaced Jews find refuge in a predominantly Arab land.

At the time the UN partition was adopted, the Jewish third of the population of Palestine owned about six per cent of the land. The Arab two-thirds of the population owned about a third of the land, and felt they had good claim on that major portion of public lands listed as government domain. At partition, the Palestinian Arabs saw themselves being forced to give up much of their lands, private and communal, to Jewish settlers as part of a grand-scale international effort at restitution and compensation to the Jews. The Palestinian Arabs, chiefly a Muslim people, concluded that they were being required to pay for the anti-Semitic sins of the Christian West.

This is obviously a simplified and only partial explanation of how the Zionist movement and the present state of Israel came to gain broad Western support, but it will be impossible to understand current Arab attitudes apart from this unflattering interpretation of why the United States and Western Europe gave support to the creation of Israel and have continued to support it. In fact, some Arabs came to feel that in Western nations pro-Zionism for Jews abroad was the natural corollary of continued anti-Semitism at home.

Partition and War

One of the first great problems faced by the infant United Nations was the collapse of the British mandate and the necessity to find some internationally acceptable solution to the Arab-Jewish conflict in Palestine. The UN study commission recommended partition as the only solution with any hope of success. This plan called for the creation of separate Jewish and Arab states and the acceptance of international status for Jerusalem with free access for all races and religions.

This United Nations plan was approved by a two-thirds vote of its then members—and made possible by agreement-for-the-moment of the United States and the Soviet Union. Partition was never accepted by the local Palestinian Arabs nor by any of the neighboring

Arab states. The Jews did accept partition and prepared to proclaim the state of Israel at the earliest possible moment, May 14, 1948. Long before the partition plan could go into effect, however, clashes developed between underground groups and paramilitary units already active on both sides. Arab terrorists, linked to the so-called Arab Liberation Army, attacked Jewish farm settlements, offices, factories, buses, and isolated individuals. Jewish terrorists inflicted similar blows upon the Arabs. On the night of April 9, 1948, Jewish extremist paramilitary groups killed 254 men, women and children in the Arab village of Deir Yassin—as some of the participants in the massacre later said, "to persuade the Arabs to get moving." On April 12, a reprisal by the Arabs resulted in the deaths of 77 Jewish doctors, nurses, university teachers and students travelling in a Red Cross convoy to Hadassah Hospital near Jerusalem.

Thus a state of civil war had already developed in Palestine over the period from December, 1947, following adoption of the UN partition plan, right through the final weeks of the British Mandate. Within hours after Dr. Chaim Weizmann and his Zionist colleagues proudly raised the Star of David flag and launched the Jewish state, military units from Jordan, Syria, Egypt, Lebanon and Iraq began an open assault upon Israel. After some initial successes for Arab arms, the Israeli forces rallied, broke the siege of Jewish West Jerusalem, and occupied substantial areas in the north of Palestine and in the south which had been assigned to Arab control under the UN partition plan. Israel wound up holding a third more territory than it would have held had the Arabs accepted the original UN partition plan.

A series of armistice agreements finally terminated hostilities in 1949. But peace did not come. Organized fighting was replaced by a propaganda war that has never ceased—and by innumerable acts of terror and counter-terror.

The Palestinian Arab state called for in the UN partition resolution was never created. Instead Jordan annexed the West Bank, including the Eastern sector of Jerusalem. Egypt assumed a kind of protectorate control over the Gaza Strip. Israel, in turn, absorbed Jewish West Jerusalem, the Negev and parts of Galilee.

The Arabs had been beaten and humiliated but neither the Israeli nor the United Nations could compel them to make peace. In the absence of peace, Israel held on to its territorial gains, as did Jordan. In the closing phases of the war of 1948–49 it became clear how weak and disorganized the Arab forces were, how competent and determined were the Israelis. Despite the disparity between the total numbers of people on the two sides, vastly favoring the Arab countries over Israel, the actual military superiority of Israel over all its Arab neighbors was made clear through the Israeli victory in early 1949. That dominance has persisted through the intervening years. It has been convincingly demonstrated by Israel's ability to strike quickly and to win spectacular victories over the Arab states in the wars of 1956 and 1967, and to dominate the military situation along the cease-fire lines and in the air to this day.

The general response of the Arabs to the establishment and consolidation of a Jewish state in their midst has continued to be one of bitterness, frustration, and a sense of humiliated impotence. Their chief satisfaction for a long time has come in a war of propaganda rarely matched in passion and vituperation and in a kind of mystical faith that in time, somehow, the Arabs would achieve the military power with which to destroy Israel. The Arabs in defeat remained weak and disorganized. But they have believed that their cause was just and that it would prevail in the end.

Meanwhile, the United Nations set up machinery and provided funds to care for the minimal subsistence needs of nearly a million Arab refugees scattered across Gaza, Jordan, Syria, Lebanon, and Egypt. Out of these refugee camps and from other Palestinians in exile came increasing cries for revenge and for a chance "to go home." Thus, through the 1940's and well into the 1950's, there seemed no hope for a resolution of the conflict. There remained only an uneasy truce, broken occasionally by acts of terror and counter-terror. Moreover, the Arabs stepped up their propaganda war into more and more blood-curdling threats of eventual revenge against Israel, a state whose very existence Arabs refused to concede. The Arabs insisted on the maintenance of belligerency against Israel and a boycott against an trade and communications across the common boundaries.

96

The Palestinian National Covenant, 1968

The document you will be reading was drawn up in the immediate aftermath of the 1967 Six Day War, in which the Arab nations were humiliated by the Israelis. The crushing defeat of Arab armies was compounded by Israeli occupation of Arab lands, including the Gaza Strip and the Sinai in Egypt; Jerusalem and the West Bank in Jordan, the home of large numbers of Palestinians; and the Golan Heights in Syria. While many Israelis believed that their victory would lead to the recognition by their opponent that only a negotiated settlement of their differences would bring peace, Palestinians were of a different mind altogether. Until 1967 many Palestinians had relied on the Arab states of Egypt, Syria, Jordan and Iraq to fight for their rights, but after the 1967 war that was no longer a reality. Therefore, one important consequence of the 1967 War was a growing sense of Palestinian nationalism and identity. The Palestine Liberation Organization (PLO), formed in 1964, would issue this covenant in a statement of their consciousness, goals, and strategies in the ongoing conflict with Israel, with al-Fatah developing as the most important group within the PLO and Yasser Arafat, its leader since 1969, an important spokesman. The excerpts presented here reflect the aspirations of the Palestinians at an important moment in the Arab-Israeli Conflict.

Discussion Questions

1. What is Palestine and what is a Palestinian? What distinction does the covenant make between Palestinians and Jews, or Israelis?

2. What do the Palestinians want? Would it be possible to achieve their goals without infringing on the rights of the Israelis?

3. What is meant by self-determination, mentioned in Article 19? Where have you seen this term used before?

4. How does the description of Zionism compare with other readings in the RGH and in your text?

5. How were the fedayeen (guerrilla fighters) to wage the struggle with the Israelis, and what would their relationship with Arab states be?

6. How do you think Israelis reacted to the covenant? The U.S.? Other Arab states? Which provision do you think is the most inflammatory from the Israeli point of view?

The Palestinian National Covenant, 1968 [Excerpts]

This Covenant will be called The Palestinian National Covenant (al-mithaq al-watani al-filastini).

Article 1: Palestine is the homeland of the Palestinian Arab people and an integral part of the great Arab homeland, and the people of Palestine is a part of the Arab nation.

Article 2: Palestine with its boundaries that existed at the time of the British mandate is an integral regional unit.

Article 3: The Palestinian Arab people possesses the legal right to its homeland, and when the liberation of its homeland is completed it will exercise self-determination solely according to its own will and choice.

Article 4: The Palestinian personality is an innate, persistent characteristic that does not disappear, and it is transferred from fathers to sons. The Zionist occupation, and the dispersal of the Palestinian Arab people as a result of the disasters which came over it, do not deprive it of its Palestinian personality and affiliation and do not nullify them.

Article 5: The Palestinians are the Arab citizens who were living permanently in Palestine until 1947, whether they were expelled from there or remained. Whoever is born to a Palestinian Arab father after this date, within Palestine or outside it, is a Palestinian.

Article 6: Jews who were living permanently in Palestine until the beginning of the Zionist invasion will be considered Palestinians. [For the dating of the Zionist invasion, considered to have begun in 1917.]

Article 7: The Palestinian affiliation and the material, spiritual and historical tie with Palestine are permanent realities. The upbringing of the Palestinian individual in an Arab and revolutionary fashion, the undertaking of all means of forging consciousness and training the Palestinian, in order to acquaint him profoundly with his homeland, spiritually and materially, and preparing him for the conflict and the armed struggle, as well as for the sacrifice of his property and his life to restore his homeland, until the liberation of all this is a national duty.

Article 8: The phase in which the people of Palestine is living is that of national *(watani)* struggle for the liberation of Palestine. Therefore, the contradictions among the Palestinian national forces are of secondary order which must be suspended in the interest of the fundamental contradiction between Zionism and colonialism on the one side and the Palestinian Arab people on the other. On this basis, the Palestinian masses, whether in the homeland or in places of exile *(mahajir)*, organizations and individuals, comprise one national front which acts to restore Palestine and liberate it through armed struggle.

Article 9: Armed struggle is the only way to liberate Palestine and is therefore a strategy and not tactics. The Palestinian Arab people affirms its absolute resolution and abiding determination to pursue the armed struggle and to march forward towards the armed popular revolution, to liberate its homeland and return to it [to maintain] its right to a natural life in it, and to exercise its right of self-determination in it and sovereignty over it.

Article 10: Fedayeen action forms the nucleus of the popular Palestinian war of liberation. This demands its promotion, extension and protection, and the mobilization of all the masses and scientific capacities of the Palestinians, their organization and involvement in the armed Palestinian revolution and cohesion in the national *(watani)* struggle among the various groups of the people of Palestine, and between them and the Arab masses, to guarantee the continuation of the revolution, its advancement and victory. . . .

Article 13: Arab unity and the liberation of Palestine are two complementary aims. Each one paves the way for realization of the other. Arab unity leads to the liberation of Palestine, and the liberation of Palestine leads to Arab unity. Working for both goes hand in hand. . . .

Article 15: The liberation of Palestine, from an Arab viewpoint, is a national *(qawmi)* duty to repulse the Zionist, Imperialist invasion from the great Arab homeland and to purge the Zionist presence from Palestine. Its full responsibility falls upon the Arab nation, peoples and governments, with the Palestinian Arab people at their head.

Article 16: The liberation of Palestine, from a spiritual viewpoint, will prepare an atmosphere of tranquility and peace for the Holy Land in the shade of which all the Holy Places will be safeguarded, and freedom of worship and visitation to all will be guaranteed, without distinction or discrimination of race, colour, language or religion. For this reason, the people of Palestine looks to the support of all the spiritual forces in the world.

Article 17: The liberation of Palestine, from a human viewpoint, will restore to the Palestinian man his dignity, glory and freedom. For this, the Palestinian Arab people looks to the support of those in the world who believe in the dignity and freedom of man. . . .

Article 19: The partitioning of Palestine in 1947 and the establishment of Israel is fundamentally null and void, whatever time has elapsed, because it was contrary to the wish of the people of Palestine and its natural right to its homeland, and contradicts the principles embodied in the Charter of the UN, the first of which is the right of self-determination.

Article 20: The Balfour Declaration, the Mandate document, and what has been based upon them are considered null and void. The claim of a historical or spiritual tie between Jews and Palestine does not tally with historical realities nor with the constituents of statehood in their true sense. Judaism, in its character as a religion of revelation, is not a nationality with an independent existence. Likewise, the Jews are not one people with an independent personality. They are rather citizens of the states to which they belong.

Article 21: The Palestinian Arab people, in expressing itself through the armed Palestinian revolution, rejects every solution that is a substitute for a complete liberation of Palestine, and rejects all plans that aim at the settlement of the Palestine issue or its internationalization.

Article 22: Zionism is a political movement organically related to world Imperialism and hostile to all movements of liberation and progress in the world. It is a racist and fanatical movement in its formation: aggressive, expansionist and colonialist in its aims; and fascist and Nazi in its means. Israel is the tool of the Zionist movement and a human and geographical base for world Imperialism. It is a concentration and jumping-off point for Imperialism in the heart of the Arab homeland, to strike at the hopes of the Arab nation for liberation, unity and progress. . . .

Article 24: The Palestinian Arab people believes in the principles of justice, freedom, sovereignty, self-determination, human dignity and the fight of people to exercise them.
. . .

Article 27: The Palestine Liberation Organization will cooperate with all Arab States, each according to its capacities, and will maintain neutrality in their mutual relations in the light of and on the basis of, the requirements of the battle of liberation and will not interfere in the internal affairs of any Arab State.

Article 28: The Palestinian Arab people insists upon the originality and independence of its national *(wataniyya)* liberation and rejects every manner of interference, guardianship and subordination. . . .

Article 33: This covenant cannot be amended except by a two-thirds majority of all the members of the National Assembly of the Palestine Liberation Organization in a special session called for this purpose.

97

Islamic Fundamentalism

One of the most widespread phenomena of the twentieth century (and today) is what is often called "Fundamentalism." In this selection, Karen Armstrong, one of the most prominent scholars of religion, places fundamentalism in its modern context and then turns to a brief discussion of its Islamic variant.

(She refers to "Afghani," a late 19th century Iranian activist who feared the encroachment of the modern West, and to "al-Nasser" who was the ruler of Egypt in the 1950s and 1960s.)

Discussion Questions

1. Why is fundamentalism a distinctively modern idea? Where did it start?

2. What do all fundamentalists have in common?

3. What forms has Islamic fundamentalism taken?

4. Is fundamentalism, generally, destined to succeed or fail? Why?

Islamic Fundamentalism

Karen Armstrong

The Western media often give the impression that the embattled and occasionally violent form of religiosity known as "fundamentalism" is a purely Islamic phenomenon. This is not the case. Fundamentalism is a global fact and has surfaced in every major faith in response to the problems of our modernity. There is fundamentalist Judaism, fundamentalist Christianity, fundamentalist Hinduism, fundamentalist Buddhism, fundamentalist Sikhism and even fundamentalist Confucianism. This type of faith surfaced first in the Christian world in the United States at the beginning of the twentieth century. This was not accidental. Fundamentalism is not a monolithic movement, each form of fundamentalism, even within the same tradition, develops independently and has its own symbols and enthusiasms, but its different manifestations all bear a family resemblance. It has been noted that a fundamentalist movement does not arise immediately, as a knee-jerk response to the advent of Western modernity, but only takes shape when the modernization process is quite far advanced. At first religious people try to reform their traditions and effect a marriage between them and modern culture, as we have seen the Muslim reformers do. But when these moderate measures are found to be of no avail, some people resort to more extreme methods, and a fundamentalist movement is born. With hindsight, we can see that it was only to be expected that fundamentalism should first make itself known in the United States, the showcase of modernity, and only appear in other parts of the world at a later date. Of the three monotheistic religions, Islam was in fact the last to develop a fundamentalist strain, when modern culture began to take root in the Muslim world in the late 1960s and 1970s. By this date, fundamentalism was quite well established among Christians and Jews, who had had a longer exposure to the modern experience.

Fundamentalist movements in all faiths share certain characteristics. They reveal a deep disappointment and disenchantment with the modern experiment, which has not fulfilled all that it promised. They also express real fear. Every single fundamentalist movement that I have studied is convinced that the secular establishment is determined to wipe religion out. This is not always a paranoid reaction. We have seen that secularism has often been imposed very aggressively in the Muslim world. Fundamentalists look back to a "golden age" before the irruption of modernity for inspiration, but they are not atavistically returning to the Middle Ages. All are intrinsically modern movements and could have appeared at no time other than our own. All are innovative and often radical in their reinterpretation of religion. As such, fundamentalism is an essential part of the modern scene. Wherever modernity takes root, a fundamentalist movement is likely to rise up alongside it in conscious reaction. Fundamentalists will often express their discontent with a modern development by overstressing those elements in their tradition that militate against it. They are all—even in the United States—highly critical of democracy and secularism. Because the emancipation of women has been one of the hallmarks of modern culture, fundamentalists tend to emphasize conventional, agrarian gender roles, putting women back into veils and into the home. The fundamentalist community can thus be seen as the shadow-side of modernity; it can also highlight some of the darker sides of the modern experiment.

Fundamentalism, therefore, exists in a symbiotic relationship with a coercive secularism. Fundamentalists nearly always feel assaulted by the liberal or modernizing establishment, and their views and behavior become more extreme as a result. After the famous Scopes Trial (1925) in Tennessee, when Protestant fundamentalists tried to prevent the teaching of evolution in the public schools, they were so ridiculed by the secularist press that their theology became more reactionary and excessively literal, and they turned from the left to the extreme right of the political spectrum. When the secularist attack has been more violent, the fundamentalist reaction is likely to be even greater. Fundamentalism therefore reveals a fissure in society, which is polarized between those who enjoy secular culture and those who regard it with dread. As time passes, the two camps become increasingly unable to understand one another. Fundamentalism thus begins as an internal dispute, with liberalizers or secularists within one's own culture or nation. In the first instance, for example, Muslim fundamentalists will often oppose their fellow countrymen or fellow Muslims who take a more positive view of modernity,

rather than such external foes as the West or Israel. Very often, fundamentalists begin by withdrawing from mainstream culture to create an enclave of pure faith (as, for example, within the ultra-Orthodox Jewish communities in Jerusalem or New York). Thence they will sometimes conduct an offensive which can take many forms, designed to bring the mainstream back to the right path and resacralize the world. All fundamentalists feel that they are fighting for survival, and because their backs are to the wall, they can believe that they have to fight their way out of the impasse. In this frame of mind, on rare occasions, some resort to terrorism. The vast majority, however, do not commit acts of violence, but simply try to revive their faith in a more conventional, lawful way.

Fundamentalists have been successful in so far as they have pushed religion from the sidelines and back to center stage, so that it now plays a major part in international affairs once again, a development that would have seemed inconceivable in the mid-twentieth century when secularism seemed in the ascendant. This has certainly been the case in the Islamic world since the 1970s. But fundamentalism is not simply a way of "using" religion for a political end. These are essentially rebellions against the secularist exclusion of the divine from public life, and a frequently desperate attempt to make spiritual values prevail in the modern world. But the desperation and fear that fuel fundamentalists also tend to distort the religious tradition, and accentuate its more aggressive aspects at the expense of those that preach toleration and reconciliation.

Muslim fundamentalism corresponds very closely to these general characteristics. It is not correct, therefore, to imagine that Islam has within it a militant, fanatic strain that impels Muslims into a crazed and violent rejection of modernity. Muslims are in tune with fundamentalists in other faiths all over the world, who share their profound misgivings about modern secular culture. It should also be said that Muslims object to the use of the term "fundamentalism," pointing out quite correctly that it was coined by American Protestants as a badge of pride, and cannot be usefully translated into Arabic. *Usul*, as we have seen, refers to the fundamental principles of Islamic jurisprudence, and as all Muslims agree on these, all Muslims could be said to subscribe to *usuliyyah* (fundamentalism). Nevertheless, for all its shortcomings, "fundamentalism" is the only term we have to describe this family of embattled religious movements, and it is difficult to come up with a more satisfactory substitute.

One of the early fundamentalist idealogues was Mawdudi, the founder of the Jamaat-i Islami in Pakistan. He saw the mighty power of the West as gathering its forces to crush Islam. Muslims, he argued, must band together to fight this encroaching secularism, if they wanted their religion and their culture to survive. Muslims had encountered hostile societies before and had experienced disasters but, starting with Afghani, a new note had crept into Islamic discourse. The Western threat had made Muslims defensive for the first time. Mawdudi defied the whole secularist ethos: he was proposing an Islamic liberation theology. Because God alone was sovereign, nobody was obliged to take orders from any other human being. Revolution against the colonial powers was not just a right but a duty. Mawdudi called for a universal *jihad*. Just as the Prophet had fought the *jahiliyyah* (the "ignorance" and barbarism of the pre-Islamic period), Muslims must use all means in their power to resist the modern *jahiliyyah* of the West. Mawdudi argued that *jihad* was the central tenet of Islam. This was an innovation. Nobody had ever claimed before that *jihad* was equivalent to the five Pillars of Islam, but Mawdudi felt that the innovation was justi-

fied by the present emergency. The stress and fear of cultural and religious annihilation had led to the development of a more extreme and potentially violent distortion of the faith.

But the real founder of Islamic fundamentalism in the Sunni world was Sayyid Qutb (1906–66), who was greatly influenced by Mawdudi. Yet he had not originally been an extremist but had been filled with enthusiasm for Western culture and secular politics. Even after he joined the Muslim Brotherhood in 1953 he had been a reformer, hoping to give Western democracy an Islamic dimension that would avoid the excesses of a wholly secularist ideology. However, in 1956 he was imprisoned by al-Nasser for membership of the Brotherhood, and in the concentration camp he became convinced that religious people and secularists could not live in peace in the same society. As he witnessed the torture and execution of the Brothers, and reflected upon al-Nasser's avowed determination to cast religion into a marginal role in Egypt, he could see all the characteristics of *jahiliyyah*, which he defined as the barbarism that was for ever and for all time the enemy of faith, and which Muslims, following the example of the Prophet Muhammad, were bound to fight to the death. Qutb went further than Mawdudi, who had seen only non-Muslim societies as *jahili*. Qutb applied the term *jahiliyyah*, which in conventional Muslim historiography had been used simply to describe the pre-Islamic period in Arabia, to contemporary Muslim society. Even though a ruler such as al-Nasser outwardly professed Islam, his words and actions proved him to be an apostate and Muslims were duty-bound to overthrow such a government, just as Muhammad had forced the pagan establishment of Mecca (the *jahiliyyah* of his day) into submission.

The violent secularism of al-Nasser had led Qutb to espouse a form of Islam that distorted both the message of the Quran and the Prophet's life. Qutb told Muslims to model themselves on Muhammad: to separate themselves from mainstream society (as Muhammad had made the *bijrah* from Mecca to Medina), and then engage in a violent *jihad*. But Muhammad had in fact finally achieved victory by an ingenious policy of non-violence; the Quran adamantly opposed force and coercion in religious matters, and its vision—far from preaching exclusion and separation—was tolerant and inclusive. Qutb insisted that the Quranic injunction to toleration could occur only *after* the political victory of Islam and the establishment of a true Muslim state. The new intransigence sprang from the profound fear that is at the core of fundamentalist religion. Qutb did not survive. At al-Nasser's personal insistence, he was executed in 1966.

98

"The Gentlemen of the Jungle"

The following famous story by Jomo Kenyatta (the "father" of independent Kenya), from his book *Facing Mt. Kenya*, presents us with a fable meant to illustrate the nature of colonialism in Africa. It should be compared with the Lugard selection on the Dual Mandate.

Discussion Questions

1. What is the point of the story?
2. What arguments do the animals use to dispossess the man?
3. Why is the man so apparently helpless?
4. What recourse did the man have in dealing with the animals? Is this an argument for the use of terrorism?

Once upon a time an elephant made a friendship with a man. One day [when] a heavy thunderstorm broke out, the elephant went to his friend, who had a little hut at the edge of the forest, and said to him: "My dear good man, will you please let me put my trunk inside your hut to keep it out of this torrential rain?" The man, seeing what situation his friend was in, replied: "My dear good elephant, my hut is very small, but there is room for your trunk and myself. Please put your trunk in gently." The elephant thanked his friend, saying: "You have done me a good deed and one day I shall return your kindness." But what followed? As soon as the elephant put his trunk inside the hut, slowly he pushed his head inside, and finally flung the man out in the rain, and then lay down comfortably inside his friend's hut, saying: "My dear good friend, your skin is harder than mine, and as there is not enough room for both of us, you can afford to remain in the rain while I am protecting my delicate skin from the hailstorm."

The man, seeing what his friend had done to him, started to grumble; the animals in the nearby forest heard the noise and came to see what was the matter. All stood around listening to the heated argument between the man and his friend the elephant. In the turmoil the lion came along roaring, and said in a loud voice: "Don't you all know that I am the King of the jungle? How dare anyone disturb the peace of my kingdom?" On hearing this the elephant, who was one of the high ministers in the jungle kingdom, replied in a soothing voice, and said: "My lord, there is no disturbance of the peace in your kingdom. I have only been having a little discussion with my friend here as to the possession of this little hut which your lordship sees me occupying." The lion, who wanted to have "peace and tranquillity" in his kingdom, replied in a noble voice, saying: "I command my ministers to appoint a Commission of Inquiry to go thoroughly into this matter and report accordingly." He then turned to the man and said: "You have done well by establishing friendship with my people, especially with the elephant, who is one of my honorable ministers of state. Do not grumble any more, your hut is not lost to you. Wait until the sitting of my Imperial Commission and there you will be given plenty of opportunity to state your case. I am sure that you will be pleased with the findings of the Commission." The man was very pleased by these sweet words from the King of the jungle, and innocently waited

for his opportunity, in the belief that, naturally, the hut would be returned to him.

The elephant, obeying the command of his master, got busy with other ministers to appoint the Commission of Inquiry. The following elders of the jungle were appointed to sit in the Commission: (1) Mr. Rhinoceros; (2) Mr. Buffalo; (3) Mr. Alligator; (4) The Rt. Hon. Mr. Fox to act as chairman; and (5) Mr. Leopard to act as Secretary to the Commission. On seeing the personnel, the man protested and asked if it was not necessary to include in this Commission a member from his side. But he was told that it was impossible, since no one from his side was well enough educated to understand the intricacy of jungle law. Further, that there was nothing to fear, for the members of the Commission were all men of repute for their impartiality in justice, and as they were gentlemen chosen by God to look after the interests of races less adequately endowed with teeth and claws, he might rest assured that they would investigate the matter with the greatest care and report impartially.

The Commission sat to take the evidence. The Rt. Hon. Mr. Elephant was first called. He came along with a superior air, brushing his tusks with a sapling which Mrs. Elephant had provided, and in an authoritative voice said: "Gentlemen of the jungle, there is no need for me to waste your valuable time in relating a story which I am sure you all know. I have always regarded it as my duty to protect the interests of my friends, and this appears to have caused the misunderstanding between myself and my friend here. He invited me to save his hut from being blown away by a hurricane. As the hurricane had gained access owing to the unoccupied space in the hut, I considered it necessary, in my friend's own interests, to turn the undeveloped space to a more economic use by sitting in it myself; a duty which any of you would undoubtedly have performed with equal readiness in similar circumstances."

After hearing the Rt. Hon. Mr. Elephant's conclusive evidence, the Commission called Mr. Hyena and other elders of the jungle, who all supported what Mr. Elephant had said. They then called the man, who began to give his own account of the dispute. But the Commission cut him short, saying: "My good man, please confine yourself to relevant issues. We have already heard the circumstances from various unbiased sources; all we wish you to tell us is whether the undeveloped space in your hut was occupied by anyone else before Mr. Elephant assumed his position?" The man began to say: "No, but—" at this point the Commission declared that they had heard sufficient evidence from both sides and retired to consider their decision. After enjoying a delicious meal at the expense of the Rt. Hon. Mr. Elephant, they reached their verdict, called the man, and declared as follows: "In our opinion this dispute has arisen through a regrettable misunderstanding due to the backwardness of your ideas. We consider that Mr. Elephant has fulfilled his sacred duty of protecting your interests. As it is clearly for your good that the space should be put to its most economic use, and as you yourself have not yet reached the stage of expansion which would enable you to fill it, we consider it necessary to arrange a compromise to suit both parties. Mr. Elephant shall continue his occupation of your hut, but we give you permission to look for a site where you can build another hut more suited to your needs, and we will see that you are well protected."

The man, having no alternative, and fearing that his refusal might expose him to the teeth and claws of members of the Commission, did as they suggested. But no sooner had he built another hut than Mr. Rhinoceros charged in with his horn lowered and ordered the man to quit the hut. A Royal Commission was again appointed to look into the matter, and the same finding was given. This procedure was repeated until Mr. Buffalo, Mr. Leopard, Mr. Hyena, and the rest were all accommodated with new huts. Then the man decided that he must adopt an effective method of protection, since Commissions of Inquiry did not seem to be of any use to him. He sat down and said: "*Ng'enda thi ndeagaga motegi,*" which literally means "there is nothing that treads on the earth that cannot be trapped," or in other words, you can fool people for a time, but not forever.

Early one morning, when the huts already occupied by the jungle lords were all beginning to decay and fall to pieces, he went out and build a bigger and better hut a little distance away. No sooner had Mr. Rhinoceros seen it than he came rushing in, only to find that Mr. Elephant was already inside, sound asleep. Mr. Leopard next came in at the window, Mr. Lion, Mr. Fox, and Mr. Buffalo entered the doors, while Mr. Hyena howled for a place in the shade and Mr. Alligator basked on the roof. Presently they all began disputing about their rights of penetration, and from disputing they came to fighting, and when they were all embroiled together the man set the hut on fire and burnt it to the ground, jungle lords and all. Then he went home saying: "Peace is costly, but it's worth the expense," and lived happily ever after.

99

The Motion of Destiny

On July 10, 1953, Kwame Nkrumah delivered the following speech before the House of Assembly of the Gold Coast in which he argued for its independence from Great Britain. Independence was granted in 1957—the first British colony south of the Sahara to achieve that status. The former Gold Coast was renamed Ghana after the great empire that went back as far as the fourth century.

Discussion Questions

1. What advantages did Nkrumah believe the Gold Coast had for becoming an independent nation?
2. Why did he think independence would be beneficial to the British themselves?
3. How did he think that history justified independence?

The right of a people to decide their own destiny, to make their way in freedom, is not to be measured by the yardstick of color or degree of social development. It is an inalienable right of peoples which they are powerless to exercise when forces, stronger than they them whatever means, for whatever reasons, take this right away from them. If there is to be a criterion of a people's preparedness for self-government, then I say it is their readiness to assume the responsibilities of ruling themselves. For who but a people themselves can say then they are prepared? . . .

There is no conflict that I can see between our claim and the professed policy of all parties and governments of the United Kingdom. We have here in our country a stable

From Kwame Nkrumah, *Ghana: The Autobiography of Kwame Nkrumah*, copyright © Panaf Books Ltd., an imprint of Zed Press Ltd., 57 Caledonian Road, London N19BU, UK.

society. Our economy is healthy, as good as any for a country of our size. In many respects, we are very much better off than many Sovereign States. And our potentialities are large. Our people are fundamentally homogeneous, nor are we plagued with religious and tribal problems. And, above all, we have hardly any color bar. In fact, the whole democratic tradition of our society precludes the *herrenvolk* doctrine. The remnants of this doctrine are now an anachronism in our midst, and their days are numbered.

We have traveled long distances from the days when our fathers came under alien subjugation to the present time. We stand now at the threshold of self-government and do not waver. The paths have been tortuous, and fraught with peril, but the positive and tactical action we have adopted is leading us to the New Jerusalem, the golden city of our hearts desire! . . .

Today, more than ever before, Britain needs more "autonomous communities freely associated." For freely associated communities make better friends than those associated by subjugation. We see today how much easier and friendlier are the bonds between Great Britain and her former dependencies of India, Pakistan and Ceylon. So much of the bitterness that poisoned the relations between these former colonies and the United Kingdom has been absolved by the healing power of a better feeling so that a new friendship has been cemented in the free association of autonomous communities. . . .

In the very early days of the Christian era, long before England had assumed any importance, long even before her people had united into a nation, our ancestors had attained a great empire, which lasted until the eleventh century, when it fell before the attacks of the Moors of the North. At its height that empire stretched from Timbuktu to Bamako, and even as far as the Atlantic. . . .

Thus may we take pride in the name of Ghana, not out of romanticism, but as an inspiration for the future. It is right and proper that we should know about our past. For just as the future moves from the present, so the present has emerged from the past. Nor need we be ashamed of our past. There was much in it of glory. What our ancestors achieved in the context of their contemporary society gives us confidence that we can create, out of that past, a glorious future, not in terms of war and military pomp, but in terms of social progress and of peace. For we repudiate war and violence. Our battles shall be against the old ideas that keep men trammeled in their own greed; against the crass stupidities that breed hatred, fear and inhumanity. The heroes of our future will be those who can lead our people out of the stifling fog of disintegration through serfdom, into the valley of light where purpose, endeavor and determination will create that brotherhood which Christ proclaimed two thousand years ago, and about which so much is said, but so little done. . . .

100

Dawn in the Heart of Africa

The author of this poem, Patrice Lumumba, was the Prime Minister of the newly independent Republic of the Congo when he was assassinated in 1961. He tried to forge a multiethnic national party based on many of the principles made popular by the nationalist leader of Ghana, Kwame Nkrumah, and was winning converts to his cause when he was killed. The former Belgian Congo had suffered long during the years of colonization, and would face years of turmoil before some stability resulted. The following selection reflects both the burdens of imperialism and the promise of independence so much a part of the African nationalist message.

Discussion Questions

1. What or who does Lumumba blame for the thousand years of suffering? What or who does he say is changing things?

2. How do his words compare with those of Nkrumah, Kenyatta and other nationalist leaders? Are there differences? If so, why do you suppose those differences exist?

3. If Lumumba were living today, how do you think he would view events in Africa?

Dawn in the Heart of Africa

Patrice Lumumba

For a thousand years, you, African, suf-
fered like a beast,
Your ashes strewn to the wind that roams
the desert.
Your tyrants built the lustrous, magic tem-
ples
To preserve your soul, preserve your suf-
fering.
Barbaric right of fist and the white right
to whip,
You had the right to die, you also could
weep.
On your totem they carved endless hunger,
endless bonds,
And even in the cover of the woods a
ghastly cruel death
Was watching, snaky, crawling to you
Like branches from the holes and heads of
trees
Embraced your body and your ailing soil.
Then they put a treacherous big viper on
your chest:
On your neck they laid the yoke of firewa-
ter,
They took your sweet wife for glitter of
cheap pearls,
Your incredible riches that nobody could
measure.
From you hut, the tom-toms sounded into
dark of night
Carrying cruel laments up might black riv-
ers

About abused girls, streams of tears and
blood,
About ships that sailed to countries where
the little man
Wallows in an anthill and where the dollar
is king,
To that damned land which they called a
motherland.
There your child, your wife were ground,
day and night,
In a frightful, merciless mill, crushing
them in dreadful pain.
You are a man like others. They preach
you to believe
That good white God will reconcile all
men at last.
By fire you grieved and sang the moaning
songs
Of a homeless beggar that stinks at strang-
ers' doors.
And when a craze possessed you
And your blood boiled through the night
You danced, you moaned, obsessed by fa-
ther's passion.
Like fury of a storm to lyrics of a manly
tune
From a thousand years of misery a
strength burst out of you
In metallic voice of jazz, in uncovered out-
cry
That thunders through the continent like
gigantic surf.

The whole world, surprised, wakes up in panic

To the violent rhythm of blood, to the violent rhythm of jazz,

The white man turning pallid over this new song

That carries torch of purple through the dark of night

The dawn is here, my brother! Dawn! Look in our faces,

A new morning breaks in our old Africa.

Ours alone will now be the land, the water, mighty rivers

Poor African surrendered for a thousand years.

Hard torches of the sun will shine for us again

They'll dry the tears in eyes and spittle on your face.

The moment when you break the chains, the heavy fetters,

The evil, cruel times will go never to come again.

A free and gallant Congo will arise from black soil,

A free and gallant Congo—black blossom from black seed!

101

Nationalism in Africa

The forces that contributed to the growth of nationalism in Africa are, in many ways, similar to those in China, India and in the Middle East. The partition of Africa in the late 19th century led to patterns of European political control, chief among them minority rule, or the exclusion of the African from political power, save in a subordinate role. Economically, the traditional patterns of African life were often disturbed, as industrialization made inroads on long-established agricultural and market systems. Socially, the missionary, the colonial official and his African counterpart contributed to important educational and cultural changes. Indigenous values and organizations would also change, but, in many ways, rebound to form the nucleus of resistance movements that, by the end of World War II, demanded "Uhuru!," freedom. The following selection, written by James Coleman, a contemporary political scientist who has studied national movements, explains the complex of factors that helped to stimulate the development of nationalism in Africa.

Discussion Questions

1. What does Coleman list as the most important factors in stimulating the rise of African nationalism? Which colonial power has done the best job of aiding the Africans in their quest for self-government?

2. What does African nationalism have in common with its counterpart in the Middle East, India, and China? What differences exist?

3. How do Coleman's comments on African nationalism correspond with the writings of African nationalists, such as Nkrumah and Kenyatta? If there are differences, why do you think they exist?

As World War II progressed, the attack on colonialism mounted, especially from the United States. The Americas Under Secretary of State, for example, declared: "Our victory must bring in its train the liberation of all peoples. . . . The age of imperialism is ended. The right of a people to their freedom must be recognized, as the civilized world long since recognized the right of an individual to his personal freedom. The principles of the Atlantic Charter must be guaranteed to the world as a whole—in all oceans and in all continents." Petitions from African colonies poured into the British Colonial Office asking for political advances and various manifestoes were drafted heralding the liquidation of imperialism. One such, on behalf of various African organizations was presented to the United Nations Conference in San Francisco in April 1945. It called for radical reforms, declaring: Simultaneously with economic development progressive steps should be taken to associate Africans with the management of their own affairs with a view toward the achievement of full self-government within a definite time limit, as in the case of the Philippine Commonwealth. The frontal attack on colonialism was not merely ideological. It stemmed from a radical transformation of the African social and economic structure. The end of colonialism was now the logical outcome of conditions and forces that had been growing in the two decades before 1939 but which accelerated with amazing speed during and immediately after the conflict. By 1945 militant nationalism could no longer be appeased. In the following material, an American professor of political science who has specialized on African affairs, especially national movements, analyzes the complex Pattern of factors that stimulated and shaped the development of nationalism in Africa.

It is far easier to define and describe nationalism than it is to generalize about the factors which have contributed to its manifestation. Put most briefly, it is the end product of the profound and complex transformation which has occurred in Africa since the European intrusion. It is a commonplace that the imposition of Western technology, socio-political institutions, and ideology upon African societies has been violently disruptive of the old familistic order in that they have created new values and symbols, new techniques for the acquisition of wealth, status, and prestige, and new groups for which the old system had no place. The crucial point here is not that nationalism as a matter of fact happened to appear at a certain point in time after the "Western impact," but rather that the transformation the latter brought about has been an indispensable precondition for the rise of nationalism. Nationalism . . . requires considerable gestation. A few of the elements constituent have been:

From James S. Coleman, "Nationalism in Tropical Africa," in the *American Political Science Review*, June 1954, pp. 404–426 passim, copyright © 1954 by the American Political Science Association.

A. Economic

1. *Change from a subsistence to a money economy.* This change, consciously encouraged by colonial governments and European enterprise in order to increase the export of primary products, introduced the cash nexus and economic individualism, altered the patterns of land tenure and capital accumulation, and, in general, widened the area of both individual prosperity and insecurity.

2. *Growth of wage-labor force.* This development has resulted in the proletarianization of substantial numbers of Africans, which has weakened communal or lineage responsibility and rendered those concerned vulnerable to economic exploitation and grievances.

3. *Rise of a new middle class.* Laissez-faire economics and African enterprise, coupled with opportunities for university and professional education, have been factors contributing to the growth of a middle class. This class is most advanced in Senegal [Ghana], and Southern Nigeria, where it has developed despite successive displacement or frustration by the intrusion of Levantines and the monopolistic practices of European firms.

B. Sociological

1. *Urbanization.* The concentration of relatively large numbers of Africans in urban centers to meet the labor demands of European enterprise has loosened kinship ties, accelerated social communication between "detribalized" ethnic groups, and, in general, contributed to "national" integration.

2. *Social mobility.* The European imposed *pax* coupled with the development of communications and transport has provided the framework for travel, the growth of an international exchange economy, and socio-political reintegration.

3. *Western education.* This has provided certain of the inhabitants of a given territory with a common lingua franca; with the knowledge and tools to acquire status and prestige and to fulfill aspirations within the new social structure; and with some of the ideas and values by which alien rule could be attacked. It has been through western education that the African has encountered the scientific method and the idea of progress with their activistic implications, namely an awareness of alternatives and the conviction that man can creatively master and shape his own destiny.

C. Religious and Psychological

1. *Christian evangelization.* The conscious Europeanization pursued by Christian missionary societies had been a frontal assault upon traditional religious systems and moral sanctions. Moreover, the Christian doctrine of equality and human brotherhood challenged the ethical assumptions of imperialism.

2. *Neglect or frustration of Western-educated elements.* Susceptibility to psychological grievance is most acute among the more acculturated Africans. Social and economic discrimination and the stigma of inferiority and backwardness have precipitated a passionate quest for equality and modernity, and latterly self-government. Rankling memories of crude, arrogant, or insulting treatment by a European have frequently been the major wellspring of racial bitterness and uncompromising nationalism.

D. Political

1. *Eclipse of traditional authorities.* Notwithstanding the British policy of indirect rule, the European superstructure

and forces of modernity have tended to weaken the traditional powers of indigenous authorities and thereby to render less meaningful precolonial sociopolitical units as objects of loyalty and attachment There has been what Professor Daryll Forde calls a "status reversal"; that is, as a result of the acquisition by youth of Western education and a command over Western techniques in all fields, there has been ". . . an increasing transfer of command over wealth and authority to younger and socially more independent men at the expense of traditional heads. . . ."

2. *Forging of new "national" symbols.* The "territorialization" of Africa by the European powers has been a step in the creation of new nations, not only through the creation of boundaries within which the intensity of social communication and economic interchange has become greater than across territorial borders, but also as a consequence of the imposition of a common administrative super-structure, a common legal system, and in some instances common political institutions which have become symbols of territorial individuality.

These are a few of the principal factors in the European presence which have been contributors to the rise of nationalism.

There are a number of explanations for these areal variations. One relates to the degree of acculturation in an area. This is a reflection of the duration and intensity of contact with European influences. The contrast between the advanced nationalism of the British West Coast and of Senegal and the nascent nationalism of British and French Central Africa is partly explicable on this basis.

A second explanation lies in the absence of presence of alien settlers. On this score the settler-free British West Coast is unique when contrasted to the rest of Africa. The possibility of a total fulfillment of nationalist objectives (i.e., African self-government) has been a powerful psychological factor which partly explains the confident and buoyant expectancy of West Coast nationalists. On the other hand, . . . the tendencies toward accommodation or terrorism in the white-settler areas is a reflection of the absence of such moderating expectancy.

Certain African groups exposed to the same forces of acculturation and the same provocation have demonstrated radically different reactions. The Kikuyu versus the Masai peoples of Kenya, the Ibo versus the Hausa peoples of Nigeria, and the Creole and Mende of Sierra Leone. It is suggested that the dynamism, militancy, and nationalist élan of the Ibo peoples of Nigeria are rooted partly in certain indigenous Ibo culture traits (general absence of chiefs, smallness in scale and the democratic character of indigenous political organization, emphasis upon achieved status, and individualism). Much of the same might be said for the Kikuyu peoples of Kenya.

Differing colonial policies constitute another cause of these areal differences. Nationalism is predominantly a phenomenon of British Africa, and to a lesser extent of French Africa. Apart from the influence of the foregoing historical, sociological, and cultural variables, this fact, in the case of British Africa, is explained by certain unique features of British colonial policy.

It was inevitable that Britain, one of the most liberal colonial powers in Africa, should have reaped the strongest nationalist reaction. A few of the principal features of British policy which have stimulated nationalism deserve mention:

1. *Self-government as the goal of policy.* Unlike the French and Portuguese who embrace their African territories as indivisible units of the motherland, or the Belgians who until

recently have been disinclined to specify the ultimate goals of policy, the British have remained indiscriminately loyal to the Durham formula. In West Africa, this has enthroned the African nationalists; in Central and East Africa, the white settlers.

2. *Emphasis upon territorial individuality.* More than any other colonial power, the British have provided the institutional and conceptual framework for the emergence of nations. Decentralization of power, budgetary autonomy, the institution of territorial legislative councils and other "national" symbols-all have facilitated the conceptualization of a "nation."

3. *Policy on missionaries and education.* The comparative freedom granted missionaries and the laissez-faire attitude toward education, and particularly post-primary education, has distinguished British policy sharply from that of non-British Africa.

4. *Neglect, frustration, and antagonism of educated elite.* Not only have more British Africans been exposed to higher education, but the British government until recently remained relatively indifferent to the claims and aspirations of this class, which forms the core of the nationalist movements.

5. *Freedom of nationalist activity.* The comparative freedom of activity (speech, association, press, and travel abroad) which British Africans have enjoyed . . . has been of decisive importance. . . .

All of this suggests that African nationalism is not merely a peasant revolt. In fact . . . nationalism where it is most advanced has been sparked and led by the so-called de-tribalized, Western-educated, middle-class intellectuals and professional Africans; by those who in terms of improved status and material standards have benefited most from colonialism; in short, by those who have come closest to the Western World but have been denied entry on full terms of equality.

102

The Declaration of Human Rights, 1948

In 1948 the newly established United Nations approved a sweeping set of proposals known as the Universal Declaration of Human Rights. Forty-eight nations voted for the document, with only eight abstentions and no vetoes. The document that follows contains the original list of rights worked out by the General Assembly in 1948, though provisions expanding the list have been added over time. Scholars have often divided the U. N. Declaration of Human Rights into three categories, civil and political rights, social and economic rights, and solidarity rights. This third category includes provisions that would require the cooperation of the global community, such as is reflected in Article 28. While there continues to be much controversy over the implementation of these rights, there is general agreement that every human being possesses certain basic rights, and that gross crimes like genocide and torture are clear violations. As the Tibetan spiritual and human rights leader, the Dalai Lama maintains, "the responsibility that we all have for each other and for all sentient beings and also for all of Nature," is key to peace in the 21st century. As this century progresses, the issue of human rights will continue to be an important component of the global community.

Discussion Questions

1. Do you think there is such a thing as universal human rights, or does each society have a unique set of rights? If you believe the latter, is the U.N. document unworkable?

2. Which of the rights belong in category one, civil and political rights? Category two, social and economic rights? Category three, solidarity rights? Are there some that are overlapping?

3. Are there any provisions of this declaration that you find either offensive, unrealistic, or contrary to U.S. principles? Are there any principles that have been omitted from this list that should be included?

4. Do you think human rights have expanded since 9/11, or has the war against terrorism led to a diminishment of some of these rights?

5. Do you agree with the Dalai Lama that we must be global citizens with responsibilities for the environment and animals, as well as humans?

Universal Declaration of Human Rights, 1948

Preamble

Whereas recognition of the inherent dignity and of the equal and inalienable rights of all members of the human family is the foundation of freedom, justice and peace in the world,

Whereas disregard and contempt for human rights have resulted in barbarous acts which have outraged the conscience of mankind, and the advent of a world in which human beings shall enjoy freedom of speech and belief and freedom from fear and want has been proclaimed as the highest aspiration of the common people,

Whereas it is essential, if man is not to be compelled to have recourse, as a last resort, to rebellion against tyranny and oppression, that human rights should be protected by the rule of law,

Whereas it is essential to promote the development of friendly relations between nations,

Whereas the peoples of the United Nations have in the Charter reaffirmed their faith in fundamental human rights, in the dignity and worth of the human person and in the equal rights of men and women and have determined to promote social progress and better standards of life in larger freedom,

Whereas Member States have pledged themselves to achieve, in co-operation with the United Nations, the promotion of universal respect for and observance of human rights and fundamental freedoms,

Whereas a common understanding of these rights and freedoms is of the greatest importance for the full realization of this pledge,

Now, therefore,

The General Assembly

Proclaims this Universal Declaration of Human Rights as a common standard of achievement for all peoples and all nations, to the end that every individual and every organ of society, keeping this Declaration constantly in mind, shall strive by teaching and education to promote respect for these rights and freedoms and by progressive measures, national and international, to secure their universal and effective recognition and observance, both among the peoples of Member States themselves and among the peoples of territories under their jurisdiction.

Article 1

All human beings are born free and equal in dignity and rights. They are endowed with reason and conscience and should act towards one another in a spirit of brotherhood.

Article 2

Everyone is entitled to all the rights and freedoms set forth in this Declaration, without distinction of any kind, such as race, color, sex, language, religion, political or other opinion, national or social origin, property, birth or other status.

Furthermore, no distinction shall be made on the basis of the political, jurisdictional or international status of the country or territory to which a person belongs, whether it be independent, trust, non-self-governing or under any other limitation of sovereignty.

Article 3

Everyone has the right to life, liberty and the security of person.

Article 4

No one shall be held in slavery or servitude; slavery and the slave trade shall be prohibited in all their forms.

Article 5

No one shall be subjected to torture or to cruel, inhuman or degrading treatment or punishment.

Article 6

Everyone has the right to recognition everywhere as a person before the law.

Article 7

All are equal before the law and are entitled without any discrimination to equal protection against any discrimination in violation of this Declaration and against any incitement to such discrimination.

Article 8

Everyone has the right to an effective remedy by the competent national tribunals for acts violating the fundamental rights granted him by the constitution or by law.

Article 9

No one shall be subjected to arbitrary arrest, detention or exile.

Article 10

Everyone is entitled in full equality to a fair, and public hearing by an independent and impartial tribunal, in the determination of his rights and obligations and of any criminal charge against him.

Article 11

1. Everyone charged with a penal offence has the right to be presumed innocent until proven guilty according to law in a public trial at which he has had all the guarantees necessary for his defence.
2. No one shall be held guilty of any penal offence on account of any act or ommision which did not constitute a penal offence, under national or international law, at the time when it was committed. Nor shall a heavier penalty be imposed than the one that was applicable at the time the penal offence was committed.

Article 12

No one shall be subjected to arbitrary interference with his privacy, family, home or correspondence, nor to attacks upon his honour and reputation. Everyone has the right to the protection of the law against such interference or attacks.

Article 13

1. Everyone has the right to freedom of movement and residence within the borders of each State.
2. Everyone has the right to leave any country, including his own, and to return to his country.

Article 14

1. Everyone has the right to seek and to enjoy in other countries asylum from persecution.
2. This right may not be invoked in the case of prosecutions genuinely arising from non-political crimes or from acts contrary to the purposes and principles of the United Nations.

Article 15

1. Everyone has the right to a nationality.
2. No one shall be arbitrarily deprived of his nationality nor denied the right to change his nationality.

Article 16

1. Men and women of full age, without any limitation due to race, nationality or religion, have the right to marry and to found a family. They are entitled to equal rights as to marriage, during marriage and at its dissolution.
2. Marriage shall be entered into only with the free and full consent of the intending spouses.

3. The family is the natural and fundamental group unit of society and is entitled to protection by society and the State.

Article 17

1. Everyone has the right to own property alone as well as in association with others.
2. No one shall be arbitrarily deprived of his property.

Article 18

Everyone has the right to freedom of thought, conscience and religion; this right includes freedom to change his religion or belief, and freedom, either alone or in community with others and in public or private, to manifest his religion or belief in teaching, practice, worship and observance.

Article 19

Everyone has the right to freedom of opinion and expression; this right includes freedom to hold opinions without interference and to seek, receive and impart information and ideas through any media and regardless of frontiers.

Article 20

1. Everyone has the right to freedom of peaceful assembly and association.
2. No one may be compelled to belong to an association.

Article 21

1. Everyone has the right to take part in the government of his country, directly or through freely chosen representatives.
2. Everyone has the right of equal access to public service in his country.
3. The will of the people shall be the basis of the authority of government; this will shall be expressed in periodic and genuine elections which shall be by universal and

equal suffrage and shall be held by secret vote or by equivalent free voting procedures.

Article 22

Everyone, as a member of society, has the right to social security and is entitled to realization, through national effort and international co-operation and in accordance with the organization and resources of each State, of the economic, social and cultural rights indispensable for his dignity and the free development of his personality.

Article 23

1. Everyone has the right to work, to free choice of employment, to just and favourable conditions of work and to protection against unemployment.
2. Everyone, without any discrimination, has the right to equal pay for equal work.
3. Everyone who works has the right to just and favourable remuneration ensuring for himself and his family an existence worthy of human dignity, and supplemented, if necessary, by other means of social protection.
4. Everyone has the right to form and to join trade unions for the protection of his interests.

Article 24

Everyone has the right to rest and leisure, including reasonable limitation of working hours and periodic holidays with pay.

Article 25

1. Everyone has the right to a standard of living adequate for the health and well-being of himself and of his family, including food, clothing, housing and medical care and necessary social services, and the right to security in the event of unemployment, sickness, disability, widowhood, old age or other lack of livelihood in circumstances beyond his control.
2. Motherhood and childhood are entitled to special care and assistance. All children, whether born in or out of wedlock, shall enjoy the same social protection.

Article 26

1. Everyone has the right to education. Education shall be free, at least in the elementary and fundamental stages. Elementary education shall be compulsory. Technical and professional education shall be made generally available and higher education shall be equally accessible to all on the basis of merit.
2. Education shall be directed to the full development of the human personality and to the strengthening of respect for human rights and fundamental freedoms. It shall promote understanding, tolerance and friendship among all nations, racial or religious groups, and shall further the activities of the United Nations for the maintenance of peace.
3. Parents have a prior right to choose the kind of education that shall be given to their children.

Article 27

1. Everyone has the right freely to participate in the cultural life of the community, to enjoy the arts and to share in scientific advancement and its benefits.
2. Everyone has the right to the protection of the moral and material interests resulting from any scientific, literary or artistic production of which he is the author.

Article 28

Everyone is entitled to a social and international order in which the rights and freedoms set forth in this Declaration can be fully realized.

Article 29

1. Everyone has duties to the community in which alone the free and full development of his personality is possible.
2. In the exercise of his rights and freedoms, everyone shall be subject only to such limitations as are determined by law solely for the purpose of securing due recognition and respect for the rights and freedoms of others and of meeting the just requirements of morality, public order and the general welfare in a democratic society.

3. These rights and freedoms may in no case be exercised contrary to the purposes and principles of the United Nations.

Article 30

Nothing in this Declaration may be interpreted as implying for any State, group or person any right to engage in any activity or to perform any act aimed at the destruction of any of the rights and freedoms set forth herein.